INQUIRY IN
EDUCATION

VOLUME II

The Educational Psychology Series
Robert J. Sternberg and Wendy M. Williams, Series Editors

INQUIRY IN EDUCATION

VOLUME II

Overcoming Barriers to Successful Implementation

Edited by

Bruce M. Shore
McGill University

Mark W. Aulls
McGill University

Marcia A. B. Delcourt
Western Connecticut State University

LEA Lawrence Erlbaum Associates
Taylor & Francis Group

New York   London

Lawrence Erlbaum Associates
Taylor & Francis Group
270 Madison Avenue
New York, NY 10016

Lawrence Erlbaum Associates
Taylor & Francis Group
2 Park Square
Milton Park, Abingdon
Oxon OX14 4RN

International Standard Book Number-13: 978-0-8058-2744-6 (Softcover) 978-0-8058-2743-9 (Hardcover)

Visit the Taylor & Francis Web site at
http://www.taylorandfrancis.com

and the LEA and Routledge Web site at
http://www.routledge.com

Contents

Preface

In the companion volume (Aulls & Shore, *Inquiry in Education: The Conceptual Foundations for Research as a Curricular Imperative*) to this compilation of case studies, reflections, and original studies, Aulls and Shore present the arguments for the necessary inclusion of inquiry-driven learning and instructional experiences in any modern school curriculum. That volume necessarily portrayed the ideal, and concentrated on what evidence exists that taking an inquiry approach to learning and instruction is philosophically, psychologically, and pedagogically important.

This book takes a step back and acknowledges that it is not at all easy to make inquiry a curricular imperative. Our challenge as editors is to convey this message in a way that does not frighten educators away from the challenge and joy of doing so. Therefore we have invited 14 authors and groups of authors to tell stories about encountering barriers to inquiry in the classroom and other settings, and how the barriers were overcome. Some of these stories are very personal adventures, given in the first-person voice of the author who was there, some are reports of original or summarized research studies with added narrative, and some are more in the nature of "thought pieces." There are common themes across many chapters, yet unique twists among them. In as many situations as possible, we have presented the words of the learners, teachers, and observers, extracted from field notes, as well as quantitative data.

Every chapter is characterized by a particular barrier or barriers. Each has a primary focus on learners, teachers, or the curriculum. The set of stories reflects highly varied learning contexts ranging from infancy to university, from the classroom to the science fair exhibition, and even to the concert stage. In every context, there are delicate interactions among barriers, focus, and contexts. The grouping and ordering of these chapters is necessarily somewhat arbitrary. We have decided to present the chapters in two principal groups, but without division. They start primarily focused on learners and the barriers learners face. Certainly, a barrier faced by a learner is a challenge for the teacher. About half way through, they shift to a primary focus on teachers and the barriers teachers face. And, of course, a barrier faced by a teacher is a challenge for the learner. Roughly in the middle of the book, somewhat anchoring this change in emphasis, is a chapter about concert pianists from infancy to adulthood and how they can make performance a creative, adaptive, original experience for themselves and their audience, how they can practice for such creative and proficient variability rather than for the perfect repetition of the curriculum, that is, the musical score. That is also the task of the learner and teacher as creative performer. McLuhan (1960) once wrote, "It's misleading to suppose there's any basic difference between education and entertainment" (p. 3). Forty years ago, McLuhan and Fiore (1967) also imagined key elements of the educational vision that embraces inquiry:

> Education must shift from instruction, from imposing of stencils, to discovery—to probing and exploration and to the recognition of the language of forms. The young today reject goals. They want roles—R-O-L-E-S. That is, total involvement. . . . The teach-in represents a creative effort, switching the educational process from package to discovery. As the audience becomes a participant in the total electric drama, the classroom becomes a scene in which the audience performs an enormous amount of work. (pp. 100–101)

We hope that the reader will recognize the following main issues in the chapters that follow, with the message developing in approximately this order.

Among the first barriers to succeeding in inquiry learning that students will encounter in classrooms is their lack of strategy skills, prior knowledge of the field, knowledge of how to co-construct curriculum with the teacher, and skills to avoid trivial noninquiry projects. Middle (junior high) school social studies provides a rich setting in which to explore these issues through a detailed case study of how one teacher overcame these hurdles (Chapter 1, Aulls). Strong parallels are found in elementary school. Elementary students, especially below third grade, are extremely variable in what they know about the prerequisites to doing or even beginning inquiry, and most are severely lacking. It is a developmental process, as well as educational, to help them succeed, this time told by a direct participant rather than observer in the classroom (Chapter 2, Starko). A critical part to beginning inquiry is having a question, problem, or project that one finds motivated to pursue. Students, however, have great difficulty coming up with a topic, a very different task from selecting one from a list or text. Strangely, it is not necessarily the difficulty of the material or even its unfamiliarity that acts as a barrier to students jumping in. Students worry about what others think, and school-related planning skills learned before high school are inadequate to more engaging sophisticated projects (Chapter 3, Delcourt).

When students have overcome the barrier of deciding on a topic, and they might even have the skills and knowledge to proceed, other challenges can interfere with the success of inquiry. Cheating or plagiarism can subvert genuine inquiry in science fairs because they lead to products that are simply not original, whatever the primary intentions. Students need support, time, and a learning structure to avoid the temptation, for example a focus on the process rather than the grade for the product (Chapter 4, Shore, Delcourt, Syer, & Schapiro). Student inquiry today typically includes Internet exploration. Watch out. The process of researching a topic from a computer is not one that can be left unguided and unsupervised any more than a field trip out in the community (Chapter 5, Cartwright, Finkelstein, & Maennling).

Inquiry is generally assumed to involve collaboration. Collaboration is implicit in the concept of a community of learners, and knowledge creation is both a private pleasure and a social activity. Initiating collaboration within inquiry, like the selection of a question or topic, is a difficult and complex task for the learner and the teacher. Students need to know the advantages and disadvantages of making a commitment to collaboration because it is not always to the advantage of a student. Teachers need to learn to read the signals accurately when students do not or choose not to collaborate well enough to make this collaboration an explicit part of building an inquiry environment (Chapter 6, Butler-Kisber). In addition to the presumption about the necessary presence of collaboration, there is also a further assumption that collaboration must be positive, cooperative, endowed with cozy feelings, and conflict is to be avoided and removed when it occurs. Conflict among creative producers, on the other hand, is probably the norm in the real world. It is one thing to totally avoid conflict. It is another to use it constructively and to learn to deal respectfully with collaborators when it occurs. Certain kinds of conflict turn out to be productive and perhaps even necessary to cognitive progress. This is illustrated in a highly structured experiment in which students' voices highlight the processes (Chapter 7, Barfurth & Shore).

As the volume shifts from a primary focus on the learner and learner-teacher interaction in classrooms to a closer look at teachers, we temporarily step outside the context of schools and schooling to focus on inquiry teaching and learning as a creative act. When inquiry or discovery is the aim, the topic is the musical score, the curriculum is a repertoire, and teacher-student interaction promotes the experience of creative variability. How they learn, for example, in the purpose of rehearsal, and in their developmental experiences, to produce creative variation in performance, and the barriers they overcome, speak to the changes teachers face in themselves and in their students when making teaching and learning an inquiry experience (Chapter 8, Cohen). Teaching is a creative performance, but moving from teaching according to a well rehearsed lesson plan to teaching that promotes inquiry is a major transformation. It is not a new set of prescriptions, but an adaptive, original approach to every learning-teaching-curriculum interaction.

Change is risky, even for professional teachers who are and think of themselves as creative professionals and achievers. The school context is not always favorable to supporting such change, and considerable inner direction, knowledge, and strength are needed. These are illustrated in a collection of teacher reflections (Chapter 9, Bramwell-Rejskind, Halliday, & McBride). On their way to taking on a new pedagogical persona, teachers as a group have many internalized models of what constitutes inquiry, but individual teachers risk being rather unidimensional in this regard. This can prevent teachers from responding appropriately to the variability in students' initial preparedness to do inquiry (cf. Chapters 2 and 3 especially). A survey study of several teachers revealed that student barriers teachers found especially challenging included the skills of articulating questions, problems, and projects (Chapter 10, Robinson & Hall). Teachers' internalized models of inquiry also vary between teachers who use inquiry and those who do not. Those who do use inquiry perceive inquiry strategy very much in the way the conceptual and research literature on inquiry portrays it. Noninquiry teachers' fundamental assumptions about good teaching are barriers to implementing inquiry. A classical collective case study compared inquiry and noninquiry teachers'—all regarded as excellent teachers—conceptualizations of inquiry (Chapter 11, Manconi, Aulls, & Shore).

Teachers do not teach and learners do not learn in a vacuum. The social context of what they learn and how they learn it reflects different learning goals and outcomes. This notably includes developing understanding of diversity among their fellow learners if, as inquiry assumes, a community of inquiry-oriented learners is to develop (as inquiry theory assumes it should). The hidden curriculum thereby becomes a barrier to full engagement in inquiry (Chapter 12, Luconi). Another important contextual element in 21st-century education is technology. Different generations react differently to the opportunities presented by instructional technology. The greatest impact is likely on roles. Teachers and learners might underestimate the importance of role changes for each other. Technology especially highlights the flattening of hierarchies of authority of knowledge in the classroom (Chapter 13, Bracewell, Le Maistre, Lajoie, & Breuleux). In between being a school child and becoming a teacher, we have the educated young adult who may or may not be heading for a career in education. Barriers to inquiry in science are evident in scientific epistemology. When inquiry is itself the content, as it is when learning about it and how to do it, incomplete and inaccurate knowledge about what it is and how to do it are serious barriers to making it happen, however wonderful and justified the imperative to include inquiry in curriculum. (Chapter 14, Butler, Pollock, Nomme, & Nakonechny).

We invite you to share these experiences and to treat the barriers to inquiry participation as the very stepping stones to successfully use this process. Whether you are a teacher, administrator, policymaker, or parent, or if you are a student looking over the pedagogical fence, this volume presents inquiry to those facilitating its establishment as a fundamental part of what is expected in the best of schooling and to those enjoying the prospect of sharing an educational experience that values the creation of new knowledge and understanding as much as accumulating knowledge that has already been conveniently wrapped and put on the shelf for quick sale and consumption.

One of our contributors, Frances Halliday, an award-winning master teacher, gifted and special education consultant, graduate student, and friend, died before her chapter and this volume were completed. Fran used to quip that ordinary education was "open head, pour in, and spit out." Being an inquiry-based learner and teacher is much more difficult, but we hope that this volume helps uncloak common barriers. We invite you to join Fran and the other authors in this volume in making the choice, weathering the voyage, and engaging in being an inquiry educator and making it an imperative in curricula at all levels and in all types of formal education.

Bruce M. Shore
Mark W. Aulls
Marcia A. B. Delcourt
Montreal and Danbury
The High Ability and Inquiry Research Group
McGill University

References

McLuhan, M. (1960). Classroom without walls. In E. Carpenter & M. McLuhan (Eds.), *Explorations in communications: An anthology* (pp. 1–3). Boston: Beacon Press.
McLuhan, M., & Fiore, M. (1967). *The medium is the massage*. New York: Random House.

Acknowledgments

Creation of an edited volume requires gratitude above all to the contributors. We especially appreciate the patience our contributors have exhibited in waiting for both volumes to be completed, and in revising and recasting their thoughts to come close to the template we prescribed for these contributed chapters, although we have tried very hard to retain the original voice and unique perspective of each contributor. None of them was aware of the details of the rest of the volume, or the content of the companion work on conceptual foundations for inquiry as a curricular imperative, but they responded with remarkably original efforts to our prompting. Each of these chapters is therefore an original work written for this volume, and we thank our contributing authors and coauthors for seeing the potential for gravity and humor in each.

Completing this volume and its companion book would not have been possible without the assistance of many students and family members who have worked with us over the years. In the final year and a half of work, Dominique (Nika) Morisano oversaw the work of three other assistants and coordinated multiple rounds of editing, reference searching, and updating the text with notes and scribbles and variably useful corrections from the authors. Working with her were Karen Borovay, Noah Edwardsen, and Monica Shore. Others who contributed to building the reference lists, text editing, and polishing the electronic files over the years of work, included Özge Akçali, Lisa R. French, Dadong (Charles) Hoa, Yuan-Jin Hong, Deanne Sauvé, Cassidy A. Syer, and especially Katherine Aulls. Several students (at the time) assisted in the creation of the original master file of hundreds of inquiry references, including Francesca Luconi, Lynn Manconi, Shelly Rohar, and Judith McBride, who also provided general feedback on the first full draft of the manuscripts.

Inevitably and happily we are especially grateful to our wives and husband, Katherine Aulls, Bettina Shore, and Jean Delcourt, all of whom have professions and lives of their own, who tolerated our absences, attachments to the computer at most unreasonable hours, and phone calls at almost unreasonable hours trying to find that elusive quotation that was absolutely essential to one chapter or another.

Finally, we thank the Social Sciences and Research Council of Canada (SSHRC) and the *Fonds du Québec de recherche sur la société et la culture* (FQRSC), *Secteur sciences humaines et sociales* [Quebec Research Funds on Society and Culture, Social Sciences and Humanities Sector] for their multiple grants over many years in support of our research on inquiry and on high ability, and specifically for the present volumes on several occasions. We also have been encouraged in this pursuit by our association with and logistical support from the multicampus Centre for Research on Learning and Performance, also supported by FQRSC.

The Editors and Authors

Mark W. Aulls is Professor of Educational Psychology, McGill University, in Montreal. His research, earlier in reading processes, is on the effects of student-teacher interaction on the development of students' intellectual skills and on the development and cultivation of inquiry learning and instruction in students, teachers, and teachers-in-training. His degrees are a BS in Education (Ball State), MEd in Reading (Indiana), and an EdD in Educational Psychology (Georgia). *mark.aulls@mcgill.ca*

Marion A. Barfurth is Associate Professor of Technology and Learning in the Faculty of Education, University of Ottawa, in Ontario. Her research is on collaborative learning in school settings, change in teaching practice, and the integration of technology in learning and teaching. She has a BA in Mathematics and Economics and MA in the Teaching of Mathematics (Concordia), and PhD in Educational Psychology (McGill). *marion.barfurth@gmail.com*

Robert J. Bracewell is Professor of Educational Psychology and Associate Dean (Research and Graduate Students) of the Faculty of Education, McGill University, in Montreal, Quebec. His research interests are in areas of ill-defined problem-solving tasks and their mastery, such as how teachers modify their instructional practices to make effective use of technology. His degrees are a BSc and MA in Psychology (McMaster) and a PhD in Educational Theory (Toronto). *robert. bracewell@mcgill.ca*

F. Gillian Bramwell-Rejskind recently retired as Associate Professor of Educational Psychology in the Department of Educational and Counselling Psychology, McGill University, in Montreal, Quebec. Her research interests are in creativity, and have also included gender differences and giftedness. Her degrees are a BA and MA in Psychology (Saskatchewan), and PhD in Psychology (Concordia). *gillian.bramwell@mcgill.ca*

Alain Breuleux is Associate Professor in the Department of Educational and Counselling Psychology, McGill University, in Montreal, Quebec. He is a cognitive psychologist collaborating with school teachers and administrators to design and investigate sustainable technology-enabled networks for learning, advanced pedagogical practices, and knowledge management in education. His degrees are a BSc, MA, and PhD in Psychology (Montreal). *alain.breuleux@mcgill.ca*

Deborah L. Butler is Associate Professor in the Department of Educational and Counselling Psychology and Special Education, and Associate Dean, Graduate Programs and Research, University of British Columbia, in Vancouver, British Columbia. Her research focuses on understanding what constitutes self-regulated, strategic engagement as situated in various kinds of academic work, barriers to students' successful engagement, and the qualities of instruction or intervention that promote self-regulated learning by diverse learners. She holds a BA (Honors) in Psychology (California, San Diego), an MA in Cognitive Psychology (British Columbia), and a PhD in Educational Psychology (Simon Fraser). *deborah.butler@ubc.ca*

Lynn Butler-Kisber is Associate Professor in the Department of Integrated Studies in Education, McGill University, in Montreal, Quebec. Her research interests are in literacy, curriculum, leadership, professional development, and qualitative methodologies. Her degrees are a BEd and an MEd in Special Education (McGill) and an EdD in Teaching, Curriculum, and Learning Environments (Harvard). *lynn.butlerkisber@mcgill.ca*

Glenn F. Cartwright is Professor of Educational Psychology and Interim Dean of Continuing Education at McGill University, in Montreal. His scholarly interests include computer applications, artificial intelligence, virtual reality, and parent-alienation syndrome. His degrees include a BA in Psychology (Sir George Williams), Teaching Diploma and MA in Education (McGill), and PhD in Educational Psychology (Alberta). *glenn.cartwright@mcgill.ca*

Philip Cohen is Emeritus Professor and Artistic Director of the Leonardo Research Project, Concordia University, in Montreal, Quebec. He is an internationally distinguished teacher, coach, performance analyst, and consultant to performing artists, and served as consultant to professional and academic programs such as the reorganization of the Conservatoire system in France. He also works with performers encountering injury, neuromuscular and perceptual disabilities, anxiety, and related performance blocks. His real-time explorations with major and aspiring performers into the art of creative variability seek a unified perspective to the aesthetic, cognitive, biological, and cultural foundations of complex human performance, and insights that point the way to a new understanding of human potential. He has a BA with double Honours in Psychology and English (McGill) and a postgraduate diploma in piano performance (Conservatoire de musique du Québec). *philipcohen@concordia.ca*

Marcia A. B. Delcourt is Professor of Education and Educational Psychology, and Coordinator of the EdD Program in Instructional Leadership, at Western Connecticut State University in Danbury, Connecticut, and Adjunct Professor in the Department of Educational and Counselling Psychology at McGill University in Montreal, Quebec. Her research interests include developing inquiry in teachers and students, encouraging talent development, analyzing program development and assessment techniques, developing student learning outcomes, encouraging teachers as researchers, and assessing the impact of computer technologies. She has a BS in Education (Bloomsburg), and an MA and PhD in Educational Psychology (Connecticut). *delcourtm@wcsu.edu*

Adam B. A. Finkelstein is the Manager of Teaching Technology Services in the Instructional Media Services of McGill University in Montreal, Quebec. He is completing a PhD in Educational Psychology, also at McGill. His research interests include the psychological implications of virtual learning environments, effective implementation of technologies in teaching and learning, and instructional design issues for online learning. He has a BSc in Biology and Psychology (McGill), and an MA in Educational Psychology (McGill). *adam.finkelstein@mcgill.ca*

Julia Hall is a social studies teacher at Benton Junior High School in Benton, Arkansas. Her professional interests focus on world history, geography, and African cultures. She holds a BA in Social Studies (Harvard) and an MEd in Gifted Education (Arkansas, Little Rock). *jwestern67@hotmail.com*

Frances Halliday was a distinguished and award-winning teacher of gifted pupils in Ontario, then a PhD candidate in Educational Psychology at McGill University in Montreal, Quebec. She also had been an Assistant Professor of Education at Bishop's University in Lennoxville, Quebec, and then curriculum-reform consultant for two regional Quebec school districts. Fran died in October 2002, before completing her PhD. Her degrees were a BEd in Elementary Education (McMaster) and an MEd and MA in Educational Psychology (McGill).

Susanne P. Lajoie is James McGill Professor and Chair of the Department of Educational and Counselling Psychology, McGill University, in Montreal, Quebec. Her research interests involve the design and evaluation of computer-based learning environments for classroom and real-world applications in science and medicine. Her degrees are a BA in Psychology and MA in Educational Psychology (McGill), and a PhD in Educational Psychology (Stanford). *susanne.lajoie@mcgill.ca*

Cathrine Le Maistre is Associate Professor in the Department of Integrated Studies in Education, McGill University, in Montreal, Quebec. Her recent research has been in the induction and support of teachers. Other interests have included mathematics education. Her degrees are BSc and Diploma in Education (Exeter), and an MEd and PhD in Educational Psychology (McGill). *kate.le.maistre@mcgill.ca*

Francesca Luconi is a PhD candidate in Educational Psychology and a consultant in continuing medical education in the Centre for Medical Education, McGill University, in Montreal, Quebec. Her research was on the hidden curriculum in schooling in relation to cultural differences and is currently on how physicians learn through the Internet. Her previous degrees include an Honors Bachelor in

Social Athropology (Iberamericana) and an MEd in Educational Psychology (McGill). *frances.luconi@sympatico.ca*

Matthew K. B. Maennling managed the instructional design and training team for the MassONE K–12 eLearning portal at the Massachusetts Department of Education. Recently based in Burlington, Ontario, he has been a consultant for Xwave Solutions, where he is designing a training strategy to deploy an ASP-based Clinical Management System for use by Ontario family physicians. He has recently moved to Ottawa, Ontario. He has a BEd in Physical Education (McGill). *matthew@maennling.com*

Lynn Manconi is a special education teacher in Montreal. Her research was on teachers' conceptualizations of inquiry. She has a BA in Early Childhood Education and an MA in Educational Technology (Concordia), and a Certificate in Special Education and PhD in Educational Psychology (McGill). *lmanconi@videotron.ca*

Judith B. McBride is a former special education teacher, now a Lecturer and Adjunct Professor in Educational Psychology at McGill University, in Montreal. Her research interests have ranged from the effects of nutrition on rats' learning, play therapy to facilitate prosocial classroom behavior, student and teacher perceptions of the mainstream school, teachers changing their practice through collaborative action research, teacher learning as perspective transformation, to how teachers emerge as researchers through immersion in the research community while undertaking graduate studies. She has a BA in Psychology and English (Concordia), Diplomas in Elementary and Special Education, and an MEd and PhD in Educational Psychology (McGill). *judy.judymcbride@gmail.com*

Joanne Nakonechny is Research Associate in the Science Centre for Learning and Teaching, Faculty of Science, University of British Columbia, in Vancouver, British Columbia. Her research interests focus on how to facilitate 1st- and 2nd-year university science students' conceptual understanding, and on developing techniques for understanding the motivational process in students' learning. She has a BA (Honours) in Anthropology and MEd in English as an Additional Language (British Columbia), MSc (Montreal) and a PhD in Anthropology (McMaster). *nakonechny@science.ubc.ca*

Kathy M. Nomme is Instructor and Laboratory Faculty in the Department of Botany and Zoology, University of British Columbia, in Vancouver, British Columbia. A plant ecologist by training, her scholarly interests focus on laboratory education for undergraduate students and motivation and attitudes in 1st-year science. She holds a Teaching Diploma (Simon Fraser) and a BSc and MSc in Plant Ecology (British Columbia). *nomme@zoology.ubc.ca*

Carol Pollock is Senior Instructor and Director of First-Year Biology in the Department of Zoology, University of British Columbia, in Vancouver, British Columbia. Her research areas of interest are the genetics of eye color in *Drosophila melanogaster*, student learning in 1st- and 2nd-year university, and laboratory education. She holds a BSc (Honours) in Microbiology and an MSc in Zoology (Manitoba), and a PhD in Zoology (British Columbia). *pollock@zoology.ubc.ca*

Ann Robinson is Professor in the Department of Educational Leadership and Director of the Center for Gifted Education at the University of Arkansas at Little Rock. Her research interests focus on school and classroom practices related to the development of talent in students and in teachers. She holds a BA and MA in English (Wyoming) and a PhD in Educational Psychology (Purdue). *aerobinson@ualr.edu*

Michelle Schapiro is a school psychologist for Jewish Family Services in Montreal, Quebec. Her research was on students' cheating in science fairs and on the stability of friendships in gifted versus other young adolescents. Her degrees are a BA in Psychology, MA in Educational Psychology, and PhD in School/Applied Child Psychology (McGill). *mschapiro@bellnet.ca*

Bruce M. Shore is Professor of Educational Psychology in the Faculty of Education at McGill University in Montreal, where he also has served as Chair of the Department and Dean of Students. His research has addressed the ways in which gifted students think and learn differently from other students, especially how the development of giftedness parallels that of expertise, and understanding learning processes in inquiry-driven environments. He has a BSc in Mathematics and Chemistry (with Psychology), a Teaching Diploma in Secondary Mathematics and Science, and an MA in Education from McGill University, and a PhD in Educational Psychology from The University of Calgary. *bruce.m.shore@mcgill.ca*

Alane J. Starko is Professor and former Head of the Department of Teacher Education at Eastern Michigan University, in Ypsilanti, Michigan. Her research has focused on problem finding and creativity, curriculum design, and teacher thinking. She has a BS in Elementary Education and Educational Psychology and an MS in Elementary Education and Reading (State University College, Oneonta), and a PhD in Educational Psychology (Connecticut). *astarko@emich.edu*

Cassidy A. Syer is a school psychologist at Summit School in Montreal. Her research has been on students' sources of help and the prevalence of cheating in science fairs, and on student teachers' understanding of the strategic demands of inquiry involvement. She has a BA in Psychology, an MA in Educational Psychology, and a PhD in School/Applied Child Psychology from McGill University. *cassidy.syer@mail.mcgill.ca*

1

Developing Students' Inquiry Strategies: A Case Study of Teaching History in the Middle Grades

MARK W. AULLS

McGill University

In this chapter, I report the results of an intrinsic case study of barriers to inquiry instruction that arise and are overcome during a year of project-based instruction in one eighth-grade teacher's integrated English and history course. This study specifically focuses on the curriculum events and instruction-learning process associated with an 18-week unit about ancient Egyptian civilization. Few case studies of the classroom enactment of a middle-grades history curriculum-in-use (Cornbleth, 1990) have been reported in the social studies and history literature. Moreover, those studies that have been reported do not offer insights into the barriers to teaching and learning interactions of inquiry that a teacher, without graduate school education, and his or her students together overcome. Some of the barriers encountered in this case study are students' lack of strategic skills needed to engage in inquiries, limited prior knowledge about the subject matter, their need to accept an unfamiliar role as co-constructor of at least parts of the curriculum and question asker, and avoiding trivial projects that do not adequately exploit the opportunity to learn through inquiry. We shall explore these through the case study of one teacher newly implementing an inquiry curriculum.

Teachers may naturally find it difficult to integrate new approaches into their existing curriculum and instructional practices (Weaver, Jantz, Farrell, & Cirrincione, 1985). Those who seek to support reforms in education, or particular kinds of instruction such as a form of inquiry instruction, sometimes forget that most teachers reinvent their own classroom culture each year by engaging a new population of students. During this process, a teacher often merges past and new plans for curriculum enactment. As the plans are enacted in the classroom, a web is spun from the interaction among the teacher, the students, and the manifest and hidden curricula (Cornbleth, 1985, 1990). The hidden curriculum is shaped by school and community forces, while the manifest curriculum is a direct function of the daily life shaped by the classroom culture. Hence, inquiry instruction entering into a teacher's classroom through new reforms is often adapted in order to fit with the instructional practices for teaching history built up over years of classroom practice.

Those teachers who decide to attempt to teach with an inquiry-oriented approach are likely already to be at a time in their career when they can give up central control of instruction and progress toward a student-centered curriculum. At least this was a finding of a recent collective case study based on interviews with eight teachers of whom six perceived themselves as inquiry-oriented, whereas the other two did not (Manconi, 2004; also see Chapter 11 in this volume). This kind of instruction raises the intellectual demands for student participation in classroom instruction. The goal of any inquiry is understanding and problem solving, not memorization or reproduction. Inquiry instruction is a complex undertaking. It fosters a deep approach to learning content among students rather than a shallow one (Brophy, 1990, 1992).

Some theorists argue that student participation in inquiry instruction demands sufficient time for students to inquire, as well as collaboration among participants, in order to reduce the inherent ambiguity and complexity of the process (Gillies & Ashman, 1998). Students must learn how to move forward intellectually in solving a problem step-by-step, or in accomplishing understanding through multiple perspectives gained from discourse and higher-order thinking (Hatano, 1993; Hicks, 1995; Wertsch & Toma, 1995). There is also the problem of students carrying out some form of inquiry in a content domain in which they lack sufficient foundational knowledge to search for and process new conceptual knowledge (Brophy, Prawat, & McMahon, 1991). Teachers who work regularly with students who are average or below average in cognitive skills may question the extent to which, and the classroom conditions under which, their students can benefit socially and intellectually from participation in inquiry-oriented instruction (Aulls, 2002; Onosko, 1991; Rossi & Pace, 1998).

Brief reviews of the nature of inquiry instruction, research on its success, and many possible barriers that arise in classrooms to hinder successful participation in project-based instruction and meaningful student learning, are helpful prefaces to the case study.

Characteristics of Inquiry-Oriented Instruction

Pressley and McCormick (1995) have systematically compared the features of what they characterized as different methods of instruction widely used in Kindergarten through 12th grade. They contrasted mastery learning, direct instruction, direct explanation, reciprocal teaching, cooperative learning, and discovery learning. The last method has been widely heralded as a method used in inquiry-oriented instruction and is attributed to theories of learning originated by Piaget (1967) and Bruner (1968). The key categories used to compare discovery learning to other methods of instruction are: (a) the amount of teacher directedness in lessons, (b) the amount or type of structure placed on student activity, (c) the teacher's role or roles, (d) the student's role or roles, and (e) the most distinguishing features of the method. These dimensions of instruction seem likely to distinguish other kinds of inquiry instruction from traditional instruction and discovery learning. Specifically, they seem to also directly apply to project-based instruction (Dewey, 1916; Dunn, 2000; Huerta & Flemmer, 2000; Tuyay, Floriani, Yeager, Dixon, & Green, 1995). In the present case study, the teacher, Paul, used a project-based form of inquiry instruction and this approach also can be described using the categories listed earlier.

Discovery learning limits the amount of teacher directedness more than any other method. Students assume the major responsibility for directing their own learning activities. In project-based learning, the teacher directedness is part of the preparation of students in basic conceptual knowledge within which domain students will carry out projects. It is also part of helping students learn how to carry out necessary strategies such as searching for resource materials, and selecting and recording information relevant to accomplishing the project. Teacher roles during discovery learning instruction are described as limited because teachers are not expected to present information. At the most, the teacher facilitates and guides students toward making discoveries.

The teacher's role in project-based learning is not limited and is more like that of a coach, guide, or resource expert. In discovery learning, instruction is student-directed and students are expected to take on many roles to actively seek and discover new knowledge. In project-based learning, the students and the teacher are both expected to take on many roles (Aulls & Peetush, 1998) but instruction is scaffolded such that, at the outset, the teacher introduces students to new concepts, engages students in dialogue about the concepts as they evolve to a critical mass, and then engages learners in the design and enactment of projects to allow students to further elaborate on the basic domain knowledge that is built up jointly with the teacher. During a year, a number of projects may be undertaken that weave together conceptual knowledge taught in (for example) English and history and strategies that are valid in both subjects as well as for inquiry learning. Exploring, manipulating, and experimenting are done by students in both discovery learning and project-based learning. Student curiosity is also cultivated and used as a source of motivation to be involved in both discovery learning and project-based learning. Discovery learning, however, also may have negative consequences. It may increase the risk of incorrect learning, and it can be inefficient in that too much time may be taken to acquire conventional knowledge through discovery, knowledge that could be obtained in much less time (and perhaps more accurately) through direct instruction by the teacher. Project-based inquiry learning, because of its scaffolding of student participation in depth into a domain, reduces the risk of incorrect learning. Empirical research on classroom instruction that emphasizes discovery learning and project-based learning suggests that the above descriptions fit many teachers' practices.

The discovery and project-based methods are only two of many approaches to an inquiry-oriented approach to teaching history in the middle grades. Others especially applicable to history instruction include (a) problem solving (Hughes, Sears, & Clarke, 1998; Son & VanSickle, 2000; Torney-Purta, 1991); (b) critical thinking (Commeyras, 1990; Facione, 1990; VanSledright & Kelly, 1998); (c) thoughtfulness (Newmann, 1990, 1991); and (d) the historical method (Spoehr & Spoehr, 1994). All of these approaches to inquiry instruction, such as discovery learning and problem-based instruction, seek to make students the center of learning more often than the teacher. For students to become the crux of classroom learning, teachers attempt to make them highly active social and cognitive participants in instruction. All of these methods engage the student in learning how to inquire while learning content through asking questions, dialogue, problem solving, investigation, or research. A project-based approach to inquiry tends to allocate more days of instruction to students negotiating, carrying out, and presenting the results of a project where the goal is to collect and analyze data that explore a topic or test a research question. The goal also must be concerned with how students present their results to various audiences.

Results of Past and Present Research on Inquiry Instruction in History

A major goal of curriculum and instruction reforms in the social studies and history has been to promote the use of these methods or approaches to construct the processes of curriculum and instruction in classrooms in elementary, middle, and secondary schools. Despite the cautions about inquiry learning being an inefficient means of teaching concepts and conceptual relationships in a school subject (Ausubel & Robinson, 1969), results of classroom research on inquiry instruction since the 1970s have generally been positive. For example, Merwin (1976a) reviewed the empirical evidence for the inquiry approach to social-studies instruction from 1960 to 1976. He found 60 studies in the educational research literature, from elementary school through college. Thirty-nine studies addressed the broad question, "Can the inquiry method generate the kinds of cognitive and affective learning outcomes necessary for citizenship in a complex world?" Nineteen of those 39 studies associated positive achievement, affect, or both with participation in inquiry and 14 studies generated no grounds to support the contribution of inquiry instruction in comparison to control groups. The methodology of six studies was inadequate for Merwin to accept the results reported as positive inquiry outcomes.

All in all, positive affective or achievement outcomes associated with inquiry methods of teaching social studies or history have been respectable. The reservations that Merwin (1976a) held regarding the results of the 60 studies he reviewed were twofold. First, socioeconomic status and cognitive ability limited the situations and populations in which inquiry instruction succeeded. Second, most studies did not control for the extent to which teachers with a positive view toward having students interact with each other were more likely to succeed in enacting inquiry instruction than those who were more negative. However, he saw a trend suggesting teachers with positive views were more successful. There has been no similar review of classroom research devoted to a variety of forms of inquiry instruction between 1976 and 2005, nor to project-based learning.

Because all the studies reviewed by Merwin were quasi-experimental or correlational studies, none actually provided a thick description of what happened as inquiry instruction. The results then could not be useful to teachers who are looking for classroom conditions similar to their own, or teachers like themselves, as the base for constructing a model of how to teach in ways that served inquiry learning. Many of the studies were far shorter than 12 weeks in duration, so could not have allowed for an extended inquiry learning opportunity for young people.

None of the studies that succeeded at inquiry instruction addressed the question of what literacy strategies and research-specific approaches had to be taught. This is a glaring omission in a multicultural society in which learning how to learn had become an important consideration (Brophy, 1990; A. L. Brown, 1994). No consideration was given to when to teach literacy or other strategies needed to carry out inquiry, or how long specific strategies needed to be taught in order for students to use them spontaneously during some form of inquiry activity such as doing research on a particular topic, question, or phenomenon. For example, Aulls and Halliday (1994) reported that at least 36 weeks were needed for middle-grade students to improve significantly in the acquisition and use of strategies to identify main ideas and to generate summaries of full text sources in middle-grade science. These strategies are necessary to the identification of important concepts, ideas, and their relationships in historical texts and are used to construct a review of literature, to solve a problem, to answer a research question, or to support hypotheses tested in simple experiments.

Many potential barriers to classroom learning during inquiry instruction have been identified in a British study that focused on discovery learning (Edwards & Mercer, 1989). However, social studies and history classrooms were not separated out from instruction in other subjects. The study was exceedingly critical of the learning outcomes associated with the government mandated curriculum built on educators' interpretations of Piagetian theory, as opposed to those of developmental psychologists. Edwards and Mercer (1989) studied the enacted curriculum (see Cornbleth, 1990) as a process in a variety of subjects and classrooms. It was published as a book entitled *Common Knowledge: The Development of Understanding in the Classroom.* The study sampled three instructional lessons taught by the same teachers in every classroom and in all the basic subjects in eight different primary, middle, and comprehensive secondary schools in lower-middle-class and middle-class communities in England.

The analysis of field notes and classroom discourse clearly showed that teacher and student discourse seldom was based on substantive shared knowledge of subject-matter content during and at the end of the lessons observed. Typically, students' participation in discovery lessons resulted in only a few organized higher-order concepts and in many misconceptions, even though students attempted to be cooperative, and teachers had invited the researchers to observe what they considered to be typical of their best lessons. Moreover, none of the lessons observed showed teachers teaching students how to learn how to carry out discovery-learning processes. Lessons often actively involved students, but, in almost all classrooms observed, the teacher still controlled the content and direction of the students' thinking. Edwards and Mercer (1989) concluded their research report with these words:

> Piagetian theory . . . no longer justifies educationists' trust. It encourages a pedagogy which over-emphasizes the individual at the expense of the social, which undervalues talk as a tool for discovery, and which discourages teachers from making explicit to children the purposes of educational activities and the criteria for success. (p. 170)

Edwards and Mercer's (1989) analysis of their results also led them to support Vygotskian theory regarding how content learning occurs. Within this "social constructivist theory" context, more emphasis is placed on the joint construction of meaning by the teacher and students. Edwards and Mercer used lesson transcripts to illustrate how classroom discourse is the key to making lesson experiences and activities meaningful for students. In their view, language and communication had to create a shared teacher and student conceptual knowledge of subject matter. The importance of instructional experience and activity had to be open and its purposes explicit. Applied to inquiry instruction, this meant that discourse, jointly constructed by the teacher and students and by students with each other, should play an important role in guiding student inquiry and enabling students to play varied roles in the collection, analysis, and presentation of the product of inquiry.

Overview of Previously Studied Barriers to Inquiry Instruction in the Middle Grades

Graduate education. Previous extended analyses of project-based history or social studies instruction in the middle grades in the United States (Collins & Green, 1992; Tuyay et al., 1995) and in Canada (Aulls, 1998, 2002) have shown that teachers who have completed a graduate degree in education and have been involved in inquiry themselves can successfully provide inquiry learning opportunities in fourth through eighth grades. In surveys of teachers' perspectives on inquiry instruction, many teachers felt they were not adequately taught to do inquiry instruction during undergraduate or graduate education (Weaver et al., 1985). Hence, the lack of sufficient and appropriate graduate education may itself act as a first barrier to many teachers succeeding in this kind of instruction.

Adapting to risk and ambiguity. A second barrier to managing project-based instruction is that participation in the inquiry process demands that students frequently encounter activities which necessarily are high in risk and ambiguity.

For example, selecting a topic on which to do research is high in both risk and ambiguity because students may choose a topic about which they have little prior knowledge, although it sounds stimulating, and it is ambiguous because so many different sources may be tapped to seek information on it; within each source, as well, what to select may be unlimited. High risk and ambiguity in academic tasks influence students to withdraw cooperation in enacting the curriculum in traditional science (Carter & Doyle, 1989) and social studies classrooms (Aulls, 1998). The nature of inquiry in history and social sciences, in any of its forms, is to present the learner with an activity that entails ambiguity and risk-taking (Gabella, 1995). What sort of tasks and social climate do or should teachers create to counteract such demands on students and to support them in accomplishing activities that are high in risk and ambiguity?

Sustaining motivation. In the social studies, teachers frequently do not attempt to teach middle-grade students how to learn to inquire or learn conceptual content but, instead, they present the conceptual content to students (Brophy, 1990). How can students, who lack the declarative and strategic knowledge to do inquiry or learn conceptual knowledge, be given more responsibility for learning without injuring motivation or self-efficacy (Aulls, 1998, 2002; Cardelle-Elawar, 1995; Delcourt & Kinzie, 1993; Frederiksen & White, 1997; Gabella, 1995; Newman & Nessim, 1997; Pirozzo, 1987; Rossi, 1995; Sandoval & Reiser, 1997; Zimmerman & Martinez-Pons, 1988)? Should a teacher expect students to learn inquiry strategies by themselves with the teacher simply coaching whatever they can do, or intervening with limited procedural facilitation that enables students to progress within a phase of inquiry that they otherwise would not be able to complete by themselves (A. L. Brown & Campione, 1993; Lubliner, 2002; Palincsar & D. A. Brown, 1987)? A. L. Brown (1994), who was one of the major contributors to advances in the application of cognitive developmental theory to strategic instruction, indicated considerable disappointment in the inability of teachers to implement strategy instruction, either demonstrated by formal research, or by teachers' own reports of their interpretations of cognitive theory. Indeed, in an extensive review in the first *Handbook of Research on Teaching,* Armento (1986) stated that social studies were literally left out of this curricular revolution. One other factor related to this third barrier is the extent to which a teacher is prepared to assess changes in inquiry strategies and the content learned through participation in inquiry instruction (Fraser, 1980; Frederiksen & White, 1997; King, 1991; Newmann, 1990; Rogers, 1990; Swanson, 1993; Swicord, 1988; Udall & High, 1989; Wilson & Ball, 1996).

Curricular pressure. A fourth potential barrier to success in inquiry learning is the press to cover all the necessary content during a project-based approach to social studies or history instruction. This places considerable pressure on teachers to abandon giving sufficient time for students to explore less content in more depth and to avoid preparing themselves to learn how to learn to carry out inquiry learning in the classroom. Efforts to recognize when productive inquiry learning is happening are also compromised (Gabella, 1995). The catalyst to inquire often stems from the intention to be thoughtful or to expect to give reasons and evidence for claims (Newmann, 1990, 1991). A related problem is the hidden curriculum, forces outside the classroom which impact negatively on student learning. It works against teaching subject matter in-depth and carrying out project-based instruction (Cornbleth, 1990). In project-based instruction, the hidden curriculum also has the potential to take class time away from participation in projects that were intentionally designed to facilitate orderly academic learning (Cross, 1995; Ehman, Glenn, Johnson, & White, 1992; Frau, Midoro, & Pedemonte, 1992; Lehrer, 1993; Martens, 1992; Prawat, 1995; Shuell, 1993; Troutner, 1988; Waddick, 1994; also see Chapter 12 in this volume).

Knowledge base.   A fifth previously recognized barrier is closely related to the fourth. It may be much more difficult for teachers to plan and implement inquiry instruction that succeeds in promoting higher-order thinking in and among students who lack discipline-based content knowledge (Cochran, DeRuiter, & King, 1993), deep conventional subject-matter knowledge in the domain of inquiry, and knowledge of inquiry procedures and strategies from firsthand experience in doing inquiry themselves (Dagher & Cossman, 1992; Hatton, 1997; Russell, 1983; Shuell, 1993; Spoehr & Spoehr, 1994; Tobin, 1986).

Classroom conditions.   The sixth reported barrier addresses the absence of social and academic classroom conditions that help overcome the impact of other barriers to inquiry teaching or learning (Aulls, 2002; Collins & Stevens, 1982; Commeyras, 1990; Dagher, 1995a,b; Dahl, 1988; Geddis, 1991; Guzzetti & Williams, 1996; Hammer, 1997; Leinhardt, 1993; Lemke, 1990; Lundeberg & Moch, 1995; Mercer, 1994; Newmann, 1990; Polman & Pea, 1997; Roth, 1995, 1996; Russell, 1983; Sommers, 1992; Watson, 1995). For example, how do teachers estimate how to guide students in planning inquiry activities together so that the members of a group have sufficient social and academic knowledge and strategies to succeed (Kleinberg & Menmuir, 1996; Lehrer, 1993; Maor, 1991; Mueller, 1997; Palincsar & D. A. Brown, 1987; Parsons & Drew, 1996; Weade, 1992)?

Overview of the Case

To analyze the nature of the project-based inquiry instruction as it evolved in Paul's classroom, Aulls (1998) attempted to address these questions: (a) Who takes responsibility for learning during instruction? (b) What are the number and variety of roles taken by the teacher and student while enacting the curriculum in the classroom? (c) What is the range of responsibilities taken for learning during the succession of curriculum events that lead to the enactment of an inquiry-oriented, project-based unit of history? (d) What evidence exists that learning has occurred? From the answers were gleaned the barriers around which this chapter is framed.

Setting and Context for the Case Study

The teacher. Paul was an experienced teacher but was untrained in inquiry-oriented instruction yet open to ways of teaching that are student-centered (Hudson-Ross, 1989). In this case study, I describe what happened as the enactment of inquiry instruction in his classroom during his second year as a member of a team of six middle-grade teachers who volunteered to integrate English and history instruction through a project-based instructional approach. Paul encountered and overcame a number of barriers to successful student participation in inquiry learning within this integrated teaching of English and history.

In the study, we asked what happened to Paul, who has not been overtly engaged in action research but who does participate in innovation programs for teaching generated by staff in his high school. Paul did not choose to attend graduate school to further his acquaintance with a new knowledge base on learning and instruction, but he kept abreast of new innovative means of instruction through his friendship with teachers who had obtained a master's degree. He entered into the integrated history and English project-based curriculum innovation because he was approached by one of these friends to participate in a project approved by the school district. Thus, in this study, the focus was on a highly experienced teacher who worked in middle grades teaching English and also in high school teaching media communications and English, but who had received only undergraduate, secondary teacher education.

The school. This study took place at Seashore High School (SHS). It was built in 1962, and buildings were added in 1968 and 1970. SHS is a two-storey, modern brick structure shaped like a banjo with the base of the instrument closest to a suburban highway. A visitor to the school would park on the blacktop driveway that forms a semicircular entrance for visitors, the principal, and two vice-principals. Directly across the road from SHS is a parking lot that is big enough to accommodate the cars of the 91 teachers, 3 guidance counselors, 10 technical aides (who offer support for students with disabilities in mainstream classes), 2 librarians, 1 community liaison coordinator, and 15 support staff, including secretaries and janitors. In the time since SHS was built as a middle-class suburban school, its local community has become more diversified socioeconomically and culturally. The curriculum, as diversified as its student clientele, offers the basic core program required for high schools, a widely acknowledged music program, a French-immersion program in which between a third and half of all courses are given in French, a vocational training program, a program to individualize instruction for students who have learning or behavioral problems, a peer-tutorial program, and a peer-mediation program to diffuse and resolve student conflicts in a manner that emphasizes prevention. SHS offers two enrichment programs, called the Alternative Learning Program: One is a French-immersion program and the other is only offered in French (at the level of a first language). Finally, SHS is a multicultural and multilingual school that, as is the norm in the Province of Quebec, includes students from 7th through 11th grades.

Paul's class.   Paul taught in the "English Stream" of eighth grade that was made up of those students who did not qualify for the French or French-immersion programs. The vice-principal pointed out that students in this program tended to come from homes where English was the only language spoken, or where some language other than French was the native language. Names such as Andy, Anik, Alain, Jamil, Jon and Katie illustrate the multiethnic distribution of the 24 students Paul taught in the observed class. The students in Paul's class ranged from above average to low achieving, based on the *Canadian Cognitive Abilities Test* (Thorndike & Hagen, 1982). Over the years, the English stream increased in size at SHS, as a result of socioeconomic changes in the community. For this reason, innovative programs were encouraged to enhance student motivation and literacy, and to reduce study-skill problems that also had lowered academic achievement.

Paul's recruitment to an inquiry-oriented curriculum project.   Paul was a member of a team of five teachers who banded together to participate in a curriculum project. The lead teacher proposed an integrated English and history period in which the teachers could use the entire block of time of 100 minutes to emphasize literacy skills while teaching history content. The use of expository and narrative writing, depicting historical events and topics from the standard history curriculum, was viewed as an advantage for students whose literacy skills were often weak. In order to increase the opportunity for the teachers to create a strong social culture with their group of students, they also taught mathematics to their class in the integrated English and history alternative curriculum, and were their groups' homeroom teachers (greeting them each morning and coordinating an overall view of their progress).

Five of the 10 eighth grade teachers agreed to participate in this project. Paul volunteered for three reasons. First, he had been a long-time social friend of the lead teacher who had developed the project and had gotten it approved by the school board and parents in the community. Second, as a result of a budget cut, and after 12 years away from teaching in the middle grades, Paul had left his position of media director for the high school and returned to teaching. Third, Paul had already used teaching materials, originally developed by the integrated English and history project leader. Paul felt that the materials were very effective as a guide for successfully teaching reading and writing skills, with both narrative and expository materials, because they had had a positive effect on his students when writing in history classes.

Paul's classroom.   Unlike most other eighth grade teachers in his school, Paul had his own classroom where his class of 24 students came at the beginning of the day for homeroom and for instruction in English, history, and mathematics. Light streamed in through nine high windows that lined the back of the classroom.

All students sat with their backs to the windows, facing the green chalkboard that ran the length of the front wall. It was cleanly washed every day. Paul used the board in a number of ways. One was to communicate the daily news, assignments, and homework. Paul's neat handwriting was seen every morning on the chalkboard, and it was easy to read. During face-to-face verbal instruction, Paul used writing and talk simultaneously to reflect the results of discussions to guide the students' thinking during a lesson, and to cue them to information that had to be remembered or further reflected upon later during group work. During a lesson, text from dialogue was usually constructed and represented in note form on the board. Paul also used it to list steps of procedures and results of brainstorming, to summarize lengthy discussions, conclusions, or decisions made by the class through consensus or debate, to note main ideas, and to produce taxonomies of concepts in diagram form. However, nothing on the chalkboard remained longer than one day. Each day began with all the students copying into their SHS Bluebook the class agenda and homework for the day.

The students' desks could be moved into various arrangements to suit the activities the students were engaged in during the week. But students did not initiate new seating arrangements without Paul's permission or full-class discussion. At the start of the year, students were asked to select two other students as partners with whom to do group work in history and English classes, and then at the end of each curriculum unit, they were given the opportunity to join a new group if they felt they could be academically more productive and offered reasons that others in the proposed group also would support. Members of groups also tended to sit near each other and kept that seat throughout most of the academic year.

Paul had two teacher's desks. A large oak top desk was in the center of the room in front of the chalkboard. It was here that students dropped off their homework in baskets marked English, history, or mathematics. Paul only sat at this desk to take attendance in the morning and occasionally to conference with individual students. The second desk was in the right-hand corner in the back of the room. It was a rolltop desk where Paul did his lesson planning, marked student papers, and ate his lunch. Next to this desk were two large file cabinets where all of Paul's lessons and student work were stored. Paul taught his students to use three-ring binders with dividers to label and date their work in all three subjects he taught. He corrected students' work in the morning, several hours before school started, and in the afternoon before going home. He was very orderly and systematic in his marking, keeping the majority of students responsible for handing in, picking up, and keeping their work for future reference, and for filing their accomplishments, and current events from school and from local, national, and international news. On another smaller chalkboard were displayed the students' messages to each other and the "Daily Agenda" and "Homework" for students to copy into their daily journals. No extra words were wasted for the agenda list or the homework. Paul taught students to develop notes, make diagrams, and make maps in as parsimonious a manner as possible while including all the important information.

There was one computer halfway between the last row of student seats and the windows. Beside it was a file with software games for students to use. Many of the diskettes were to be used by students during the lunch hour when Paul left his room open to whoever wished to use it with his permission. In that time, his students and those from other classes often used the software games.

The wall on the entrance side of the room had three gigantic bulletin boards and a long narrow table on which Paul placed the work he had marked for students to pick up. Student work was mounted on the bulletin boards, and each school term, Paul left a public record of student team memberships and the results of weekly academic assignments. Students were responsible for keeping up with this information themselves. Each week the content of the bulletin boards changed. Most student work found its way to this bright and colorful board. The students and Paul also posted current events, cartoons related to classroom issues, or events and academically related material. The results of individual and small group student projects were always displayed on these bulletin boards, while student writing from English assignments was always put on display on the bulletin board in the rear of the room. The general impression of Paul's classroom was one of things happening and a sense of community where students were interested in peer accomplishments, discoveries, and observations about life.

Shaping the classroom climate.   To offer a better feel for Paul's classroom and his students, consider the results of Aulls's interview with him about the classroom climate he tried to create:

Interviewer: Would you consider, then, that for a lot of these kids, your classroom was a safe place for them to be, a secure place for them to be?

Paul: That's what I try to do, it's the feeling I try to create. It is a haven, or an oasis, hopefully, that the place is always presentable for them. It's their home to use as they see fit. When they are in there, I am not doting over them. I don't kibitz with them. I am not there to socialize with them. I'm the teacher. But I am always there. You know I keep the room open for the lunch hour, so they have a place to socialize and do anything they want to generally relax and they can do academic work if they have to. I was there if they needed me at the end of every day . . . for personal help.

Interviewer: Were they free to come in anytime other than during those three periods?

Paul: Oh yes!

Interviewer: Did they come at lunch?

Paul: Oh yes! And they came when I asked them to come for specific reasons or they came and they learned from playing chess, or playing computer games, or getting caught up on work, and of course, students from other rooms were in there as well.

Interviewer: So they were welcome to bring their friends?

Paul: Oh yes. Yes! And there were students who came in who didn't come in with somebody from our class.

Interviewer: Oh, they just came because it was a nice place to be to play chess or chat with you.

Paul: And some to play on our computers or get help.

Interviewer: When they came at lunch, did they sometimes chat with you, too?

Paul: Not too much, I'm unapproachable. I'm not too approachable. I have certain things I do at lunch as well. Most of the time they'd see me there working, correcting, I had a full load and I take advantage of it. I don't like to take a lot of work home with me and I tend to get it done at lunch and after school.

Interviewer: You stay a little later?

Paul: Oh, I do. Most days 4:00 or 4:30, which is a good two hours, when you think about it, after the students leave. So a lot of the . . . time, even though the class is open, it is my lunch hour too. They respected that.

Paul's Beliefs Regarding Teaching and Learning

Teaching.   Anderson and Burns (1989), after reviewing a decade of research on classroom instruction, took the position that "teaching" is part of "instruction." It is what the teacher does. Other factors enter into instruction such as activities and the co-constructed academic discourse that arises during lessons. Qualitative classroom researchers (Aulls, 2002; Collins & Green, 1992; Tuyay et al., 1995) reported that instruction and learning interact with each other on a minute-by-minute basis as the teacher and students strive to construct classroom life and the curriculum as a process. It is a dynamic, complex, and often messy endeavor in which it is difficult for the participants and observers to identify how one variable affects another within a sequence of lessons making up the events of the curriculum-in-use. To understand the teaching component of instruction, it is necessary to have some understanding of the teacher and how she or he views teaching and learning. During a two-year period of observation, Paul was asked a series of questions about his views of teaching and learning. These are his answers to questions about teaching, and later about learning.

Interviewer: What is teaching?

Paul: It's everything you do when you are at school. It involves monitoring, feedback, and the various processes of directly teaching subject matter face-to-face. Teaching includes taking on different roles and especially modeling to students. It is teaching content within a set of social rules so people can coexist with each other in my classroom. The content is taught in a particular order by units.

Interviewer: What do you do to teach history?

Paul: I use lecture format but not a great deal. I want them to be more active in their learning. I want them to lecture, do a bristol-board oral presentation, develop a time-line presentation, focus them on manipulating content through dialogue. I want them to create categories and say, "What can I put under those?" I want them to do activities and assignments. I want them to go find content and organize it themselves. They should be able to take notes from assigned readings. I'd model and put notes on the board in order to get them to paraphrase. O.K.? What can we say about what you read? They have to come up with their own ways to say things in the texts that mean more for them. And they have to talk about content relationships.

Interviewer: How does a teacher facilitate the students' learning of skills?

Paul: Modeling them. I even use diagrams on the blackboard to show levels of importance, relationships between concepts by arrows.

Interviewer: What do you do to teach content?

Paul: I use analogies, synonyms, superordinate categories, and subordinate ones. I do modeling. Like, I often use graphics to illustrate ideas. I also demonstrate different alternatives for solving problems.

Interviewer: How do you see yourself when teaching in the classroom?

Paul: How? I make clear the kinds of standards I expect. I also stress student self-organization and their taking responsibility, so students can recognize self-progress and learn to become better at doing things on a regular basis. For example, you know, I get kids verbalizing to me, "I never have known anyone as organized as you." They come to my desk and see piles of things and they ask me for something, they know that I can find whatever it is, and they say, "Sir, how do you do that?" If I live this way, they eventually will come to remember and see the importance of being able to be organized. I want them to apply that sort of disposition or mentality. I have a cyclical program. The student keeps going back on things or they are not going to do well. I want them to recognize from their own results that if they keep up with the work, they will achieve well. They are given the opportunity to redo assignments and learn from doing it again. So I have to give them some scope and flexibility. I think achieving this is an important part of teaching. I'll look at their work but first they will do it themselves. I see to it that students do what I expect, that they are prompt, that they are organized, and that they can accomplish what I design. I take care of that early in the school year. I get under control early and make sure the parents and the students are accountable for their behaviors. Of course, they are free to go to other students to get help. I give that kind of freedom. How I teach is a reciprocal kind of thing. This year, social studies is done in groups. In social studies, you have to be responsible, cooperate, and [be] able to make decisions based on the information that you are given. But you have to follow directions, too. It is a hard lesson for them to learn, and it is going on constantly in my classroom.

Instruction that supports an inquiry-oriented approach to history entails not only understanding what the teacher does in the classroom but also seeing the image the teacher holds of inquiry as a curriculum process that takes place over an entire year. In an August interview focused on his plan for the history curriculum to be taught for the coming year, Paul revealed that he was aware that this was an important part of his instruction, and revealed that he not only thought of himself as a teacher; he also called himself "a designer."

Paul: Well, a designer sees things a certain way. You have a vision. You live your vision and you would like to see others also live it. I am flexible at times, and at times I am adamant about my vision of instruction and learning in history. I do not import materials or activities of others into my classroom. I couldn't use it, because even if it were perfect, it may not do the kind of thing that I want to do to suit my learning goals for students. Like, rather than do all the lecturing myself, I want students to do some of it. I give up control over the content, because I think kids are capable of making meaning themselves. Still, a designer has to be flexible, when students say they are not buying the full package I have in mind for their instruction. When the kids don't think they are as capable as I think they are of doing the learning, then I have no choice but to teach the content by lecture or even do the notes for them and hand the notes out. The bottom line is the students themselves.

Learning.   During the first interview, when Paul was asked "What is teaching?," he was also asked what he thought of learning.

Paul: Learning is acquiring a variety of skills, techniques that allow the student to acquire knowledge, to learn how to organize themselves in a way that they can refer to past work in order to help them with current or future work. Learning is becoming more and more independent and not having to rely on others to give you the answers to become more self-reliant.

In a subsequent interview, Paul was asked, "What does learning content mean?" He responded the following way.

Paul: In the history program, it would mean awareness of the development of man, and why mankind blossomed at various points in the development of various places in the world like Egypt. It's learning how to think about man's development, and what questions to

ask. How did man organize his life, actions, and desires? It's seeing categories of man's activity, understanding content at different
levels, seeing changes in man's behavior, and giving reasons for
the changes observed. In English it's learning to recognize general
concepts and main ideas, learning to understand that comprehension is what's important.

Interviewer: How do you imagine students learn content?
Paul: It's more than learning facts. They have to learn concepts about the
Egyptian civilization such as what criteria are used to explain the
nature of a civilization; its economic, social, and political dimensions. These are concepts that will be repeated as students study
other people and societies.

Goals for student learning in integrated English and history instruction.   Paul's
views on teaching and learning corresponded to the sorts of goals he set for his
students for the integrated English and history program in eighth grade. At the
beginning of the school year, a goals interview was also conducted with Paul.
Based on that interview, the following long-term learning goals for students were
derived. He also set immediate goals for specific units of instruction.

The long-term academic goals for his students were:

- To learn to recognize the knowledge they possess and to use it to
  respond to questions that are raised by themselves, other students, or
  the teacher.
- To record, discuss, and evaluate new subject matter concepts and
  information.
- To become highly skilled in written and verbal communications.

The long-term social goals for his students were:

- To respect the daily classroom processes and environment as a whole.
- To become more organized, responsible, and accountable for actions taken.
- To cooperate with others in small group meetings.
- To come to value interpersonal relations in order to produce meaningful
  and productive responses to assignments.

The immediate learning goal for the unit on Ancient Egyptian Civilization was:

- To learn to think critically.

In the previous year, learning to think critically had not been the stated goal
for the unit on Ancient Egyptian Civilization. Even at the outset of teaching this
unit, Paul was not sure of the overarching immediate goal of the curriculum unit.
He knew his long-term goal was to teach content to and strategies for how to make
maps, how to make notes, and how to relate prior knowledge to the interpretation
of new history concepts and events. At the time the unit on Egyptian Civilization
was introduced, Paul and his class had reached the middle of the year. In the

previous history unit on "Early Man," he had had success with helping students learn together in groups to study and make sense of assigned readings from the history text, and he had involved them in a short research project in the library. This may have led him to decide to make learning to think critically about history the focus of his instruction.

The critical-thinking goal was directly related to two of the three projects arising during the curriculum unit. For the unit on Ancient Egyptian Civilization, Paul had in mind doing several projects, and probably one large one at the end of the unit. He had done one small project at the beginning of the history unit on Early Man, from September to December. Within the context of project-based teaching as part of his curriculum and instruction, he was torn by the issue of what his obligation was: To have the students think critically about history, to have them learn strategies for learning how to learn in history, and to remember important concepts about Egypt and civilizations in general which they could draw upon later in high school history. The following excerpt from an interview done after the unit was completed offers some insight into Paul's thoughts about his learning goals for his students.

Interviewer: And did you have any overall, global content goals with regard to the English program, and more specifically the Ancient Egyptian program that you wanted everybody to understand?

Paul: Yeah, I'd say my constant emphasis throughout the year was backing up statements or ideas with facts, how and why, . . . giving reasons. We seemed to stress those two terms, and it tied in with the English program. It's where I bring in supporting details, in other words, learning how something was, and why it was.

Interviewer: What do you mean by reasons?

Paul: I would expect they would have learned to justify something in terms of actual evidence.

Interviewer: OK, so when you're talking about justification of factual evidence, you're talking about something beyond what they think is important?

Paul: Not necessarily. I mean what they think is important. But they're working out of ignorance mostly, so what they're learning is paramount. But whatever statement they make that they could think about reasons why, I encouraged them to give them. In other words, I guess that brings in relationships and why certain things are and how they happened. The students will provide more details, and become more cognizant of what is going on.

Interviewer: And those reasons can come from themselves, their own prior knowledge.

Paul: Yes. Also it's from accepting new history knowledge. In the English program, it's also whether they're going to decide if they're going to write something important that they elaborate on.

A Description of the Enacted Curriculum
To understand Paul's orientation to history instruction, one must directly observe what happened across a unit of history. The unit on Ancient Egyptian Civilization began January 28 and ended 18 weeks later on May 28 at the end of the school year. This time period is characteristic of what some researchers have called in-depth instruction (Rossi, 1995). In fact, the team only taught two curriculum units in history during the entire year. The instruction allowed sustained time for (a) encoding history concepts and for relating the network of concepts embedded in the lesson events to those presented in assigned readings in a textbook, and (b) for collecting project data from the SHS library, local community libraries, and a collection of donated books.

The curriculum unit content.   The history of Ancient Egyptian civilization spans a time period of more than a 3,000 years from its emergence as the most advanced civilization on earth to its fall. Its core concepts include civilization, culture, politics, religious beliefs, dynasties, kingdoms, government, economics, technology, geography, the effects of geography, the effects of historical events on each other, and the effects of individuals and groups inside and outside the country on Egyptian society and its civilization. In addition to these history concepts, there were others that defined how thinking was to be directed. These include the concepts of (a) criteria; (b) evidence; (c) making notes on details, dates, and elaborations; (d) lecture; (e) debate; (f) relevant criteria for a civilization (set out by historians); and (g) producing reports, charts, and time lines. The pursuit of concepts such as these takes time for a class of eighth-grade students of mixed ability. All of the students had to be given time to build new knowledge of these and other relevant concepts since almost none already existed in their memories. In-depth study also depends on the use of knowledge gained about new concepts, and a spirit of inquiry that offers opportunities and support to students to manipulate ideas in ways that would lead to finding out new facts and gaining new understanding (Rossi & Pace, 1998; Torney-Purta, 1991).

Students' prior knowledge of content presented during the unit.   At the outset of the unit, students in Paul's class were asked to write down all the words that came to mind when he said "ancient Egypt." As a class, the words most frequently listed created a profile of what students knew. The class as a whole said that "ancient Egypt was made up of an exotic people who built pyramids and the sphinx," "had kings," "had queens like Cleopatra," "had pharaohs," "had mummies," "kept slaves to do all the labor and services," "possessed jewels," "lived in a desert," "the Nile river," and "owned cats and had cobra snakes." The average student could not think of more than six words in association with the phrase ancient Egypt. Obviously, the typical student had a limited repertoire of relevant concepts to bring to reading and writing about ancient Egyptian society, and to listening to their teacher talk about this civilization. According to most students, the sources of their knowledge were movies on television and pop culture. This absence of prior knowledge of history concepts considerably increased the difficulty students had in learning and understanding new history content simply by reading the material in the textbook (Sinatra, Beck, & McKeown, 1992).

Curriculum events 1, 2, and 3.   Curriculum events (Aulls, 1998, 2002) are sequences of lesson events that contribute to an overarching topic, in turn, the focus of discourse and activities through which the teacher and students jointly construct the curriculum unit as a process and as content. Curriculum event one was made up of the lessons from the first 2 weeks of the curriculum unit. In most lessons, the content was either declarative knowledge about the properties of a civilization of which Egypt was a shining example, or strategies for manipulating that declarative content to put it into the memories of individual students so it could be recalled and used to gain further understanding about Egyptian civilization. Curriculum events conceptually helped the teachers think about what really counted as history and English instruction, and what was enacted as the weeks flew by in the classroom.

The curriculum events making up 3 months entailed in the enactment of the civilization curriculum unit on Ancient Egypt were organized into three major curriculum events that hierarchically organized the presentation of key concepts and engaged students differently in how to learn that content.

Curriculum event one (weeks 1 and 2).   Instruction was devoted to building new upon prior knowledge of what were the properties of a civilized society, and how this applied to ancient Egyptian society. Simultaneously, students were taught strategies Paul believed would help them encode seven properties of a civilization and relate them to one another. He did this by directly explaining a group notemaking strategy as students read assigned reading material, a group semantic map construction procedure, and a strategy for group study and reflection on the notes they were generating.

Curriculum event two (weeks 3 to 9).   Instruction was devoted to analytic thinking as the content of instruction. This event was made up of three components of both content and strategy. The components of declarative knowledge in week 3 involved various influences on the history of Egypt. In week 4, the meaning of dynasty was developed, and the various dynasties or kingdoms of Egypt were sketched. In weeks 5 through 7, technology, religion, science, and their interrelationships were explored. Simultaneously with each content focus, students learned particular strategies needed to manipulate the content being taught. For instance, in week 3, map construction and interpretation had to be learned in order to discover how the geography of Egypt influenced the development of several of the properties of a civilization and sheltered the society from invasion by other people for many centuries. In week 4, students learned to use descriptions as evidence for inferences about dynasties from the notes they had recorded while reading about them. In weeks 5 to 7, students acquired new knowledge about religions of Egypt, and about technological advances and scientific inventions. They also learned to collect data, organize it into topics and concepts, statements of relationship between concepts, and questions about relationships, as well as how to make diagrams to represent their thinking. Then, for the first time, they presented their findings to classmates. In the last 2 weeks (8 and 9), further opportunity was given for students to hone their newly acquired skills in data collection and analysis, leading to a product that could be presented to others and that informed them about history. During week 8, time was also spent planning what the students would do for a multicultural week in which the entire school would participate, and inviting parents and other community members to attend. This project was to take place two weeks after the spring break (April 29 to May 3) and constituted part of the hidden curriculum (Cornbleth, 1990). Paul and other members of his special project team had not been made aware in advance by the vice-principal that they were supposed to devote at least 1 week's preparation and 1 week of celebration of multiculturalism during the time previously assigned to the history and English curriculum. Because students had already covered an extensive body of information about Egypt by week 8, Paul had all student groups design a test to give to another group, based on reviewing their notes and then writing the questions for a 50-item multiple-choice and short-answer test. This activity was supported by directly teaching how to write unambiguous questions beginning with who, what, when, where, how, and why. Students also learned that the answer to each question had to be stated directly in the original source or inferred from main idea statements. Each group developed an answer key for its test, so a person could score it privately. The students enjoyed taking on this responsibility, and very few disputes arose about the fairness of the test items.

In week 9 of the unit, the academic activity shifted from student-generated questions that elicited recall of concepts, ideas, and facts presented in the unit to groups using their collective knowledge about Egyptian civilization. They had to list and defend the 10 most important facts and ideas the members of their group had learned thus far about ancient Egyptian society and its history. Last, individual students were asked by Paul to explain in a short essay whether the properties of a modern civilization would be the same as those for ancient Egyptian civilization. The result was an excellent discussion that demonstrated the new understanding students had gained about the nature of civilization. Hence, the activities of week 9 pushed the students' collaborative and individual thinking about Egyptian civilization to a higher level.

Curriculum event three (weeks 10 to 14). The content for the history course was largely generated by the students from library resources, interviews with experts, and dialogue with each other and the teacher. During this event, two extended research projects were done, and a historical time line was developed of the dynasties of Egypt. In week 10, preparation and enactment for the multicultural week offered an authentic opportunity for students to use their knowledge of analytical thinking to do and present their first research project on a topic they had selected as a class, and the completion of the project demanded that they act as a community of researchers holding different kinds of expertise needed to accomplish the project goals. The students decided to do research on Pakistan as an ancient and as a modern society. The ancient society was studied much in the same way as students had learned to study Egypt. This resulted in products that described Pakistan as a society, the geography, and its culture including the religious practices, and daily family life in the home. To gain knowledge about modern-day Pakistan, the class proposed to make use of the five Pakistani students in the class, who offered their expertise to plan original ethnic food dishes, to organize modeling traditional clothing, to provide a parent lecture, and to create a videotaped demonstration of two popular sports (cricket and soccer). Research took on an authentic purpose for many students during this project-based study of Pakistani history. In weeks 11 and 12, nine groups of students presented research on historical events associated with the kingdoms of Egypt between 3000 b.c. and 500 b.c. The library research was started on April 12, and oral presentations to classmates and the teacher occurred between May 6 and May 23. At this point in the unit, students took over the teacher's role as lecturer, and were held accountable by their peers and the teacher through dialogue. It was important that in week 8 students had created their own self-evaluation of what they had learned during curriculum event 2. Now, in event 3, Paul's students were trying out the role of lecturer, after having done team research. Although different in kind, each activity enabled students to take greater responsibility for their own learning. Subsequently, I will describe some of these presentations and offer an analysis of the extent to which the students were the center of the instruction-learning interaction.

In weeks 13 through 18, the class created a museum-style time line of historical events across all the dynasties of the Egyptian civilization until the period when ancient Egypt was conquered and declined in power and influence. Each group dealt with a different time period and produced a bristol-board display of it. During this time, students also were being assessed to determine their growth of knowledge of Egypt, writing and study skills.

Paul balanced the learning of knowledge about Egyptian history with knowledge about strategies for learning how to read, think, and talk about what was being learned. This balance between the different kinds of knowledge occurred across sequences of lessons. Projects emerged in each of the three curriculum events. The interviews with Paul and field notes across the year suggest that only the third project was formally planned by Paul. The other projects were undertaken because they were invoked by the hidden curriculum sources.

It was essential to determine how this enactment pattern facilitated student participation in projects and supported critical thinking. The emphasis Paul placed on having students use strategies he taught in English to study history also may be an important means to explain how project-based instruction succeeds. Merwin's (1976b) review of classroom research on an inquiry approach to social studies and history instruction found that the most successful learning outcomes were associated with teachers who placed a consistent emphasis on small-group learning opportunities, but he was not able to explain why this made a difference. Since then, Gillies and Ashman (1998) and Cohen, Lotan, Abram, Scarloss, and Schultz (2002) responded that students in more structured small-group work are cooperative and offer more elaborated help to peers as they strive to accomplish the task. Students using a strategy as a group are offered more structure for making meaning together. The strategies taught explicitly by Paul are presented in Table 1.1.

There was another very important dimension of Paul's instruction that helped him structure students' higher-order thinking during teacher-class academic discourse. By lesson 9, Paul had made the chalkboard an integral tool in his instruction. He used it to show diagrams, notes, and other representations that he actively constructed with students as he talked to them about history content or a strategy for how to learn such content. It was a tool for students, too, because it allowed them to come closer to Paul's mental image during a lesson on procedures and the relationships among concepts and ideas. It helped both the teacher and the students follow closely the consequences of teacher-class discourse. Eventually, it reflected both the language and thinking of the teacher and the students. Paul's creative use of the chalkboard and the neat shorthand symbols that he had invented offered an anchor for higher-order thinking in whole-class academic conversations.

Classroom researchers and theorists in social studies education have argued that inquiry-oriented instruction has to offer an opportunity for students to engage in higher-order thinking about history content (Cornbleth, 1985). Newmann (1991) found that higher-order thinking challenged high school students to manipulate, analyze, or interpret information because a question to be answered or a problem to be solved could not be resolved through the routine application of previously learned knowledge. It was a regular practice for Paul to deliberately challenge students to give reasons for their answers to questions raised by him or other students.

Higher-Order Thinking
Higher-order thinking occurs when a person brings new information to the information stored in memory and interrelates, rearranges, and extends it to achieve a purpose or find possible answers for perplexing situations (Newmann, 1991). Higher-order thinking could be seen in Paul's enactment of the curriculum unit by tracing the acquisition of new knowledge by students through teacher assistance along sequences of lesson events. The students used this new knowledge to accomplish academic activities, and eventually they drew on new knowledge about Egyptian history and on new strategies to raise questions and issues, collect data, and then present them as a project.

For example, in curriculum event 1, Paul's students initially had very limited knowledge about civilization. With time and meaningful instruction, they overcame this barrier to their learning. For example, they internalized the properties of a civilization that were easily recalled when requested by Paul. After this, they

Table 1.1 Strategies Taught during History

Declarative Knowledge Used in Dialogue and Literacy	Student-Teacher Teaching	Student Generative	Time Line Relevant	Research Tools	Dialogue	Transformative Instructional Situations
Kinds of questions • what types • how to types Author's grouping of topics • general • specific in paragraphs • paragraphs of a selection Recognizing main idea statements • Selecting the main idea from notes for paragraph or essay writing • Selecting main ideas for illustrations in visual displays "Point formatting" of notes Diagramming levels of concepts and ideas and relationships between notes concepts and ideas	Student-to-student modeling of "how to" Student-Teacher modeling of • spatial note formats for students • guidelines • lecturing • parameter setting • objectives (purposefulness) Working hard toward an end Making interpretation from narrative and film	Question asking • sets of questions related to each other Making • notes • maps • headings with main ideas • main points • notes from film notes Organizing • large amounts of info from multiple sources • point-form notes taken during oral presentations Predicting answers Self-checking of answers Summing up research note data in writing	History time-lines showing • main events • important dates • details • organized by time Using notes from unit as data and library research data to select time line information Representing what happened, not why it happened Deciding what information can and should be illustrated	Using • periodical index • historical and other atlases • general historical reference books • film documentaries • CD ROMs Selecting and using periodicals and books Note making strategies	Group decisions • content • organization of time-lines Group analysis and decisions about headings for notes Group member critiques of each other, processes or products Group editing of paragraphs or notes Debating results of research Presenting results of research to an audience Teacher-class discussion	Students • using multiple strategies to help each other accomplish activities • listening to and viewing content and notes • converting notes to paragraphs or paragraphs back to posters and bulletin boards Writing • paragraphs from notes • questions from notes Recycling • the same content through different student generative strategies • the same strategy through different academic activities

began to relate the concepts attributed to Egyptian civilization into a hierarchical conceptual organization during the following two curriculum events. In curriculum event 2, in week 9, students were asked to select the most important facts about the various properties of civilization and give reasons for their choices, as well as to generate criteria for the properties of a modern civilization, and then address whether they would or would not be different than those of an ancient civilization such as ancient Egypt. Over a period of 7 weeks, most students moved from a level of factual acquaintance with properties of civilization to a conceptual understanding, then to being able to use this understanding with other knowledge to compare modern and ancient civilizations. Finally, in curriculum event 3, students drew on all this knowledge without Paul's assistance to carry out projects that investigated various dynasties of Egypt, and then they presented the results to the class and to Paul. Although many students struggled to present a coherent lecture to their peers, a smaller number were able to present fairly coherent lectures. Most students could answer the questions raised by their peers about the content of their lecture.

The ordering of the curriculum events suggests that the students in Paul's class were approaching history by building up a hierarchical body of concepts about ancient Egypt in their memory. They learned how to learn such content with greater interdependence as a group and then individually when strategies became internalized. This is a very important claim, tested by counting the number of elaborated concepts and the cohesion and coherence of the ideas presented in student essays prior to and after the unit on ancient Egyptian civilization. The differences between the pretest and posttest essays were significant on all three standards. Indeed, the average student scored 38% on the pre-essay and 88% on the postessay. One pair of essays by a student, whom Paul considered to be of average ability, exemplifies this improvement.

Pretest essay

The people of Egypt built pyramids to keep out of the sun and also to keep their valuable treasures. A valuable treasure that they had was coins from different countries brought by travelers and many other treasures that they would supply their god with. When a pharaoh died he would be wrapped in clothes so that his body would be preserved and they would put him in a casing with all of the treasure.

Another thing about their civilization is that they had transportation by camels. That was very important, because they could have trading. They could trade their gold, also their furs for their food because they wouldn't need it.

The temperature was very hot. They needed the pyramids because it would keep them out of the sun. For their camels they built little huts of nearby trees, and the leaves were used as roof, usually the leaves of a banana tree or coconut tree.

Posttest essay

In ancient Egypt the stuff that was most important was their industry. How they managed to feed themselves, such as agriculture and mining. Another thing that I found important was their trade. In ancient Egypt the weather was very hot, enabling them to grow wheat and rice, but probably at a certain time such as when the rising of the Nile brought nutrients up to the top of the soil and enriching their soil and food.

Their trade was also extremely important because olive oil; and spices that were needed to make their foods tastier were found in other countries, so they traveled by boat. They used sledges to transport rock up and down the banks of the Nile, then from there it could be transported elsewhere. Cypress and cedar are some of the woods needed to build boats. In ancient Egypt they used a method called bartering, it was the exchange of goods without money.

Another important fact was their social classes. They were needed to keep the countries in order and in total harmony. The different classes were God-king the mightiest. Then there were the nobles and city dwellers, they were very powerful. The last group that was very unimportant was the slaves. All they did was work for the city dwellers and the nobles.

Other evidence is that the class average score was 68% on a researcher-developed, 100-item multiple-choice quiz that had tested the facts and concepts of the entire 18-week unit. Although one might consider this mean to be low, it was higher than the scores obtained by a secondary history teacher and a college lecturer on history education who were given the test questions to answer before being given the chance to read the materials the students had studied. After reading, the two teachers scored over 95%, but before having had this opportunity, each one obtained a score below 50%. On the pretest, the teachers had not had a chance to revive memories of their knowledge of ancient Egypt, but, after reading, their access to prior knowledge was much greater. When we tested an Egyptologist, she scored above 95% on the pretest and 100% on the posttest.

Building Strategic Knowledge for Learning How to Learn Content
For Paul to engage his students in the process of inquiry, he either had to motivate them to participate or slowly show them how to use cognitive strategies for actively encoding new declarative knowledge. This effort is warranted in teaching social studies. For example, Knight, Waxman, and Padron (1989) stated that later elementary-grade students do not frequently use such strategies to solve critical thinking problems in social studies. Moreover, a social studies teacher should be aware of and selectively teach a range of strategies that students can use to solve academic problems and accomplish academic assignments. Similar conclusions were reached by Hara (1997).

In the first unit of the history curriculum, devoted to prehistory and the evolution of ancient people, Paul had relied mostly on motivating students. Perhaps this was because students held a good deal of native curiosity about how the earth began, the age of dinosaurs, and the cave dwellers' evolution into people who could create civilizations. Little emphasis was given to teaching literacy strategies in history lessons. However, in English classes, students were introduced to concepts of general and specific categories as a way of organizing concepts and ideas in informational prose and writing paragraphs. In history, this basic knowledge was applied to creating poster boards combining pictures and titles to illustrate new conceptual knowledge learned about ancient people.

During the unit on Ancient Egypt, Paul began by teaching students note-making strategies for actively recording concepts and ideas about Ancient Egyptian civilization. Students were expected to define key concepts in assigned reading and to relate new concepts to each other as well as to prior knowledge. Paul was teaching note-making to have students make a record of facts, concepts, and ideas, and also to actively engage their attention to understanding what they read. The meaning of, and strategies for, understanding were built up over time. He started with making brief notes as paraphrases of the history textbook and to further develop all students' conceptual grasp of the general topics and their relationships to subtopics that elaborated their meaning. Every student had to make notes in Paul's class, not only for later use when studying for tests but, more importantly, to use as means of data collection and evidence for their answers to the teacher's questions, as a record of the important information to refer to at a later date, and as stimuli for asking the teacher or other students questions during a lesson in history.

Here is a brief excerpt from curriculum event 1, week 1. Paul was reviewing one of the seven properties of a civilization explained in a reading assignment that students took notes on as homework for that day's class. At the same time, he was trying to model on the chalkboard how to construct the notes to show relationships between concepts.

Paul:	Number 2, emergence of cities. Please, tell me what you have written as your very short heading, and show me your indentation. I don't want to see notes down this same margin. This is our heading of the note, *Emergence of cities.* I want to see your notes with an indentation when I look at them. These are some points that we're writing: definitions, results of, causes of, succinct note with a few possible words with a little bit of indentation.
Student:	What does emergence of cities mean?
Paul:	Do we have to define the term emergence of cities?
Student:	To grow, maybe.
Paul:	Yes, grow, build up, those are words you could use.
Student:	Develop.
Paul:	Develop is another. Good.
Paul:	Anybody else not understand what emergence is? When you're making notes here, the author assumes that you understand the vocabulary. When you're in a group and you meet something or one of your peers

is reading something to you and you don't understand the word, then you'd better ask about it. That would seem the logical way to start. Do we have to talk about how to define the terms? Yes. Does anybody have to write down what emergence of cities means? Do you understand what the concept of cities is?

Student: Yes.

Paul: Emergence, what does that mean? It sounds like emerging city. What is emergence?

Student: Emerge.

Paul: What's another word for emergence? If something emerges out of the water.

Student: Developed.

Paul: Developed, we said developed.

Student: Rises?

Paul: Rises. Yes, the rising of cities. Alright, what is the first note?

Student: Houses are built in the cities.

Paul: Permanent housing develops. O.K., as a result of what?

Student: Food?

Paul: Permanent houses as a result of . . . ?

Student: Well, I think it was farming.

Paul: Yes . . . food, permanent homes, houses, as a result of food supply. Which we dealt with in the previous note, right?

Paul writes on the blackboard: Abundant food supply or dependable food supply [draws arrow]. Permanent houses as a result. . . .

Paul had to figure out how to help students succeed with strategies, including making notes, which facilitated students in how to explicitly relate two or more concepts. Making notes required selection and reduction of information. But these two conditions did not guarantee the importance of that information. If the students had much prior knowledge about the information being read, they were likely to select the most important information. If they lacked sufficient prior knowledge, then they were not as likely to know what information was important. In the latter case, notes allowed repetition of information as the primary mediator of learning.

In the 2nd week of the unit, Paul attempted to teach students a notation system that made them more active by using the following steps: (a) Define or explain all key concepts, and (b) ask questions about how each relates to previous concepts noted or what you already know. Categories of relationships presented to students included "reasons for," "causes of," "antecedent and consequence," "kinds of," "cause-effect," and "means-ends." By week 5 of the unit, Paul was guiding students to use notes to gather evidence for each of the criteria for a civilization. The results took the form of a list of the criteria in the first column of a table, and dates and details in the second and third columns, and then forms of evidence ranging from statements from original reading sources that could be disproved, to inferences from these sources that suggested clues to hypotheses about possible evidence. Students worked in groups and used their notes to follow these steps as a team, and Paul devised questions that engaged them in sharing and using their results to answer his questions. This condition seemed very successful in supporting learner understanding.

It is clear from the patterning of content and strategy lessons shown that Paul intended to have students simultaneously learn the history content and be able to internalize the strategies introduced for content learning. The full range of strategies Paul stated in interviews that he was teaching, and that were actually observed, were given in Table 1.1. These strategies, used as tools by members of each of the small groups, led to greater understanding than might have occurred if used by individuals alone. They also helped individuals remember assigned reading content.

Teacher and Student Roles during the Enactment of the Unit

The analysis of teacher interviews and lesson field notes showed that Paul played many different roles in the classroom during the curriculum's enactment. This finding also corresponds to results reported by Peetush (1998). Teachers remembered as very good teachers in general differ from very good inquiry teachers. This is because inquiry teachers provided more and different roles for the teacher and the students to play during the enactment of a course.

The most prominent roles taken by Paul during the unit were (a) lecturer, (b) question asker, (c) guide who gives clear purposes for activities, (d) planner who recycles content and strategies to optimize them for students to learn, and (e) facilitator who explains purposes for activities, shows steps for how to do something, models (i) how to identify general and specific topics while reading a paragraph, (ii) note-making procedures, (iii) how to brainstorm and relate the results, (iv) giving reasons, (v) self-questioning, (vi) how to represent relationships as notes, (vii) antecedent-consequences thinking, (viii) argument during verbal class discussions, and (ix) critical thinking during discussion. In addition to modeling, Paul provided diagrams on the blackboard.

Students often played the roles of (a) collaborator in group projects and routine study, (b) poser of questions, (c) lecturer during one project, (d) note maker, (e) monitor of events, (f) responder to questions, (g) peer critic, and (h) investigator during projects. Some of the roles stayed constant across curriculum events, whereas others changed during the unit. For example, as the unit evolved, students moved from note maker and question answerer (curriculum event 1) to lecturer and question asker (curriculum event 3). Finally, the variety of teacher and student roles in Paul's classroom indicates that he became more student-centered than teacher-centered.

The Function of Dialogue in Project-Based History Instruction

Classroom dialogue and discourse is deeply embedded in classroom life. Classroom discourse was a central part of Paul's instruction. Classroom research shows that discourse arises from talk which becomes coherent and cohesive. Of course, not all talk in classrooms becomes discourse. Paul had an ample vocabulary, spoke precisely about most topics, used many examples to elaborate main ideas and concepts, and used many metaphors and analogies. He was humorous, witty, and nimble of thought. Students enjoyed listening to him because his voice was usually soothing, vital, and sometimes dramatic. At the same time, he had organized the learning environment strictly, stood for zero tolerance for students fooling around in class, being off-task, speaking out of turn, not doing one's part, and being unprepared.

Paul's students ranked him as follows on classroom management skills identified by classroom research (Wittrock, 1990):

- Has control, Most of the time: 93%
- Accomplishes lesson goals, Most of the time: 78%
- Corrects student work right away, Most of the time: 95%
- Effectiveness, Most of the time: 85%
- Wants us to learn, Most of the time: 95%
- Is enthusiastic, Most of the time: 76%

The engagement of students in academic teacher-class conversation that rises to the quality of discourse depends upon many factors. One is the managerial skill of the teacher (Hicks, 1995). To engage students to participate successfully in teacher-class discourse that accompanies projects requires putting students into the center of the curriculum. At a minimum, this appears to mean that class time cannot be dominated by the teacher lecturing to students about subject matter. As well, students must have ample opportunity to engage peers and the teacher in academic discourse.

Promoting Critical Thinking and
Classroom Discourse across Curriculum Events

In Paul's classroom, the primary goal for student learning in history was to promote critical thinking. How did Paul's conversation with students achieve this goal? Table 1.2 shows a frequency count of a variety of properties of classroom conversation based on the observation of 18 lessons. Three lessons are sampled from those taught in January when the unit began, seven come from lessons in February, and the last eight are from lessons in May when the unit ended. The most obvious pattern in Table 1.2 is the significant increase in student-initiated topics during the lessons observed in the month of May compared to January or February. This increase was a direct reflection of students taking over roles earlier assumed by the teacher. A second pattern is the dramatic increase in student explanation arising during a typical lesson.

A third trend is an increase in student academic questions in May, with a corresponding decrease in teacher questions. Student lectures only occurred in May and were based on the results of team projects investigating various dynasties of ancient Egypt. For students to increase their understanding of content, they had to become more active in processing information and relating it conceptually. Table 1.2 also shows that in May students were more engaged within the lecture context than they had previously shown in lessons in January and February. They were giving reasons and asking questions that related history concepts during the project presentations. Finally, the table shows that discourse arose more often in May when student discussion revolved around the meaning of their own research rather than around content presented in the textbook, as had been the case in the lessons selected in January and February. A key feature of discourse is that the content of conversation is organized hierarchically and relates the meanings of concepts to each other. These properties are associated with better recall and understanding of history content (Aulls, 1998).

It might be assumed that students will go off-task when the teacher no longer asks most of the questions, and that classroom academic conversation will become less focused and semantically less coherent. The data in Table 1.2 show that this assumption is wrong. The number of occasions of discourse arising during Paul's history unit actually increased during student's project presentations, compared to lessons during which the teacher had initiated most of the topics, statements, and questions. Hence, in a classroom culture such as the one constructed jointly by Paul and his students, giving them the responsibility for lecturing on history and preparing questions to ask, and holding the expectation that they should be able to answer questions asked by others, seemed to offer specific conditions supporting the occurrence of discourse during history lessons. During the school year, there had been a consistent emphasis on students taking the initiative to attempt to relate broad and narrow concepts and ideas and to give reasons for their statements and responses to questions posed by others. But change in the students' reasons for their thinking was not gradual during the unit of instruction. To the contrary, it was abrupt and tied to agreeing to take on new roles and responsibility for student participation in classroom processes and learning.

Lessons Learned Through the Enactment of Curriculum Event 3
As Paul's class reached the end of the third curriculum event, they were struggling once again to collect data, organize results, then write them up in a manner that could be presented to peers. Students felt the stress of having to organize the information for consumption by others. Indeed, after the first student presentation, many students were upset because too many questions were being asked during the lecture, disrupting the planned flow of the presentation.

The following lesson field notes are excerpts from student lectures. They primarily include conversation with peers and the teacher. Lesson time is shown as it was noted. T designates the teacher and S is a student other than the presenter identified by his or her initial. Field-note remarks on the lesson offer added insight into what happened.

Table 1.2 Frequencies of Categories of Classroom Academic Conversations across 18 Lessons

| | Lesson | | | | | | | |
| | Topic Initiated | | Question | | Explanations | | Topics | |
Date	Teacher	Student	Teacher	Student	Teacher	Student	Relating	Discourse
01/28	4	0	13	4	1	0	0	3
01/29	1	0	27	16	2	0	0	1
01/30	3	0	12	12	2	0	0	3
02/04	4	0	10	7	0	0	0	2
02/05	5	0	8	0	0	0	0	5
02/06	3	0	26	0	0	0	0	3
02/07	2	1	7	0	0	0	0	2
02/08	4	1	19	0	0	0	0	4
02/26	4	1	24	0	0	0	0	4
02/28	4	0	20	0	0	0	0	4
05/13	0	5	6	18	0	28	0	4
05/14	4	0	3	5	0	5	1	4
05/16	1	4	4	10	0	20	0	5
05/17	0	7	9	16	0	19	2	7
05/21	0	8	9	9	0	29	0	8
05/22	0	6	14	6	0	11	4	6
05/23	0	9	2	1	0	7	0	9
05/29	0	7	3	6	0	5	0	7

May 13:
9:13

M: I'll be talking about different groups [of people] and the important people. Pharaoh, city dwellers, slaves, nobles.

T: Stops Mike to remind class of what the lecturer's responsibilities are to them and to hold him accountable.

9:15

M: Stands again to give out handouts.

S: Asks about the spelling of Amenhotep on the handout.

S: How high is 60 meters?

M: Draws step pyramid on board.

M: There were grave robbers, so they built pyramids so they would get trapped going out.

S: What dynasty was it built in?

M: In the third. So the king could walk up the pyramid to meet Ra.

S: What was the height?
M: Oh, it's 200 meters!
S: How were they built?
M: I don't know.
S: Who was the most important guy in that period?
M: Zoswer was the important one.
T: Where did you get the spelling of Zoswer on the board?
M: From the Filch video.
S: The spelling I have is from the encyclopedia.
S: Who was the most important guy during the period?
M: Amenhotep.
J: What was Amenhotep's influence on Zoswer or the step pyramid?
M: He was the architect and built it in Giza.

The next school day, students asked Paul for an open class discussion to re-evaluate the rules for presenting and participating in a lecture. Here is some of that discussion:

May 16:
[History group lectures—activity sheet—question-answer note making.
History—Egypt lecture—independent preparation?]

T: How's it going?
S: Too much attention on questions [during the presentation].
S: Ask questions after [refers to "after" as an option to the practice the previ-
        ous day of asking questions at any time during a student's presentation.].
S: If we wait, we'll forget.
S: One way is to divide into sections for notes and then questions.
T: How did you feel when you had to wait [referring to a student presenting
        the previous day]?
S: Questions really got in the way of my presentation. We should field ques-
        tions afterward.
T: And which do you prefer [referring to a different presenter the previous day]?
S: I think we should lecture, and ask questions after the lecture is over.
T: How could a listener do this?
S: Write beside the notes [being shown to the class using an overhead
        transparency].
S: Put an "*" or a "?" next to the one [question] you want to ask about.
T: (He hesitates.) What about the kind of question?
S: Why did this happen? Where?
S: A lot of questions are competitive and try to test what has not been pre-
        sented by lecturer.
S: Questions have to be on what is presented.
T: You could challenge later, or add info to info on questions.

10:03

T: What if we limit questions to one per person?
S: If a question on an activity sheet obviously comes up . . .
S: Ask your big questions at the end, spelling of name stuff, etc.
S: If questions are at the end, maybe both class and presenter could go over the answers to questions (his voice is so low now, it is just between him and the teacher).

Paul wants to start the lesson. He's satisfied the air has been cleared.

Based on survey questions given to his class at the end of the unit and the school year, the students seemed motivated. First, 49% of the students thought history was sort of interesting and 28% very interesting. Second, when asked how important they felt the subject was, 48% said sort of important and 35% said very important. Third, 45% reported they sometimes get excited about ideas in history and 14% said they often did so. Fourth, only 20% thought friends in other history classes did more interesting things than they did most of the time. When asked to list the most interesting part of the history course, 80% of the students listed the lecture project on the dynasties of Egypt, and 20% listed the Pakistan project done for Multi-Cultural Week. Projects were an important source of motivation to Paul's students.

Discussion

Paul's instruction has been characterized as a project-based inquiry approach to teaching history. The origins of the project-based approach have been interpreted by Kliebard (1987, 2004) to be a product of the merger, in the 1930s reforms to education, between the child-centered "developmentalists" and those reformers advocating a more socially relevant curriculum. Paul is a student-centered teacher who held as his first concern the students' growth, socially and cognitively, as responsible citizens. His secondary concern was to help them learn to think critically about the past and present. He saw projects as a way to get students to use conceptual knowledge about the history of Egypt and strategic knowledge he had taught them, to go beyond the textbook information. He saw the project as a source of motivation to continue an interest in history and a context for promoting critical thinking. The other "hidden curriculum" projects, while shaped by Paul and his students, were originated by the vice-principal and the Moral and Religious Education program. He was expected to comply with their directives. The end result was a much longer history unit than Paul had originally designed. Project participation took up one third of the total lessons occurring in the unit. These projects emerged through the initiative of the teacher. Paul also stressed continuity in his curriculum. One way to preserve continuity was to make critical thinking the common thread that pulled together what happened in both project and nonproject history lessons.

Tanner (1991) proposed that Dewey (1933) did not envision the curriculum as a series of projects. Although often called a project advocate, Dewey appeared to be at least somewhat uncomfortable with this categorization. He stated, "Many so-called projects are of such short time span and are entered upon for such casual reasons, that the extension of acquaintance with facts and principles is at a minimum"; in short, "They are too trivial to be educative" (pp. 442–423). Paul avoided involving students in projects that were too trivial to be educative. The first evidence for this interpretation was the keen interest students took in the projects. Second, the projects always culminated in higher-level discussion with the teacher and peers, as well as parents and a school administrator in project two. Third, all the projects lasted between one and three weeks and involved identifying the issue or topic to investigate, collecting relevant information, organizing the information for presentation and sufficient understanding of the results to be able to ask others questions about it, responding to others' questions, and giving reasons for the responses given.

Dewey (1931) believed that instruction of subject matter should be compelling and suggested that it be taught by organizing content into broad themes as inclusive as "the study of civilization." Moreover, he stressed that powerful ideas from the disciplines be incorporated into every facet of the overall plan of study. Paul's unit exemplified several of these properties. For example, in the study of Ancient Egyptian civilization, the unit started by explaining to students the nature of a civilization and using that concept as a framework for learning about the contributions its geography made to the classic features of a civilization. Later, the conceptual properties of a civilization were used to initiate the study of its social organization, economics, religion, and leaders. At the start of the unit, the typical student in Paul's class could cite no more than six of the more than 60 key concepts making up the history unit and nearly half as many propositions linking pairs of concepts. This is another reason why an eighth-grade history class made up entirely of projects would simply not be feasible for his students. Because tests of factual knowledge, conceptual knowledge, and the organization of concepts about Ancient Egyptian civilization indicated that students had learned a great deal by the end of the unit, it seems warranted to infer that the enacted curriculum was associated with deep as well as shallow content learning.

Paul stated that a major goal of his instruction in this unit was to promote critical thinking. This goal was not among those stated prior to teaching the unit. Instead it emerged following the conclusion of the first project on religious beliefs and practices. This is very interesting because the final project was imagined prior to enacting the unit as part of his instruction. During the interview, Paul revealed that he wanted students to be able to take more responsibility for learning during projects as a community. He talked about having students make their own tests of what they were learning last year. He was impressed with the students' ability to write both factual and conceptual test items with a minimum of training, but he was even more intrigued with the satisfaction they got from making a test for peers, taking a test a peer had written, and scoring the test results. His original idea for the lecture project was to take the question asking one step further by combining it with student lectures, and by the audience taking notes good enough to be able do well on the lecturer's test on what was presented. At the outset, he could not imagine that, when students do research and present it to peers followed by the requirement to ask and answer questions on the presentations, it would change the learning conditions sufficiently to encourage students to engage in genuine discussions of a critical nature. Schermerhorn, Goldschmid, and Shore (1975), in a cross-age study in which learners from primary to graduate school added question asking to normal reading and review, then peer discussion and comparison of answers to each other's anticipated replies to their own questions, demonstrated that using questions and answers in these ways also contributed to superior performance on measures of knowledge and understanding.

After observing genuine critical discussions during the unit's first project, it became clear to him that this was a learning outcome that he genuinely valued because it reflected a more genuinely democratic social context for learning. Being a good citizen entails critically responding to concepts from the past that are of substantial relevance today, for example, being open to understanding the reasons underlying religious beliefs and practices that are different from one's own.

Dewey (1933) defined reflective thought as "Active, persistent, and careful consideration of any belief or supposed form of knowledge in light of the grounds that support it and the further conclusions to which it tends . . ." (p. 9). VanSickle (1985) defined reflective thought as a process which begins with intellectualizing a problem. It is followed by refinement of inferences, and then clarification of definitions. One describes the conditions and causes of the problematic situation as fully as possible. Later, it may be revised and elaborated as new information and relationships are recognized.

In Paul's class, equipping students with relevant inquiry-learning strategies played a very important role in helping them actively participate in processing and encoding. He taught students to use strategies in reading the textbook to identify and remember important information and how to find primary sources from the library. He taught them note-taking strategies for establishing the important ideas, recording them as brief paraphrases, and determining the supporting facts for those ideas when presented as reasons, arguments, causes, or consequences. They were practiced throughout the unit as one of the routines emphasized for small-group work used to study assigned readings in the basic textbook and later sources selected by the students from the library. During these activities, Paul would circulate around the room to model how to use the strategies and to coach those who had begun to put steps together. He gave immediate written feedback on group and individual notes, and he modeled to the whole class at the blackboard how he would make critical notes, stopping periodically to have the groups ask clarifying questions, to make comments on the strategy, or to question the resulting organization of history concepts and ideas.

During projects, reflective thought becomes part of inquiry through the collection of data, use of note-making strategies such as the one described above, and through the accompanying conversation between members of a group as they confer with each other about how to interpret the data, how much to present, and the sufficiency of the evidence for the interpretations made. Rossi (1995) reported that 10th-grade students who were engaged in in-depth instruction in history were not given the opportunity by the teacher to establish the grounds for analysis of project data. During the present study, too, there was limited evidence that Paul's students actually analyzed the data based on criteria they developed themselves. However, Paul did perceive that students would need criteria to critically respond to the results of their data collection. He facilitated this at the start of each project by offering students a general problem or an organizing set of questions or statements to address as they collected data and presented it to peers. To some extent, then, Paul was following procedures envisioned by Dewey (1933) as part of what he called "reflective thought." This practice helped students in all three projects to generate their own questions to peers and to keep remarks about presentations focused on important or relevant data. A remarkable finding was that in half the group lectures the discussion led to a "collective" analysis of reported findings. Together the students fashioned criteria for interpreting historical facts through discussion.

The inquiry process necessarily creates a good deal of ambiguity and excitement for students, which the teacher must learn to manage rather than squelch. Paul maintained most students' excitement during the project. Gabella (1995) argued that ambiguity and uncertainty are essential to inquiry across domains of the school curriculum, but they are rarely welcomed by teachers and are systematically suppressed by the way time and space are organized as well as by the teacher and students. For example, doing inquiry projects, compared to teaching solely with a textbook, requires more planning time for the teacher to determine that ample resource material is available, to see that students have access to it, and to figure out how to grade students in equitable ways when many different ways of interpreting inquiry results are feasible. Even after overcoming many of the barriers to inquiry mentioned in the introduction to this chapter, criteria for marking students remained a barrier for Paul at the conclusion of the history unit.

Secondary students have been shown to resist academic activities that are high in ambiguity and risk (Doyle, 1992) by reducing social cooperation with the teacher and rates of participation in lessons. This often forces teachers to reduce the risk or ambiguity (or both) of an academic activity. Yet, by doing this, the original and intended learning outcome may be altered. For example, Gabella's study (1995) of an entire secondary school's one that embraced a problem-based approach to instruction in all subjects, demonstrated that teachers overcome negative responses to ambiguity and uncertainty by creating social conditions of care such that students who could not cope with this pedagogical regime received help from peers and their teacher. In addition, the teachers demonstrated reflectivity and often changed how they taught as well as helped students perceive the connectedness of what they were learning.

Paul demonstrated the characteristic of caring by holding his room open to all students during lunch time to engage in hobbies, games, and conversation.

In addition, he counterbalanced the inherent ambiguity of higher-order thinking demands and inquiry projects by selecting mixed ability and gender groups to be more successful in establishing positive interdependence among team members and to make collaboration in carrying out inquiry more likely. Mixed-ability grouping is not supported in the literature on gifted education, but was defensible in Paul's class; it also provided a window through which Barfurth and Shore (in this volume) were able to observe the importance to cognitive progress of disagreement and social "moves." Paul also allowed students the opportunity to change groups for each new project. Lastly, he was spontaneous and flexible in shifting his ways of teaching to improve students' responsiveness to conceptual content and strategies that he was attempting to teach.

According to A. L. Brown and Campione (1994), another important means of reducing student uneasiness with the demands placed on them in carrying out inquiry projects is to directly teach them relevant strategies for how to accomplish the projects. As shown earlier, throughout the year, Paul taught students strategies for recording important information from oral and written discourse and film. Because of this, students needed progressively less assistance on this dimension of data collection from primary or secondary sources. Because establishing important concepts became a routine part of his instruction, it prepared students to extract more of the important information and less of the trivial information that they read. During projects, students had plenty of opportunity together to demonstrate these strategies to other team members as an aid to interpreting historical data. Hence, it is not simply teaching the individual student a strategy that has the largest payoff. Instead, it is potential to empower more students to help each other in small groups than the teacher could possibly do alone.

Within the spirit of demonstrating a commitment to democracy in the classroom, students must come to value intellectual responsibility for the validity of the data they collect and present to others. Each project arising during the history unit resulted in students presenting information to an audience with the expectation that they would be accountable for the information presented. In projects 1 and 3, the primary audience comprised the teacher and fellow students. In the second project the audience members were parents, peers in the school, other teachers, school administrators, and invited members of the school community. The nature of accountability to peers and the teacher appeared to be different from accountability to parents and members of the local community. Students' own peers were very critical of a peer who presented information for which they could not perceive valid evidence. For example, one of the groups presented claims about one of the religious group's practices, for which they had cited no original sources. The other students were not pleased by the lack of sufficient respect for evidence reflected in the selection and presentation of a tertiary source of information rather than comparing the tertiary source to an available primary source for the same information.

After showing their displeasure publicly to the student lecturers whom they had criticized for making statements without appropriate evidence, they courteously accepted a request from that group to obtain the missing primary source and to share it with the class. Moreover, they made a public apology to those who practiced the religion in their class. As a result of this outcome, during the last project, only a few students were criticized for ignoring primary sources of information when available. Certainly this outcome speaks to the theory that the students acted as a "community of learners" that valued inquiry seriously. Moreover, it suggests that the students implicitly perceived that ideas are developed through a social dialogic process within which statements of relationship must be verifiable and dependent upon the accuracy of facts used to support them. Dewey (1925) regarded this learning outcome as very desirable. He stated, "To understand is to anticipate together, it is to make cross-reference which, when acted upon, brings about a partaking in a common, inclusive undertaking" (p. 141).

Garrison (1994) argued that Dewey (1925) saw human learning largely as a socially constructed phenomenon. In a classroom culture, the enactment of projects by groups of children is fueled by linguistic participation in the group, the roles arising, and, especially, through dialogue among members of the group. Meanings come about through linguistic participation in groups. Meaning is seated in the coordination of an actor's mental and motor activities (Dewey, 1925). Dewey stated, "Education is not an affair of telling or being told but an active constructive process" (1916, pp. 8–9). This perspective on learning places emphasis on the quality of the classroom discourse and the variety of roles and responsibilities taken by teacher and students that, in turn, signal the nature of dialogue that is ongoing to direct the shape of inquiry as it evolves during a project.

All projects during the Ancient Egyptian civilization unit were accompanied by discourse among the students, between the teacher and the students, and between the students and others outside the classroom, such as a librarian or member of the community. Analysis of classroom talk for 18 lessons distributed across the three curriculum units (see Table 1.2) indicated that more classroom discourse involving student initiated statements and questions occurred during the third project than in the first or second curriculum events. This may be evidence that students learned sufficient strategies and conceptual and factual knowledge about Egyptian civilization to collectively carry out more sustained dialogue than they were able to do earlier in the unit.

Another interesting feature of the teacher and class discourse accompanying a sequence of lessons devoted to a project is the extent to which it engages the students and sometimes the teacher in genuine discussion. Wilen (1990) defined discussion between the teacher and students as "an educative, reflective, and structured group conversation with students" (p. 5). A conversation is a relatively informal exchange of thoughts and feelings. It is reflective because it encourages students to think critically and creatively. It is structured when questions and statements are related and participants honor an order of speakers. It is educative when it has relevance to what has been presented as academic content. Dillon (1988) pointed out that, in discussion, fewer questions will be asked by the teacher, and there will be a mix of statements and questions by teachers and students. Roby (1988) concluded that discussions do not need to be teacher led, and teachers need to seek more opportunities for students to assume more leadership, being more like teachers.

In all projects in Paul's class, students were directed to ask each other questions based on the research results being reported. However, in the last project, students were expected to lecture, thereby being like the teacher (in at least one respect) or, more generally, like an expert in the field. In both the first and last projects, many genuine questions and statements were raised by the student audience with the student lecturers. The evidence is overwhelming (again, see Table 1.2) that the teacher moved into the background in the last project.

During student-led discussions, students revealed empathy with each other. For example, they consoled each other when they could not find as much information as they would have desired on particular issues. On other occasions, students shared reference sources as preparation for a future discussion on an issue. Finally, during the last project, two of the groups who lectured asked for more time on a following day to discuss further issues or questions asked by other students that they could not answer. Not only does this suggest the high level of motivation these students experienced, but it also indicates that extended student-initiated conversation occurred about some aspect of dynasties which, in turn, raised the likelihood that this information would be understood more deeply and remembered. Wertsch and Toma (1995) also reported observing children in Japanese classrooms who similarly attempted to work with each other and with the teacher to test student-generated hypotheses as part of scientific inquiry.

Conclusion

Paul's classroom culture favored projects to promote the development of individual students as investigators and members of a learning community in which rules for critical thought emerged through (a) teacher-directed classroom discourse, (b) the teaching of strategies for establishing importance and levels of evidence, and (c) the opportunities students had during projects to replace ambiguity with reasons for claims. History was taught by teaching strategies and concepts simultaneously over an extended period of time. Sixty percent of the allocation of time in the unit went to reading and responding to a textbook and the accomplishment of teacher-designed activities. Forty percent of the time was spent in projects.

Miller (1990), after a year-long observation of three secondary teachers who actively promoted discussion in social studies classes, found that the teacher who relied on a textbook alone to teach social studies had the least amount of discussions. Her students believed that, because the textbook was not open to interpretation, there was no point in engaging in classroom discussion. In contrast, Paul used a variety of sources of information including a textbook. Of the 60% of class time spent on nonproject activity, at least 40% was spent reading, taking notes from, and talking about information in the textbook. During time devoted to textbook topics, Paul, and not the students, generated by far the largest proportion of questions. This finding agrees with Miller's observations. Therefore, one added benefit of projects is to create conditions wherein students believe that it is worthwhile to generate questions and wherein they expect to give the answer, or they expect the teacher and other students to answer it or to elicit a question as response to a question they ask. In these kinds of circumstances, students move from Socratic thought to discovery thinking, and then to genuine inquiry (Keegan, 1993).

Miller (1990) also reported that, in all classrooms, the movement toward sustained discussion was slow and nonlinear. A similar pattern was found in this case study. Hence, it may be that a teacher should expect that the preparation for students to be inquirers takes time and persistence. Teachers may give up too early. Paul did not give up. He believed that students must be guided intentionally toward greater competence and responsibility. Some teachers, like Paul, who have no direct education in teaching through project-based instruction in history, may be able to overcome barriers to inquiry instruction with the indirect support of a team. Middle-grade students need well-defined skills to learn how to ask and address nontrivial historical questions. Paul believed that the simultaneous teaching of content and a variety of strategies was worthwhile.

The use of projects and their systematic pedagogical presentation enabled students to overcome several learner barriers to being able to engage in inquiry. These typically included taking on classroom roles that are largely reserved for the teacher in more traditional classes. Key examples included building upon their interests to define and co-construct important components of their curriculum, asking questions that matter, devoting extended time to topics in order to move from trivial to profound consideration, working with other learners to amplify the quality of learning, and acquire high level, generalizable, independent learning skills. This case study also demonstrated that, in an inquiry-oriented context, the principle of social constructivism operates in two complementary directions. At the same time that the learners acquired new knowledge, skills, roles, and expertise, so did the teacher as he better understood the dynamics of classroom learning, found ways to balance control and opportunity, accommodated unexpected administrative demands, and thereby took on some of the characteristics of the learners. Helping students develop inquiry strategies also may strengthen the teacher's professional repertoire.

References

Anderson, L. W., & Burns, R. B. (1989). *Research in classrooms: The study of teachers, teaching and instruction*. New York: Pergamon Press.

Armento, B. J. (1986). Research on teaching social studies. In M. C. Wittrock (Ed.), *Handbook of research on teaching* (pp. 279–314). New York: Macmillan.

Aulls, M. W. (1998). Contributions of classroom discourse to what content students learn during curriculum enactment. *Journal of Educational Psychology, 90*, 56–69.

Aulls, M. W. (2002). The contribution of co-occurring forms of classroom discourse and academic activities to curriculum events and instruction. *Journal of Educational Psychology, 94,* 520–538.

Aulls, M. W., & Halliday, F. E. (1994, November). *How students of different abilities respond to instruction in literary strategies.* Paper presented at the annual meeting of the National Association for Gifted Children, Salt Lake City, UT.

Aulls, M. W., & Peetush, A. K. (1998, April). *Students' perceptions of good college teaching: Are good instruction and good inquiry instruction essentially the same?* Paper presented at the annual meeting of the American Educational Research Association, San Diego, CA.

Ausubel, D. P., & Robinson, F. G. (1969). *School learning: An introduction to educational psychology.* New York: Holt Rinehart and Winston.

Brophy, J. (1990). Teaching social studies for understanding and higher order applications. *The Elementary School Journal, 90,* 351–417.

Brophy, J. E. (1992). Fifth grade U.S. history: How one teacher arranged to focus on key ideas in depth. *Theory and Research in Social Education, 20,* 141–155.

Brophy, J., Prawat, R. S., & McMahon, S. (1991). Social education professors and elementary teachers: Two purviews on elementary studies. *Theory and Research in Social Education, 19,* 173–188.

Brown, A. L. (1994). The advancement of learning. *Educational Researcher, 23,* 4–12.

Brown, A. L., & Campione, J. C. (1993). Collaborative research classrooms: Grade school environments that promote scientific literacy. In *Restructuring learning: Analysis and recommendations of the Council of Chief State School Officers* (pp. 85–97). Washington, DC: Council of Chief State School Officers.

Brown, A. L., & Campione, J. C. (1994). Guided discovery in a community of learners. In K. McGilly (Ed.), *Classroom lessons: integrating cognitive theory and classroom practice* (pp. 229–270). Cambridge, MA: MIT Press.

Bruner, J. S. (1968). Some elements of discovery. In R. F. Allen, J. V. Fleckenstein, & P. M. Lyon (Eds.), *Inquiry in the social studies: Theory and examples for classroom teachers* (pp. 14–28). Washington, DC: National Council for the Social Studies.

Cardelle-Elawar, M. (1995). Effects of metacognitive instruction on low achievers in mathematics problems. *Teaching and Teacher Education, 11,* 81–95.

Carter, K., & Doyle, W. (1989). Classroom research as a resource for the graduate preparation of teachers. In A. E. Woolfolk (Ed.), *Research perspectives on the graduate preparation of teachers* (pp. 51–68). Englewood Cliffs, NJ: Prentice Hall.

Cochran, K. F., DeRuiter, J. A., & King, R. A. (1993). Pedagogical content knowing: An integrative model for teacher preparation. *Journal of Teacher Education, 44,* 263–272.

Cohen, E. G., Lotan, R. A., Abram, P. L. Scarloss, B. A., & Schultz, S. E. (2002). Can groups learn? *Teachers College Record, 104,* 1045–1068.

Collins, A., & Stevens, A. L. (1982). Goals and strategies of inquiry teachers. In R. Glaser (Ed.), *Advances in instructional psychology, vol. 2* (pp. 65–119). Hillsdale, NJ: Erlbaum.

Collins, E., & Green, J. L. (1992). Learning in classroom settings: Making or breaking a culture. In H. H. Marshall (Ed.), *Redefining student learning* (pp. 85–98). Norwood, NJ: Ablex.

Commeyras, M. (1990). Analyzing a critical-thinking reading lesson. *Teaching and Teacher Education, 6,* 201–214.

Cornbleth, C. (1985). Critical thinking and cognitive process. In W. B. Stanley (Ed.), *Review of research in social studies education 1976–1985* (pp. 11–63). Washington, DC: National Council for the Social Studies, Bulletin No. 75.

Cornbleth, C. (1990). *Curriculum in context.* New York: Falmer.

Cross, L. (1995). Preparing students for the future with project presentations. *Learning and Leading With Technology, 23,* 24–26.

Dagher, Z. R., & Cossman, G. (1992). Verbal explanations given by science teachers; their nature and implications. *Journal of Research in Science Teaching, 29,* 361–374.

Dagher, Z. R. (1995a). Analysis of analogies used by science teachers. *Journal of Research in Science Teaching, 32,* 259–270.

Dagher, Z. R. (1995b). Review of studies on the effectiveness of instructional analogies in science education. *Science Education, 79,* 295–312.

Dahl, K. L. (1988). Writers teaching writers: What children learn in peer conferences. *English Quarterly, 21,* 164–173.

Delcourt, M. A. B., & Kinzie, M. B. (1993). Computer technologies in teacher education: The measurement of attitudes and self-efficacy. *Journal of Research and Development in Education, 27,* 35–41.

Dewey, J. (1916). Method in science teaching. *Science Education, 1,* 3–9.

Dewey, J. (1925). Experience and nature. In J. Boydston (Ed.), *John Dewey: The later works, 1925–1953, vol. 1.* Carbondale, IL: Southern Illinois University Press, 1981.

Dewey, J. (1933). *How we think. A restatement of the relation of reflective thinking to the educative process.* Boston: Heath.

Dillon, J. T. (1988). The remedial status of student questioning. *Journal of Curriculum Studies, 20,* 197–210.

Doyle, W. (1992). Curriculum pedagogy. In P. W. Jackson (Ed.), *Handbook of research on curriculum* (pp. 486–516). New York: Macmillan.

Dunn, M. A. (2000). Closing the book on social studies: Four classroom teachers go beyond the text. *Social Studies, 91,* 132–136.

Edwards, D., & Mercer, N. (1989). *Common knowledge: The development of understanding in the classroom.* London: Routledge.

Ehman, L. H., Glenn, A. D., Johnson, V., & White, C. S. (1992). Using computer databases in student problem solving: A study of eight social studies teachers' classrooms. *Theory and Research in Social Education, 20,* 179–206.

Facione, P. A. (1990). *Critical thinking: A statement of expert consensus for purposes of educational assessment and instruction.* Fullerton, CA: American Philosophical Association.

Fraser, B. J. (1980). Development and evaluation of a test of enquiry skills. *Journal of Research in Science Teaching, 17,* 7–16.

Frau, E., Midoro, V., & Pedemonte, G. M. (1992). Do hypermedia systems really enhance learning? Case study on earthquake education. *Education and Training Technology International, 29,* 43–51.

Frederiksen, J. R., & White, B. Y. (1997, March). *Reflective assessment of students' research within an inquiry-based middle school science curriculum.* Paper presented at the annual meeting of the American Educational Research Association, Chicago, IL.

Gabella, M. S. (1995). Unlearning uncertainty: Toward a culture of student inquiry. *Theory into Practice, 34,* 236–242.

Garrison, J. (1994). Realism, Deweyan pragmatism, and educational research. *Educational Researcher, 23,* 5–14.

Geddis, A. N. (1991). Improving the quality of science classroom discourse on controversial issues. *Science Education, 75,* 169–183.

Gillies, R. M., & Ashman, A. F. (1998). Behavior and interactions of children in cooperative groups in lower and middle elementary grades. *Journal of Educational Psychology, 90,* 746–757.

Guzzetti, B. J., & Williams, W. O. (1996). Gender, text, and discussion: Examining intellectual safety in the science classroom. *Journal of Research in Science Teaching, 33,* 5–20.

Hammer, D. (1997, March). *Discovery learning and discovery teaching.* Paper presented at the annual conference of the American Educational Research Association, Chicago, IL.

Hara, K. (1997). Significance of formal instruction for information skills in elementary schools. *Education, 118,* 111–122.

Hatano, G. (1993). Time to merge Vygotskian and constructivist conceptions of knowledge acquisition. In E. A. Forman, N. Minick, & C. A. Stone (Eds.), *Contexts for learning: Sociocultural dynamics in children development* (pp. 153–166). New York: Oxford University Press.

Hatton, E. (1997). Teacher educators and the production of bricoleurs: An ethnographic study. *International Journal of Qualitative Studies in Education, 10,* 237–257.

Hicks, D. (1995). Discourse, learning, and teaching. *Review of Research in Education, 21,* 49–95.

Hudson-Ross, S. (1989). Student questions: Moving naturally into the student-centered classroom. *Social Studies, 80,* 110–113.

Huerta, G. C., & Flemmer, L. A. (2000). Using student-generated oral history research in the secondary classroom. *Social Studies, 91,* 110–115.

Hughes, A. S., Sears, A. M., & Clarke, G. M. (1998). Adapting problem-based learning to social studies teacher education. *Theory and Research in Social Education, 26,* 531–548.

Keegan, M. (1993). Optimizing the instructional moment: A guide to using Socratic, didactic, inquiry, and discovery methods. *Educational Technology, 33,* 17–22.

King, M. B. (1991). Leadership efforts that facilitate classroom thoughtfulness in social studies. *Theory and Research in Social Education, 19,* 367–390.

Kleinberg, S., & Menmuir, J. (1996). Young children and inquiry. *Scottish Educational Review, 28,* 113–119.

Kliebard, H. M. (1987). *The struggle for the American curriculum, 1893–1958.* New York: Routledge & Kegan Paul.

Kliebard, H. M. (2004). *The struggle for the American curriculum, 1893–1958* (3rd ed.). New York: Routledge Falmer.

Knight, S. L., Waxman, H. C., & Padron, Y. N. (1989). Students' perceptions of relationships between social studies instruction and cognitive strategies. *Journal of Educational Research, 82,* 270–276.

Lehrer, R. (1993). Authors of knowledge: Patterns of hypermedia design. In S. P. Lajoie & S. J. Derry (Eds.), *Computers as cognitive tools: Technology in education* (pp. 197–227). Hillsdale, NJ: Erlbaum.

Leinhardt, G. (1993). Instructional explanations in history and mathematics. In W. Kintsch (Ed.), *Proceedings of the fifteenth annual conference of the Cognitive Science Society* (pp. 5–16). Hillsdale, NJ: Erlbaum.

Lemke, J. L. (1990). *Talking science: Language, learning, and values.* Norwood, NJ: Ablex.

Lubliner, S. (2002, April). *The power of clarifying: A comparative analysis of strategies that strengthen comprehension* (Report No. TM 034270). Paper presented at the annual meeting of the American Educational Research Association, New Orleans, LA. (ERIC Document Reproduction Service No. ED466691)

Lundeberg, M. A., & Moch, S. D. (1995). Influence of social interaction on cognition: Connected learning in science. *Journal of Higher Education, 66,* 312–335.

Manconi, L. (2004). *Teacher's understanding of inquiry.* Unpublished doctoral dissertation in educational psychology, McGill University, Montreal, QC.

Maor, D. (1991). *Development of student inquiry skills: A constructive approach in a computerized classroom environment.* (ERIC Document Reproduction Service No. ED336261)

Martens, M. L. (1992). Inhibitors to implementing a problem-solving approach to teaching elementary science: Case study of a teacher in change. *School Science and Mathematics, 92,* 150–156.

Mercer, N. (1994). The quality of talk in children's joint activity at the computer. *Journal of Computer Assisted Learning, 10,* 24–32.

Merwin, W. C. (1976a). The inquiry method. In S. E. Goodman (Ed.), *Handbook on contemporary education* (pp. 388–392). New York: Bowker.

Merwin, W. C. (1976b). An inquiry into inquiry teaching. *High School Journal, 59,* 159–162.

Miller, S. (1990, April). *Critical thinking in classroom discussion of texts: An ethnographic perspective.* Paper presented at the annual meeting of the American Educational Research Association, Boston, MA.

Mueller, A. (1997). Discourse of scientific inquiry in the elementary classroom. *Journal of Elementary Science Education, 9,* 15–33.

Newman, E., & Nessim, A. (1997). *How gifted students engage in the process of inquiry: A comparative case study.* Unpublished MEd joint research report in Educational Psychology, Department of Educational and Counselling Psychology, McGill University, Montreal, QC.

Newmann, F. M. (1990). Qualities of thoughtful social studies classes: An empirical profile. *Journal of Curriculum Studies, 22,* 253–275.

Newmann, F. M. (1991). Classroom thoughtfulness and students' higher-order thinking: Common indicators and diverse social studies courses. *Theory and Research in Social Education, 19,* 410–433.

Onosko, J. J. (1991). Barriers to the promotion of higher order thinking in social studies. *Theory and Research in Social Education, 19,* 341–366.

Palincsar, A. S., & Brown, D. A. (1987). Enhancing instructional time through attention to metacognition. *Journal of Learning Disabilities, 20,* 66–75.

Parsons, D. E., & Drew, S. K. (1996). Designing group project work to enhance learning: Key elements. *Teaching in Higher Education, 1,* 65–80.

Peetush, A. K. (1998). *Students' perceptions of effective teachers: those who promote inquiry and those who do not.* MEd special activity report in Educational Psychology, Department of Educational and Counselling Psychology, McGill University, Montreal, QC.

Piaget, J. (1967). *The language and thought of the child* (3rd ed.). London: Routledge & Kegan Paul.

Pirozzo, R. (1987). Breaking away: A self-directed, independent approach to learning science: Ontario, Canada. *Gifted Child Today, 10,* 22–24.

Polman, J. L., & Pea, R. D. (1997, March). *Transformative communication in project science learning discourse.* Paper presented at the annual meeting of the American Educational Research Association, Chicago, IL.

Prawat, R. S. (1995). Misreading Dewey: Reform, projects, and the language game. *Educational Researcher, 24,* 13–22.

Pressley, M., & McCormick, C. B. (1995). *Advanced educational psychology for educators, researchers and policymakers.* New York: Harper Collins.

Roby, T. W. (1988). Models of discussion. In J. T. Dillon (Ed.), *Questioning and discussion: A multidisciplinary study* (pp.163–191). Norwood, NJ: Ablex.

Rogers, P. (1990). 'Discovery', learning, critical thinking, and the nature of knowledge. *British Journal of Educational Studies, 38,* 3–14.

Rossi, J. A. (1995). In-depth study in an issues-oriented social studies classroom. *Theory and Research in Social Education, 23,* 88–120.

Rossi, J. A., & Pace, C. M. (1998). Issues-centered instruction with low achieving high school students: The dilemma of two teachers. *Theory and Research in Social Education, 26,* 380–409.

Roth, W.-M. (1995). Affordance of computers in teacher-student interactions: The case of interactive physics. *Journal of Research in Science Teaching, 32,* 329–347.

Roth, W.-M. (1996). Teacher questioning in an open-inquiry learning environment: Interactions of context, content, and student responses. *Journal of Research in Science Teaching, 33,* 709–736.

Russell, T. L. (1983). Analyzing arguments in science classroom discourse: Can teachers' questions distort scientific authority? *Journal of Research in Science Teaching, 20,* 27–45.

Sandoval, W. A., & Reiser, B. J. (1997, March). *Evolving explanation in high school biology.* Paper presented at the annual meeting of the American Educational Research Association, Chicago, IL.

Schermerhorn, S. M., Goldschmid, M. L., & Shore, B. M. (1975). Learning basic principles of probability in student dyads: A cross-age comparison. *Journal of Educational Psychology, 67,* 551–557.

Shuell, T. J. (1993). Toward an integrated theory of teaching and learning. *Educational Psychologist, 28,* 291–311.

Sinatra, G. M., Beck, I. L., & McKeown, M. G. (1992). A longitudinal characterization of young students' knowledge of their country's government. *American Educational Research Journal, 29,* 633–661.

Sommers, E. (1992, March). *Peer groups in evolution: Inventing classroom communities.* Paper presented at the annual meeting of the Conference on College Composition and Communication, Cincinnati, OH.

Son, B., & VanSickle, R. L. (2000). Problem-solving instruction and students' acquisition, retention, and structuring of economics knowledge. *Journal of Research and Development in Education, 33,* 95–105.

Spoehr, K. T., & Spoehr, L. W. (1994). Learning to think historically. *Educational Psychologist, 29,* 71–77.

Swanson, H. L. (1993). An information processing analysis of learning disabled children's problem solving. *American Educational Research Journal, 30,* 861–893.

Swicord, B. (1988). Maximizing the relationship between self-esteem and independent study in an urban gifted program. *Roeper Review, 11,* 31–33.

Tanner, L. N. (1991). The meaning of curriculum in Dewey's laboratory school (1896–1904). *Journal of Curriculum Studies, 23,* 101–117.

Thorndike, R. L., & Hagen, E. P. (Eds.). (1982). *Canadian Cognitive Abilities Test. Multilevel edition, Level A-H, Form 3.* Scarborough, ON: Nelson.

Tobin, K. (1986). Student task involvement and achievement in process-oriented science activities. *Science Education, 70,* 61–72.

Torney-Purta, J. (1991). Schema theory and cognitive psychology: Implications for social studies. *Theory and Research in Social Education, 19,* 189–210.

Troutner, J. (1988). Teaching geometry through inquiry. *Journal of Computers in Mathematics and Science Teaching, 7,* 9–11.

Tuyay, S., Floriani, A., Yeager, B., Dixon, C., & Green, J. L. (1995). Constructing an integrated, inquiry-oriented approach in classrooms: A cross-case analysis of social, literate and academic practices. *Journal of Classroom Interaction, 30,* 1–15.

Udall, A. J., & High, M. H. (1989). What are they thinking when we're teaching critical thinking? *Gifted Child Quarterly, 33,* 156–160.

VanSickle, R. L. (1985). Research implications of a theoretical analysis of John Dewey's "How We Think." *Theory and Research in Social Education, 13,* 1–20.

VanSledright, B. A., & Kelly, C. (1998). Reading American history: The influence of multiple sources on six fifth-graders. *Elementary School Journal, 98,* 239–265.

Waddick, J. (1994). Case study: The creation of a computer learning environment as an alternative to traditional lecturing methods in chemistry. *Educational and Training Technology International, 31,* 98–103.

Watson, J. (1995). Teacher talk and pupil thought. *Educational Psychology, 15,* 57–67.

Weade, G. (1992). Locating learning in the times and spaces of teaching. In H. H. Marshall (Ed.), *Redefining student learning: Roots of educational change* (pp. 87–118). Norwood, NJ: Ablex.

Weaver, V. P., Jantz, R. K., Farrell, R. T., & Cirrincione, J. M. (1985). A case study in curriculum innovation: Whatever happened to inquiry? *Social Studies, 76,* 160–164.

Wertsch, J. V., & Toma, C. (1995). Discourse and learning in the classroom: A sociocultural approach. In L. P. Steffe & J. Gale (Eds.), *Constructivism in education* (pp. 159–174). Hillsdale, NJ: Erlbaum.

Wilen, W. W. (1990, April). *Instructional discussions: Forms and interaction patterns.* Paper presented at the annual meeting of the American Educational Research Association, Boston, MA.

Wilson, S. M., & Ball, D. L. (1996). Helping teachers meet standards: New challenges for teacher educators. *Elementary School Journal, 97,* 121–138.

Wittrock, M. C. (1990). Generative processes of comprehension. *Educational Psychologist, 24,* 345–376.

Zimmerman, B. J., & Martinez-Pons, M. (1988). Construct validation of a strategy model of student self-regulated learning. *Journal of Educational Psychology, 80,* 284–290.

2

Teaching Problem Finding to Elementary Students: Views from the Trenches

ALANE J. STARKO

Eastern Michigan University

Problem finding, or the ways in which individuals identify and focus their creative tasks, has almost certainly fascinated much of humankind since the beginning of civilization. We wonder how great storytellers find the worlds of their imagination, how artists find images where none existed before, how scientists decide to investigate an idea no one else thought fruitful. My own curiosity about problem finding has centered on the processes used by children to choose their topics for art, writing, and scientific investigations.

Although none of the studies I have pursued thus far yielded clearly identifiable exploratory behaviors linked to creativity, each one provided additional evidence that such behaviors are used by some children, and can be effective in generating original problems. One field test (Starko, 1996) attempted to develop exploratory behavior by providing children with specific lessons on how creative individuals identify and select problems for invention, writing, or scientific investigation. It was clear that teachers varied considerably in their responses to such lessons. Even among volunteers, some teachers approached the activities with ease and fluency, tying ideas to class activities and problems and showing considerable enthusiasm for the unpredictable nature of the processes. Others, although following the suggested lessons to the letter, did not seem to be having any fun. They seldom used the lesson ideas spontaneously, and rarely did they tie them to other school-content or real-world opportunities. The less comfort evidenced by the teacher, the fewer opportunities for transfer seemed evident, and the less likely it seemed that students would apply the ideas taught in any situations outside the lessons.

This chapter centers on an extension of that research stemming from a very personal question. Could I do what I was asking teachers to do? What would this type of teaching demand of me and of the students? What would it be like to try to teach problem finding? Such musings may have remained in the realm of personal introspection had not an opportunity arisen to teach an exploratory class at a local elementary school. For 6 weeks, Jane, a 7-year veteran teacher then graduate assistant, and I went back to school twice a week to teach problem finding to a group of third, fourth, and fifth graders. For 9 of the 12 classes, I taught while Jane took field notes. After each class, I made my own field notes, and then we met to review the events of the day, clarify the notes, discuss our responses to the day, and plan for the next class. The remaining three classes, while I was out of town, Jane taught alone and kept a single set of notes.

This chapter describes reflections around that experience. It is divided into three sections. The first section reviews research regarding problem finding in children. The second describes the lessons. The final section of the paper comprises thoughts about our experiences as they relate to problem finding, to inquiry teaching, and to the fundamental demands of learning and teaching.

Research on Problem Finding

Described by Dillon (1982) as "those activities, processes and events which precede the solving of a clearly posed problem" (p. 102), problem finding has been investigated in diverse disciplines (see, for example, Jay & Perkins, 1997; Starko, 1999). It is possible to conceptualize problem finding in varied ways, emphasizing different aspects of the process. Problem finding entails sensitivity to needs or an awareness of possibilities in a given situation. It may demand focusing and clarifying a problem, or analyzing data to determine a broad issue underlying several seemingly disparate situations. It also might include an evaluative component, selecting which problems are worthy of pursuit.

Few efforts to date have examined developmental changes in problem finding or how problem finding in children may differ from that in adults. A key question in such investigations must be the relationship of problem finding to the development of other cognitive processes. Arlin (1975, 1990) postulated that problem finding can only develop after formal operational reasoning. In a similar vein, Smilansky (1984) asserted that one can only become a problem finder after one is capable of solving similar problems. If problem finding only emerges as postoperational thought, efforts to identify it as a variable in young children may be futile. However, such an assertion is based on a tightly defined view of problem-finding processes. It is still unclear whether problem finding is a single construct, or whether it may be multidimensional or domain-specific. It is possible that various types of problem finding may develop along different time lines or that individuals may have profiles of problem finding, perhaps paralleling Gardner's (1983, 2000) multiple intelligences.

Problem finding has been studied in students of various ages. Some studies have examined students' created problems. Created problems are distinguished from found problems because they do not already exist in problem form. For example, a good office manager may discover a practice that is hampering the company's efficiency. That practice was a found problem. If that same office manager undertook to create a completely new type of office design or write a play about her colleagues, she would be creating a new problem to solve. Starko (1989) examined the problem-finding strategies of four groups: professional writers, high school students identified as possessing specific interest and ability in creative writing, students in above average ability language arts classes, and students in average ability language arts classes. In the problem-finding task, participants were presented with a collection of 18 objects and asked to generate ideas for writing that could relate to one or more objects. More able writers were more likely than other groups to deliberately manipulate ideas in order to generate ideas for writing, and were more fluent in the number of ideas generated. Less able writers were more likely to wait for ideas to "pop out" without any strategies to enhance that possibility. There were no significant ties between originality of ideas and any of the described strategies.

Moore (1985) followed procedures closely paralleling those of Getzels and Csikszentmihalyi (1976). Working with college art students, Getzels and Csikszentmihalyi had found that exploratory behaviors in choosing and shaping an art task were associated with originality. Moore presented middle school students identified as creative and less creative with a collection of objects on one table and asked to arrange some of them on a second table and then produce a piece of writing based on the objects. Patterns of scores for problem finding and problem solution in the creative and less creative groups differed in the directions predicted based on the art research, although not always significantly. The relationship between problem-finding strategies and originality of solution was significant and positive.

A series of studies (Starko, 1993) examined problem-finding behaviors in elementary school students presented with an art task. In the first study, students in kindergarten, Grade 2, and Grade 4 were presented with an assortment of materials and asked to make something. Data analysis provided little evidence of the types of exploratory behaviors found in other studies. Most students plunged immediately into the task (occasionally before the researcher had completed the directions!). However, discussions after the task gave clues to emergent problem-finding processes. Some children described beginning the task and discovering midway what the creation was going to be, "I started sticking things together and then it turned into a dog, so I made a dog."

Two subsequent investigations (Starko, 1995) examined the possibility of problem finding during the construction process. Students in Grades 2, 4, and 6 were presented with the same building task and asked to tell the researcher when they first had an idea what they were going to make, any time they changed their idea, and when they completed the building task. This study provided evidence that young children continued to define the building problem while pursuing the task at hand. In the first, total number of ideas, time before final idea, total time used, and the ratio of time to final idea to total time all increased with one measure of originality, although none significantly.

In the second, exploratory time before selecting a final idea, total time used, and the number of items used all increased as originality increased. However, the number of items handled but not used was greatest in the middle group, whereas the number of ideas generated was the reverse of the expected order, with students whose products were rated lowest in originality generating the greatest number of ideas. These puzzling results brought to light a seeming conflict with Getzels and Csikszentmihalyi's original study (1976). Some students seem to have explored several ideas but did not select the one most likely to be judged as original. Such choices may reflect the importance of evaluative thinking in problem finding. In order to be a creative problem finder one must not only generate potential problems but also must select problems that lend themselves to effective, original solutions (Runco, 1991, 1993; Runco & Chand, 1994).

Other studies have examined students' problem finding in other types of problems. Hoover and Feldhusen (1990) studied problem finding in natural science by examining the questions of gifted ninth grade students presented with ill-defined situations. They determined that hypothesis generation was not related to intelligence or attitude toward science. Hoover (1992, 1994) cited similar results with fifth grade students. In that study, it was also determined that problem finding in science did not correlate with any part of the Torrance Tests of Creative Thinking. Subotnik (1988) examined the relationship between factors from the Structure of the Intellect model and problem finding in science. Westinghouse Talent Search Winners who, as gifted adolescents, had independently selected their projects (problems) were more likely to name processes of cognition, convergent production, and evaluation as crucial to the selection of their research questions. Students who selected their own problems also were more likely to be involved in research even years after winning the Talent Search (Subotnik & Steiner, 1994).

Delcourt (1993) also noted problem-finding activity in adolescents identified as creative producers in secondary school. Students were described as "continuously explor[ing] their many interests as they actively sought project ideas through a variety of techniques including reading, sharing information with others, and taking courses both in and out of school" (p. 28). In that study, the opportunities and encouragement for students to identify and pursue individual problems occurred during specialized services for gifted students. Without a comparison group, it is impossible to tell whether Delcourt's students' problem-finding processes were affected by their participation in a program designed to facilitate individual investigations.

Burns (1990) examined a similar program for elementary students. Although not writing specifically about problem finding, she investigated the effects of training activities on students' initiation of creative investigations. Students who engaged in a series of lessons on identifying interests and problem focusing initiated significantly more investigations than students not receiving such training. Her results were echoed by Kay (1994) who described the use of a discovery unit in assisting elementary students to conduct original investigations.

To date, no research has investigated the effects of specialized training in problem finding on heterogeneous groups of children. The lessons described in this chapter were designed to do just that. This chapter addresses the processes of teaching problem finding, the challenges for the teacher, and reflections on the experience.

The Lessons

There were 10 lessons originally written for the problem-finding research. They were designed for fourth-grade classes. When we were invited to teach the exploratory classes, it was necessary to fit into the school's 12-session exploratory calendar. Exploratory classes occur three times per year and include a variety of topics and instructors. Students sign up for their preferred classes, then they are divided into groups taking into account their preferences and ages, and class composition. This exploratory class included nine students: four in Grade 3, two in Grade 4 and three in Grade 5. There were three girls and six boys (three African American students, five Caucasian students, and one Asian student). The variation in number of lessons and grade levels, and the normal revisions that take place in any teaching experience focused on children's responses, caused a series of alterations in the original lesson plans. The lessons are described here as taught rather than as planned.

Lesson 1. Why would anyone want to find a problem? This lesson focused on inventors and the situations that inspired their inventions. Students cut pictures out of catalogues and speculated on the circumstances that might have spurred someone to invent the object.

Lesson 2. Finding invention problems. This lesson provided practice and reinforcement for Lesson 1 and introduced the importance of fluency. Students were provided with descriptions of two individuals with disabilities, both friends of the author. In groups, they brainstormed daily activities that might cause problems for one of the individuals and drew an invention that could assist.

Lesson 3. How do writers find problems? The lesson examined how authors find story ideas, using picture books and authors' descriptions of their processes. A key idea was the importance of careful observation and persistence. Students selected a picture book and hypothesized how the author got the idea for the story.

Lesson 4. Finding stories in objects. This lesson used authors' stories and a series of questions to show how story ideas can be generated from interesting objects. Students wrote stories using a selected object.

Lesson 5. Students continued working on their stories, trying to make them interesting through detail.

Lesson 6. Finding stories in characters. In a manner paralleling Lesson 4, students learned to generate story ideas through the creation of interesting characters. They had the choice of drawing or writing about their characters. All students chose to draw.

Lesson 7. How do artists find problems? This lesson, added to the sequence because of the students' interest in drawing, used the book *A Rainbow at Night* (Hucko, 1996) to discuss how Native American children chose the subjects for their art works. Students used a variety of media and described their processes in selecting a project.

Lesson 8. How do scientists find questions? This lesson focused on "what," "when," and "how" questions, and on scientists' use of observation and curiosity. Students dissected candies and generated questions about them.

Lesson 9. Using comparison questions. Lesson 8 used two stories of elementary students' research to introduce comparison questions. In teams, students generated comparison questions about two brands of paper towels and designed experiments to test them.

Lesson 10. Using "what if" questions. This lesson asked students to generate "what if" questions from a story about an ordinary day at school.

Lesson 11. Trapping ideas. This lesson focused on recording ideas and creating a problem-finding notebook for interesting questions and problems.

Lesson 12. Habits of mind. The final lesson asked students to summarize what they had learned about being a problem finder and to discuss the habits of mind that a good problem finder might have. These included being alert and interested in the world, being a careful observer, wondering how to solve things rather than complaining, thinking of many ideas, and not being afraid to try. It ended with the opportunity to go outside with notebook in hand, to look for interesting problems.

Observations from the Field

Teaching problem finding is an interesting paradox. We used a combination of direct teaching and discussion to help students learn a process that forms the foundation of inquiry. Although every effort was made to help students draw conclusions from stories and examples, much of the teaching about this discovery process was not done through inquiry teaching. Of course, practice activities in which the processes were used provided different kinds of experiences.

From the beginning, it was clear that teaching the lessons was going to be a challenge. On the first day only five students arrived: two fifth graders, one fourth grader, and two third graders. Within 5 minutes, I found myself with my first dilemma. I asked the children why anyone would want to find a problem. I had anticipated this would lead to puzzled expressions and a lively discussion. After the discussion, I hoped to tell several stories leading to the idea that inventors often find their inspiration in problems around them. However, when I asked the question, one student answered quickly by saying that inventors needed to find problems. He even told one of the stories I'd planned. This led to two immediate difficulties. First, it was clear my carefully planned lesson was blown. Second, it was clear that everyone except the child who had answered the question was completely lost. The leaps of reasoning taken by this child were too large or too quick for the others to follow. I found myself, an oftentimes advocate for gifted children, trying to figure out how I could slow this child down before the rest of the small class became any more confused.

This was the first of many times during the 6 weeks I thought about the intricate dance between student and teacher necessary during inquiry teaching. The nature of inquiry suggests that students must make discoveries and inferences. Discoveries and inferences happen only when (a) the student doesn't already know the information to be learned (otherwise no discovery is necessary or relevant) and (b) the student has enough prior knowledge and accessible information to draw the necessary conclusions. In any class on any given day—even a class as tiny as this one—there are likely to be students for whom the necessary conditions for inquiry are not present. Either they already have the needed information or they are not able, for any of a variety of reasons, to draw conclusions from the information available.

The same two conditions for learning—a need for information and conditions sufficient to gain it—are required for any learning situation. Certainly my initial question had not constituted an inquiry activity. It had, however, brought to light one of the quandaries of inquiry teaching. Whereas in direct instruction it is possible for the teacher to imagine that learning is taking place as long as the teacher is talking, no such illusions are possible with inquiry teaching and learning. If a student already knows the information the teacher wishes to convey, he or she is likely to short-cut the entire planned investigation before it begins. And, as I was to learn in later lessons, if students do not draw the conclusions from data that seem obvious to the teacher who planned the activity, the resulting blank stares and expressions of confusion quickly quash any illusions that active learning is taking place. Inquiry teaching and learning progress only as rapidly as the students' thought processes. Without careful diagnosis of students' prior knowledge, it is easy to ask questions that are either overly obvious or completely incomprehensible.

Furthermore, teaching in which the progress of the lesson is dependent on conclusions drawn by participants makes variations in students' knowledge, skills, and capabilities particularly challenging. In this case, I had not yet started any inquiry activity. Yet, the answer to one question made it clear that if I followed up on the accurate and appropriate response given by one student, the remaining students would be lost almost instantaneously. If I spent the time to allow the rest of the class to build the information necessary for them to draw a similar conclusion, the first student was going to be bored to tears. All this, and I'd only been teaching for 5 minutes! I was worried that it was going to be a very long 6 weeks.

Adrift Without an Answer Key

I like inquiry. I loved discovery activities as a student and I enjoy planning them as a teacher. Yet, in this series of lessons I experienced considerable anxiety. Some of it could be credited to a not-unreasonable fear that I would say or do something completely foolish in front of someone who had spent a lot of time listening to me pontificate about the teaching and learning process. I truly hoped for no complete flops in front of my graduate assistant—as experienced, understanding, and congenial as she was. Any time a teacher is with a group of students he or she does not know well, there are multiple opportunities for disaster. We had a few.

Even more anxiety-provoking was the nature of the content itself. I have spent many years teaching students basic skills. I've even spent a number of years teaching problem solving and the skills of independent learning. I am pretty confident in my ability to teach those things. I have never taught content like this, nor watched anyone else teach it. I did not know if the ideas presented were too abstract for elementary school students, or even if the problem-finding processes I had gleaned from reading that research and self-reports would actually work for children. Would they, in fact, be able to use these tools to generate new ideas for stories, or pictures, or experiments? I did not know.

And, of course, there was much more I did not know. Because the lessons were designed largely around stories of creative adults, and attempts to model their processes, I was hoping students would be able to draw conclusions from the stories and use them to build the concept of problem finding across disciplines. I was determined not to engage in the false sense of discovery that is an easy teacher trap, in which the teacher guides the discussion with such a heavy hand that no conclusions or observations, other than those planned in advance, are possible or accepted. For example, all too many school "discussions" sound like this dialogue intended to help students discover advertising strategies.

> "What do you notice about the advertisements? What kinds of clusters did you form?"
> "Some have a lot of colors and some don't."
> "But what do you notice behind the ideas in the ads?"
> "The colored ones are more exciting."
> "Some ads do use color but look at these three ads. They all feature famous people. Do you think people might want to buy things those people use? How will we write that on our list?"

The teacher was so concerned that students discover the specific categories identified in the text that the class lost the opportunity to examine the use of color and discuss its impact on the buyer.

One of the high points of the research for me was when I read Jane's field notes. They indicated that I was listening carefully to the students and seemed to really care about their responses. It was true; I was and I did. I was determined to hear their conclusions, even as I looked for opportunities to share mine.

As I have thought about this experience, it brought home again the courage necessary for a teacher to engage in inquiry with children for any length of time. I was an experienced teacher faced with a small group of children in a relatively low-risk situation. Neither my job nor the students' core learning depended on my activities. And yet there were times I felt positively insecure. It is easy to do an activity one period and go back to the usual present-and-check routine the next day. Such deviations from the norm provide a welcome diversion. But to continue in exploration day after day, no answer key in sight, takes courage, strength of will, and a keen sense of direction in the teacher—particularly when using such activities to teach core curriculum. If you know you are heading in the right direction, making judgments about how much time will be adequate, and how much the investment in student-guided activities will "pay off" in added learning, demands sophisticated judgments not easily managed by a beginning teacher.

Seeking a Safe Haven

If the teacher in a new inquiry situation feels adrift, some students feel like passengers on an unfamiliar ship, hoping desperately it is not the *Titanic*. In this small group of students, responses to the activities ranged from immediate almost constant enthusiasm to equally persistent resistance. Many of these students were accustomed to familiar questions posed in familiar forms. They did not know how inventors got their ideas or why someone might have written a particular book. But if a teacher had asked, surely, they were supposed to know. In those moments when the answer was unclear, some students easily and comfortably let their imaginations wander. Others looked frightened, making repeated guesses in an attempt to "get it right." In one case, a student appeared to deal with any unfamiliar material with open hostility. The student's strategies included multiple forms of distraction, covering pages with the word "No," and loud refusals to participate. I was informed in no uncertain terms that the lessons were too hard, the student did not like them, and did not want to come to class anymore. Even though we had some successes after this low point (during the lessons on authors), the student never demonstrated clear understanding of the concepts addressed.

I am sure this type of resistance was not unique to the exploratory class. The student sometimes arrived quite happily describing the consequences suffered in other classes ("I'm not allowed in the cafeteria for a week" or "I can't sit near Sue anymore"). Yet, the stressors of the critical thinking required when our class operated in a problem-solving mode clearly made matters worse. If I was telling stories or asking concrete questions, there were few problems. It was only when the tasks were perceived as "hard" that serious management challenges sometimes evolved. As I watched this process and struggled to find ways to support the student's learning so as to make the resistance unnecessary, it struck me that the classroom management challenges sometimes associated with more open-ended teaching may not be simply the result of more opportunities for movement or conversation. If the activity asks for types of thinking not commonly required in school tasks, students who are uncomfortable or fearful can avoid focusing on the risks of exploration by remaining off task.

The Development of Problem Finding

Although it is risky to speculate on the basis of a single instance with a small group, our experience with the exploratory class did provide evidence in support of a developmental process undergirding problem finding. These lessons had been previously taught in four classes, fourth grade and up. Although there had been isolated difficulties for particular children, teachers were confident that students were able to comprehend and use the ideas taught. Activities were successfully completed, and some improvement in problem-finding processes was shown. I have no such confidence regarding any of the third graders in this small sample. One third grader was my most resistant child, but the others generally worked hard to do what was asked. Often, they attempted to use context clues to figure out what was "right," using the appropriate vocabulary but without the necessary links of logic.

For example, in one activity, students looked through catalogues for pictures of inventions and tried to imagine what circumstances might have led someone to invent such a thing. Typical fourth or fifth grade responses were, "He got sick of getting athlete's foot so he invented shower shoes," or "A guy named Brita didn't like the nasty taste of water." A third-grade response was, "I think he invented the cellular phone because he might have a problem with it." The student understood that we were discussing problems, but the abstraction of identifying an underlying problem appeared too challenging, at least on that day.

In a similar fashion, all the fourth and fifth graders were able to imagine an event that could have triggered an author's idea for a story. Only one third grader did so. It seems reasonable to assume that if students are unable to conceptualize how such a process might work for others, it would be difficult for them to use it purposefully themselves. In fact, when students were asked to use a purposeful strategy, focusing on a series of questions about an object, to generate a story idea, the results were identical. All the third graders needed considerable prompting and support to generate story ideas. The older students all used the strategy effectively. However, the age differences were not uniform. When asked to generate questions that a scientist might ask about a piece of candy, there were no discernible trends by age, at least in fluency. Older students were more successful in generating and testing hypotheses regarding the effectiveness of various brands of paper towels. Such differences raise some questions and offer ties to developmental theories.

Certainly, Vygotsky's linking of children's creative imagination "with meaning-making, a higher psychological function that has connections not only with emotions but also with intellectual functions" (Gajdamaschko, 2005, p. 18) would support a gradual development of volitional problem-finding. Vygotsky believed that mature creativity developed when the creative imagination of childhood—in which symbolic play may be largely imitative or initiated by others—is linked with thought. Mature creativity, in Vygotsky's mind, was purposeful. He envisioned the coming together of thought and imagination as a task of adolescence, and possibly earlier (Gajdamaschko, 2005). Even though none of the students in this small study was an adolescent, there were trends that mirrored Vygotsky's ideas. Although the younger children often tried to take their cues from the adults' language and examples, the older children were more successful in using strategies purposefully to address a given task. Similar ties to Vygotsky can be seen in the earlier (Starko, 1993) study in which a second-grade child described his art project as "turning into a dog." The child looked to external cues to guide his creative process rather than intentionally attempting creative processes.

Solving the Problem You've Found
Finally, this small investigation reminded me, yet again, of the inseparable relationship between problem finding and problem solving. Smilansky (1984) suggested that individuals cannot "find" a problem unless they have the skills to solve it. The conceptualization of problem finding as a skill more complex than problem solving—and perhaps requiring problem solving as a prerequisite—is supported by Smilansky and Halberstadt (1986) and Arlin (1975, 1990). In the story-writing task, much of the younger students' trouble generating story ideas may have stemmed from their difficulties conceptualizing basic story structure. Although the older students knew without discussion that a story would need characters, that something would have to happen, and that it would need a beginning and middle and an end, the younger students appeared to bring no such knowledge to the task. It was only with considerable prompting that their stories took on those characteristics (e.g., "All right, you want to write a story about a bear in the woods. What do you think the bear is going to do? Will something happen to the bear?"). Without the conceptual framework of what a story entails, and some notion of how to go about creating one, finding a story idea is a difficult, if not impossible, task.

In addition, problem finding is, in any real-world setting, only step one. Individuals find problems in order to solve them. Activities in which we simply generated ideas appeared to be less motivating than those in which we followed the ideas to their natural conclusions. The most motivating activity was that in which students generated hypotheses about paper towels and then had the chance to test them. Although some of the excitement can be attributed to the opportunity to "play" with water, towels, and other variables, the process of becoming curious and then satisfying that curiosity is a powerful one. Efforts to teach students problem finding must, in the end, be linked to problem solving if they are to have maximum impact.

Many Roads Not Traveled

The questions raised by my foray into problem finding are far more numerous than those answered. Can we teach elementary school students to purposefully generate ideas for inventions, stories, art projects, or scientific investigations? Probably, at least older elementary students. Beyond that, much remains unknown. The development of problem finding, the general or specific nature of the process, the range of problem-finding abilities in young students, and the optimum way to teach such abilities remain open to investigation. Effective problem-finding strategies themselves remain to be identified. These lessons taught strategies that could be identified in successful creative individuals. Whether they are likely to be effective for others remains to be investigated. Surely there are other strategies left to be identified. The problems remaining to be found in the area of problem finding are many, varied, and interesting.

Beyond the immediate issues of problem finding, the experiences in my small class illustrate the dilemmas facing teachers wishing to use inductive teaching or inquiry teaching more generally. These cluster into challenges rooted in student needs and those originating more from teacher needs—although the intricate weaving of teaching and learning make the division tenuous at best.

Inquiry teaching assumes that students are cognitively situated in the space between already knowing and having the necessary prerequisites. The more students are involved in inquiry, the more likely that some will fall outside the range—shortcutting others' processes by immediate conclusions or frustrated by unsuccessful attempts at understanding. The range of students is not usually greater in an inquiry activity, but our awareness of it may be. If students are not able to draw the necessary conclusions (or they draw them "prematurely"), the process can be stymied for all concerned.

Additionally, inquiry, by its very nature, fosters uncertainty. Puzzling questions are an essential part of the process—but questions without clearly defined answers are not an accustomed part of many schools' cultures. It is just a short step from uncertainty to its much less helpful cousin, insecurity. The difficulty can be compounded by the "visibility" of many kinds of inquiry. A confused student in a lecture can sit silently with no one the wiser. In many inquiry situations, students' repeated attempts and responses are visible to all. Even though uncertainty and ambiguity are part and parcel of the creative process, insecurity can lead to frustration, premature closure, anger, and a host of management problems.

Students are not the only ones who may feel insecure in an inquiry situation. Teachers, too, are accustomed to clear problems and neat answers. Most are comfortable with familiar teaching routines. Inquiry is messy—often physically as well as cognitively—unaccustomed and uncomfortable. Because it must be led by students' responses, it is impossible to plan in detail. It forces improvisation and can never be completely predicted. In accountability-driven school environments it is daunting to take the longer and less predictable route. Even as an experienced teacher, I found that the parts of these lessons that involved direct teaching—telling stories of inventors or teaching specific problem-finding strategies—almost never brought me any concerns. My insecure moments virtually always came when I was trying to help students draw conclusions on their own and was not quite sure I would be able to manage it.

The set of challenges would be daunting except that inquiry teaching is so important, with such rich opportunities for in-depth understanding, higher-level thinking, and the excitement of new insights. I do not begin to claim to have the solutions but here are a few thoughts on conditions that will facilitate successful inquiry.

1. It is essential that the classroom atmosphere be supportive of risk-taking. The essential trust necessary among teacher and students it at the heart of what I have called elsewhere a "problem-friendly environment" (Starko, 2001). An inquiry classroom must be one in which mistakes are recognized as a necessary part of learning and the teacher can be counted on to maintain an encouraging relationship in the midst of academic struggles. Everyone needs a safe community in order to engage in activities that are inherently uncertain.

   Part of the building of community is the explicit understanding that individuals learn and think differently and that it is to be expected that some students will "get" some activities quicker than others. Some students understand this best through sports analogies. Individual "hits" or laps of a relay are great, but it takes a team effort to win. Good team members cheer one another on until everyone is successful.

2. Teachers must develop strategies to deal with the range of prerequisite knowledge and skills in the room to maximize the number of students who have the opportunity to draw conclusions individually. Part of this process may be acknowledging the difficulty to the class and soliciting their help. Even young students can understand that the fun and the learning comes from figuring things out yourself and that other students will be happier if they get to figure out on their own. In some cases teachers may devise strategies for students to record or share conclusions with the teacher without sharing with other students—whispering ideas or writing them down. New technologies can allow students to communicate with the teacher electronically, inputting conclusions in computers or personal digital assistants (PDAs).

   Although many activities may take place in a large group or heterogeneous small groups, in some cases students may work individually (either with physical materials or on an individual computer) and in some cases students may be divided into groups based on prerequisite knowledge or skills so that there is a smaller range of experience within each group. In such a case, all groups need not receive the same information, allowing more scaffolding for students with less background.

3. Content for inquiry lessons should be selected carefully. Not only should the content lend itself to analysis and conclusions, but the time invested in inquiry teaching makes it only logical that the content selected also be of

sufficient importance to merit the extra investment. Key concepts that form the basis for further learning and areas with common misconceptions are particularly appropriate.

It is also important to consider the prerequisite skills, knowledge, and reasoning necessary to draw the conclusions targeted. For example, students from language-rich homes and backgrounds enter school with experiences with many different kinds of stories. Such students are much more likely to be successful in an inquiry lesson designed to discover "circle stories" than students whose language experiences are more limited—at least until the teacher has provided multiple in-school story experiences.

4. Finally, although inquiry lessons can never be perfectly scripted, planning successful inquiries involves "getting inside students' heads," following the train of logic not from our own perspectives but from theirs. It can be easy to confuse "active" or "hands on" activities with inquiry. Many fine practice or demonstration activities are active but require the teacher as the major initiator and presenter of ideas. Inquiry teaching, at least as I define it, requires students to combine data, examples, or instances and draw their own conclusions. They must do this within the sphere of their own reasoning. Teachers must look at the evidence to be presented with new eyes, thinking carefully through the train of logic necessary to travel the cognitive distance from where the students are to the conclusions to be drawn. Planning bridging questions or illustrative examples in advance can enhance students' likelihood of success. However, in some cases the logic necessary may not be developmentally appropriate for the group and thus the activity not a wise choice.

In many ways, an inquiry lesson is like a good home-cooked meal. It is both tastier and more nutritious than a fast-food drive-through meal or a box of easy-to-assemble ingredients. But home-cooked meals are messy and time-consuming. And, of course, there's always the risk of going to a lot of trouble and then burning the main course! We might love to have completely home-cooked meals every day, but the pressures of life and time constraints can make it impossible. Similarly, many teachers find the time, preparation, and risk involved in inquiry daunting. Nonetheless, just as a periodic home-cooked meal (probably on a holiday) is better than none, periodic inquiry lessons organized around the most important content are better than none at all. And, as it is better to add a salad to the burgers and fries, so it is better to add small doses of inquiry whenever possible than to throw up our hands and say that because it is impossible to do all the time we won't try to do it at all.

I believe the benefits of inquiry also will parallel our best culinary efforts. I do not remember many of the ordinary meals I ate growing up (although they clearly brought me nutrition), but I do remember the special ones. The stories told, the interactions with family, even the foods we ate, remain vivid memories. Similarly, students will remember the science experiments they really wondered about, the history investigation that allowed them to enter the world of the nineteenth century, and maybe even the manipulatives that made the mathematics problems real far longer than they will remember other lessons more easily taught.

References

Arlin, P. K. (1975). A cognitive process model of problem finding. *Educational Horizons, 54(1)*, 99–106.

Arlin, P. K. (1990). Wisdom: the art of problem finding. In R. J. Sternberg (Ed.), *Wisdom: Its nature, origins, and development* (pp. 230–243). New York: Cambridge University Press.

Burns, D. E. (1990). The effects of group training activities on students' initiation of creative investigations. *Gifted Child Quarterly, 34*, 31–36.

Delcourt, M. A. B. (1993). Creative productivity among secondary school students: Combining energy, interest and imagination. *Gifted Child Quarterly, 37*, 23–31.

Dillon, J. T. (1982). Problem finding and solving. *Journal of Creative Behavior, 16*, 97–111.

Gajdamaschko, N. (2005). Vygotsky on imagination: Why an understanding of the imagination is an important issue for schoolteachers. *Teaching Education, 16*, 15–24.

Gardner, H. (1983). *Frames of mind*. New York: Basic Books.

Gardner, H. (2000). *Intelligence reframed: Multiple intelligences for the 21st century*. New York: Basic Books.

Getzels, J. W., & Csikszentmihalyi, M. (1976). *The creative vision: A longitudinal study of problem finding in art*. New York: Wiley.

Hoover, S. M. (1992, February). *Constructs and processes of problem finding ability among gifted individuals*. Paper presented at the Esther Katz Rosen Symposium on the Psychological Development of Gifted Children, Lawrence, KS.

Hoover, S. M. (1994). Scientific problem-finding in gifted fifth grade students. *Roeper Review, 16*, 156–159.

Hoover, S. M., & Feldhusen, J. F. (1990). The scientific hypothesis formulation ability of gifted ninth-grade students. *Journal of Educational Psychology, 82*, 838–848.

Hucko, B. (1996). *A rainbow at night: The world in words and pictures by Navajo children*. San Francisco: Chronicle Books.

Jay, E. S., & Perkins, D. N. (1997). Problem finding: The search for mechanism. In M.A. Runco (Ed.), *Creativity research handbook* (pp. 257–293). Cresskill, NJ: Hampton Press.

Kay, S. I. (1994). From theory to practice: Promoting problem-finding behavior in children. *Roeper Review, 16*, 195–197.

Moore, M. T. (1985). The relationship between the originality of essays and variables in the problem-discovery process: A study of creative and noncreative middle school students. *Research in the Teaching of English, 19*, 84–95.

Runco, M. A. (1991). The evaluative, valuative, and divergent thinking of children. *Journal of Creative Behavior, 25*, 311–319.

Runco, M. A. (1993). Divergent thinking, creativity and giftedness. *Gifted Child Quarterly, 37*, 16–22.

Runco, M. A., & Chand, I. (1994). Problem finding, evaluative thinking and creativity. In M. A. Runco (Ed.), *Problem finding, problem solving and creativity* (pp. 40–76). Norwood, NJ: Ablex.

Smilansky, J. (1984). Problem solving and the quality of invention: An empirical investigation. *Journal of Educational Psychology, 76*, 377–386.

Smilansky, J., & Halberstadt, N. (1986). Inventors versus problem solvers: An empirical investigation. *Journal of Creative Behavior, 20,* 183–201.

Starko, A. J. (1989). Problem finding in creative writing: An exploratory study. *Journal for the Education of the Gifted, 12,* 172–186.

Starko, A. J. (1993, November). *Problem finding in elementary students: Two explorations.* Paper presented at the annual meeting of the National Association for Gifted Children, Atlanta, GA.

Starko, A. J. (1995, May). *Problem finding in elementary students: Continuing explorations.* Paper presented at the Henry B. and Jocelyn Wallace National Research Symposium on Talent Development, Iowa City, IA.

Starko, A. J. (1996). [Problem finding lessons]. Unpublished raw data.

Starko, A. J. (1999). Problem finding: A key to creative productivity. In A. S. Fishkin, B. Cramond, & P. Olszewski-Kubilius (Eds.), *Investigating creativity in youth* (pp. 75–96). Cresskill, NJ: Hampton Press.

Starko, A. J. (2001). *Creativity in the classroom: Schools of curious delight* (2nd ed). Mahwah, NJ: Erlbaum.

Subotnik, R. F. (1988). Factors from the structure of intellect model associated with gifted adolescents' problem finding in science: Research with Westinghouse Science Talent Search winners. *Journal of Creative Behavior, 22,* 42–54.

Subotnik, R. F., & Steiner, C. L. (1994). Problem identification in academic research: A longitudinal case study from adolescence to early adulthood. In M. A. Runco (Ed.), *Problem finding, problem solving, and creativity* (pp. 188–200). Norwood, NJ: Ablex.

3

Where Students Get Creative-Productive Ideas for Major Projects in the Natural and Social Sciences

Marcia A. B. Delcourt
Western Connecticut State University

How can we best help students to pursue scientific investigations? By understanding and developing their own creative productive behavior, students report that they are better prepared to think of new ideas for projects. This information is related to the development of self-regulatory behavior in adolescents, namely: forethought regarding actions, actual performance, and self-reflection after activities are completed. This research focuses on nine secondary school students from districts employing Renzulli's Enrichment Triad Model (Renzulli & Reis, 1986), a program stressing the development of creative productivity. As a result of this study, self-regulatory behavior is viewed by studying characteristics of youths who pursued and completed scientific investigations based on their interests. This information was collected through parent and student surveys and student interviews. Based on experiences in their respective school programs, students revealed insights into how they matched their interests with ideas for projects (forethought), how they carried out their investigations (performance), and what they learned from their efforts (self-reflection).

When a science project is assigned at school, how should we as parents and teachers help students start working on their submissions? Several guides written for students begin by suggesting that topics be selected based on interest (Brisk, 1999; Tocci, 1997). Another reference commenced by admonishing students not to copy from a book (Bochinski, 1996), thus setting the stage for a description of regulatory standards for science fair projects. On the lighter side, Iritz (1987) stressed that, regardless of the topic, projects should be fun. This cumulative advice is meant to help youths get started on their paths to completing highly satisfying science projects. Additionally, with titles such as *1001 Ideas for Science Projects* (Brisk, 1999), books containing over 100 project ideas (Adams & Gardner, 1997), and chapters describing 50 award-winning science projects (Bochinski, 1996), there are numerous texts providing idea starters and project models that students should be able to relate to their interests.

Certainly, the concept that a science project should be of interest is not new and, with so many references available, the issue of searching for a topic should be greatly assisted. Unfortunately, the number of topic ideas can be overwhelming, so that students have difficulty matching their interests with possible topics. How then do students know, or perhaps learn what is of interest to them? What quality of project idea can be expected from a young mind? Can students really produce unique ideas or are they only able to repeat the experiments or the demonstrations of others?

In considering our expectations for student ideas and therefore their projects, a perspective of human growth and development needs review in terms of creative productive behavior. Several researchers view creative productivity as a characteristic unique to adults, contending that youths are best classified as consumers of information rather than producers (Simonton, 1984; Tannenbaum, 1986). After all, regarding investigations such as science projects, it is generally recognized that "Most projects have been done before in one form or another" (Bochinski, 1996, p. 17). Whether a project is developed for a science-fair competition or not, teachers of science are hoping to turn the tide of the complacent or reluctant science fair participant, but also fully realize that somewhere in the discussion about how to investigate a science project, they will inevitably say,

> With little time and practically no preparation, you might resort to constructing a poster display of pictures from magazines, writing a report from an encyclopedia, or performing a lab exercise obtained from a textbook. Such projects are not real science but only "cookbook" chemistry—just follow the recipe and the result is guaranteed. (Tocci, 1997, p. 8)

How can students be assisted to go beyond the "cookbook" stage? Can students participate in "real science"? Some researchers, most notably Renzulli, believe that students can be producers of quality ideas as well as consumers of information (Renzulli & Reis, 1985, 1986). This statement presupposes that students can think not only of ideas for projects but also of valuable solutions. To support this concept, Delcourt (1993) has documented the products of secondary school students and found that, among several types of audiences (local, regional, state and national), students can pose problems and seek solutions that are unique for their developmental levels with some being on the level of adult creativity.

Thus, the purpose of this study was to identify secondary school students who were highly creative-productive in either the natural or social sciences. These students were nominated from programs for the gifted and talented which focused on the development of creative-productive behaviors. This information was then related to self-regulation theory to analyze the stages of project development.

What Factors Promote Creative-Productive Behavior?

Creative productivity involves the process of applying one's abilities to an area of personal interest, with the intended result being "the development of original materials and products that are purposely designed to have an impact on one or more target audiences" (Renzulli, 1986, p. 58). This view of gifted behavior focuses on the interaction between three clusters of traits: above average ability, task commitment, and creativity. Not all traits will be of equal size or stability for each person, thus the model considers individual differences among students. This conception of giftedness is part of a larger educational plan employing the Enrichment Triad Model. At the core of this model are three types of activities: Type I (general exploratory activities), Type II (skill-building activities), and Type III (individual or small-group investigations of self-initiated topics).

Students participating in programs that employ the Enrichment Triad Model are encouraged to develop their interests by having new topics or Type I activities available to them on a regular basis. These topics are not typically included in the regular curriculum and are presented through demonstrations, interest centers, guest speakers, and cluster groups (groups of students with similar interests), among other techniques. For example, a cellist demonstrating a new piece, an interest center about producing a radio program, and an author describing her writing process are all Type I activities.

Once students learn about a topic, they may want to gain the skills required to perform it themselves. These skills or Type II activities are planned as part of class lessons or are additional lessons that are available for all or some of the students in a class. They may be incorporated into interest centers and can include topics such as conducting surveys, using a computer spreadsheet, developing architectural graphing techniques, and writing original song lyrics. Projects are self-initiated by the student, either individually or in small groups, are called Type III activities. Opportunities for these activities need to be incorporated into the school day and can also be pursued before or after school. For these activities, the student matches his or her interest area with an idea and proceeds to seek a solution to a self-selected problem. Projects vary as do their outlets. Ideas can include finding the environmental hazards related to pressure treated wood and presenting the results at a local science fair as well as sending findings to the EPA (Environmental Protection Agency), or inventing an automatic page turner for sheet music that is used by a local pianist and entered in a young inventors' competition. Some of these projects are designed as true experiments, whereas others represent solutions to problems that develop through a trial-and-error process. A satisfactory result is a completed project with or without external deadlines.

Effectiveness of the Enrichment Triad Model

Several studies have been conducted to review this model's effect on creative productivity. Reis (1981) reported that creative productivity, in terms of completing Type III projects, was not reserved for those considered to be gifted, approximately the top 3 to 5% of the student population in ability. In fact, she found no significant differences in product quality between students in the top 5% of the population and those in the next 15 to 20%. This result supports the use of this model with a larger portion of students than the gifted population. In fact, Type I and Type II activities are promoted for use with all students, whereas Type III projects can be used with at least the top 25% of the student population, or those students who want to pursue these projects. Reis also noted that of the 1,162 students in her study, 64% did not choose to complete an advanced level product. This observation suggests a need for additional research focusing on students who continuously choose to engage in self-selected investigations as well as those who never begin projects or those who do not complete them.

When Gubbins (1982) researched characteristics of high ability students, a final phase of her data collection included the use of a questionnaire designed for gathering information from students who did not complete products. From their responses, she identified four factors that interfered with product development: low interest level; poor task commitment; inadequate time commitment; and lack of human and material resources. Burns (1990), on the other hand, found that students trained in managing, focusing, and planning an investigation were more likely to initiate projects than were students who did not receive the training.

Starko (1988) also investigated the relationship between creative productivity and project initiation. When comparing students who complete Type III investigations in school and those who do not, she concluded that "students who engage in creative productivity in school have higher self-efficacy with regard to creative productivity and are more likely to pursue creative productivity outside of school" (1986, p. 92).

Self-Regulation Learning Strategies

The combination of building confidence or self-efficacy in students and training them in managing an investigation led to more recent work in developing self-regulation strategies in students across ability levels. Based on Bandura's (1986) social cognitive theory describing reciprocal determinism, self-regulation refers to students' efforts to monitor and influence learning based on three factors: personal processes, environmental influences, and specific behaviors (Zimmerman, 1989). Personal processes refer to those characteristics and abilities that are brought to the learning situation. Environmental influences include all external sources of information which impact an activity. Specific behaviors are the actions required to execute activities (Pajares, 1996).

In a study comparing gifted and nongifted students, Zimmerman and Martinez-Pons (1990) found that, in comparison with their nongifted peers, gifted middle and secondary school students displayed higher self-efficacy or confidence in their verbal and mathematical abilities as well as greater skills in self-regulated learning: organizing and transforming information (personal processes), imagining consequences (specific behavior), seeking peer assistance, and reviewing notes (environmental influences). Self-regulatory strategies also were used to transfer effective learning procedures from an arts program to academics in the classroom (Baum, Owen, & Oreck, 1997). These authors described specific self-regulatory behaviors in the classroom and arts environment as well as a specific plan for assisting teachers to identify these behaviors and incorporate them into the curriculum.

Zimmerman (1998a) also developed a three-stage model for promoting self-regulatory behaviors among students. This model includes forethought, performance, and self-reflection. The first stage represents the prethinking involved in any project. This includes understanding one's capabilities and making early decisions before actually initiating an activity. This is the "getting ready" period. Performance, in stage two, encompasses all of the actions needed to accomplish the task. This includes, for example, actively planning the project, seeking information, keeping records and monitoring progress, making alterations to the plan, and predicting outcomes. The third phase, self-reflection, is used to review the entire project. It is an assessment of what has been learned and what should be changed in the future.

Zimmerman (1998b) also provided an explanation of the cyclical self-regulation phases and the subprocesses related to each phase. His work includes an insightful explanation of the differences between naive self-regulation and skillful self-regulation. Although a recent review of motivation and self-regulation with respect to gifted learners is found in Schunk (1998), the literature does not examine the self-regulatory behaviors of high ability students who consistently produce high quality products. This study was conducted to investigate self-regulation techniques among highly creative productive secondary students and to uncover techniques for promoting these behaviors in other students.

Method and Procedures

Research Questions

In order to understand the match between student interests and the self-regulatory strategies leading to the completion of a satisfactory scientific investigation, the following questions were posed: (a) How do students who are recognized for their creative-productive behavior obtain ideas for science projects? (b) What self-regulatory skills do these students use to initiate and complete their science projects?

Research Design

This study used a qualitative research design with multicase studies. Triangulation of data methods and sources was employed to overcome the weaknesses and biases that prevail in a single-method design. This technique provided checks for both reliability and validity of collected data (Smith, 1975). The sources and types of information were parent questionnaires, student questionnaires, and student interviews.

Table 3.1   Distribution of the Sample According to Grade Level and Gender

Participants	Grade				
	9	10	11	12	
Females	0	0	3	1	4
Males	1	1	2	2	6
Total	1	1	5	3	10

$n = 10$

Sample

The sample consisted of 10 students in Grades 9 through 12 from four sites in three different states in the northeast of the United States. The distribution of the sample according to age and gender is presented in Table 3.1. All sites were recommended by experts in the field of gifted and talented education and were located in typical high schools rather than special schools for the gifted. Each program employed the Enrichment Triad Model (Renzulli, 1977, 1986) which encourages student productivity within student-initiated interest areas. Program services at the sites also included advanced placement courses, honors classes, special seminars, and mentorships, along with opportunities for individual investigations.

At all four sites, one teacher of the gifted was selected as the coordinating teacher. Each had completed coursework in gifted and talented education. These teachers were given a checklist of creative-productive behaviors and asked to nominate students based on three criteria. First, only high-school aged students were included in the study because their age and experience provided more pertinent information for exploring creative processes over a period of time. Second, to assure student familiarity with the goals of the program for the gifted and talented, only subjects with four or more years of participation in a program were eligible. Third, to be accepted for the study, students also were screened according to the quality and numbers (at least three) of their performances or products. Whenever possible, actual products were examined if students still retained copies of their published or presented projects such as scientific papers, project outlines, or computer programs. The impact of a project was also considered by categorizing the type of audience as local, regional, state, or national. Using this system, students were selected based on their outstanding performances, such as solving a problem in cancer cell growth for a chemist, conducting experiments in plant hybridization for a local florist, and experimenting with holographic images. See Table 3.2 for examples of student projects, which were used to make decisions in the nomination process.

All four sites based their programs on multiple selection criteria. Even though the identification systems for each program used either achievement scores, IQ test scores, or grades as criteria, or some combination thereof, "alternate pathways" also were considered. These nontraditional methods for selection into programs for the gifted and talented included parent, peer, and self-nomination, writing

Table 3.2   Examples of Student Products Used to Determine Nomination for the Study

Student # (Sex)	Title/Topic*	Product	Audience**
1 (Male)	Physics Newton's Laws of Motion	Research Paper and Experiments	Citywide Science Fairand Middle School Art Fair
	Political Science Stock Market	Game	Middle School Social Studies Class
	Collecting Baseball Cards	Organized Collection	Collector's Conventions in the Northeast
	Journalism Newspaper	Organized and Co-edited	Middle School Open House
2 (Female)	Architecture "Dream House"	Blueprint of a Model Home to Scale	Architects and Classmates
	Theater "Peter Pan"	Performed in and Produced a play	Students and Parents in the School District
	Theater "The Secret of Fairyland"	Wrote, Performed in, and Directed a Play	Students and Parents in the School District
	Computer Science Math Baseball	Wrote a Computer Game	Middle School Students
	Biology Pediatric Physical Therapy	Organized an Internship	Local Therapist
3 (Male)	Computer Science Computer Graphics	Created a Short Movie on Several Linked Computers	Regional Media Festival (Won Overall Prize)
	Physics Creative Competition	Team Organizer/ Developed the Electrical Components for the Project	Regional Competition
	Physics Holography	Wrote Grant to Obtain Laser	State Grant Evaluators
	Physics Holography	Created Holograms	Traveled to Secondary Schools in the State to Make Presentations
	Chemical Engineering and Computer Science "Computer Simulations and Cancer Research: A New Solution to a Complex Problem"	Researched and Wrote a Paper, Developed a Computer Program to Solve a Problem Simulating Cancer Growth	Classmates, Deans and Engineering Profs. of Engineering School at the University of Southern California
4 (Male)	Computer Science Computer Graphics	Wrote Programs	Went through Marketing Process for a Computer Program

Table 3.2 *(continued)*   Examples of Student Products Used to Determine Nomination
for the Study

Student # (Sex)	Title/Topic*	Product	Audience**
	Videography Adventure Film	Wrote and Directed Video	Middle School Students
	Musical Theater	Performed in and Produced a Musical	Elementary School Students in District
	Ham Radio Operating	Wrote Computer Program to Learn Operating Commands	Local Ham Radio Operators
5 (Male)	Physics Holography	Wrote Grant to Obtain Laser	State Grant Evaluators
	Physics Holography	Created Holograms	Traveled to Secondary Schools in the State
	Theater Orientation to Gifted and Talented Program	Wrote and Created a Puppet Show	Elementary School Students, Parents
	Creative Competition	Created Board Game	Regional Competition
6 (Male)	Physics Fractal Geometry	Computer Program	School and Regional Science Fair, State Science Fair (Won Award)
	Computer Science	Computer Video Yearbook	Secondary Students, Parents
	Physics "Octaves and Sine Waves"	Experiment and Display	Local Science Fair
	Astronomy	Organized Internship	Local College Planetarium
7 (Male)	Solar Energy	Created a Solar Hot Dog Cooker	Students, Local Newspaper
	Computer Science	Wrote Several Computer Graphics Programs	Community Fair
	Nature	Created Weekly Nature Segment for TV Show	Local Cable TV Program
	Biology Plant Hybridization	Growing and Selling Plants	Local Florist
8 (Female)	Writing	Wrote a French Play	Classmates
	Theater Writing	Wrote and Performed in a Play	Elementary School Students
	Computer Science	Wrote a Program to Teach Mathematics Facts	Elementary School Students

Table 3.2 *(continued)*   Examples of Student Products Used to Determine Nomination for the Study

Student # (Sex)	Title/Topic*	Product	Audience**
	Psychology	Developed a Learning Center	Secondary School Students
9 (Female)	Psychology Wrote Story About Typical Student Problems	Short Story	Young Author's Contest (Won Award), Local TV Show
	"Nutrition for Everyone"	Wrote and Directed Puppet Show	Elementary School Students
	Nature Experiences	Wrote a Book	Young Author's Contest (Won Award)
	Photography	Photographic Display	Local Schools, Banks, Fairs
10 (Female)	Humanities Seminars for Gifted and Talented Students	Organized Seminars and Served as Discussion Leader	Secondary Students, Teachers, Profs.
	Political Science	Organized Internship at State Capitol and Served as Research Assistant	Senator and Staff at State Capitol
	Journalism "Free Thought"	Founded and Organized Newspaper for Student Activists	Students throughout State
	Political Science Student Activist Conference	Organized Seminars	Conference for Regional Secondary School Students

* Project Titles/Topics are listed in chronological order for each student.
** All audiences were composed of individuals interested in the presented topics.

samples, and estimates of creative behavior. No one criterion determined selection into the program at any site.

Data Collection

The data were collected using three methods: parent questionnaires, student questionnaires, and student interviews. Documents such as any available projects also were collected and analyzed. Triangulation of data methods and sources was sought.

Parents completed two questionnaires. The first one detailed family background including parents' occupations and educational level and the second one surveyed the quantity and quality of student projects completed in and outside of school as well as the amount of effort invested by the student. A parallel form of this survey was completed by the students.

Each student also participated in a 1.5- to 2-hour interview, which was tape-recorded and later transcribed. The 26 interview questions were divided into three categories related to the student's family background and childhood, educational experience, and perception about project development. Each student responded to all questions. Follow-up questions were used to clarify responses during the course of the interview and each student received a copy of the transcription in order to make any corrections. (The interview protocol is available from the author.)

Limitations

According to Campbell and Stanley (1963), every research design is susceptible to both internal and external threats to validity. The qualitative research design accommodates reduced sample size by allowing for an in-depth view of the phenomenon under investigation. Considering the sample size, internal consistency of programmatic format as well as student and community demographics were sought. Yet no two profiles are ever identical. Each program for the gifted varies depending upon the needs and views of the community, and every student differs in personal characteristics and background experiences. These variations were taken into account during data analysis and interpretation.

In addition to this limitation, responses were confined to a historical point in time, thus reducing generalizability of the findings. Biases also may enter the analysis during data interpretation. However, appropriate coding and classification of the data can strengthen the formation of consistent and accurate results.

Another major limitation to qualitative research is replicability, yet a precise description of the research design and methodology should provide a strong foundation for developing a close approximation of the procedures. Finally, conclusions and recommendations from this study may or may not be applicable to programs that are not already based on promoting creative-productive behavior in students.

Analysis

The data were collected according to methods described in the design section. Confidentiality was assured and a coding system employed for all data sources. Analysis of the data proceeded with the formation of case records (Patton, 1980). The unit of analysis per record was the student. The information obtained from the interview data underwent content analysis in a search for patterns and themes (Spradley, 1979). After each record was analyzed, all records were compared and contrasted regarding patterns, themes, and categories (Miles & Huberman, 1984).

Results

In this section, both of the research questions were addressed: (a) How do students who are recognized for their creative-productive behavior obtain ideas for science projects? (b) What self-regulatory skills do these students use to initiate and complete their science projects?

These questions are answered through the analysis of individual and group data. First, student profiles provide analyses within each case. Second, a synthesis across cases is presented.

Student Profiles

These overviews include descriptions of each student's family background, interests, and projects. Data were collected and synthesized using all of the sources and methods described in the triangulated research methodology.

As mentioned earlier, the students were selected for this study based on the quality and quantity of their creative-productive behaviors. In this selection process, cooperating teachers were not instructed to confine their judgments to high scholastic achievers or to sample from grade levels. All students were selected for their interest in either natural or social science. Although school-related variables were contained in the profiles, this information was not collected until after students had been nominated and selected for the study. Likewise, grade levels and gender do not meet any specific quota.

Student 1: Greg. Greg is an extremely confident 14-year-old. He also has known for a long time that politics and economics are an important part of his life. He plans to have a career in this combined field. He remembers being 5 or 6 years old and trying to organize his family into committees. In this way, he could have more influence in areas such as the amount of television time allowed each week. Greg also tried to set up a Rules Committee. "Usually I would try to set those up right after I got in trouble so we could change the rules." He is the oldest of three sons and finds that his brothers generally tolerate his ideas. Greg has been involved in a program for the gifted and talented for the past four years. Within that time, he has completed 5 major projects and 15 minor ones. The major science projects include demonstrations of several of his own computer adventure games and a science-fair project displaying experiments with Newton's Laws of Motion. He also has presented his extensive baseball card collection, is the editor for the school newspaper, has developed a game about the stock market, and was a participant in a national creative problem-solving competition. The audiences for these products have ranged from local peers to regional groups.

An excellent student, he is interested in "any sort of challenge," which he actively seeks. His creativity pertains to "ideas, not designs or pictures." When giving advice to another student regarding topic selection, he recommends that you do what you like best and not be an "impulsive buyer."

Student 2: Cindy. Seventeen-year-old Cindy describes herself as an outgoing person who is happy with her life. Although she has played the piano since she was in the sixth grade and has performed in plays since Grade 5, she also enjoys the company of children.

The first thing I can remember [about a career] was when I was ten years old. I don't know how it came about but I realized that I loved children. And I've liked science throughout my years of schooling and I just tried to look for a career that had children and science, and [what I] came up with was a pediatrician . . . or a pediatric physical therapist.

This decision grew from a project which she began several years ago. She has been researching child development and plans to share her findings of many years in a learning center for other students.

Cindy has been in a program for the gifted and talented since Grade 2 and has completed seven projects. Her science projects have included pediatrics, hydroponics, and computer science. Other topics were related to architectural design, play writing and production, music composition, and creative problem solving. The projects have been presented to a variety of audiences including local, regional, and national groups.

Her favorite school subjects are biology and chemistry because "they involve experiments and answer questions about the human body and other scientific phenomena." She is concerned about her grades but relatively satisfied with her school accomplishments. Her mother felt that her many projects have taken the boredom out of school for her. She likes to be creative and said she is "willing to be different and a nonconformist." Through her risk-taking, she said that she has learned a lot from "things that don't work."

Student 3:   Chris. When Chris was 16, his interest in engineering led to his acceptance in a competitive summer science internship at the University of Southern California. Paired with a research scientist in chemical engineering, Chris was assigned a project to investigate a specific type of cancer cell growth. During the 7-week internship, he researched the topic, wrote a computer program in Pascal, solved the cell-growth problem, then wrote and presented a paper entitled "Computer Simulations and Cancer Research: A New Solution to a Complex Problem?" During Chris's seven years in a program for the gifted and talented, he has completed at least five major projects. In addition to the summer internship, he has:

1. Produced a short movie on several linked computers for which he won an overall prize at a regional media festival
2. Assisted in building a battery-powered vehicle for a problem-solving program in which he competed on a national level
3. Jointly wrote a grant to build a holographic display which was presented at his own school as well as regional secondary schools
4. Competed in a national problem-solving program

At age 17, Chris admitted, "I'm self-motivated. I try to do the best I can in everything. I'm disappointed if I don't. There's no pressure on me—I just want to." For instance, during one of his summer vacations, he taught himself a computer language. His parents are proud of his efforts and support his progress both in and out of school. He has one younger sister, age 14. He commented that they do not share his many interests.

In four years of high school, Chris has taken courses that cover six years of mathematics. He would like to see more advanced level courses offered to high school students. Chris regrets that living in a rural area provides few opportunities for a great variety of experiences, but he does take advantage of courses at a local university, where he recently completed a Calculus II course.

Chris's other interests include track, playing the French horn, and reading. His greatest reward in his projects is "to get something done that works." He plans a career in aerospace engineering and believes that people should work in areas in which they have the greatest interest. His motto: "Don't give up and don't procrastinate."

Student 4: James. Altering the expression "a self-made man," James is a "self-taught student." He is a ham-radio operator, a certified scuba diver, a sailor, and a computer programmer. Although he has had to take licensing courses, he has learned most of these activities on his own. James is also a competitive swimmer and he enjoys outdoor activities. In the future, he would like to pursue a military career, one relating to the outdoors, or one in computer science. When asked to describe himself, James said that he is definitely independent. He also notes that he is different "from other people in the student body, in many ways besides just creativity. Perhaps in ideals and goals or opinions about things."

James has an IQ in the very superior range. He prefers to work with applying concepts rather than memorizing linear facts. In school, James says that there is not enough opportunity to apply information or to take interesting courses such as drafting or music. He does prefer his computer science course to all other courses.

James has written several computer programs. They usually serve to fulfill a need, such as a program that taught him Morse Code or one that reviewed Latin vocabulary. He regrets that he has not been successful in locating appropriate audiences for his programs. Other projects have included the production of a videotape and a play. When he finds new interests, he usually attends lectures on the subject at the local university.

James is the oldest of three children. He has been in the gifted and talented program since the sixth grade. He is now in the 11th grade.

Student 5: Tim. Tim's interests relate to mathematics and computer science. As a 17-year-old in the 12th grade, Tim has been taking accelerated mathematics courses since the seventh grade. Although he has performed well in these classes, he describes himself as someone who is "not highly motivated." With his "easygoing" personality, he tries not to be affected by the pressures of academic competition, but he is disappointed with himself when he does not achieve his goals. For example, he enrolled in a Calculus II course at a local university but withdrew when the work became too difficult. He knew how disappointed other people would be, but he said he was not yet prepared for the demands of such a course.

He may try it again next year, as he would like to pursue a career in science or mathematics. Tim's parents are proud of his work and they do not put pressure on him to perform academically. Tim has both a younger brother (age 13) and a younger sister (age 7). He enjoys being with them because he said, "They keep me thinking younger." They also brainstorm project ideas with him, but they are not involved with his actual work.

Tim collects baseball cards in order to complete the sets and to study the statistics. Another interest of Tim's is making holograms. He has been involved with this topic since the seventh grade. Not only has he designed several holographic images, but he was also a member of the group that wrote the grant that enabled his school to acquire a laser for making holograms.

During his eight years in a program for the gifted and talented, Tim has completed four major projects, all science-related. He also has participated in a problem-solving program on both local and national levels. He said that all of these projects have allowed him to be more creative, given him the opportunity to work with others, developed his self-confidence, and assisted in decreasing his tendency to procrastinate. Although he described his learning process as a combination of reading and discussing, he knows that he does not spend enough time applying information.

Student 6:   Ed. Ed, at age 15, has always been fascinated by science, stating, "I cannot remember a single time when I was not interested in science." In trying to recall an early experience, he stated, "I was so into mechanics and the way things work that when I was about four or five, I saw a clock and I pointed to it and I said, 'gears.'" Ed describes himself as someone who relates his "overall interest in technology, mechanics, and science [to] the way things work. That's just where it's all at as far as I'm concerned, understanding the universe"! Toward that end, Ed's favorite project was a computer program describing the function and growth patterns of fractals. This study of fractal geometry took place in the seventh grade. He entered his project in an eighth-grade science fair and tied for first place. Winning the award went beyond all his expectations, as did his satisfaction in the completed project. Having been in a program for the gifted and talented for the past five years, Ed has focused his attention on the natural sciences. Setting his sights on being accepted to M.I.T., he plans to become an astrophysicist.

Ed is also interested in the technical side of music and has an interest in video production. He knows that other people do not always understand his enthusiasm. When asked what his family thinks about his projects, he made the following reply:

> I drive them nuts with technical details occasionally, just because there's no one else to tell technical details to. Do you know what a single ray ratio is? I can go on and on about them. But seriously, they understand that I really like this stuff and they're supportive of it as long as I don't impose it on them. I've gotten better about that, but it's just . . . I've gotta tell someone. You know?

Ed does not like the cliques that form in school, but he is satisfied with his relationships with other students and with teachers. He sees school as a place to learn and a stepping stone to a good college. Outside of school, Ed is motivated by his interests as stated in this comment, "What I want to do is defined by what I've enjoyed doing."

Student 7: Oliver. "I don't ever remember being interested in anything before I got interested in science. There wasn't anything before that. [My interest started in] the second or third grade." At age 17, Oliver finds that his interests are centered on science and art. Possible career plans include landscape architecture and engineering. Oliver has participated in a program for the gifted and talented since the second grade and has completed the following projects:

1. A solar hot dog cooker
2. Several computer graphics programs
3. A weekly nature segment for a children's television program
4. A video movie
5. A plant growing business for a local florist

Oliver's humor is dry and cynical. He explained that even the worst of his many projects was better than going to school. He admitted that several of his projects were completed because people reminded him of his deadlines.

Oliver is also interested in writing, listening to music, and reading. He incorporates these interests into his passion for nature. On weekends and during the summer he works for a local florist. This gives him the opportunity to experiment with plant hybridization and to make money. He will only work on a project as long as it does not bore him so he has many different types of planting projects happening at once. He says, "I have no short term patience, but long term I can generally manage to stick with something if I really want to do it."

His three older brothers do not influence his work since there is a nine-year age difference between Oliver and the next sibling. Oliver's parents do not interfere with his projects and he likes to work alone. However, his parents were role models for his interest area because they are garden enthusiasts. He is presently discovering his own learning style and knows that he has to get away from his ideas in order to reconsider the problems he encounters.

Student 8: Karen. Karen is 16 years old. She describes herself as "enthusiastic, easy-going, optimistic, and sentimental." She also views problems as a challenge. Karen loves music and acting, which she pursues by taking ballet, guitar, and voice lessons. Her interests do not stop with these classes, as Karen is an actress in a summer theater and has performed with a state ballet company. Her love of the arts is balanced by an interest in the logics of computer science. Reading has always been an important form of relaxation for Karen, but she has had to decrease the amount of time she spends on that activity in order to make time for her other interests. Karen enjoys the independence of doing projects on her own and she is disappointed with society's focus on numbers as indicators of success. Instead, she believes that people should be able to creatively and accurately express themselves.

Identified for the gifted and talented program in elementary school, Karen has been involved with a variety of projects. She completed at least six projects, including writing an extensive computer program, producing a play, writing and performing a play based on a myth, and founding a school newspaper.

When working on a project, Karen brainstorms ideas with other people in order to clarify her thoughts. She also thinks it is helpful to "get away from" a project in order to obtain a better perspective of the situation. Major influences in her life have been her teachers in the gifted program. Her time in the resource room has helped her to expand her knowledge and improve her organization. When asked about her creativity, Karen said that she likes to discover "new things and new ways to do them."

She always prefers firsthand resources and advises any student to stick to a task in order to accomplish it. Working on projects has given her more opportunity to express her individuality, provided her with independence, and given her access to new ideas.

Student 9:   Mary. Mary, at age 18, combines her love of the outdoors with her curiosity for exploration. As she explores, she continually hunts with her camera. When she was 17, she arranged a trip to Caracas, Venezuela, for seven weeks to discover the Amazon jungle and another culture. This experience certainly added new entries to her study of nature and her photography portfolio. Mary would like to major in zoology with a double major in photography and outdoor education. Her goal is to become a wildlife photographer. Presently, she is pursuing a mentorship with a professional in this field. Her other interests include writing and health care. Mary has been a member of both a volunteer and a professional medical team since she received her Emergency Medical Team (EMT) license last year. Her attainment of this certificate marked the first time someone from her state was allowed to take this exam under the age of 18.

As a participant of the gifted program since the second grade, Mary has competed six major projects. On two distinct occasions, she has received regional awards for writing short stories. She has also written and performed in a play for children as well as displayed a collection of her photographs in various community settings such as local schools and banks.

She realizes that she sometimes overextends herself, but she also finds that engaging in new activities provides much self-satisfaction. Mary describes her activities as stimulating and revitalizing. She says that her many interests have "made school more tedious and boring in comparison." She comments that, "In class, I don't feel the same satisfaction and enjoyment as I do from these projects." Although her grades remain high, she has been decreasing the amount of time spent on her courses and this concerns her mother. Her twin brother does not have the same passion for exploring, nor do her older brother or sister.

When asked about her motivation to pursue her interests, Mary stated, "I have always had motivation and initiative. These projects have given me the chance to pursue some of my interests."

Student 10:   Becky. Becky, a 17-year-old, is very politically oriented. Much of her time is consumed by investigating causes such as injustice in Central America. How does a high school student support a political cause? Becky was the founder of a newspaper that promotes political awareness in high school students. She also works to bring AIDS education to students and has assisted in organizing a statewide political march against injustice. Her favorite project was a self-arranged mentorship with a prominent state politician in her state's capitol. Becky enjoys working with people. She loves to coordinate events and has even sought the advice of professional politicians to obtain tips for working effectively with people. As a child, Becky enjoyed playing the piano. She quit a few years ago, however, because as she says, "I couldn't stand listening to myself play." Her mother agrees that she is a perfectionist. This may hinder her performance in some areas, because she also claims to lack self-esteem.

Although Becky has great respect for her teachers, she said, "I am not willing to make school the overall thing in my life." Her mother comments that she wishes Becky would perform better in school. She prefers to learn on her own and has even taken textbooks home to read them over the summer. Her teacher in the gifted and talented program admits that she learns better that way, by herself.

Becky is best characterized as someone who gets as deeply involved in her work as possible. She looks for a need and begins her projects immediately. This energy is applied toward interests related to humanity and in the near future, she would like to volunteer her services in Central America.

Where Ideas Come From

Preparation for learning includes gathering both data and resources. According to Zimmerman (1998b), five types of forethought processes include goal setting, strategic planning, self-efficacy beliefs, goal orientation, and intrinsic interest. Goal setting refers to knowing the outcomes of learning and of the project, whereas strategic planning includes the methods for attaining the goal or goals. Perceived self-efficacy reflects an individual's confidence in his or her ability to perform a behavior to produce specific outcomes; it is thought to directly impact the choice to engage in a task, as well as the effort that will be expended and the persistence that will be exhibited (Bandura, 1977).

The fourth process cited by Zimmerman is goal orientation, which includes learning and performance goals. The former refers to the fact that the student is concerned with the mastery of skills while the latter means that an individual is focusing on how he or she is being judged when completing a task goal (Elliott & Dweck, 1988; Ames & Archer, 1988). Individuals recognized as expert or skillful self-regulators focus on developing skills and improving their learning rather than on what others think about their behaviors. For example, both types of students may be high achievers, but are motivated for different reasons. Finally, having intrinsic interest in a topic means that an individual has selected an idea based on his or her own priorities and reasons for pursuing that topic.

Selecting a topic. Prior to acting on a particular interest, students need to get an idea for a project. According to Csikszentmihalyi (1994), getting ideas or problem finding is the most crucial stage in creative achievement. In the case of self-regu-lation in learning, getting an idea is included in the first phase, that of forethought. This precedes an actual investigation or performance and prepares the learner for delving into a project (Zimmerman, 1998b). These students continuously explored their many interests, as they actively sought project ideas through a vari-ety of techniques including reading, sharing information with others, and taking courses both in and out of school. Intrinsic interest was sometimes expressed as shear passion for a topic. The concept of "falling in love" with an idea appeared frequently in the interviews as demonstrated by a student who explains how he first became interested in fractal geometry:

> I really enjoyed that project . . . It started in June. It was kind of almost "romantic" because I saw this article in *Scientific American* . . . and I said, "Gee, that's neat." And it just kind of built on itself.

Just as this student was able to recognize a topic that was suited to his inter-ests and abilities, all subjects said they investigated topics that they already liked or knew something about. As one student put it, "What I want to do is defined by what I've enjoyed doing." Five of the 10 students said that others were involved with their idea selection processes, at least some of the time. Students reported brainstorming ideas with siblings, friends, parents, or teachers.

As students work at getting their ideas, "think time" plays an important role in product development. One student refers to this as "mind intervention." The following response illustrates how a student employed incubation while deciding to investigate the difference between diamonds and graphite.

> It starts out as an insignificant thing. You think: "Why is that diamond hard?" But then it will just develop . . . your mind will just keep turning the idea over and over. . . . If you get to the point where you just can't figure it out and you really want to know, then it starts to seem important to you and you think—"This is something I should try and figure out."

This student's desire to understand a phenomenon for its own sake repre-sents a learning-goal (Ames & Archer, 1988; Elliott & Dweck, 1988) rather than a performance-goal orientation. When searching for a topic, intrinsic curios-ity is assisted by a disciplined or strategic approach to getting ideas. Another student, who sets aside time each day for thinking, gets ideas in the following manner:

Basically, I just hear about something and then it just strikes me that that would be something good to do a project on. I don't . . . consciously sit down and say: "What project I am going to do next?" It . . . starts as a like, or a thought and just turns into a project.

This may not seem like a replicable methodology or strategic planning, but he does actively think about his project ideas on a daily basis. When asked, "Do you ever do anything to purposely bring ideas together?" another student, who also consistently seeks ideas, replied with this analogy:

I try to [make myself look for ideas], but it doesn't work as well as serendipity. Serendipity isn't very dependable, but I suppose that's . . . like the chance of one atom [decaying today]. If you only had one of them and it only [decays] once every million years, [the chance] is very small. But if you have a trillion of those atoms and each of them decays once every million years, then the chances are very good that one of them will decay in one day. And it's the same kind of thing. There are so many ideas out there that I'm bound to come up serendipitously with some good idea to research.

If "chance favors the prepared mind," then students who consciously and unconsciously scan their environments for ideas are more likely to find one they like. When asked to provide advice to another student regarding topic selection, students stressed that you should "choose something that you enjoy, otherwise you're going to get bored with it after a while." All students believed that a topic needed to be personal, as one student said, "You should select a topic that you like. [You] can't choose something to please other people, choose something you want to do." Assigned topics or those picked from a list are not as satisfying according to the following comments:

I like doing research. . . . It's enjoyable to me, like science projects in a topic that I enjoy doing. If the topic is given to me and I don't like it, I don't enjoy researching it. But if it's a topic that I want to learn about I can research forever on it. (Learning-goal orientation)

It depends whether or not they're assigned or on my own. If I do it on my own, I tend to start on it sooner than if it was assigned. If it's assigned, you tend to put it off until the last couple of days. (Intrinsic interest)

Resources.   Major reasons for disliking projects were related to the forethought stage and to strategic planning, in particular. Specifically, inadequate preparation led students to mention these criteria when describing their least-liked investigations:

1. Lack of group or personal commitment
2. Lack of interest in the topic
3. Inadequate amount of time for working on the project
4. Poor selection of human and material resources
5. Inadequate information or skills prior to commencing an investigation

These criteria are similar to those described by Haensly and Roberts (1983) in a study of the creative processes of professionals in six different fields. In their study, the participants reported the following necessary ingredients for successful product development: task commitment, the ability to select an appropriate audience for presenting one's contribution, and energy to overcome obstacles such as a lack of time, money, or cooperation. In the present study, environmental and personal resources not only include equipment, mentors, books, funds, background information, time, group management skills, and imagination, but also feedback.

One student said that she needs a lot of positive reinforcement for working on a project. She thinks about how this could happen before the project starts, stating, "If I don't know what I'm doing, I like people to point me in the right direction." She likes to know who can help her ahead of time. Another student said that it's a problem for him when there is no one around to help him with an idea. Students need to talk about their projects. They need feedback before, during, and after project development.

These students say that they are not consciously looking for projects, but their conscious minds are absorbing information that can be used for an investigation when the right combination of factors presents itself: interest, curiosity, background information, and available resources.

Planning.   Most of the students do not regard planning in a lock-step fashion. They do not consider their approach to these activities as structured. This attitude is reflected in the following three quotes:

> There's no schedule. I try to break it down into smaller pieces to make it easier, but there's no formal plan that I spend hours working on to get everything straightened out and [to figure out] the amount of time I'm going to spend on everything.

> I just try to generally find a couple of things to start with and then wherever that leads me that's where I go. . . . I know where I'm going, I just don't know how I'm getting there. If I find something better, I'll change it. I won't go with what I had. Usually my original idea is one of the best things that I can turn it in to (flexible goal structure).

> How would I solve this particular problem? [I] break everything down into smaller problems and think about different ways [I] could get this section to work.

This ability to have a goal in mind, to break a task into its component parts while maintaining a tolerance for the partial successes along the way, is a characteristic of expert problem solvers. Although all students in this study employ problem-solving behaviors to complete their projects, they each made a point of detailing this less structured format during their interviews. So prevalent was the concept of flexibility in these students' planning processes that the coding in the analysis procedure became "flexible strategy." In fact, these students almost resented the fact that the researcher asked how they "planned" their projects. Planning was what you had to do with assignments directed by the teacher. Their projects were thought of as their own creations, not scheduled tasks with inflexible due dates. There may have been final deadlines for some of the projects such as those submitted to science fairs, but the majority of the projects completed by these students were not required. The following conversations reveal distinctions between teacher-directed and student-directed projects.

Researcher: So there's no particular way that you plan anything?

Student #1: No. Not really, because I do that on school projects. I used to at least, and I didn't really seem to get it done as well. I would still get a good grade and everything but I just didn't feel I had done as good a job as possible.

Researcher: Do you know why that might have happened?

Student #1: Maybe when I set up the time schedule, I wouldn't allow any change. If I set it up I'd want to do it that way. But I think it works better where you just come up with a couple of things to start with and then see where that takes [you] to.

Researcher: How do you set up the projects you want to do?

Student #4: I leave lots of time for things that I want to do. . . . Most of them do not start out with the idea of the whole concept that it ends up with in the end. Lots and lots of things get added on as you work.

Researcher: What is most important as you begin a project?

Student #7: To find a way to do it that's easy enough for me to be capable of doing it. . . . I don't have to state what direction they are going to take right away. I can change [them] around or modify them.

Researcher: How do you decide how to plan a project, what do you do?

Student #6: Basically, it's just kind of automatic. You read about it and you have the process where you get the idea, you learn more about it, and just research. This is a scientific method. And then you come up with your own idea for something to do with it. And then you do that. And then you polish your project and then you display it. And that's basically the process and it's kind of obvious. I mean, you just have to decide at what time you want to have each stage of the game done.

Student #6: I don't have a calendar.

Researcher: So you don't really write anything down.

Student #6: Generally [not]. Although I'm doing that more simply because the projects are getting bigger and bigger. The bigger a project is the more planning it takes.

You can't always have concrete planning because things change. . . . You have to be flexible. You can never be completely concrete.

Given the quality and quantity of the projects, it is not surprising that these students allocate a great deal of time and energy to working on their investigations. Students reported spending approximately 1 to 10 hours a week working on a project, including thinking time. One student explained that his devotion to a project is sporadic:

> If interest comes and something is really happening at a certain time, it will be a lot. It could be five hours a day, late into the night. If nothing is happening, nothing happens for weeks.

Another student had a more balanced work pattern, stating, "I try to work on something of my own every day." The time and energy spent on an investigation depends on the student's interest and commitment. Deadlines for projects may be imposed by a formal organization, but the goal itself and the distribution of effort is largely determined and controlled by the student.

Performance

Zimmerman (1998b) suggested that the second self-regulatory phase of performance/ volitional control has three subprocesses: attention focusing, self-instruction/imagery, and self-monitoring. Attention focusing relates to an individual's ability to stay on task. When too many distractions interfere with the completion of a project, a student is in jeopardy of abandoning an investigation. The distractions might result from competing projects or assignments as well as inadequate resources. The second process, self-instruction, takes place when a student tells himself or herself how to proceed with a task (Schunk, 1982). It can take the form of imagery (imagining what to do in a situation) or self-talk (giving oneself verbal directions as with a pep talk). Third, an individual practicing self-monitoring uses feedback to determine how well a task is being performed. Constant use of this process can interfere with an individual's progress if he or she is overly self-critical.

Although all students conceive of their projects using different approaches and develop their ideas using different methods, they do employ these three subprocesses. Once students select topics they like, think are fun, and find intriguing, they are more motivated to pursue them. One student even commented that he needs to slow down because he can be so eager to finish, he might make mistakes. By recognizing this potential problem, he takes his personality into consideration and adjusts his behavior appropriately.

After beginning a project, a few students work steadily until completion, but most take breaks along the way. These breaks are not periods of disinterest. All students reported consciously stopping work on a project in order to "get away from it." These periods of incubation occur at intervals during the process, as the students accomplish subtasks toward the completion of their goals. These lapses are used to reorganize ideas and resources. Unfortunately, there may also be competing interests making it difficult for even the most practiced problem-solver to get back to work. Students report being able to give themselves "pep talks" to continue. Here's how one may sound: "You've chosen to do this project. You like it, so just don't sit around and procrastinate about it. Start doing something!"

Based on their reflections from prior projects, these students were realistic about lapses of interest after choosing a topic, and provide this advice for others:

> If they don't like it, get out of it. Or . . . try to be optimistic and find something that is good about it and say, 'Even though I don't like this I am learning something, so I'll continue" . . . And not say this is stupid and a waste of time. (Self-instruction: self-encouraging statements)

> One thing is definitely stick to it because a lot of times you can get frustrated by the little things that happen. When you think everything is together then you'll find a flaw in it and it will seem like everything is falling apart. So just stick to it and keep seeing the end result. Then, even once you get there, as I've experienced, I've even wanted to go further in some cases. A lot of times you just have to try new things and it doesn't always come easily. (Self-efficacy)

> If you're doing it with a group, choose carefully who you're working with. Don't just say you'll go with anybody. And think carefully before you just randomly pick something. Don't be an impulse chooser like an impulse buyer. Think about the different options, or think about the different ideas you can come up with. Figure out which one you like the best and which one you could do the best job with, and then make the determination. (Intrinsic interest and Self-monitoring)

> Don't give up on it once you start, because in the end you'll realize that you usually liked it, you enjoyed what you did . . . Just work on something that you're interested in, something that suits your own needs, but don't let other people tell you what to do: do stuff on your own that you like to do. (Intrinsic interest and Self-efficacy)

Their advice to students is summarized in Table 3.3.

Self-Reflection

Does feedback about these projects make an impact on students? Why do they continue to participate in science projects? What do students learn from these experiences? These are the kinds of questions related to self-reflection, the third stage in the self-regulation process. Four processes related to this phase are self-evaluation, attributions, self-reactions, and adaptivity (Zimmerman, 1998b). These related processes include comparing oneself to others or to a standard or goal (self-evaluation); determining the source of one's successes or failures such as luck, the difficulty of the task, ability or effort (attributions) (Weiner, 1979, 1985); responses to performances (self-reactions); and modifying behaviors to suit the situation (adaptation). These students reported that they reflected on their work during the investigation as well as after a project was completed.

Table 3.3   Student Advice to Peers about Conducting a Project

Student Advice	Self-Regulatory Subprocesses
1. Choose a topic of interest (unanimous response).	Intrinsic interest
2. Have task commitment, "stick-to-itiveness."	Attention focusing
3. Don't choose a topic to please other people, select something you want to do.	Learning goal orientation
4. When working in groups, make certain that everyone in the group gets along and is interested in the topic.	Intrinsic interest
5. If you don't like the topic, get out or find something you can like about the topic.	Self-monitoring
6. Tell yourself to be optimistic.	Self-instruction: Self-encouraging statements
7. Be prepared to try something new as you proceed with your investigation. You don't know exactly where it will take you.	Self-efficacy
8. Find time on a regular basis to think about your project ideas.	Strategic planning and self-monitoring
9. Know about the types of resources you will need as you prepare your project.	Strategic planning
10. Use feedback to judge progress on a regular basis.	Self-monitoring and Self-evaluation

The role of the audience.   Students in this study believed that it was essential to show their work to the appropriate audience. These are people who understand the topic, appreciate the student's effort, and supply constructive criticism, not just flattery. When asked why an audience was necessary, subjects responded:

> Because you don't really have anybody's comment on what you've done. If you just do it yourself, you can't really say as easily that some things should have been better, because you're looking at the fact that you worked for a long time on this, and worked really hard, so it's got to be the best possible. So it usually takes someone else, on the outside, to get you thinking about some of the mistakes that were made or things that could have been done better.

> Actually, it's one of the rewards; being able to explain something to somebody and having them understand it. You get a real sense of satisfaction out of being able to show your understanding for [your project] and create an understanding in other people. . . . You've just given them something. It's a gift!

Not only do the students want an evaluation of their work, they find it necessary to interact with people who have similar interests, sharing what they have learned with those who can appreciate it.

Why do students engage in creative-productive behavior? Students agreed that the projects assisted in meeting the following needs: interest and inquisitiveness, self-satisfaction, increased learning, challenge, and self-expression.

Why do I write (computer) programs? When I see something, and I don't know how it works, I wonder. So that may be part of it.

Everything I've done . . . was geared for someone else. . . . I want someone else to understand something.

Because I enjoy it . . . It provides a challenge that I like to look for and an outlet for some of my skills, or non-skills when I'm trying to improve.

I guess it's just something different for me to do in the classes, more exposure to different things than you'd get in the normal class study. And if you have a group that's interested in it, you'll get more done. Like in class we have some kids that really don't care.

I guess it's basically the idea in general that these things really make a difference. That they're significant. They can really explain some natural phenomenon that couldn't be explained before. . . . That's basically the purpose of my science fair projects: you ask a question and then you try and create a background for yourself to get an understanding. That's what it's all about.

Many students have completed projects in more than one subject area, yet their favorite project usually relates to their favorite school subject, present area of interest, and potential career path. In describing their most successful investigations, student responses included the following criteria:

1. Genuine interest in the topic (seen as vital)
2. Self-satisfaction and enjoyment
3. Audience recognition and helpful feedback
4. Opportunities for creative expression
5. The project did what it was supposed to do, "It worked"

What was learned? As they continued to work on their projects, these students learned to better organize their activities despite the fact that they did not believe they were actually planning any events. They did not necessarily report that each project is more satisfying than the last one because some found that earlier projects were their favorites. Perhaps an early project represented the "hook." In this case, the sense of accomplishment derived from a project well done overcame the novice level of sophistication in early activities, resulting in a favorable memory of the early project. Students also learned that long-term projects can be frustrating. One student remarked that he learned to make himself stop his work before he got too frustrated with it. Then he would go back to it after a break. Although they learned how to manage a project, everything did not turn out as well as expected. Another remarked that when you put more time into a project than you thought you would and the results are not what you expect, the project falls below your expectations.

> When you're younger you want to start it faster and you're more eager to do it. . . . Now you realize that it's a lot of work and sometimes [a particular project] isn't worth it.

According to the students, there were positive and negative aspects to project development. Despite the problems, students were able to overcome obstacles through such methods as giving themselves "pep talks" when motivation slumped, shifting to other interests in order to have time to think about their ideas (incubation), or even terminating their work on a project when the appropriate resources and energy were not available. Ending one creative-productive activity did not interfere with beginning another and at least two students reported working on more than one project at a time, just for more variety.

Overall, students did see improvements in their skills for pursuing investigations. Their cumulative comments are reported in Table 3.4.

Table 3.4   Changes over Time

---

1. The project itself resulted in
   a. Increased interest and task commitment
   b. Improvements in the quality of projects
   c. The ability to get more ideas
   d. Better organizational strategies
   e. Future selection of more challenging projects
   f. The ability to accept criticism more realistically
2. Skill acquisition or development occurred in
   a. Research
   b. Writing
   c. Communication
   d. Technical abilities
3. Personality traits showed improvement in
   a. Self-satisfaction
   b. Patience
   c. Self-assurance
   d. Responsibility
   e. Attitude toward learning
   f. Independence
   g. Enjoyment
   h. Passion for a topic
4. Possible careers were explored
   a. Career topics were generated
   b. Work skills were developed

Self-reflection occurs as students make decisions to pursue specific stages of their work as well as after a project is completed. Reflection should reveal not only what students think about their performances but also what they realize about themselves, as this student indicates:

> I don't know. [My projects] haven't changed me; they've just changed how much I know about me.

Discussion and Conclusions

Self-Regulation among Gifted and Nongifted Students

Zimmerman and Martinez-Pons (1990) identified 10 strategies related to self-regulation: Organizing and transforming information, imagining consequences, seeking peer assistance, reviewing notes, self-evaluating progress, goal setting and planning, seeking information, keeping records and monitoring progress, structuring the environment, and rehearsing information. Zimmerman and Martinez-Pons found that the first four strategies were exhibited by gifted students to a greater degree than by their nongifted peers. Given these results, these two researchers were surprised to find that goal setting and planning were not characteristics of the gifted sample. In fact, although planning skills increased for all students from Grade 5 to Grade 8, this construct actually decreased for all students when they reached Grade 11.

The present study provides some insight into this result because these secondary school students also admitted that they did not plan their creative-productive projects. The following two related explanations provide possible reasons for the reduction in reported planning skills. First, the studies by Zimmerman and Martinez-Pons (1990) as well as the present one asked students for self-reports of their planning abilities. Neither study employed actual observations of student planning. This may result in students' misrepresenting or underestimating their planning abilities because, for them, planning is not a new skill, may not have been expanded over time (since Grade 8), and may be taken for granted. For many of these students, the expectations for their planning skills have not changed over time and their method has, therefore, become so automatic that the students do not recognize what they are specifically doing when planning.

Another explanation is that school-related planning operations reach a peak around Grade 8 and are actually not useful for more complex procedures. The reported decline is due to the fact that students are not using these less sophisticated skills. Another aspect to this latter explanation is the value that students in this study placed on the term "planning." They relegated the concept to a lock-step process that was only required and used in school. They had refined their planning skills from a concrete model based on an outline to a more flexible strategy where the goal was in view but the procedures for achieving that goal could and did vary. These are the characteristics of expert problem solvers. Perhaps this behavior is not being adequately recognized and developed in most students.

How can Science Inquiry be Developed Using
Self-Regulation of Learning Processes?
The stages of self-regulatory behavior outlined by Zimmerman (1998a) were certainly represented by these students. The students gathered information to determine the pertinence of topic ideas for their interest areas. By reviewing their own skills and resources, they were able to select satisfying topics resulting in high quality projects. These preproject activities showed considerable evidence of forethought. Therefore, the first phase of project development should include an examination of a student's abilities, preferences, and resources. In order to fully explore one's personal traits, this phase must begin as early as possible, not just when a mandatory science fair project is due. Students need to learn how to understand themselves and their learning processes. Techniques for developing these skills could include: completing and analyzing an interest inventory, maintaining a journal of possible project ideas, participating in a workshop about learning styles, and developing a talent portfolio.

Regarding the performance phase, these students knew how to keep track of their progress, what to do about interruptions to their work, and how to change the direction of their plans to seek a satisfying goal. What sustained students through this stage was the identification of a problem of value to the student which was selected by the student. The steps for solving the problem seem not to be a primary focus as students admitted that they did not construct a detailed plan prior to beginning a project. As the students in this project reported, their ability to participate in creative-productive activities was influenced by the support they received in their programs for the gifted and talented and by the initiation and completion of projects. Projects students liked and disliked were instrumental in the development of their self-regulatory behaviors. Many of these strategies can be directly taught and improved in students (Schunk & Zimmerman, 1998). Suggestions for preparing other students for this stage include: Attending presentations by students who have already succeeded in this process; maintaining some type of project journal although it does not have to be organized in a linear fashion; meeting with mentors who can facilitate project development throughout the investigation; and reviewing strategies for representing ideas schematically, verbally, or in writing.

Stage three of the self-regulation process, self-reflection, was easily identified in the advice these students gave to their peers and in what they learned from their ventures. Although evaluation was incorporated into the presentation of the project to an audience, students were also reflecting on the degree of success at each stage of their work: Do I have the necessary time and resources to learn about hydroponics before I need to develop an experiment related to this form of plant growing? Have I included all the details that the science-fair judges want to see? Do I tap the appropriate resources to complete this project about graphite and diamonds? Students could benefit from self-reflection by keeping a record of their reactions to their progress and by sharing their ideas with peers, mentors, teachers, and parents during their investigations.

Students learned more about themselves and their learning patterns. According to all of these students, involvement in their creative productive activities has improved their self-regulatory behaviors (refer to Table 3.3) and provided them with critical skills for today as much as for their future careers.

References

Adams, R. C., & Gardner, R. (1997). *Ideas for science projects* (rev. ed.). New York: Franklin Watts.

Ames, C., & Archer, J. (1988). Achievement goals in the classroom: Students' learning strategies and motivation processes. *Journal of Educational Psychology, 80,* 260–267.

Bandura, A. (1977). Self-efficacy: Toward a unifying theory of behavioral change. *Psychological Review, 84,* 191–215.

Bandura, A. (1986). *Social foundations of thought and action: A social cognitive theory.* Englewood Cliffs, NJ: Prentice Hall.

Baum, S. M., Owen, S. V., & Oreck, B. A. (1997). Transferring individual self-regulation process from arts to academics. *Arts Education Policy Review, 98,* 32–39.

Bochinski, J. B. (1996). *The complete handbook of science fair projects* (rev. ed.). New York: Wiley.

Brisk, M. A. (1999). *1001 ideas for science projects* (3rd ed.). New York: Macmillan.

Burns, D. E. (1990). The effects of group training activities on students' initiation of creative investigations. *Gifted Child Quarterly, 34,* 31–36.

Campbell, D. T., & Stanley, J. C. (1963). Experimental and quasi-experimental designs for research on teaching. In N. L. Gage (Ed.), *Handbook of research on teaching; a project of the American Educational Research Association* (pp. 171–246). Chicago: Rand McNally.

Csikszentmihalyi, M. (1994). The domain of creativity. In D. H. Feldman, M. Csikszentmihalyi, & H. Gardner (Eds.), *Changing the world: A framework for the study of creativity.* Westport, CT: Praeger.

Delcourt, M. A. B. (1993). Creative productivity among secondary school students: Combining energy, interest, and imagination. *Gifted Child Quarterly, 37,* 23–31.

Elliott, E. S., & Dweck, C. S. (1988). Goals: An approach to motivation and achievement. *Journal of Personality and Social Psychology, 54*(1), 5–12.

Gubbins, E. J. (1982). *Revolving door identification model: Characteristics of talent pool students.* Unpublished doctoral dissertation in educational psychology, The University of Connecticut, Storrs.

Haensly, P. A., & Roberts, N. M. (1983). The professional productive process and its implications for gifted studies. *Gifted Child Quarterly, 27,* 9–12.

Iritz, M. H. (1987). *Science fair: developing a successful and fun project.* Blue Ridge Summit, PA: Tab Books.

Miles, M. B., & Huberman, A. M. (1984). *Qualitative data analysis: A sourcebook of new methods.* Beverly Hills, CA: Sage.

Pajares, M. F. (1996). Self-efficacy beliefs in academic settings. *Review of Educational Research, 66,* 543–578.

Patton, M. Q. (1980). *Qualitative evaluation methods.* Beverly Hills, CA: Sage.

Reis, S. M. (1981). *An analysis of the productivity of gifted students participating in programs using the Revolving Door Identification Model.* Unpublished doctoral dissertation in educational psychology, The University of Connecticut, Storrs.

Renzulli, J. S. (1977). *The enrichment triad model: A guide for developing defensible programs for the gifted and talented.* Wethersfield, CT: Creative Learning Press.

Renzulli, J. S. (1986). The three-ring conception of giftedness: A developmental model for creative productivity. In R. J. Sternberg & J. E. Davidson (Eds.), *Conceptions of giftedness* (pp. 53–92). New York: Cambridge University Press.

Renzulli, J. S., & Reis, S. M. (1985). *The schoolwide enrichment model: A comprehensive plan for educational excellence.* Mansfield Center, CT: Creative Learning Press.

Renzulli, J. S., & Reis, S. M. (1986). The enrichment triad/revolving door model: A schoolwide plan for the development of creative productivity. In J. S. Renzulli (Ed.), *Systems and models for developing programs for the gifted and talented* (pp. 216–266). Mansfield Center, CT: Creative Learning Press.

Schunk, D. H. (1982). Effects of effort attributional feedback on children's perceived self-efficacy and achievement. *Journal of Educational Psychology, 74,* 548–556.

Schunk, D. H. (1998, November). *Motivation and self-regulation among gifted learners.* Paper presented at the annual meeting of the National Association for Gifted Children, Louisville, KY.

Schunk, D. H., & Zimmerman, B. J. (1998). *Self-regulated learning: From teaching to self-reflective practice.* New York: Guilford.

Simonton, D. K. (1984). Creative productivity and age: A mathematical model based on a two-step cognitive process. *Developmental Review, 4,* 77–111.

Smith, H. W. (1975). Triangulation: The necessity for multimethod approaches. In H. W. Smith (Ed.), *Strategies of social research: The methodological imagination* (pp. 271–292). Englewood Cliffs, NJ: Prentice Hall.

Spradley, J. P. (1979). *The ethnographic interview.* New York: Holt, Rinehart, & Winston.

Starko, A. J. (1988). Effects of the revolving door identification model on creative productivity and self-efficacy. *Gifted Child Quarterly, 32,* 291–297.

Tannenbaum, A. J. (1986). Giftedness: A psychosocial approach. In R. J. Sternberg & J. E. Davidson (Eds.), *Conceptions of giftedness* (pp. 21–52). New York: Cambridge University Press.

Tocci, S. (1997). *How to do a science fair project* (rev. ed.). New York: Franklin Watts.

Weiner, B. (1979). A theory of motivation for some classroom experiences. *Journal of Educational Psychology, 71,* 3–25.

Weiner, B. (1985). An attributional theory of achievement motivation and emotion. *Psychological Review, 92,* 548–573.

Zimmerman, B. J. (1989). A social cognitive view of self-regulated academic learning. *Journal of Educational Psychology, 81,* 329–339.

Zimmerman, B. J. (1998a). Academic studying and the development of personal skill: A self-regulatory perspective. *Educational Psychologist, 33,* 73–86.

Zimmerman, B. J. (1998b). Developing self-fulfilling cycles of academic regulation: An analysis of exemplary instructional models. In D. H. Schunk & B. J. Zimmerman (Eds.), *Self-regulated learning: From teaching to self-reflective practice* (pp. 1–19). New York: Guilford Press.

Zimmerman, B. J., & Martinez-Pons, M. (1990). Student differences in self-regulated learning: Relating grade, sex, and giftedness to self-efficacy and strategy use. *Journal of Educational Psychology, 82,* 51–59.

4

The Phantom of the Science Fair

BRUCE M. SHORE, MARCIA A. B. DELCOURT,
CASSIDY A. SYER, AND MICHELLE SCHAPIRO
McGill University

One of the most common ways that inquiry is introduced to the general school curriculum is through the involvement of students in science fairs, and there are hundreds, even thousands of these from the classroom level to international. A science fair is an exhibition of students' scientific experiments or investigations that they have completed over the course of the school year. Science fairs are the most widespread type of knowledge fair; however, social science fairs, such as history fairs, are becoming increasingly popular. There are many handbooks that are available to teachers about how to conduct science fairs and science projects (e.g., Cothron, Giese, & Rezba, 2000; Finkelstein, 2002; National Science Teachers Association, 2003), but the literature does not provide any warnings about some of the pitfalls that lie in the way.

The purpose of a science fair is to permit students to learn by doing and to understand science by actually being a scientist. It is an opportunity for students to do an in-depth investigation of a topic of their own interest and to play the role of knowledge producer (Renzulli, 1986). When students complete a science-fair project, they are participating in a research process that involves problem finding, asking questions without known answers, and discovering new knowledge. This process is essential to inquiry-based learning (Starko & Schack, 1998). In this way, science fairs facilitate curriculum reform objectives, namely to help students have authentic learning experiences and to become life-long learners.

The way science fairs are currently conducted, however, is sometimes antithetical to the nature of science and to good pedagogy. By emphasizing prizes and competition, for example, rather than intrinsically motivated learning and cooperation, science fairs do not accurately reflect the meaning of science. Students may actually know very little about their projects when they are forced to prove their competency to an audience, as perhaps their parents completed most of the project to help their child win. This is inconsistent with the goal of science fairs, namely to gain an in-depth understanding of a topic of interest to the student. Given their ancillary place in instruction, the current role of science fairs inadequately reflects curriculum-reform objectives. Students may receive little guidance through the research process because teachers are expected to teach content that students will be tested on at the end of the year, which, in turn, gives little class time for students to work on their science projects.

Potential pitfalls of engaging in inquiry-driven activities, such as science fairs, that our research has uncovered are cheating on science-fair projects and a lack of support for students involved in this process. The present chapter addresses the problem of cheating in science fairs, places this problem in context, provides empirical evidence for the existence of the problem, and discusses some of the steps that can be taken to mitigate the potential ill effects.

The General Problem of Academic Cheating

Adolescent Cheating

Although the problem of scientific misconduct arises in the popular press, the link to cheating by young scientists at science fairs has been given no attention in the literature, and the amount of research on adolescent cheating, in general, is scarce. We found one study, however, that illustrates the increasing prevalence of cheating among high-school students. Schab (1991) examined adolescents' cheating behaviors across the span of 30 years. He administered questionnaires to 1,629 students in 1969, 1,100 students in 1979, and 1,291 students in 1989. The number of students admitting to cheating increased over the years. Students reported using a cheat sheet on an exam, letting others copy their work, and plagiarizing material for their papers. Fear of failure was the most commonly reported reason for cheating. Other reasons included laziness to study, parental demands for good grades, desire to keep up with others, ease of cheating, and pressure for time. Cheating occurred most frequently in mathematics and science courses.

Oftentimes students may act so as to avoid meeting parental expectations or their own feelings of frustration. The alternatives may be contradictory to societal or school rules or generally avowed standards, and may include cheating in one form or another (Calabrese & Cochran, 1990). Some adolescents might eschew school values or policies and undertake unethical paths to reach their goals. Pressures to succeed encountered by teenagers in school, and in what they may perceive as their financial futures, may regard school, both as an organization and as a home base for rules of behavior, as an impediment to their own successes, especially if they measure their success by external criteria (Calabrese & Cochran, 1990). As a result, they may be drawn toward giving greater weight to their personal priorities. High levels of competition for entry to prestigious universities or selective programs can thereby place extra pressures to cheat on matriculating students.

Before the Internet, school cheating was accomplished most readily by mail order or otherwise purchasing or selling papers and examinations. Ready access to the World Wide Web now presents opportunities, largely in private, to down-loading assignments from Web sites with such irreverent names as Schoolsucks. com. These sites offer students complete essays and projects, enabling students to (a) submit ready-made assignments when insufficient time is allowed for their honest completion; (b) tender products that are better quality than what they could create on their own; or (c) impress schoolmates who are generally more success-ful and gain social acceptance.

Schools may unknowingly condone or promote this kind of unethical behav-ior, and may create situations that leave students with little or no option but to cheat (Shore & Delcourt, 1995). For instance, teenagers might react to societal or parental pressure with a degree of cynicism because the pressure to complete a project may reflect an environment in which cheating and other unethical behav-ior appears in practice to be condoned and perceived to be a condition associ-ated with survival in the face of tough competition. Be they subtle or explicit, such pressures are substantial in the lives of adolescents. Such pressures are evident in rising standards for college admission, more public external testing, tightening graduation criteria, and a curriculum that adds new courses and mate-rial, but sheds very little (Calabrese & Cochran, 1990). Pressures on teenagers to compete for educational, social, or financial advantage may exaggerate the importance of personal gain over community well-being. There also might be socioeconomically variable pressures on students to cheat. For example, stu-dents from wealthy circumstances may not be motivated initially to cheat for fiscal reasons, but they may encounter strong family pressures to gain entry to prestigious colleges and universities where their success may not be guaranteed, standards may require effort they do not want to expend, or they may not feel competent to achieve on their own (Calabrese & Cochran, 1990). Successful cheating may also be rewarded (let us assume unknowingly) by families and by schools, thereby increasing the likelihood of more such behavior. For example, a school may place a student on the honor role for ill-gotten grades. Through such sequences of events, even if not condoned, unethical actions may be accepted de facto. In the absence of less competitive and individualistic means to achieve personal educational objectives, students, from elementary school to graduate school, are hardly likely to forego dishonesty from their repertoires of strategies (Schab, 1991).

Schab (1991) concluded from several years of surveys that home was a far superior venue than school to teach the importance of honesty. Even with this built in handicap, schools cannot shirk their duty to do their part, communicating as best they can with parents and guardians. Responsibility, honesty, and trust are the essential foundations for models of personal action in academic activities. Because successes derived from cheating may reinforce the persistence of subse-quent dishonest actions (McLaughlin & Ross, 1989), a long-term societal dilemma is connected to students' cheating and other unethical behavior in school. School cheaters can eventually find themselves in positions of responsibility in private or public sector enterprises.

In order to illustrate the risks anticipated in this line of reasoning, the following sections review examples of college-level cheating and of prestigious and influential scientists and professionals who behaved unethically by producing fraudulent data and research.

College-Level Cheating

Although most prior publications about cheating are descriptive, the overall literature provides consistent evidence that cheating, especially among college and university students, is a widespread phenomenon (Syer & Shore, 2001). D. L. McCabe and Trevino (1996) surveyed 1,800 students at 31 campuses across the United States in the 1990 to 1991 academic year. Students were asked about their own academic integrity on tests and examinations, and on major written assignments while in college. McCabe and Trevino compared the students' replies to those of students who completed similar questionnaires at the same universities by a fellow researcher, Bowers, in 1963 (Bowers, 1964, as cited by D. L. McCabe & Trevino, 1996). Approximately two-thirds of the students admitted to having engaged in at least one of 14 questionable academic behaviors in 1963, and males more frequently reported cheating than females. The number of students who admitted cheating increased modestly between 1963 and 1990. However, the authors reported that students were engaged in a much larger variety of test-cheating behaviors and other types of academic cheating more often over the years. For example, between 1963 and 1990 the number of students who admitted to copying the work of another on a test increased from 26% to 52%. Students who confessed to using crib sheets on a test increased from 23% in 1963 to 37% in 1990. Cheating on written work increased as well. For instance, 49% of students admitted to copying material without footnoting it in 1963 compared to 54% in 1993. The proportion of students who admitted to collaborating on assignments requiring individual work jumped from 11% in 1963 to 49% in 1990.

Not surprisingly, the problem of cheating does not seem to be limited to North American students. Poltorak (1995) surveyed 248 college students at four Moscow universities. The majority of participants were Russian, and all students were in their second year of study or higher. The questionnaire attempted to elicit respondents' definition of cheating and to assess its frequency. Approximately 84% of the 248 Moscow college students admitted to cheating at least once on items including exams, homework, or term papers. Specifically, 70% admitted to cheating on exams, 84% admitted to cheating on homework, and 62% of students admitted to cheating on term papers. Students were most accepting of using crib sheets for tests, copying another person's work, peeking at someone else's exam, using their own notes on an exam, and using someone else's homework or laboratory report. Although this study described students' various cheating behaviors, it failed to explore reasons why students cheated.

A study conducted in the United Kingdom probed the possibility of cheating among college students and searched for an explanation of why cheating occurred. Newstead, Franklyn-Stokes, and Armstead (1996) developed a questionnaire that asked students about their cheating behaviors and potential causes for cheating. Participants were 943 2nd-year students from 19 disciplines at a British university. Students were asked to indicate whether they had engaged in any of the 21 cheating behaviors listed on the questionnaire by answering either "yes" or "no." They were then required to select a reason for cheating from another list if they answered "yes" or a reason for not cheating if their answer was "no." Students most often reported paraphrasing material from another source without citing the author, making up data, allowing another student to copy their work, fabricating references or a bibliography, and copying material without acknowledging the source. Cheating was more common among men than women, more common among lower performing students than higher performing students, more common among younger students than older students, and most common in science and technology. The most frequently reported reasons for cheating by students were pressure for time and to increase a grade. In order to examine the generalizability of these findings, Newstead et al. gave the same questionnaires to 180 psychology students from another university. Students at both universities responded similarly, however there was a higher incidence of reported cheating at one of the universities. Therefore, one can have some confidence in the generality of these results.

Most college-level students appear to have cheated at least once in their student career. Students engage in a variety of cheating behaviors related to examinations, written work, and homework, usually in response to pressure for time and pressure to get good grades. Is cheating by high school and college students a unique phenomenon? Perhaps not; consider the case of cheating in academic and professional settings.

Cheating Among Professionals and Scientists

Because we are talking about cheating at science fairs, we shall now look more closely at scientific and related misconduct later in life. Cheating by career scientists is frequently reported in both the academic and popular press; *The Chronicle of Higher Education* uncovered "a political scientist who swiped five pages of his book from a journal article, a historian who cribbed from an unpublished dissertation, and a geographer whose verbatim copying appears to span his lengthy career. . . . While this article delves into a few cases we uncovered, our reporting suggests that what we found is not exceptional" (Bartlett & Smallwood, 2004, p. A8). The scientific profession and research establishment seem to be under increased scrutiny. According to the National Science Foundation, fraud and plagiarism are the most common grounds for allegations of scientific misbehavior (Glick, 1992).

A 1993 report from the U.S. Office for Research Integrity concluded that Dr. Roger Poisson falsified data on some of the 1,511 women he had recruited to clinical trials at the Hôpital Saint-Luc in Montreal as part of the National Surgical Adjuvant Breast and Bowel project (Weijer, 1995). He provided the experimental treatment to 99 women who were in the control group of the study and reported them as having not experienced the treatment. Poisson provided about 18% or 19% of the cases in that larger study. The credibility of the entire study and the conclusions that had been reached were brought into question; Dr. Poisson argued that he provided the treatment because of his moral commitment to the well-being of these patients. It was not honest science and the clinical benefits of the treatment, tested under controlled conditions, had not been confirmed.

Sir Cyril Burt was a famous and influential British psychologist who died in 1971 at the age of 88. He directed a considerable part of his publishing, including several years as editor of the *British Journal of Educational Psychology,* to demonstrating the impact of genes on human intelligence. His most famous studies reported very high correlations of IQ between twins, correlations that only slightly changed when the twins had been raised in different environments. In the late 1970s, Burt was judged to have fabricated some of his data, disguised the sources of some information, and invented one and perhaps more of his coresearchers (Science, 1986). Davison (1992) wrote, "When I first read Burt's research papers in 1972, it was at once obvious that I was reading the words of a liar and a fraud. . . . The data invented by Burt were simply a conscious (and successful) effort to influence social and educational policy" (Section 5, p. 1). Burt's influence on British educational and social policy from the 1920s to the 1940s was exemplified by the Eleven Plus selection procedure that redefined secondary schooling in England and Wales throughout most of the last century. The standardized Eleven Plus examinations in Verbal Reasoning, English, and Arithmetic screened the top 20% of students leaving elementary school for admission to grammar schools; the remaining 80% were restricted to state secondary schools that were less well regarded and offered many fewer later opportunities to enter university. This system underselected children whose superior ability was not recognized until after the age of 12, and such children came predominantly from working-class families (Vernon, 1979) or the United Kingdom's increasing immigrant population. In 1976, Cyril Burt's research was criticized and the situation labeled "the most sensational charge of scientific fraud in this century" (Davison, 1992, Section 5, p. 1). One of the missing research assistants was apparently found in the 1990s, but the doubts remain.

Henry H. Goddard published *The Kallikak family: A study in the heredity of feeble-mindedness* in 1912. Karagiannis (1999) wrote an extensive review of the major impact of this study on how disabilities were viewed in North America and beyond for the better part of a century: Goddard's was a case study of a family that Goddard asserted comprised two distinct genetic branches. The "Kali" part of the family branch (from pure or good in Greek) were mentally superior, and the "Kaki" were mentally or morally defective. Goddard based his distinctions on facial features from family photographs. Years later, it was alleged that Goddard tampered with the data by penciling in facial modifications on some of the photographs of the purported Kaki branch of the family. In much the same manner as Burt's influence on English education, Goddard's contributions to the eugenics argument had long-lasting impact, even up to the 1970s when sterilization was still advocated and practiced for persons with disabilities or disadvantages in many places in North America.

Late in the 20th century, Interleuken-4A was announced as a potential breakthrough in the treatment of cancer and infectious diseases. However, the event was a hoax and the material did not exist. Postdoctoral researcher Dr. Claudio Milanese, the Dana Farber Cancer Institute in Boston, confessed to having manipulated data to create falsified outcomes. He stated, "There was a lot of pressure in the lab and I didn't have the courage to tell them" (Faked data, 1988, p. F8). This forced researchers to withdraw papers from two prestigious scientific journals, other unpublished materials, and to cancel a patent application (Faked data, 1988).

Cardiovascular researcher John Darsee, of the Harvard Medical School, was the author of a hundred articles and abstracts between 1979 and 1981 during which time he held a National Institutes of Health (NIH) Fellowship. This prodigious output, however, was the outcome of fabricated experiments and data. Emory University, where Darsee had worked five years before going to Harvard, then conducted a further review that uncovered even more fraudulent publications. One of the Emory papers acknowledged the work of two nonexistent physicians (Danforth & Schoenhoff, 1992).

In 1994, two widely reported papers in the *British Journal of Obstetrics and Gynaecology* were declared invalid after the authors were found to have built their cases on fraudulent data. The papers reported a case entitled "Term delivery after intrauterine relocation of an ectopic pregnancy" and in which a 29-year-old woman experienced a third ectopic pregnancy. The fetus was reportedly moved to her uterus, and allegedly remained there until a successful birth with no ill effects. However, there was no evidence that the operation took place or that the patient actually existed (Richmond, 1995).

The head of one of Harvard Medical School's major teaching hospitals, former director of the National Institute of Mental Health, and a past president of the American College of Psychiatrists in the mid-1980s, Dr. Shervert Frazier, resigned after he acknowledged plagiarizing substantial portions of four articles in medical journals and textbooks (Eminent psychiatrist, 1988). A Philosophy graduate student from the University of Rochester initiated the complaint in a letter to Harvard. A university investigative committee concluded that there was evidence of plagiarism in four papers and careless scholarship in three of them. The papers in question were general reviews about pain and did not proffer original data. Dr. Frazier had been respected as a significant policy maker and advocate for high quality research, and rational policies, and excellence for the mental health field.

Unhappy with the advent of managed care, family physician Robert Fiddes left medicine to pursue a law degree and was admitted to the California bar. He then recognized a new business opportunity and created a medical practice around a profitable research-related enterprise, aggressively engaging large numbers of his patients in drug experiments. Dr. Fiddes' success made him extremely attractive to the drug industry that was increasingly in needs of clinical trial patients. Companies paid him millions of dollars to conduct nearly 200 studies. However, his clinical trials turned out to be scams. He "was conducting research fraud of audacious proportions, cutting corners and inventing data to keep the money flowing from the drug industry. Fictitious patients were enrolled in studies. Blood pressure readings were fabricated. Bodily fluids that met certain lab values were kept on hand in the office refrigerator, ready to be substituted for the urine or blood of patients who did not qualify for studies" (Eichenwald & Kolata, 1999, p. 1). Government and industry monitors were not alerted by the apparently accurate paperwork. A government auditor got hints of problems from the manager at a colleague's office who, in turn, was alerted by a disquieted former employee. After many years investigating Fiddes's Southern California Research Institute, he and three collaborators admitted to the fraud. The conspiracy compromised drug studies for almost every pharmaceutical company, and raised public suspicions of the private system for clinical trials of new medicines. The *New York Times* quoted the former chief financial officer of Fiddes's company, Alan Knox, who was not involved in the conspiracy, as stating that Fiddes "was putting the health of all these patients at risk, but he was also skewing samples that could affect the whole American public" (p. 2). Reports of plagiarism and fabricated or falsified data continue to appear in print and electronic media, on topics as diverse as stem-cell research ("Korean scientist resigns," 2005), women's health, aging, lupus, and malaria (Mendoza, 2005).

Finally, teachers cheat, too. Jacob and Levitt (2002) showed how many Chicago schoolteachers, and sometimes school administrators, were falsely reporting inflated English test scores for students, following the introduction of U.S. federal legislation that tied school funding to test results. Large increases in the years in which testing was done, followed by flatter gains in other years, combinations of many correct replies to hard questions and wrong answers to easy questions, and high correlations among the scores within classrooms were the best predictors. The actions were a good fit to an economics model perspective, one that highlighted the incentives and the blocks, both occurring in three categories—moral, social, and economic—and the impact of high-stakes testing (Levitt & Dubner, 2005).

The preceding examples of fraudulent scientific research suggest that perhaps the "scientific society" or the "working environment" itself must be carefully evaluated. Unintentionally, the very context that outwardly advocates honesty and integrity may actually be creating a forum that is covertly encouraging dishonest acts by the high-stakes nature of the system's operation. For example, the fact that the scientific researchers have to apply repeatedly for grants to fund their projects, and also face competition for academic posts, may push some researchers over the edge and lead them to engage in fraudulent or other unethical behavior (Lowry, 1995). The grants councils themselves have had to deal with declining or frozen budgets at a time when competition among researchers for grants has increased (D. McCabe, 1995). When an academic career hinges on doing work that is deemed good enough to merit research grants and publications, the temptation to fake results or make other false claims may be too great for some people to resist (Lowry, 1995). Perhaps the "working environment" itself has to change. For example, in order to take unreasonable pressure off researchers, the universities and granting councils should focus more on quality rather than on quantity. Although there is some movement in that direction, there is still a tendency to be overly impressed by the number of publications or by the amount of grant money professors and researchers receive. Integrity is not easily factored into these considerations; it is probably reasonably assumed in most cases. It remains, however, much more difficult to qualitatively assess the impact than the inputs of someone's contribution (D. McCabe, 1995).

The literature on academic cheating shows that students are most often dishonest when faced with pressure to perform, namely, to get good grades and to finish projects on time. Career scientists sometimes cheat, too, as they are under tremendous pressure to publish their research and to earn recognition and awards. The life of a professional scientist appears to involve living up to high performance expectations while working in an area of relative resource scarcity. Does the experience of a science-fair participant resemble this reality of career scientists? Research looking at many capable young people indicates that they show positive characteristics of adult experts. So a perfectly natural question is, of course, do they also show the negative characteristics?

Empirical Support for Cheating in Science Fairs

In an attempt to explore the circumstances surrounding science-fair participation, and how the experience is similar to the reality of career scientists, we conducted three studies. We shall describe the three studies and then discuss the findings of each in terms of evidence for our suspicion that cheating occurs at science fairs, and data related to potential causes of cheating.

We Didn't Know the House Was Haunted

Our suspicion that cheating occurs at science fairs arose from a study conducted by Shore and Delcourt (1995). Shore and Delcourt replicated and extended the paradigm of previous comparisons of the development of high ability and performance in children with adult expertise on a creative-productive task. They were working within a theoretical framework that proposed that giftedness is a step in the developmental process toward adult expertise (see Pelletier & Shore, 2003). This process includes having experience with and creating open-ended or problem-finding tasks as well as convergent or problem-solving tasks.

Haensly and Roberts (1983) provided an important impetus for raising this question. They interviewed six prominent professionals, one each in communications, liberal arts, fine arts, science, education, and business administration. They asked the experts about different elements of the creative process and remarked that these processes seemed similar to the needs and experiences of gifted children. Shore and Delcourt thus set out to empirically explore the question of whether the learning and thinking processes of high performing school-age children resembled those observed in adult experts.

With the help of Patricia Haensly, who kindly supplied copies of their interview schedule and other materials and data, Shore and Delcourt were able to replicate and extend their study to two groups of experts, academic scientists and graduate students, and three groups of school children, voluntary (invited and self-initiated), and required participants in science fairs. Participants included (a) 18 science faculty members from two universities, (b) 19 science graduate students from the same universities, (c) 67 Grades 5 to 10 public school students who voluntarily presented projects at a district science fair, (d) 33 Grade 11 students from a trilingual parochial school who were required to take part in a science fair as part of their course, and (e) 26 Grade 7 children from public and private schools who were invited to exhibit their projects at a science fair sponsored by a community college. All students finished and actually entered their projects.

The questionnaire was slightly adapted from Haensly and Roberts (1983), principally in providing multiple choices based on the most frequent categories of replies obtained by the original authors. Questions tapped into (a) the sources of inspiration for their ideas; (b) new skills and preparation needed in order to follow up their inspirations; (c) how they progressed toward the completion of "products" they sought to develop; (d) how they maintained task commitment; (e) the obstacles to completion and how they overcame them; (f) and the role of the potential audience in the conceptualization and development of their projects. Experts, responding to the survey, were asked to base their replies on one specific product or service that had given them the most personal satisfaction, and pupils were asked to reply based on their science-fair project.

Shore and Delcourt's (1995) data were a combination of multiple-choice selections and summaries of narrative replies. The results for both groups of student volunteers were very similar and were collapsed into a single category. The results are best observed in summary, as presented in Table 4.1. Cells in which the information is presented in italics are especially to be noted and are discussed in detail later.

Table 4.1 indicates that most of the scientists and graduate students were highly self-motivated to pursue their ideas. For example, their inspiration either came from personal interest, to clarify their own thinking, or to expand their horizons. Volunteer science-fair participants' ideas were also mostly self-motivated; however, children who were required to participate in a science fair were assigned topics for the most part. When asked about preparation for the product, experts and students required to participate in a science fair most often indicated needing additional skills to carry out their ideas, including character improvement, management skills, general skills, and specific skills. Half of the students who volunteered to participate in a science fair claimed that they did not need new skills to complete their project. Scientists and both groups of children reported that while some projects proceeded as originally planned, the majority evolved

Table 4.1 Summary and Comparison of Replies

Question	Scientists n = 18	Graduates n = 19	Volunteers n = 93	Required n = 33
Inspiration	13 self-motivated and personal interest	12 self-motivated	74 self-motivated	*22 were assigned their topics*
Preparation	12 needed new skills	13 needed new skills	*47 said new skills not needed*	22 needed new skills
Products	6 remained as conceived; others evolved	*1 remained as conceived*	22 remained as conceived	4 remained as conceived
Commitment	5 worked up to 10 years, 6 more than 5 years	7 worked for 2 to 7 years, rest were less than 2 years	*46 took an average of 1.5 months*	*25 took under 6 months*
Obstacles	11 said time and 5 said money	*8 said time and 8 said money*	67 said time and 19 said money	20 said time and 14 said money
Audience	0 said none; 13 scientific community	0 said none; 15 scientific community	Younger pupils (gr. 5 and 6): "Fair Visitors" 3 said none; 11 older students said scientific community	8 admitted making up their data so as to finish! 9 said none; 12 scientific community
Note	Very similar to the experts in Haensly and Roberts (1983) data	Very similar to experts except for Commitment	Similar to experts except for new skills (see Preparation) and Commitment	Assigned topics and admitted to making up data

over time. Very few of the graduate student's projects remained as conceived. Products usually became larger, more concrete, and more complex, or the product took on a different dimension or implication. Only a couple of the students' projects became smaller, which is reasonable, but perhaps should have occurred more often because students frequently need to narrow their focus when completing independent research projects; this narrowing might, however, be more likely to occur when students receive supervisory input at many stages of their work. When groups were asked about their task commitment, experts reported spending up to 10 years in some cases developing the same product. More than half of the volunteer science-fair participants took an average of six weeks to complete their project and the majority of required science-fair participants took under six months. The most frequently faced obstacle by all groups of participants (except for graduate students) was pressure for time, which was closely followed by lack of money and lack of necessary knowledge. When asked about the role of the audience in the completion of the product, scientists and graduate students recognized the scientific community as a general audience, as did some of the older science-fair participants. The only ones who did not produce their product for an intended (and external) audience were science-fair participants who had been required to exhibit a project.

The academic scientists in this sample and the professionals in the Haensly and Roberts (1983) study responded alike. Graduate students engaged in a similar process to academic scientists except that their projects were more likely to change with time, primarily to grow in size and complexity. In addition, money, rather than time was a slightly greater constraint. Both of these diversions from the pattern of experts' replies were minor and reasonably reflected the context of graduate students, namely, being answerable to their supervisors regarding their research and constantly reading and updating, and having long hours and limited funds devoted to their own research.

The pupils who voluntarily took part in science fairs took the main initiative for their topics and were driven by interest. These students were mostly in Grades 5 to 7. Additionally, there were community college students exhibiting at the invitational science fair. These participants recognized a legitimate external audience in the people who would come to visit the science fair. The unexpected result was the small majority who felt they did not require new skills to pursue their projects and the great speed with which they completed their exhibits. This last combination raises the issue of whether or not they were sufficiently challenged by the assignments they chose, largely on their own, as many students selected projects that could easily be accomplished using the skills they already possessed.

The pupils who were required to enter an exhibit in a science fair took or were given far less independence in selecting their topics. However, they more resembled the experts in acknowledging the need for help with new skills required to accomplish the projects. The greatest surprise was the open admission, by a quarter of this group of graduating high school students, that they had made up data in order to expedite the completion of their projects! Half of the eight participants who reported making up their data also indicated that the project was intended for no particular audience. Shore and Delcourt did not ask students if they completed the project for a grade.

The Shore and Delcourt (1995) study illustrates that many young capable children perform similarly to adult experts when engaging in a creative-productive task as offered by participation in a science fair. The main differences between volunteer science-fair participants and experts, namely, fewer reports of the need for new skills and spending less time on the project, suggest that a relatively high level of teacher guidance may be desirable in order to ensure that sufficiently challenging projects are chosen and that students acquire the knowledge and skills to identify the additional learning they need in order to conduct an independent science project.

Students whose participation was required by the school were more like the experts in their recognition of the need for additional skills. Their having been assigned the majority of their project topics may not have been as inappropriate as first thought upon encountering these data, because many students did not have the guidance to select topics on their own. Note that even the graduate students changed their initial projects in great proportion. Data most challenging to interpretation were the open confessions by students who were required to participate in a science fair to fabricating data in order to bring the projects to conclusion. Perhaps cheating may have been a result of the compulsory nature of the participation and the pressure to complete the project within the semester, despite a likely absence of personal interest. These factors may have made the experience a less genuine one for the learners, reducing their commitment and the veracity of their data. Is this a risk when the reward system for scientific activity is extrinsic rather than intrinsic?

In a creative-productive activity such as offered by participation in a science fair, school children perform like professionals in most respects, notably with regard to the production and use of professional end-products, except (a) when participation is voluntary, more students claim not to require additional skills, possibly because they are insufficiently challenged as a result of having the freedom to choose their topics they had previously mastered; perhaps such assignments should emphasize the exploration of new topics; (b) when participation is compulsory, ideas are generally not self-initiated (this could be the result of lower motivation or the inclusion of students with less relevant prior knowledge, ability, or skills), the role of the audience becomes greater, knowledge perhaps being pursued because it is expected by others, and there can be some cheating to meet these expectations.

This study set out to ask a fairly innocent question, namely, do children participating in a science fair get inspiration for ideas in the same way as adults deemed as experts? We answered the question, but we got more than we bargained for. Science-fair participants seem to go through a similar creative process as experts, however, to our surprise, some of them admitted to cheating in order to complete their projects!

The Phantom Has Been Sighted Before
From our first study, we know that the terms of engagement by students in a science fair are similar to those of experts. In our second study, we set out to investigate whether the facilitators and inhibitors for students in science fairs are parallel to those encountered by professional scientists. Schapiro (1997) examined the types and sources of help that students considered fair and reasonable and those they actually received for their science-fair project. She recruited participants from four school-level science fairs in the greater Montreal area. In total, 41 Grade 10 and 11 students participated in this study. Only six of the 41 participants volunteered to participate in their school science fair, so the replies of students who volunteered and who were required to participate in the science fair were combined.

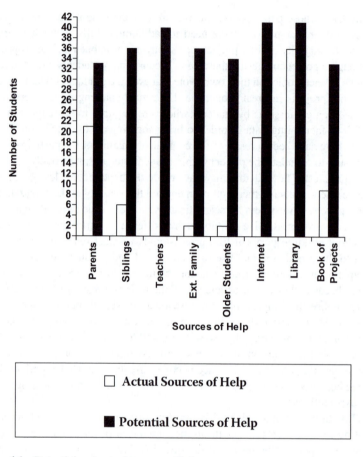

Figure 4.1   Potential and actual sources of help

In a structured interview, Schapiro (1997) asked participants, in general, from whom they considered it acceptable to get help, and about the kinds of help they deemed reasonable. With regard to their science-fair project, in particular, she asked from whom they received help, and about the types of help they actually received. Students were given the choice of eight sources and eight types of help from which they could indicate the ones they considered appropriate and the ones they actually received. The interview data are best observed in two frequency distributions. The first distribution permits the comparison of sources of help deemed fair and reasonable in contrast to the sources of help actually used, and the second distribution represents the eight types of help deemed fair and reasonable compared to those received (refer to Figures 4.1 and 4.2). The Wilcoxen sign test for differences between related samples was carried out for each of these two comparisons.

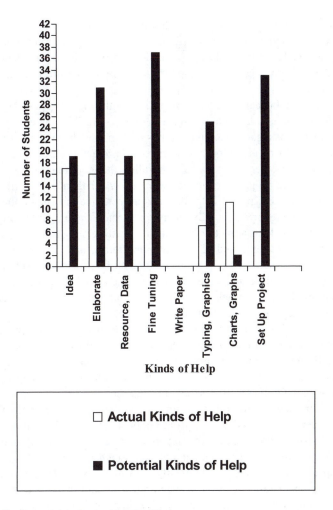

Figure 4.2 Potential and actual kinds of help

Students replied that, in general, it was fair and reasonable to receive help from all of the eight sources of help; however, students did not receive the help they deemed appropriate. Figure 4.1 illustrates the discrepancy between the potential and actual sources of help for students in science fairs. All 41 participants unanimously agreed that the Internet and the library were acceptable sources of help for students in science fairs. However, when students actually had to complete their own projects, only 19 students reported actually using the Internet, and only 36 students reported using the library as a resource when completing their science projects. The majority of students also considered parents and teachers acceptable sources of help, but only about half of the students actually received help from these two sources. Siblings, extended family, and older students were the least popular sources of help. Although most students considered help from these groups acceptable, between two and four students actually received help from siblings, extended family, and older students. Therefore, students do not receive all of the help from the sources they deem appropriate for science fairs.

Figure 4.2 indicates that students considered the eight types of help acceptable, with the exception of having someone else write their paper. Once again, however, there was a gap between the types of help they deemed appropriate and those they actually received for their science-fair project. For example, the majority of students considered help with elaborating the idea, fine-tuning the paper, and setting up the project acceptable; however, fewer than half of the students received these three types of help for their project. The most common types of help that students reported actually receiving, included help with coming up with an idea, help with elaborating the idea, and help with getting resources or collecting data. Only between 6 and 11 students reported actually receiving help with typing, charts, and setting up the project. None of the students considered having someone else write the paper to be appropriate, and not one student reported actually receiving this type of help. In summary, students are also not receiving the kinds of help they consider acceptable.

The most striking result is the extent to which the science-fair projects were independent in the sense of being private or individual work. This is echoed by the virtually nonexistent help provided from other students, which suggests an absence of peer collaboration. The two students who received help from older students were in Grade 11, the last year of high school. These students must have been receiving help from college or university students. None of the Grade 10 students received this kind of help from Grade 11 students. This finding is particularly disconcerting given the official cooperative learning policy of one of the schools from which participants entered their science projects. Adolescents in this sample did not interact academically with more experienced students, thus missing the opportunity to be in a mentored role, and to engage in curiosity-driven learning with other adolescents who share their interests. Perhaps peer collaboration should not have been operationalized in terms of receiving help from older students; rather, the question could be broadened to include all other classmates regardless of age or grade level.

An interesting and unanticipated outcome was that the most commonly provided sources of assistance were individual rather than collaborative. The world of student-scientist may be rather similar to that of the professional scientist in this regard, but in both cases, the pressure is toward increased collaboration. Unfortunately, even after many years of advocating inquiry-driven, discovery, and collaborative learning models, this study depicted a considerable gap between ideals and practice. In addition, the students' general experience of participation in science fairs did not emulate a community of learning. These results suggest that the learning environment surrounding science-fair participation may be far from optimal, and it may have parallels in the real world of science.

In this study, we also gained more insight than we expected. Children appeared to feel pressure to perform; however, they are also undersupported. The entire literature on adult cheating shows us that professional scientists can be dishonest, and perhaps cheating is a consequence of a lack of support. Children in science fairs look like real scientists in terms of support. We know that some researchers cheat, so a natural question to ask is whether a directly posed question (in contrast to the unexpected outcome of the Shore and Delcourt [1995] study) would reveal that students do, too.

The Phantom Is Real

We conducted a third study to see if the students in a science fair who felt unsupported would admit to cheating when explicitly asked, compared to children who felt they received the help they considered appropriate. Syer and Shore (2001) surveyed 27 students between the 7th and 11th grades from six high schools in the Montreal area. Twenty-four of the participants in the study had been required to participate in a science fair and three had volunteered. Because only a few students volunteered to participate, data discussed here are based on the 24 students whose participation was compulsory.

Participants anonymously completed a questionnaire asking them about the obstacles they faced and the ways they dealt with those obstacles when completing their science-fair projects. Students checked off as many of the 10 obstacles listed as applied to their science-fair experience. For example, they would answer "yes" or "no" to the question, "Did you have trouble coming up with an idea for your project?" In addition, students checked off as many of the 15 means of coping as applied to their project. Some of these choices were positive and adaptive ways of dealing with difficulties, for example, implementing their parents' and teachers' feedback as well as relying on self-perseverance, whereas others were maladaptive means of coping, including cheating. We defined cheating as making up data or results, copying the work of someone else, or having someone else write the paper. Students also completed a second questionnaire, based for the most part on Schapiro's instrument.

Syer and Shore (2001) confirmed that between 20 and 25% of students required to participate in a science fair admit to cheating. Five of the 24 students reported having cheated in the form of making up their data or results. None of the participants indicated having someone else write their paper. However, two of the students who reported making up their data, and none of the other students reported copying the work of someone else.

Only two students who admitted to cheating, neither of whom made up their data, chose topics about which they were already expert. Syer and Shore (2001) speculated that perhaps the risk of working on something new and unfamiliar was too big of a leap into the unknown and that is why some students felt sufficient pressure to cheat. Indeed, three of the students who reported having cheated expressed difficulties with coming up with an idea and experiencing disappointment or disillusion, which may be explained by their working in an area of ignorance and not capitalizing on their strengths. In addition, a greater proportion of students who made up their data indicated they lacked the necessary knowledge to complete their projects, compared to the proportion of students who did not make up their data.

Although the students in the Syer and Shore (2001) study who reported cheating lacked appropriate strategies for dealing with obstacles, they may not have necessarily lacked moral values. Syer and Shore reported that one student objected to all forms of help, was very adamant that participation in science fairs be compulsory, that one not do a topic on which one is already expert, and that the idea for the project be entirely the student's idea. Furthermore, a few students reported not wanting much help from teachers and preferring to do the project on their own. Syer and Shore thus surmised that perhaps students were cheating not because they were deceitful, rather because they lacked or did not make use of adaptive mechanisms or resources.

Syer and Shore (2001) also confirmed the discrepancy between the sources and types of help students consider fair and reasonable, and the actual help they receive for their projects (Schapiro, 1997). Most students in both the Schapiro and Syer and Shore studies considered parents an acceptable source of help; however, a greater proportion of students in the Syer and Shore study actually received a parent's help. In addition, most students in both studies indicated that the Internet was an appropriate source of help; however, only about half of the students in the Schapiro study made use of this resource, compared to 23 of the 24 students in the Syer and Shore study. This difference may merely reflect greater access to the World Wide Web a few years later. Consistent with the Schapiro study, some participants rated the eight kinds of help as fair and reasonable, with the exception of having someone else write the paper.

Syer and Shore (2001) failed to find differences between students who reported having had cheated and those who did not when they traced the replies of students. Students who reported making up their data did not face more obstacles, nor did they receive less support for their project than students who did not report cheating. The science-fair experience of students who admitted to cheating did not differ from the experience of those who did not cheat.

There is certainly a phantom of the science fair! Some students cheat. Intriguing is the semblance between the reports of science-fair participants and career scientists regarding obstacles encountered and support available. Is the experience of a professional scientist the reality against which the experience of science-fair students should be gauged?

Suspicion of Cheating Confirmed

We know that one of the subject areas in which cheating is most common is science (Newstead, Franklyn-Stokes, & Aarmstead, 1996; Schab, 1991) and that professionals sometimes cheat in order to meet high performance expectations. In the process of examining the inspiration of students' ideas, some of the science-fair participants in the Shore and Delcourt study spontaneously admitted to cheating. When Syer and Shore (2001) asked students explicitly if they cheated in a science fair, some students admitted to making up their data or results. It appears as though children in science fairs not only show the adaptive traits of adult scientists, but they also show the maladaptive ones, namely, cheating. The literature points out some of the reasons for cheating by professional scientists, namely pressure to perform, and pressure for time. In the world of researchers, this combination of pressure is known as publish or perish. Do students in science fairs also cheat because of the pressure for time and to perform, in this case to get good grades?

Potential Causes of Cheating
Why is there a phantom haunting science fairs? We searched for potential causes of cheating in terms of compulsory versus voluntary participation in a science fair, obstacles faced, and in terms of resources available to students. Only the students who were required to participate in a science fair reported having cheated in the Shore and Delcourt (1995) study. None of the students who volunteered to participate in a science fair reported having engaged in cheating. Syer and Shore (2001) had difficulty confirming or refuting the possible relation between compulsory participation in a science fair and cheating given the small number of respondents who had volunteered in a science fair. In an attempt to further explore this relation the 27 participants in the Syer and Shore study were mailed the questionnaire a second time, and were asked to complete them based on a science-fair experience for which they had volunteered. Thirteen students returned questionnaires stating that they had never volunteered for a science fair and six students replied about a science-fair experience in which they volunteered to participate. One student indicated that someone else wrote the paper. Although questionnaires were anonymous, the participant wrote identifying markers on the questionnaire; thus, we were able to connect this particular participant's questionnaire based on a volunteer experience to the corresponding questionnaire based on a compulsory experience. Replies on both questionnaires were very similar, as were the comments added in the margins, and it was apparent that the student was reporting on the same science-fair project. This participant indicated having made up data on the first questionnaire; however, on the second questionnaire the participant reported having had someone else write the paper. Furthermore, the student reported that the partner's parents did the entire project. The student appeared not to have welcomed the partner's parent's help as exemplified by replies that the amount of help received was not fair and reasonable and that only a minimal amount of help was wanted. Therefore, only students required to participate in a science fair reported having cheated, with the exception of one volunteer who indicated having cheated on two questionnaires based on the same project. These findings suggest that another potential cause of cheating may be compulsory participation in a science fair.

We also looked at potential causes of cheating in terms of obstacles faced. Expert participants in the Shore and Delcourt study indicated that pressure for time was the most frequently faced obstacle in the creative process, closely followed by lack of money and knowledge. Syer and Shore confirmed that pressure for time was also the most common obstacle faced by students required to participate in a science fair. This was the only obstacle faced by all students who reported having cheated. College-level students in the Newstead et al. (1996) study and adolescents in the Schab (1991) study also indicated that lack of time was a common reason for cheating. Therefore, there appears to be a relation between pressure for time and cheating.

A third barrier that may lead to cheating involves difficulty choosing a topic. Many students in the Syer and Shore (2001) study experienced frustration coming up with an idea and only two students, neither of whom made up their data, chose a topic about which they had extensive previous knowledge. Furthermore, more students who admitted to making up their data, compared to those who did not, reported lacking the necessary knowledge to complete their project. Students in the Shore and Delcourt study who were required to participate in a science fair also indicated needing additional skills and knowledge in order to complete their projects. Volunteer participants, on the other hand, said they did not need new skills or knowledge. This suggests that students need guidance when selecting a topic. The emphasis needs to be on choosing a problem for which the student has some prior knowledge but that has not yet been mastered. This way, students are challenged to develop new skills to complete their project, but at the same time, they can work from their strengths.

The last potential cause for cheating that we explored was a lack of support for students. Schapiro (1997) and Syer and Shore (2001) found a gap between potential and actual sources and types of help for students in science fairs. Like professional scientists, children in science fairs are working in an area of resource scarcity, which could lead to cheating as a coping strategy.

Data from our three studies support our suspicion that the circumstances surrounding participation at a science fair closely resembles, both positively and negatively, the world of career scientists. We found a phantom haunting the science fair! Some students admitted to making up their data in order to meet time limitations. This ghost is indeed real; professional scientists cheat sometimes, too. Our data support four potential causes of cheating in science fairs. The first may be the pressure of compulsory participation in a science fair. None of the students who volunteered to participate in a science fair reported having had cheated (Shore & Delcourt, 1995; Syer & Shore, 2001). A second potential cause of cheating involves pressure for time. Pressure for time was the most frequently faced obstacle by professionals engaged in a creative process, by students required to participate in a science fair, and the only obstacle unanimously faced by students who reported having had cheated in a science fair (Shore & Delcourt, 1995; Syer and Shore, 2001). Third, students had difficulty choosing a topic. Perhaps students used cheating as a means of coping for working on a topic about which they did not have a solid knowledge base. A final cause of cheating we explored was resources and adaptive mechanisms used by students.

Students do not make use of or receive the sources or kinds of help they consider fair and reasonable.

We now know that cheating does occur with some regularity at science fairs and we have gained insight into possible reasons for cheating. We found patterns in students' replies that would suggest possible reasons for feeling sufficient pressure to cheat; however, future research would benefit from asking students explicitly about their reasons for cheating. Whether students are cheating because they are deceitful or because they lack or do not make use of adaptive mechanisms also warrants more direct probing. We have a suspicion that the unresolved problem surrounding science fairs involves similar difficulties experienced by career scientists, namely working unsupported in an area with high performance expectations. We have entered the science-fair house and found a ghost; now our task is to exorcise the restless spirit that haunts students' science experiences.

Implications

There appear to be several discernable implications for educators managing science fairs. The first is that students would benefit from guidance with the initial stages of completing an independent research project. Students in the Shore and Delcourt (1995) study were either assigned topics that may not have interested them, or chose their own topics that did not require additional skills. Similarly, students in the Syer and Shore (2001) study reported having difficulties coming up with an idea, experiencing disappointment, and staying motivated. Perhaps teachers need to use language such as "finding a problem" and "formulating a question" to better facilitate the research process (Bishop, 2000). Teachers conducting science fairs may need to take more time in the initial stages helping students to find and explore different problems, and to give students practice asking and refining research questions.

A second implication is that teachers and students need to be aware of the help that librarians can provide. Although librarians were not one of the choices of sources of help offered to students to check off, Schapiro (1997), and Syer and Shore (2001) found that students were not receiving help that librarians are trained to provide. For example, only 16 of the 41 students in the Schapiro study, and 8 of the 24 students in the Syer and Shore study, who were required to participate in a science fair received help gathering the necessary background information, research information, data, or finding the research site or participants. Librarians are "trained in the teaching of the research process and the integration of library skills into the research process" (Bishop, 2000, p. 62). They are skilled at teaching students how to access information resources, for example, finding background information from periodicals or effectively and efficiently searching the World Wide Web (Tabatabai & Shore, 2005). Teachers and students need to be aware that librarians and other technology support staff are excellent resources to be used for science-fair projects.

In addition, deadlines for projects need to be considered with care. The most frequently faced obstacle in the Shore and Delcourt (1995) and the Syer and Shore (2001) studies was pressure for time. An approach that might best suit the need of the teacher to have students complete their projects on time, and to promote a sense of responsibility for the student would be for students to have individual interviews with the teacher where both parties agree upon particular deadlines.

The ways that science fairs are conducted may give students a false impression of what science in the real world is, or, at least what it should be. We are teaching students that science is not cooperative, interactive, or collaborative, and that it is extrinsically motivated by prizes. In reality, science is increasingly a cooperative endeavor in which scientists routinely extend, correct, and adapt the work of their mentors, predecessors, and colleagues to increase our knowledge. Science embraces a tremendous body of knowledge accumulated through the worldwide diverse efforts of investigators who are building on the data, theories, and conclusions of other scientists (Grobman, 1993).

According to Grobman (1993), cooperation in science is so common that it is rarely reported, compared to competition for prizes, which is so rare that it becomes newsworthy. For example, the popular media announce the awarding of Nobel prizes; however, they rarely mention or celebrate the numerous cooperative endeavors that have resulted in our current body of scientific knowledge. Despite this, the way in which we currently conduct science fairs gives students exactly the opposite impression (Grobman, 1993). For example, students generally work independently on their projects without expert or peer assistance, without a plan, and without the resources they value most highly, and prizes are often awarded. A missing element is therefore likely explicit experience with collaboration toward shared goals. Students appear to be particularly aware of two choices: working honestly alone or cheating alone. Working honestly in appropriately chosen groups would provide close-up experience with cooperation. Barrett and Cox (2005), however, alerted us to the fact that students may not fully appreciate the difference between cooperation and collusion because they deduce that "some learning is taking place" (p. 107).

The preceding research suggests that alternatives that provide all students with the chance to succeed and receive recognition are desperately needed. For a climate that fosters success, cooperation, fun, and a sense of pride and accomplishment, teachers and schools should consider different approaches to science fairs. Here are some suggestions that have been offered in the literature.

Noncompetitive Science Fairs
According to McBride and Silverman (1988), science fairs can impact students' self-images. They explained that competition is an effective way to sort a class into winners and losers. The winners risk being boastful rather than gracious, and the losers are exposed to the risk of anger or jealousy, or they can even feel rejected because their projects were not judged worthy. Not surprisingly, young

children sincerely believe that they will win; thus, the loss feels like a personal failure, making the students feel worthless and incapable.

Given the most common form of outcomes of judging in science fairs, namely, first, second, and third place, there are naturally going to be more winners than losers. Moreover, as McBride and Silverman (1988) also argued, this method of judging usually rewards the most able students. As a result, less capable but equally hard-working students do not often win. Therefore, one recommendation is a noncompetitive science fair.

Science Fairs with Alternative Awards

One alternative method of judging a science fair is based on the mastery approach. McBride and Silverman (1988) suggested that once a student has completed the prespecified requirements for a science-fair project, either as set up by the teacher or negotiated with the teacher, the student should receive a participation award. They also recommended different standards for students of different academic and ability levels. The projects would then be showcased in the science fair, and all projects would receive a certificate of achievement or acknowledgment of participation. This alternative science fair rewards individual or group accomplishments, curiosity, and initiative, rather than competition with others.

Show-and-tell is another alternative noncompetitive method of conducting science fairs. It emphasizes a different type of reward, that is, attention and acknowledgment for a job well done (McBride & Silverman, 1988). For example, a student produces a project and then shares it with the class in a "show-and-tell" fashion. In such a situation, the student stands beside his or her project, displays it, and explains the project to classmates, students from other classes, and possibly parents. Also, a video recording can be made of the presentations.

Invention Projects

According to Kuehn (1988), the purpose of science-fair projects is to allow students to ask questions that interest them, to apply their knowledge to solving the problem, to demonstrate their use of science-process skills, and to encourage unique or creative participation. Most existing guidelines, however, provide a particular "scientific method," and require a written report delineating step-by-step procedures and conclusions. Science-fair projects can be creative as well as productive, yet students often follow a cookbook style approach to experimenting and little creative thinking is employed (Kuehn, 1988).

As an alternative to the traditional science fair, "an invention fair can be an enjoyable, exciting, and educationally sound addition to the science curriculum" (Kuehn, 1988, p. 7). To understand this concept, the definition of invention must be spelled out.

> An invention is something new or original—a method, a process, or device developed through investigation. Although they never existed until generated by the inventors, most inventions are rarely entirely new.

They are combinations of previously existing objects and ideas combined in a new way for a new purpose. Inventing, therefore, can be defined as that process which produces something previously unknown by the use of imagination or ingenuity. (Kuehn, 1988, p. 6)

Kuehn (1988) viewed invention in science as an integration of at least five components: (a) a science knowledge base, (b) basic science process skills, (c) creative thinking skills, (d) visual thinking skills, and (e) manual skills.

The second stage, research skills, is the active part of inventing, the step that actually creates the invention. It is in this stage creative skills are emphasized, generating ideas, which might be repeated many times throughout the process as a result of trial and error. This stage is also the one that students consider most creative and exciting. Kuehn (1988) wrote, "although very little similarity is found between these steps and what is typically included in the science curriculum, students find these activities fun and rewarding" (p. 6).

"Since inventing is not dependent on verbal skills or on traditional literacy skills, invention fairs can be a fun-filled challenge and a rewarding experience for a wide range of students from those with severe learning problems to the academically able" (Kuehn, 1988, p. 7). Inventing could be an effective alternative for bypassing learning problems associated with reading and writing, and can provide an opportunity for students with nonverbal strengths and talents to experience success in such school-based inquiry-related activities. Therefore, by using this alternative approach to science fairs, the total school population can have the opportunity to apply science principles in a creative scientific endeavor and experience the creative nature of science (Kuehn, 1988). Although many open-ended guidelines may be provided, the students are encouraged to foster investigative skills such as trial and error and independent and critical thinking.

According to Romjue and Clementson (1992), if our objective as educators is to promote higher achievement, greater self-esteem, and improved attitudes toward science, or learning in general, then teachers and the educational community must consider an alternative to the norm of competition found in many situations. The noncompetitive science fair, in its various forms, encourages students to view and experience science as a process, to feel pride in accomplishment, and to understand the role of science in our society (Romjue & Clementson), and without the specter of cheating.

ACKNOWLEDGMENTS

We are very grateful to Sheila Glazer and Sari Fridell for their considerable and diligent assistance in collecting the raw data for the Shore and Delcourt study and for organizing the data in a manner that facilitated the preparation of the 1995 conference presentation and ultimately this chapter.

References

Barrett, R., & Cox, A. L. (2005). "At least they're learning something": The hazy line between collaboration and collusion. *Assessment and Evaluation in Higher Education, 30,* 107–122.

Bartlett, T., & Smallwood, S. (2004). Professor copycat—Four academic plagiarists you've never heard of: How many more are out there? *The Chronicle of Higher Education, 51*(17), A8–A12.

Bishop, K. (2000). The research processes of gifted students: A case study. *Gifted Child Quarterly, 44,* 54–64.

Bowers, W. J. (1964). *Student dishonesty and its control in college.* New York: Columbia University, Bureau of Applied Social Science.

Calabrese, R. L., & Cochran, J. T. (1990). The relationship of alienation to cheating among a sample of American adolescents. *Journal of Research and Development in Education, 23,* 65–72.

Cothron, J. H., Giese, R. N., & Rezba, R. J. (2000). *Science experiments and projects for students* (3rd ed.). Dubuque, IA: Kendall/Hunt.

Danforth, W. H., & Schoenhoff, D. M. (1992). Fostering integrity in scientific research. *Academic Medicine, 67,* 351–356.

Davison, J. (1992, February 23). 'Great Fraudster' may have been right after all. *The Sunday Times* (London), Section 5, p. 1.

Eichenwald, K., & Kolata, G. (1999, May 17). A doctor's drug studies turn into fraud. *The New York Times,* pp. A1, A16. (The copy referred to in this chapter was downloaded June 18, 2005, from http://www.contac.org/contaclibrary/research6.htm, 11 printed pages.)

Eminent psychiatrist resigns from Harvard after plagiarism charge. (1988, November 29). *The Gazette (Montreal),* pp. F9.

Faked data led to report of cancer breakthrough. (1988, November 24). *The Boston Globe,* p. F8.

Finkelstein, A. (2002). *Science is golden: A problem-solving approach to doing science with children.* East Lansing, MI: Michigan State University Press.

Glick, S. M. (1992). Research in a hierarchy of values. *The Mount Sinai Journal of Medicine, 59,* 102–107.

Goddard, H. H. (1912). *The Kallikak family: A study in the heredity of feeble-mindedness.* New York: Macmillan.

Grobman, A. (1993). A fair proposition? *The Science Teacher, 60*(1), 40–41.

Haensly, P. A., & Roberts, N. M. (1983). The professional productive process and its implications for gifted students. *Gifted Child Quarterly, 27,* 9–12.

Jacob, B. A., & Levitt, S. D. (2002). *Catching cheating teachers: The results of an unusual experiment in implementing theory.* Cambridge, MA: National Bureau of Economic Research, Working Paper No. 9414. (Downloaded June 18, 2005, from http://www.nber.org/papers/w9414, 33 pages in .pdf format.)

Karagiannis, A. (1999). The prophecy of the Kallikak family: "Disability" in postmodern schools. *Journal of Educational Administration and Foundations, 13*(2), 11–26.

Korean scientist resigns over fake stem cell research. (2005). Associated Press as reported in the *Guardian Unlimited,* December 23, 2005. Retrieved August 23, 2006, from http://www.guardian.co.uk/genes/article/0,2763,1673508,00.html

Kuehn, C. (1988). Inventing: Creative sciencing. *Childhood Education, 65*(1), 5–7.

Levitt, S. D., & Dubner, S. J. (2005). *Freakonomics: A rogue economist explores the hidden side of everything.* New York: William Morrow (HarperCollins).

Lowry, F. (1995). Create culture of integrity to defeat research fraud, funding agencies say. *Canadian Medical Association Journal, 152,* 1507–1508.

McBride, J. W., & Silverman, F. L. (1988). Judging fairs fairly. *Science and Children, 25*(6), 15–18.

McCabe, D. (1995, February). New ethics code on the way. *The McGill Reporter, 27*(10), 1, 4.

McCabe, D. L., & Trevino, L. K. (1996). What we know about cheating in college: Longitudinal trends and recent developments. *Change, 28,* 28–33.

McLaughlin, R. D., & Ross, S. M. (1989). Student cheating in high school: A case of moral reasoning vs. "fuzzy logic." *The High School Journal, 72,* 97–104.

Mendoza, M. (2005). *Managing science: Allegations of fake research hit new high.* Associated Press as reported on ABC News, July 17, 2005. Retrieved August 23, 2006, from http://www.spinwatch.org/modules.php?name=News&file=article&sid=1265

National Science Teachers Association (Ed.). (2003). *Science fairs plus: Reinventing a favorite, K-8.* Arlington, VA: National Science Teachers Association Press.

Newstead, S. E., Franklyn-Stokes, A., & Armstead, P. (1996). Individual differences in student cheating. *Journal of Educational Psychology, 88,* 229–241.

Pelletier, S., & Shore, B. M. (2003). The gifted learner, the novice, and the expert: Sharpening emerging views of giftedness. In D. C. Ambrose, L. M. Cohen, & A. J. Tannenbaum (Eds.), *Creative intelligence: Toward theoretic integration* (pp. 237–281). New York: Hampton Press.

Poltorak, Y. (1995). Cheating behavior among students of four Moscow universities. *Higher Education, 30,* 225–246.

Renzulli, J. S. (1986). The three ring conception of giftedness: A developmental model for creative productivity. In R. J. Sternberg & J. E. Davidson (Eds.), *Conceptions of giftedness* (pp. 53–92). New York: Cambridge University Press.

Richmond, C. (1995). Different fates await authors after two journal reports declared invalid in UK. *Canadian Medical Association Journal, 152,* 1129–1130.

Romjue, M. K., & Clementson, J. J. (1992). An alternative science fair. *Science and Children, 30*(2), 22–24.

Schab, F. (1991). Schooling without learning: Thirty years of cheating in high school. *Adolescence, 26,* 839–847.

Schapiro, M. (1997). *Sources of help for students in science fairs.* Unpublished master's thesis in educational psychology, McGill University, Montreal, QC.

Science and the Citizen. (1986, February). *Scientific American, 245,* 56–57.

Shore, B. M., & Delcourt, M. A. B. (1995, November). *Understanding inquiry: Lessons in scientific thinking and fraud from students' participation in science fairs.* Paper presented at the annual meeting of the National Association for Gifted Children, Salt Lake City, UT.

Starko, A. J., & Schack, G. D. (1998). *Research comes alive! A guidebook for conducting original research with middle and high school students.* Mansfield Center, CT: Creative Learning Press.

Syer, C. A., & Shore, B. M. (2001). Science fairs: What are the sources of help for students and how prevalent is cheating? *School Science and Mathematics, 101,* 206–220.

Tabatabai, D., & Shore, B. M. (2005). How experts and novices search the Web. *Library and Information Science Research, 27,* 222–248.

Vernon, P. E. (1979). *Intelligence, heredity and environment.* San Francisco: Freeman.

Weijer, C. (1995). The breast cancer research scandal: Addressing the issues. *Canadian Medical Association Journal, 152,* 1195–1197.

5

Caught in the Web:
Internet Risks for Children*

GLENN F. CARTWRIGHT, ADAM B. A. FINKELSTEIN,
AND MATTHEW K. B. MAENNLING
McGill University

Television late-night talk show host David Letterman once had a list of "Signs your child is spending too much time on the Internet." Among these were:

- Named the hamsters, I., B., and M.,
- Been in bed all week with a computer virus,
- Refers to sex as "logging on,"
- The bedroom walls are covered with printouts of naked Bill Gates, and
- Calls you www.daddy.com.

Although tongue-in-cheek, the list underscores serious parental concerns about the Internet and its effect on children. We wondered what the dangers were, if the Internet might affect the gifted more than other children, and if there were particular risks to the gifted.

Development of the Internet and the World Wide Web
In the late 1960s, the United States was steadily moving into a Cold War. A threat of nuclear attack was perceived and relationships between United States and the Soviet Union were tense. At that time, the United States Department of Defense posed a perplexing problem to the RAND Corporation, a public policy think-tank: In the event of a nuclear attack, how might communications continue? To solve this problem, the RAND Corporation proposed a communications network that respected two important principles. First, no central command should be

---

* Based in part on a paper presented at the midyear conference of the National Association for Gifted Children, Montreal, May 2–4, 1997.

vital to the sustainability of this network, as a central command would be immediately targeted in a first strike. Second, the network should be assumed to be
unreliable at all times. Each node or link in the network should be independent
and have equal status with all others in the system.

Originally designed for military communications, this early network became
the foundation of what was to eventually become the Internet. Over a period of 20
years, more and more computers were connected to this communications network,
and more and more networks joined together with each link independent from all
others. Eventually, the military network was merged with research and university
networks. As more computers were connected, the network became stronger.

One of the most popular metaphors for the Internet was that of a superhigh-
way. The original network consisted of four specific lanes: electronic mail (e-
mail), file transfer protocol (ftp), news discussions (usenet), and remote computer
control (telnet). Other lanes also were added. Despite this growth, the Internet did
not become infused in popular culture until Tim Berners-Lee proposed HTML
or HyperText Markup Language in the early 1990s (Berners-Lee, 1989; Berners-
Lee & Cailliau, 1990). Berners-Lee expanded Vanevar Bush's original concept
of Hypertext, or the linking of relevant information, by allowing authors to link
various media to written textual information (Bush, 1945). Hypertext allowed
authors to create links between ideas, rather than using a conventional, linear
organization of information (such as a book). The concept of Hypertext became
a reality when Marc Andreessen designed a "viewer" for Berners-Lee's HTML.
This was the final link that enabled authors to easily link ideas and various types
of media, but allowed anyone in the world to examine these HTML pages by simply knowing where the page was on the network. These two simple ideas were the
beginning of the World Wide Web (WWW). The World Wide Web soon became
the most popular lane on the Internet highway (Sterling, 1993).

Andreessen's first creation, Mosaic, was the HTML viewer (Web browser)
that he designed while attending university. He provided it at no cost and did
not expect the overwhelming response. In 1993, the WWW grew by 341,634%
(Schlender, 1995). Still growing in 1994, WWW growth was up by 1713% (Berners-Lee, 1996). Andreessen soon left university and founded Netscape which
became one of the world's largest software companies.

Recently, the Internet has grown at a rate of 20% per month, from its original
4 nodes in 1969 to over 6.6 million by July, 1995 (Sterling, 1993; Zakon, 1995).
Although this growth has slowed slightly in the 21st century, the increase in Web
users is still climbing at an astonishing rate. The White House, the Queen, and
the Pope all have their own Web pages. Current Web use is estimated at over
580 million users (Nua Internet Surveys, 2002). Two-thousand-year-old Vatican
documents and the 5,000-year-old Dead Sea Scrolls can now be accessed from
the comfort of one's home. The World Wide Web has become the world's largest
repository of information. Any question can be answered (www.askjeeves.com)
and any known information can be uncovered (www.britannica.com). Internet
resources are so numerous that even computerized search engines such as Google

(www.google.com) cannot hope to catalogue every web page on the Internet. Could the World Wide Web be the beginning of humankind's global brain?

The World Wide Web is also a perfect domain for inquiry. It offers open (www.google.com), categorized (www.yahoo.com), or guided (www.askjeeves.com) search and inquiry capabilities. Students can embark on WebQuests, Internet scavenger hunts, virtual tours, and even gather real-world data for analysis. Students can gather real-world data from locations such as the National Center for Health Statistics (www.cdc.gov/nchswww/) for a biology course on birth rates and the National Oceanic and Atmospheric Administration (www.noaa.gov) to analyze atmospheric phenomena all with the facilitation of a teacher looking to improve mathematical concepts (Drier, Dawson, & Garofalo, 2003). Wilson and Lowry (2001) proposed three principles for effective use of the WWW for learning: providing access to rich sources of information (perhaps the richest ever compiled by any society), encouraging meaningful interactions with content (through webquests, simulations, etc.), and bringing people together to challenge, support, or respond to each other (through online discussions and other interactions). They proposed that the WWW is a perfect medium by which students can construct knowledge through self-directed inquiry.

General Benefits and Risks

The Internet is generally a positive development. All the world's knowledge can be locally available. All humans are potentially linked: This results in improved communication and (hopefully) better understanding. There is immediacy of information and information flows around the planet in an accelerated form.

There are, however, serious risks to the general population. Getnetwise.org lists a number of important types of risks that are available to children:

- Meeting Someone On-line
- Loss of Privacy
- Getting Into On-line "Fights"
- Making Threats/Law Breaking
- Inappropriate Material
- If I read it on-line is it true?
- Putting People In Jeopardy
- Drugs and Other Substances (http://www.getnetwise.org, August 22, 2005)

We posit that the highest risks for children are among the following: Exposure to inappropriate material, meeting dangerous strangers, harassment, power without accountability, anonymity, gender-swapping, and loss of personality.

The Risky Gifted

Are the gifted at any greater risk? No one knows for sure, but it is possible that some proportion of the gifted may be at greater risk than others.

Who are the risky gifted? We define the risky gifted as that portion of the gifted population who may be at greater risk of danger on the Internet, possibly even as a result of their giftedness. Among the gifted who may be more at risk are those who are more curious, energetic, or imaginative. If so, they may be more exploratory, more prone to intellectual risk taking, more sensitive, and more affected by tragedy. Internet risks to children in general are now receiving mainstream attention (Jackson, von Eye, & Biocca, 2003). The particular characteristics of many gifted children invite us to speculate about curiosity or inquiry driven activity using the Internet. Let us consider several of these possible risks in more detail.

Exposure to Inappropriate Material

Sexual content.   Among the most frequently accessed are pornographic Web sites. These Web sites include exposure to inappropriate sexual content, deviancy, solicitation, prostitution (e.g., escort services), and live-video sex shows. Even mainstream "erotic" adult sites may be inappropriate for young viewers. Because the architecture of the Internet was designed to avoid central control for security reasons, this results in the inability to centrally censor content. Nearly 30% of teenage girls have been harassed online. Many girls report exposure to pornographic sites accidentally by either unsolicited e-mail, or inadvertently accessing one (Nua Internet Surveys, March 11, 2002). Although not 100% effective, computer software such as Cyberpatrol (www.cyberpatrol.com) allows for local or familial control of content. Because the Internet is a global communication system (and even extraglobal, reaching space shuttles), national laws are ineffective in controlling global content.

Hate literature.   Because the Internet cannot be controlled and has unclear jurisdictional boundaries, it becomes the perfect medium to nurture hatred. Young children have access to sites about the National Socialist Movement and can purchase Nazi propaganda and memorabilia online. According to the Simon Wiesenthal Center, in just one year after the World Trade destruction of September 11, 2001, the number of hate Web sites rose by nearly one-third, from roughly 2000 to 3000 (Nua Internet Surveys, July 10, 2002). The National Association for the Advancement of Colored People (NAACP) has purchased the domain name containing derogatory labels to prevent later misuse by hate groups. The Anti-Defamation League has registered anti-Semitic domain names for the same reason (Festa, 1998; Who Owns the N-Word Dot Com?, 1999).

Illegal activities.   The Web harbors illegal and unethical information that can be garnered without much cost or effort. Everything from buying term papers to finding "81 ways to trash your school" is easily accessible. Adolescents have been known to purchase drugs, illegal firearms, and alcohol online with their parents' credit-card numbers. Online fraud has exploded in the last few years, resulting in a loss of over 700 million dollars to consumers. In a recent GartnerG2 survey, 5% of online consumers have been victimized by credit-card fraud, contesting charges on their bills that they did not purchase (Nua Internet Surveys, March 4, 2002). Also in this category is downloading stolen software (Hawaleshka & Scott, 1999).

Cultist activities. Anyone can retrieve information about joining bizarre organizations. Some cult warning referral services have now been taken over by cults themselves to provide inaccurate information. Even on examining cult Web sites or anticult Web sites, it becomes difficult to know the true motives behind each.

Traumatic news. Young minds eager to explore information, for example, on the wars in East Timor, Afghanistan, or Iraq, might be psychologically unprepared for the visuals they encounter (e.g., www.easttimor.com). Those looking for resources on the September 11th attack on the World Trade Center may not be able to comprehend the tragedy. There are a number of Web sites dedicated to the posting of tragic events. These sites post pictures of car accidents (taken by ambulance technicians), war photography, and other graphic scenes. Recently, a suicide note was found posted on the Web. Although this was upsetting in itself, there was no way of knowing its authenticity or what action should have been taken. With the increased popularity of live webcams, the danger of disturbance to traumatic information increases. Is the information viewed on these webcams authentic?

Incorrect information and role models. The lack of editorial content control means that much of the information on the Internet may be inaccurate. Birth-control information may be wrong, information on sexually transmitted diseases may be incomplete, and sites may exist that slant information to push particular agendas. In September 1994, *Mirabella* magazine's cover featured America's most beautiful woman: Called the Face of America, thousands of teenage girls were exposed to this particular view of "perfection." As later reported, the famous photograph by Hiro was actually an artificial creation. The image was a computer generated composite of a woman who never existed. Online bullying is also a growing problem. Nearly 25% of children in the United Kingdom have reported to have been victimized by online bullies. Unfortunately, one-third of online bullying goes unreported (Nua Internet Surveys, April 15, 2002).

Temptation to hack and crack. Adolescents have broken into corporate Web sites, security installations, defense systems, and even the Pentagon itself. It is important to examine the difference between intellectual curiosity and criminal intent. Specifically, is there a difference between an adolescent exploring computer systems, Web sites, and networks, and an adolescent who tries to break into a computer with devious intent? The temptation to hack may be rooted in intellectual curiosity, but the end result is the same, a criminal act. Often adolescents are given powerful tools, such as computers connected to the Internet, but lack the necessary experience or ethical structures to guide them in the use of these tools.   Criminal intent was the deciding factor in the now infamous case of Mafiaboy. Mafiaboy, an intelligent 17-year-old adolescent, was arrested, charged, and convicted of initiating major attacks on a number of Web sites including Yahoo, eBay, Amazon, and others. Although he claimed that he perpetrated these acts without criminal intent, the judge thought otherwise and sentenced him to eight months' detention (Mafiaboy, September 13, 2001).

Meeting Dangerous Strangers

Consider the case of Sharon Lopatka. A married woman, Sharon Lopatka met a man on the Internet who said he would like to kill her. She agreed, left her husband a note, and met the stranger in another state, where he killed her. The stranger's e-mail (Robert Glass) was found later on her home computer with a detailed account of how he would torture her and eventually kill her (Associated Press, February 28, 1999). Might the gifted more likely to be lured into strange and dangerous encounters because of their curiosity or willingness to take intellectual risks?

Harassment

In southern Ontario, the Tamai family reported being "spooked" by someone by the name of "Sommy" who interrupted their phone calls with a strange voice, slashed investigating police's tires, and switched lights on and off in the family home. Neither the telephone company, investigators, nor the police were able to ascertain the source of the problem. Two American TV networks sent correspondents to report on the phenomenon. Finally, 15-year-old son Billy Tamai, confessed to being the electronic intruder. He had taken the name "Sommy" from a cat on a television fix-it show. He was sent for psychiatric treatment (Cable News Network, April 22, 1997).

In another incident, a major university was forced to discipline a student for making anonymous death threats to other students on the Internet. Might some gifted children be more likely to be enticed into harassing others on the Internet?

Power without Accountability

Web authors use the Internet to amplify their thoughts and relay them to a wide variety of individuals around the world. However, unlike other powerful media, there is little or no accountability. Web authors are not required to reference their sources, prove their points, or back up their claims. Most Web sites are not peer reviewed. Although such power without accountability is dangerous and irresponsible, it seems to be the very nature of the Internet. In a democracy, individuals can say almost whatever they like (and are protected under free speech laws). However, laws are inconsistent across international boundaries. The Internet ignores these artificial boundaries; sites that may be outlawed in Canada because of tougher hate laws, may be legal in the United States. On the Internet, one's physical location becomes irrelevant. Highly creative, imaginative, or subversive gifted students may be more likely to author and explore such sites.

Anonymity
Anonymous slander magnifies power without accountability. Like rumors, slan-
derous statements take on a life of their own and spread globally while their
sources remain untraceable. Software can be used to make it impossible to determine the source of an offending e-mail. Universities are being forced to redraft
their policies to accommodate for the anonymity that the Internet provides (Rogerson, 2000). There is a danger that the gifted may be more likely to use the Internet as an amplifying and transmitting instrument of their thoughts.

Gender-Swapping
Although it was originally thought that pretending to be the opposite sex on the
Internet was deviant, it is now recognized for many that it may be a legitimate
way of exploring sex roles. Sherry Turkle (1995) at MIT reported the case of a
man who pretended to be a woman pretending to be a man. Although such exploration may not be dangerous for the pretender, it may well prove to be dangerous
to or at least embarrassing for the correspondent. An adolescent might develop
feelings for another person over the Internet only to discover that the sex of their
correspondent was not what was expected. This raises two questions: (a) Are the
gifted more likely to swap genders? (b) Are the gifted more likely to be recipients
of unwanted attention by gender swappers?

Loss of Personality
Overuse of the Internet may interfere with normal personality growth and interaction with real people in the real world. Online relationships are a poor substitute
for healthy emotional relationships with real people. Excessive Internet use, at the
expense of other social activities, may interfere with the development of normal
social skills, empathy, nonverbal skills and other facets of communication long
thought to be the basis of what we consider to be human. The Center for On-line
Addiction (http://www.netaddiction.com) was created to consider this phenomenon. According to a survey conducted by the Center, 6% of the nearly 20,000
Internet users studied demonstrated signs of compulsive use. Perhaps the most
poignant suggestion by the Center is that the Internet presents the illusion of inti-
macy within a faceless community.

What Can Parents and Teachers Do?

1. *Recognize that the Internet is here to stay, cannot be shut off, and will not
go away.* Although overall a generally positive development, parents and
teachers recognize some of the dangers listed earlier. Technically, the Internet was designed as a communication system built to withstand nuclear
devastation. There is no central command structure and every node is independent. "Turning it off" is a technical improbability. Pragmatically, its use
has become intertwined with the economy with most industries now reliant
upon its existence.

2. *Know your child.* Try to be aware of what interests your children have, and what attracts them on the Internet. This may give some indication as to what sites they may wish to visit. Remember that though the Internet can help solve many problems, it also can make other problems worse.

3. *Open a "hailing frequency" with your child.* Keep the lines of communication open. Should problems develop later, they will be easier to discuss and resolve if parents and teachers can interact easily with children. The Internet is a powerful tool and in the hands of an unaware and uneducated student can inflict harm on other individuals and themselves.

4. *Participate with your child.* The Internet can be a catalyst for social interaction and can strengthen family and educational activities through joint participation. Find games and activities children like and participate in them together as a family.

5. *Recognize that guiding Internet content must be done at the local level.* Use filtering software where necessary to help guide children to appropriate sites, and be aware that this type of software can never be 100% effective—an even better reason for more teacher and parent involvement.

The information highway is indeed a rapid expressway with great risks and great potential for our youth. As with any journey, it is important to watch out for bad drivers, use your map, go with the flow, avoid tickets, and enjoy the ride.

References

Associated Press. (1999, February 28). E-mail indicates woman may have agreed to be slain. USA Today. Retrieved April 1, 2005, from http://www.usatoday.com/life/cyber/tech/ct309.htm (This source is available only by subscription. A publicly available report on the same event is available in an article by Rachel Bell at the following website as of April 1, 2005: http://www.crimelibrary.com/notorious_murders/classics/sharon_lopatka/1.html.)

Berners-Lee, T. (1989). *Information management: A proposal.* Unpublished proposal submitted to European Organization for Nuclear Research (CERN). Retrieved August 22, 2005, from http://www.w3.org/History/1989/proposal.html

Berners-Lee, T. (1996). *The World Wide Web: Past, present and future.* Retrieved September 23, 2005, from http://www.w3.org/People/Berners-Lee/1996/ppf.html

Berners-Lee, T., & Cailliau, R. (1990). *WorldWideWeb: Proposal for a HyperText Project.* Unpublished proposal submitted to European Organization for Nuclear Research (CERN). Retrieved August 22, 2005, from http://www.w3.org/Proposal.html

Bush, V. (1945). As we may think. *The Atlantic Monthly, 176,* 101–108.

Cable News Network. (1997, April, 22). High-tech stalker turns out to be an insider. Retrieved August 22, 2005, from http://www.cnn.com/WORLD/9704/22/cyber.punk/

Drier, H. S., Dawson, K. M., & Garofalo, J. (2003). *Using technology and real world connections to teach secondary mathematics concepts.* Eisenhower National Clearinghouse for Mathematics and Science Education (ENC). Retrieved August 22, 2005, from http://www.enc.org/topics/inquiry/internet/document.shtm?input=FOC-000706-index

Festa, P. (1998, May 1). *Controversial domains go to civil rights groups.* CNET News.com. Retrieved August 22, from http://news.com.com/2100–1023–210803.html?legacy=cnet

Hawaleshka, D., & Scott, R. (1999). Beware the Internet Underground. A secret passage is leading kids to stolen software and hard-core porn. *Maclean's* (Newsmagazine), *112* (45), 42–46.

Jackson, L. A., von Eye, A., & Biocca, F. (2003, December). Children and Internet Use: Social, Psychological and Academic Consequences for Low-income Children. *Psychological Science Agenda, 17*(2). Retrieved August 22, 2005, from http://www. apa.org/science/psa/sbjacksonprt.html

Mafiaboy sentenced to 8 months. (2001, Sept 13). Wired News Report. Retrieved August 22, 2005, from http://www.wired.com/news/print/0,1294,46791,00.html

Nua Internet Surveys. (2002, May). *How many on-line? Worldwide.* Retrieved August 22, 2005, from http://www.nua.com/surveys/how_many_online/world.html

Nua Internet Surveys. (2002, April 15). *A quarter of UK kids have been bullied on-line.* Retrieved August 22, 2005, from http://www.nua.com/surveys/index.cgi?f=VS& art_id=905357849&rel=true

Nua Internet Surveys. (2002, July 10). *Hate spreads across the Internet.* Retrieved August 22, 2005, from http://www.nua.com/surveys/index.cgi?f=VS&art_id=905358152& rel=true

Nua Internet Surveys. (2002, March 11). *Many teenage girls harassed on-line.* Retrieved August 22, 2005, from http://www.nua.com/surveys/index.cgi?f=VS&art_id= 905357736&rel=true

Nua Internet Surveys. (2002, March 4). *On-line credit card fraud soaring.* Retrieved August 22, 2005, from http://www.nua.com/surveys/index.cgi?f=VS&art_id=905357713&rel= true

Rogerson, S. (2000). Computer based harassment on college campuses. *Student Affairs On-line 1* (1). Retrieved August 22, 2005, from http://www.studentaffairs.com/ ejournal/Spring_2000/article5.html

Schlender, B. (1995). Whose Internet is it, anyway? *Fortune Magazine, 132*(12). Retrieved October 16, 2005, from http://www.fortune.com/fortune/articles/0,15114,377170,00. html

Sterling, B. (1993). Short history of the Internet by Bruce Sterling. *The Magazine of Fantasy and Science Fiction.* February. Retrieved August 22, 2005, from http://www. library.yale.edu/div/instruct/internet/history.htm

Turkle, S. (1995). *Life on the screen: Identity in the age of the Internet.* New York: Touchstone.

Who Owns the N-Word Dot Com? (September 22, 1999). Wired News Report. Retrieved August 22, 2005, from http://www.wired.com/news/culture/0,1284,21873,00.html

Wilson, B. G., & Lowry, M. (2001). Constructivist learning on the web. In E. J. Burge (Ed.), *The strategic use of technologies: Reflective and strategic thinking* (pp. 79–88). San Francisco: Jossey-Bass, New Directions for Adult and Continuing Education.

Zakon, R. H. (1995). *Hobbes' Internet timeline.* Retrieved April 7, 2005, from http://web. bilkent.edu.tr/History/isoc/guest/zakon/Internet/History/HIT.html

6

Collaboration in Student-Oriented Teacher Inquiry

Lynn Butler-Kisber

McGill University

The purpose of this chapter is to examine a teacher-as-researcher experience (Cochran-Smith & Lytle, 1993) I had several years ago in a graduate class at my university. The chapter includes how I became interested in conducting this work, the context in which the research took place, and the qualitative methodology that I used for the study. It outlines how personal stories shared in class nurtured the sense of community, and provided me with insights about my teaching. An examination, in particular, of the collaborative work of two students shed light on some important dimensions of collaboration, and the role inquiry played in the teaching and learning process, suggesting implications for further work.

The context for this story was the early 1990s in a university setting in a large urban city in Canada. Having recently completed a qualitative thesis for my doctoral work (Butler-Kisber, 1988), I was heavily committed to qualitative research, and found myself increasingly attracted to the growing body of literature on teacher-as-researcher studies. These studies resonated deeply with the kind of partnership that developed between the classroom teacher and me during the time I did my study on peer collaboration (Butler-Kisber, 1991). As a result of this experience, I became more and more sensitive to the issues of voice and ownership in research (Belenky, Clinchy, Goldberger, & Tarule, 1986), and began to include teacher-as-researcher work in the content of my courses.

The following is a retrospective examination of a graduate course I taught in 1993 during which time I documented what transpired in my classroom, from a teacher-as-researcher perspective, to understand more fully my own practice, and to model what I was advocating for education students. It is a form of "conceptual research" (Cochran-Smith & Lytle, 1993) where one "researches" (Berthoff, 1987) what was learned at the time of an experience, as well as what has been learned since. It is a move toward praxis, that integration of action and reflection to create change (Lather, 1986), and has potential for improving the quality of learning and living in educational contexts.

Student-Oriented Teacher Inquiry

The plan to systematically monitor a graduate class I was teaching was grounded in both my general and specific experiences at the university. At the time, I was continuing my work on peer collaboration among young children (Butler-Kisber, 1988, 2000) and approaches to literacy (Butler-Kisber, 1997). In addition, I was teaching about literacy and qualitative research, and exploring the burgeoning literature on reflective practice and teacher research. It was the intersection of this work that led to this study.

The unique features of the questions that prompt teacher research is that they emanate from neither theory nor practice alone but from critical reflection on the intersection of the two (Cochran-Smith & Lytle, 1993, p. 15).

A product of preservice teacher education of the 1960s, I had been schooled in Dewey's work as well as the progressive education movement of the time. I experimented with project (inquiry) learning with various cohorts of elementary students (Butler-Kisber, 1997), and then tried to transpose elements of this work to the university context. I was to discover later that what I was attempting to implement was based on constructivist approaches to teaching and learning (Fosnot, 1992), and the theory of multiple intelligences (Gardner, 1983, 2000). A constructivist approach entails "a learner and life-centered curriculum, enriched environments, interactive settings, differentiated instruction, inquiry, experimentation and investigation, mediation and facilitation, and metacognitive reflection" (Fogarty, 1999, p. 78). Gardner (1983) has proposed there are seven kinds of intelligences, and later postulated as many as eleven (2000). He suggested that we must create learning situations that engage students by building on these different strengths, rather than limiting learners by acknowledging only the traditional "academic intelligences"—the logical-mathematical and linguistic-based modes.

At first my experimentation revolved mainly around the kinds of work I assigned to students. I tried to promote what Perkins (1999) would call active, social, and creative learners. I encouraged them to do inquiry on issues of interest and need, to benefit from each other by working collaboratively, and to share understandings in exhibitions or performances, and by means of "portfolio portraits" (Graves & Sunstein, 1992; see Figure 6.1). The goal was to make the work more meaningful and reflective, and each time the results were encouraging. The students responded with enthusiasm, energy, and high standards. The potential for expanding these possibilities was always limited, however, by the compartmentalized nature of courses at the university, and the lack of flexibility of time and space. On two occasions this changed.

Our students doing a postdegree, 1-year, preservice teacher-education program were required to do two intensive courses over a three-week period before their final field experience. I was scheduled to teach one of the courses, the second half of a six-credit language arts requirement, meeting every day for three hours with the students. As a result, we were able to take over a classroom and transform it from the usual sterile place into a multifaceted environment. This included working, meeting, and socializing spaces, a library corner, display areas, and a

Figure 6.1 Exhibition of portfolio portraits.

spot where we enthusiastically hatched and nurtured chickens (see Figure 6.2). We reflected on the process, and how this kind of inquiry, or something like it, might be incorporated into language arts teaching in elementary classrooms.

We arranged to have the room open all day so work could continue whether or not I was present. As we negotiated the curriculum, I tried to model what they were reading by presenting "mini-lessons" (Calkins, 1991) and conducting conferences as needed, by journaling with them, and by facilitating the inquiry in which they were involved. It was an exciting time for all of us. We became close, and shared both our personal beliefs about education and professional experiences we had in our classrooms to help inform our understandings and questions (Ford Slack, 1995). I found the work very labor intensive, however, and not easily transferable to the kinds of classes that meet twice a week, in cramped, desk-filled rooms where groups of students follow on the heels of each other. In subsequent courses, I tried within the latter constraints to reproduce some elements of community, inquiry, and reflection with varying degrees of success. These experiences made me decide it was time to document systematically what transpired in my classes, and I began a teacher-as-researcher inquiry during a course I was teaching in 1993. By doing this, I hoped to gain a deeper understanding of my own practice while modeling the notions of reflective practice (Schön, 1983, 1987) and teacher inquiry or research (Goswami & Stillman, 1987) because these were two important dimensions of the course content.

The course in question was at the graduate level and entitled "Teaching Language Arts: Trends and Issues." It attracted nine women students, three of

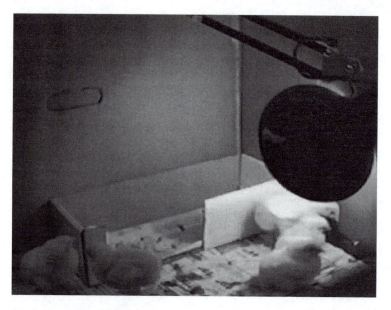

Figure 6.2   Hatching chickens.

whom were enrolled in a master's program in Second Language Education; the other six were in Curriculum Studies. Apart from two recent graduates, most were teachers with considerable experience at the elementary, secondary, and adult education levels in various geographical areas including Canada, the Caribbean, and the Middle East. Several of the students had been together in previous courses, but this was the first time all nine had been in the same group.

It was the second time I had taught the course and I wanted to make it as student-oriented as possible in spite of the constraints that resulted from one three-hour meeting per week. To accomplish this I took the role of facilitator whenever possible, and invited students to help shape the direction of the course within certain parameters. The main assignment for the course was to conduct an inquiry of interest related to trends or issues in literacy. I encouraged students to conduct qualitative inquiries in their own or colleagues' classrooms. I hoped these kinds of projects would be engaging, and help them reap some practical benefits in terms of their own teaching. I anticipated the work would also develop some of the qualitative research skills they needed for completing the monograph, an extensive research paper that was required to complete the program. To help with the process, I hired a research assistant who had taken the course the previous year. Kelly participated in classes, scripted what was transpiring, and helped operate a drop-in time in the "action room." Here, for an additional three hours per week, students came on an optional basis to discuss issues with us that related to either the course content or their research projects. I envisioned Kelly's role would include an informal teaching component that would be helpful to the others because of her previous experience in the course.

The room was located conveniently across the hall from my office from which information and resources (computer, books, articles, and telephone) could be accessed easily. This alleviated the need to set up anything permanently, and cut down on some of the extra investment in time that operating the room required.

Two students chose to do library research, three carried out inquiry in other teachers' classrooms because they were not teaching themselves, and four did teacher-research projects in their own classrooms. Additional assignments included mini-proposals submitted for feedback before they began their research, and individual or collaborative presentations on a particular literacy issue of their choice.

The classes were conducted in a seminar style with discussions emanating around a critical examination of both the historical and current sociopolitical issues in language-arts pedagogy (Edelsky, Altwerger, & Flores, 1991; Willinsky, 1990). There were several guest presentations, and at times I took a more teacher-directed role to pursue a topic or question that merited attention. Because most of the students were working during the day and registered part-time, they tended to come to the university on the evening of the course, and then on Saturdays to use the library. As a result, they did not use the action room on a regular basis. At first, this was disappointing, but eventually the richness of the data, collected on the work of two students in particular, far outweighed this concern.

A qualitative approach was used to document in detail what transpired during both the course and action-room time, as well as during my planning time with Kelly. A tripod-mounted, stationary video camera recorded all classes and drop-in times. This did not always permit a total visual record, but the group was small enough to obtain a very complete audio recording of all verbatim interactions. This allowed me to revisit what transpired (Erickson & Wilson, 1982) with a clarity that otherwise would not have been possible. Field notes recorded by Kelly and me augmented the videotaped data. Balancing the teaching and researcher role is arduous, and as a result, my notes tended to be sketchy, raising my respect for those teachers who do this on a regular basis. Kelly's were much more detailed, and her transcriptions included useful reflective and interpretive comments (Maykut & Morehouse, 1994) providing a different perspective on what was happening. We also carefully compiled an artifact collection of all student work and in-class evaluations. After the course was over, the mandatory departmental teaching evaluations were added to these data. Formal and informal interviews with Kelly and some students both during the course and subsequent to it added to the richness of the data, helped focus the study, and validated the results (Seidman, 1998). Kelly and I worked on an initial "coarse-grained" analysis, the early data analysis that accompanies the data collection (Butler-Kisber, 1988). This included a preliminary viewing of the videotapes and a sharing of our field and reflective notes and memos that we then integrated with the student artifacts. Some initial patterns emerged, permitting us to successively refine our focus. We began to look more carefully at the amount of storying that went on among us in classes, the personal anecdotes and professional experiences that we shared to make a point, or to elaborate on something we were reading. We also focused on a very unique collaboration between two students, Ann and Debbie.

A more fine-grained analysis took place after the course was over. This included a detailed cataloguing of all the videotapes (Corsaro, 1979) where class phases and events were delineated and timed. As well, a topic and contributors summary was prepared using an adaptation of Tannen's (1984) format. Each time the topic shifted, we recorded the number on the digital counter, the name of the speaker, and the first couple of lines of the verbatim interaction. This record permitted easy retrieval of data and verbatim text as needed, and also helped to uncover global patterns more quickly. The videotaped sessions of all the action-room sessions, and four classes selected as a result of the cataloguing, were transcribed in their entirety. These data were merged with the field notes and artifact collection to further refine and classify the emerging patterns (Maykut & Morehouse, 1994). Kelly's participation in the early part of the analyses provided a useful perspective on the process. Finally, almost a year later, a length of time frequently required for qualitative analysis of this sort, Ann and Debbie, the two students who used the action room most often, were videotaped for several hours. During that time they reflected on their experiences of working together. As well I shared videotaped excerpts of various patterns that had emerged. They responded to these to help corroborate or question my interpretations of what had occurred.

What became apparent, as a rather startling revelation, was the amount of time and frequency that was devoted to the sharing of personal experiences. Not all of our classroom talk was in personalized terms. We also interacted in the more typical ways, such as discussing and questioning how our ideas were related to concepts in the course readings. But none of us escaped using the "storytelling" mode. Our stories were used to explain and extend ideas, set examples, negotiate, contest, resist, and joke. Although the storying theme is not the focus of this chapter, it merits some elaboration as it provided a context for examining the collaboration between Ann and Debbie, and the work that went on in the action room. The transcripts are replete with these personal narratives that are part of discussions that tended to focus on course content, qualitative research skills, individual projects, and program issues. For example, one student recounted how she was grappling with definitions of holistic versus direct instruction in language arts:

> and then they (referring to her own children) come home and I've got to sit with them and do the actual work. And, it's all, and like yesterday (pause), every night I have to sit with my son and read for fifteen minutes. Well, I like to read to him on MY time, at the "teachable moment" which we do a lot of because like I said, I have a holistic approach. But now it seems I'm getting instructed to sit for fifteen minutes every day—let the parents do the real work, we'll do the holistic thing here. You know what I mean? (video transcript/Class/Jan. 12, 1993)

And in a discussion about the canon and political correctness, this student shared how she decided not to introduce the nursery rhyme "The Old Woman Who Lived in a Shoe":

> It's funny, this relates, but this weekend I was planning for school, and uh, and I, I thought, OK, I had finished one nursery rhyme and which one was I going to do next. And I thought, well, gee, "The Old Woman that Lived in a Shoe" is just such a great springboard, you know counting, sorting by different colors. . . . And when I was going through it, I thought, oh no, she fed them without any bread and spanked them all soundly. And I said this is not right, but it's a classic, they'll have to know it. Anyway, I chose not to do it. (video transcript/Class/Mar. 16, 1993)

During class time, Kelly's role tended to be more that of a researcher because she was occupied taking field notes. She interjected something only occasionally, or when I specifically called on her. In the action room she participated more as a coinstructor, taking full responsibility for helping those who dropped in when I was not present, and working collaboratively with me when we both were there. She drew extensively on her personal experiences of being in the course the year before and on the school-based qualitative research she was doing for her MEd monograph. This gave her peer status, and reduced her social distance in ways that I could not. She helped to explain and justify aspects of the work to our students. For example, she shared how she went about doing her project for the course the year before, and how in retrospect the experience contributed to her subsequent work. Her unsolicited examples and attestations helped legitimize my role in the eyes of the students and, as might be expected, made my work easier. Kelly was able to transcend the boundaries between teacher and student, and to provide them with a "referential perspective" (Cazden, 1988, p. 111), a way of understanding and seeing the situation similarly and thereby providing a higher degree of inter-subjectivity.

I, too, used personal anecdotes in our classes to explain and justify things to students. As well, I recounted stories to offer an alternative perspective or to redirect the discussion. These stories were pulled from my early experiences as a classroom teacher, from experiences in other university courses, the university at large, my own graduate work, and my life at home. When I began to examine the data, the use and range of my stories did not surprise me. I knew this was part of my teaching style. What was startling was the frequency and length of my contributions. It raised two serious reservations. One of these was the amount of "air time" (Cazden, 1988) my stories involved. Almost without exception they were twice as long as those of the students. I believe it is through sharing our narratives in relation to others that we define our understandings and ourselves (Bruner, 1986; Cooper, 1995), but I worry about the power differential that the length of my stories implied, the message that as the instructor my stories were more important or valuable.

The other concern was that even though I believed I was attempting to communicate empathy and understanding, as a "perceived expert," my stories could be misconstrued, and make things more difficult for some students. This was corroborated in a discussion about the demands involved in doing a qualitative project. It took place between Ann and Kelly in the action room when I was not present:

Ann: Yeah that's it. Did you guys ever feel . . . did you ever feel overwhelmed when you were doing this (the qualitative inquiry)?
Kelly: Always.
Ann: Well, Lynn said she never did when she did it.
Kelly: Yeah, but Lynn was doing a doctorate after a master's, this is your first course.
Ann: Yeah, I suppose. . . . (video transcript/Action Room/Mar. 2, 1993)

I revisited the portion in the transcripts to which Ann had referred. Interestingly, although the discussion focused on my first experience of doing a qualitative project as a requirement for a course in my doctoral program, nothing in the transcript indicated that I had not been overwhelmed. The story was, rather, about the elation I felt when immersed in qualitative inquiry, and how at the time I felt I had finally found a research "niche" for myself, one that resonated with my epistemological stance. It was apparent I had painted a retrospective, enthusiastic "big picture," and although it was accurate in terms of my feelings for qualitative work, I had failed to reflect the arduousness of the process, particularly the first time around; it did not deal with what Ann, and perhaps others, needed to hear. This is a lesson I have carried with me ever since, although I have not abandoned using stories in my teaching. I believe stories can serve as an instructional scaffold, "a supporting structure to move the learner forward" (Wood, Bruner, & Ross 1980, p. 281). They also provide a way of developing a more personal and "particular landscape of action" (Bruner, 1986, p. 12) than other more conventional instructional strategies, and one to which the students responded positively. One of the students corroborated this when she voiced in our last class her satisfaction with how we shared our personal experiences:

> During the course of my schooling I encountered at least one teacher that I wanted to pour my heart out to, but there was no vehicle with which to dialogue on that level. As well, I went to a school where the undue display of emotion in any form was frowned on. Teachers and pupils were kept at a safe emotional distance from each other. I think that both teachers and students suffered.

Later, when Ann and Debbie were responding to excerpts from the videotapes, and discussing our use of personal experiences in class they said:

Ann: I think personal stories ground everything, for me, anyway.
Debbie: And for me, too. It makes it tangible.

Ann: And context, that's . . .

Debbie: (overlapping) . . . that's meaningful. Again, it, it just makes it. I think it was also a very safe classroom, to be able to do that. (validation interview/July 1994)

I do, however, pay more attention to the frequency and length of my stories, and try to be more aware of the particular context and needs of the listeners.

In spite of the sense of safety, and closeness that developed as a result of our classes together, the interaction still contrasted with that of the action room. This closeness was perhaps due to the smallness of the group, the emphasis on personal sharing (Hollingsworth, 1994), because we were all women (Belenky, Clinchy, Goldberger, & Tarule, 1986), or some combination of these, yet the classes were clearly under my direction. In the action room, however, the students directed the discussions, and Kelly and I stepped back and responded as needed. We still shared personal experiences, and no doubt what occurred in classes spilled over into this work, and vice versa. But the contributions of the students were more frequent and longer. The discussions were student-oriented, and focused on their research projects. And as a result, we were able to learn much more about how this work played out. We learned things in this setting that never would have been apparent in class, such as how much time is needed to revisit ideas discussed in class, how transparent the methodology for inquiry must be made, and how necessary it is to provide spaces for these things to occur. By doing teacher research in a student-oriented inquiry context, I have learned not to gloss over these needs just because students are at the graduate level and have modified my teaching as a result. In some more specific ways, I learned from the work of Ann and Debbie, to which I now turn.

The Collaboration between Ann and Debbie

Ann and Debbie were among the few students who were full-time in the program. They were also the only two that decided to work together even though I had encouraged the whole group to do collaborative projects during our first class, and Kelly had endorsed the notion by explaining how helpful she found working with a peer the previous year. The benefits of collaboration are well known and have long been touted (Lee & Smagorinsky, 2000): gaining from other perspectives, growing cognitively from dissonance, interacting from relatively equal status, sharing some of the workload, and negotiating meaning and understanding. The drawbacks are not articulated as frequently: the extra time and energy required to arrange the work, the potential for conflict, and the possibility that some members of the group will do most of the work while others slack off and reap the benefit of a good grade.

It became apparent, while examining the transcripts of the discussions that took place in the action room, that Ann had experienced some very negative effects of collaboration in another graduate course and had been profoundly

affected by it, vowing never to work in a group again. Ann explained further in
our interview after the course was over:

Ann: Yeah, you [referring to Debbie] were just sitting in the chair and you
            said, "Do you want to do one [a project together]?" I DIDN'T want to do
            one . . . because I had one terrible experience . . . I mean I really learned
            my lesson. And, uh, and then when I went home and told my family
            (that she was going to work with Debbie), they said, "My god, you're
            not going to do that again!" Everybody in the whole family knew what
            I had gone through . . . plus all my friends, because I had bitched a lot.
            (interview, July 4, 1994)

Yet, she ended up with Debbie in what we came to see was a very special
relationship. I decided to examine their collaboration to try to understand what
occurred. It seemed particularly important to do so at a time when increasingly
students are required to work together on assignments both in and out of classes.
Part of this trend in my Faculty of Education may be a response to the increasing
class sizes. More frequently, it is attributed to the benefits of collaborative learning (Dixon-Krauss, 1996), and to the need to mirror the collaborative activity
expected in school classrooms nowadays, also among teachers, administrators,
and their colleagues.

I began by examining all of our interactions with Ann and Debbie in the
action room and selected videotapes from our classes that appeared to be relevant. As mentioned earlier, these tapes were transcribed in their entirety, and
the data categorized using rather general codes to get an initial understanding of
their collaborative process (Bogdan & Biklen, 1992). The more refined patterns
that emerged over time became much more meaningful when Ann and Debbie's
perceptions were included, the ones they expressed during the long, subsequent,
retrospective interview and when they responded to the videotaped excerpts.

I approached this interview as an entity, and after several "close readings"
began unitizing the data and assigning code names and rules of inclusion for the
resulting categories (Maykut & Morehouse, 1994). I attempted to account for all
the pieces of the text by assigning everything to some category, allowing, but not
paying too much attention at this time, to overlapping segments. When I could,
I used insider (emic) terms for code names. Initially the categories tended to be
more descriptive. Later in the process I was able to collapse them under broader,
more conceptual ones. For example, codes such as "good vibes," "before class
chat," "chance encounter," and "in-class talk" all became part of a category called
"affinity" (see below). The results of this exercise were then juxtaposed with Ann
and Debbie's reflective logs, their drafts and final submission of their inquiry
project, and their preparation for a conference presentation. All of this helped to
fine-tune the analysis.

What emerged was a collaborative process comprising three phases. The collaboration occurred in part because I had encouraged everyone to work together

on the inquiry-oriented tasks (the qualitative research projects) to produce a joint product. What ultimately occurred between Ann and Debbie, however, showed evidence of other elements at work.

The first two phases took place quickly during the first night of the course, but were crucial as they served to "seal" their agreement to work together. And although the possibility always existed to reverse this arrangement, time, investment of energy, and perhaps inherent expectations (both theirs and mine) mitigated against this.

In phase I, the phenomenon that emerged I labeled "collaborative searching." It included a sense of "affinity," "comfort," and "low stakes." It became apparent that both Ann and Debbie felt an immediate, unconscious affinity for each other. This was initiated when by chance they met in the corridor and chatted just before class. Right away, they recognized similarities between themselves as each had been away from teaching for some time. Debbie explained this during the retrospective interview:

Debbie: I was talking to you before class started and you [Ann] said, "Oh no, I'm not you know. I was a teacher 22 years ago in PEI [Prince Edward Island] and this is what I do, and I'm taking these courses for fun." And I thought, oh, then I can be here, too. I'm sure that's what it was. It was like all of a sudden (pause), okay then, she's doing this. I can do this. This will be great fun. And I just relaxed, well, relaxed (pause), as much as you can relax for a first class. (validation interview, July 4, 1994)

During this encounter, and subsequently during discussion the night of the first class, they also felt intuitively comfortable with each other. They concluded because it was so early on in the course that the stakes involved in collaborative work were relatively low, as Ann explained:

Ann: That's one important thing. And I thought I'd get with her. Now, I don't know where that came from. It just felt that she was comfortable, she wasn't putting on airs. Some people put all this bull that they know everything, and on and on (pause), that you just feel like saying, "I don't want to work with them." . . . And it looked like someone looking for someone right at the beginning, that was the first class, before anything was even mentioned about anything. (validation interview, July 4, 1994)

Their strategy for coming together occurred during break time when by chance they were both looking for some materials in my office. This second phase I labeled "collaborative affiliation." During this period, they "weighed the odds" and "traded off" the advantages and disadvantages of working together and agreed to collaborate, and as time would demonstrate, without the loss of their individual identities. They realized because they were not teaching, neither of them had a potential setting for their qualitative inquiry projects and so they "seized the moment" to make a tentative agreement to work together. I had indicated earlier in class that I knew a teacher in a central location who might be willing to make her classroom available for a project. Ann was more tentative because of her previous experience mentioned earlier, but the agreement remained:

Debbie: It was, you know . . . but we ended being there and just seized the moment. And I said, "Ann, would you like to do this with me?"

Ann: (jumping in). I said, "Yeah, it'd be a good idea, I'll think about it." (validation interview, July 4, 1994)

It would seem, under conditions where collaboration is encouraged as part of an educational task, that early in the process there is an unconscious searching and sizing up activity that occurs. Images, impressions, and interactions are retrieved and then juxtaposed to weigh the merits of entering a collaborative working relationship. In this case, Ann and Debbie sized up the situation, seized the moment, and a tentative agreement was made. It indicates that informal and implicit interactions and behaviors appear to play at least as important a role as the more formal and explicit ones in making decisions and taking actions. This illustrates how complex the collaborative process is, and the need for educators to give more thought to how collaborative tasks are assigned in order to avoid compromising the cognitive advantages touted by Vygotsky, Piaget, Bruner, and others (Lee & Smagorinsky, 2000). Things to consider might be when, and how collaborative groups should be formed, what role, if any, the teacher should play in forming groups, what size groups should be, and what kinds of activities are best suited to collaborative work (Butler-Kisber, 1988). Further, it suggests the need to allow more time for collaborative work to get under way. If this preliminary dimension is as important as it was for two adults, one wonders about the implications for younger participants, in terms of both preservice students, and those in elementary and high schools.

I labeled the third phase in the process "collaborative negotiation." This was the interaction and communication that transpired between them, from the time the collaboration was agreed upon until the work was completed. The data revealed that this period was an ongoing process of negotiation. The process was bolstered by the high degree of affinity they had for each other, the supportive reciprocity they exhibited, and the high level of trust they built. This reciprocity was manifested in many ways. For example, they were always quick to jump in and respond positively to bolster the other, or to underscore the other's strengths. Yet this was done in a very honest and direct way. There was never any sense of insincerity. An example of this occurred when we were discussing some of the frustration that occurred when they were trying to write their paper. In fact, they became so attuned to each other that they regularly completed each other's thoughts without a pause in the conversation. Ann and Debbie explained after they had viewed an excerpt of videotape from the action room:

Ann: I felt, no I don't mind her cutting [portions of the paper], but I wasn't quite sure why she was cutting.

Lynn: I see.

Ann: I didn't mind her cutting at all, but I knew, I knew, yeah, I had just written everything I could think of, and that's usually what I do when I go back . . . I don't think we were focusing on the question at that point. We were . . .

Debbie: (overlapping) No we were still scrambling.

Ann: We were working on the background. We were looking to get the literature stuff.

Debbie: Yes . . .

Ann: . . . to get, uh . . .

Debbie: . . . the lit review done . . .

Ann: . . . and all that stuff in . . . but I had enough stuff I could have put in, but I put half of it in 'cause you figured we'll just do some of it and then go right to the question. And that made sense, too 'cause there was so much to do, you know?

Debbie: But that's where I really drew on your expertise 'cause I really didn't know what a lit review was or how you did it, and you were really good at that. You said, "This is what we do." You knew how to do it! That was the important thing. (interview, July 4, 1994)

According to John-Steiner and Meehan (2000), a large percentage of co-constructed sentences in interaction signify that collaborators are deeply engaged in joint thinking. Co-construction was a common occurrence between Debbie and Ann throughout the videotapes, suggesting joint thinking was an integral part of their collaboration.

Their project was a qualitative inquiry about how a Grade 5 classroom teacher implemented language arts with her students. They went to the school together to collect the data (field notes and interviews with the teacher and some students), and conducted the analysis collaboratively, informally in the drive to and from the school, and more formally in each others' homes, and then cowrote the resulting research paper. They spent an enormous amount of time together, probably much more than most students can or will do, and this intensive interaction was not free of tension and frustrations. The data revealed, however, that Ann and Debbie were able to manage such moments by using humor and role delineation, and having a high degree of accessibility to each other. These features of their collaboration enabled them to disagree yet make consensual choices that satisfied each of them.

The videotapes are replete with the laughter and joking that transpired between Ann and Debbie (see Figure 6.3). It was playful and supportive humor, never sarcastic or a form of veiled criticism. Ann and Debbie summed it up very well when they presented their collaborative work (Matthews & Payne, 1993) at a local conference on teacher research with Kelly and me just after the course was over:

Figure 6.3   Debbie and Ann at work.

The third plus of this experience has been the sheer enjoyment and fun we have had all the way through. For all the frustrations and complaints, there have been as many, and more, moments of laughter, joking pleasure, and yes, fun. I can't remember when I have so much enjoyed working so hard, for something so elusive. This, for me, is learning at its best. (p. 9)

Another example occurred when they were trying to create a concept map with some of their data in an attempt to understand how the expectations and reflective process inherent in the classroom in which they were observing was related to the positive forms and results of evaluation:

Debbie: Oh, I'm going to throw a monkey wrench in all of this. Maybe it's because the teacher expects all these things to happen that she makes that happen. That's what I mean about your starting point.

Ann: Oh, okay.

Debbie: And then you can just say, you can say it just goes around in circles.

Ann: I like that.

Debbie: Now that's another way of looking at that. Because she EXPECTS these things to happen and part of her expectations are that kids enjoy themselves, and there's mutual respect, THEN she creates a situation which is all of this (pointing to the diagram).

Ann: Oh God, Debbie please, I had it all in order.

Debbie: No, we still somewhere have to, like, make a break and start it.

Ann: Yeah, but we can always say we're not sure which comes first, the chicken or the egg (everyone laughs and for several more minutes there is continued repartee about the chicken and egg). (videotape transcript, Action Room, Mar. 30, 1993)

The goodwill between them and the work they were doing overshadowed any tensions, frustrations, and disagreements. When these did occur, they seemed to naturally dissipate into moments of humor and laughter.

The tacit sense of affinity they felt during their first encounters played out into very tangible and complementary roles. They acknowledged during their research process how, when collecting their data, Debbie had situated herself physically where she was able to focus on the global aspects of what was going on in the classroom, whereas Ann located herself where she could record the more particular aspects of events and interactions. This occurred spontaneously, and once they realized they had assumed these roles they decided consciously to switch places for a day and felt quite frustrated with the experience:

Debbie: In the car coming home, and we said, "It was awful. I want to go back to my place tomorrow."

Ann: I couldn't get my structures. I couldn't get everything . . . I couldn't get the tidbits . . . your place was more global. (interview, July 4, 1994)

This theme carried over into their writing in which they referred to each other as the "slasher" and the "embellisher." Debbie wanted to get at the "big picture," whereas Ann preferred to deal with the details first. Their complementary strengths were positive forces in their relationship, and enhanced rather than detracted from their work. And, as they indicated later, this had helped to scaffold what they were doing (Hogan & Pressley, 1997):

Ann: I did try to write like her in some ways . . . I tried, I got, at times I'd read it out loud to myself, and uh, I knew when I was sounding more like me and trying to sound more like her in a way.

Debbie: Even the reflection notes, when we'd cook them up, and, and give them to each other, what Ann would do is she would start citing these people. And I was so impressed, I thought, I started trying to do it. (interview, July 4, 1994)

In addition to their reflective time together traveling to and from their research site, they were frequently in touch by telephone, and spent a lot of time working together in each other's homes. This no doubt contributed to how they were able to develop their complementary roles.

Discussion

In previous work with young children (Butler-Kisber, 1988), I discovered that, in most educational tasks, there are very legitimate reasons why collaborative groups should not exceed three or four in number. Interactions and negotiations become too complex, the work takes longer, and certain group members seek to dominate the group. The positive collaboration between Ann and Debbie suggests that group size and task also deserve attention when adults collaborate, and that complicated tasks, such as those involved in conducting an inquiry, merit small groups or pairs. The process of their collaboration in conjunction with their inquiry had reciprocal benefits for them. They benefited from each other's strengths, perspectives, and support. And although not within the scope of this paper, Ann found that she discovered the ability to use her own insights and voice in the process (Butler-Kisber, 2002), something she had never been able to do before in her graduate courses. Yet the work required an extensive and intensive amount of time, energy, and ongoing negotiation. In addition, it required the extra three hours per week in the action room, and a research assistant to support the process. Overall, the experience had excellent rewards for everyone involved, but it had high costs, too.

The understandings I gleaned from closely examining the collaboration between Ann and Debbie have made me rethink when, where, and how I suggest or encourage collaboration when students are involved in inquiry assignments such as research projects. I now make explicit the advantages and disadvantages of collaboration by sharing some of these examples with my students so they can make informed and careful choices when they are embarking on a collaborative journey. More generally, the work with Ann and Debbie has helped me see the need to approach all other classroom processes more metacognitively (Zimmerman, 1995). My original constructivist leanings have developed more fully (Walker, 1995), and I believe as a result, have enhanced my teaching.

Cochran-Smith and Lytle (1993) have defined teacher research as:

> Systematic, intentional inquiry by teachers about their own school and classroom work . . . ordered ways of gathering and recording information, documenting experiences inside and outside of classrooms, and making some kind of written record. (Teacher research) . . . is an activity that is planned rather than spontaneous (and) . . . stems from or generates questions and reflects teachers' desires to make sense of their experiences . . . (pp. 23–24)

I have suggested that initially I began my teacher research in an effort to better understand my practice, and to model what I was advocating my students should do. I hoped that a deeper understanding of what was transpiring in my classes would help me to find ways of becoming more inquiry and constructivist oriented within the constraints of university classes. As well, I have outlined some of the costs involved for both students and the instructor in implementing this kind of teaching and learning. I learned firsthand in my graduate classroom context, for example, about the impact of stories for establishing a sense of community and safety. This established a positive tone for inquiry, but also revealed the power differential that exists between the stories of the teacher and those of the students. As a result, I am more sensitive about balancing the number and length of stories that I inject into the situation, and careful that because of my distance from these experiences, my stories do not gloss over details that could be useful to students. I also discussed the serious demands on time, energy, and interpersonal skills that are necessary to implement inquiry approaches, particularly collaborative ones.

In the context of the action room where, for an additional three hours per week, students could get help with their qualitative inquiries, I learned about the very interesting collaborative process that developed between Ann and Debbie. I became aware of their process in much more detail than would have been possible in the corresponding graduate class, even though the class size was small (there were only nine students). Part of this was because I was attending to fewer people at one time. But I believe that much more importantly it was because they were conducting an inquiry. A student-oriented, constructivist curriculum engages the learners in meaningful inquiry, puts the responsibility for the learning in the hands of the learners, and requires the teacher to step back and act as facilitator. In that role, I followed their leads, and listened attentively to their discussions. This allowed me to examine their process in a much more detailed and thorough way. I was able to not only understand their collaborative process more deeply, but could also see clearly the advantages and disadvantages of working together, and have become much more sensitive about how, when, and why I encourage collaborative work. The detail and depth of my understanding of what transpired has helped me to change my practice in positive ways. It has built action into reflection, and vice versa, in subtle and not so subtle ways.

Overall, I would say I have become even more student-oriented by involving students in various kinds of inquiry tasks, by paying attention to collaboration as discussed earlier, and by stepping back and watching, listening, documenting, and facilitating without abdicating my responsibility as the instructor. I have discovered that student-oriented teacher research that documents and reflects on the teacher's actions, and is conducted around student inquiry such as described here, necessarily includes participants and provides the kind of insights that engender actions that make a difference in classroom teaching and learning. Student-oriented teacher research forces the researcher into a participatory and self-critical stance (Weiler, 1988). It permits a closer and deeper examination of what is transpiring in an educational context because the focus is on the students. This results in richer understandings that foster a more critical stance and open up the possibilities for action and change.

References

Belenky, M. F., Clinchy, B. M., Goldberger, N. R., & Tarule, J. M. (1986). *Women's ways of knowing*. New York: Basic Books.

Berthoff, E. (1987). The teacher as researcher. In D. Goswami & P. Stillman (Eds.), *Reclaiming the classroom: Teacher research as an agency for change*. Upper Montclair, NJ: Boynton/Cook.

Bogdan, R. C., & Biklen, S. (1992). *Qualitative research for education: An introduction to theory and methods* (2nd ed.). Needham Heights, MA: Allyn & Bacon.

Bruner, J. S. (1986). *Actual minds, possible worlds*. Cambridge, MA: Harvard University Press.

Butler-Kisber, L. (1988). *Peer collaboration around educational tasks: A classroom ethnography*. Unpublished doctoral dissertation, Graduate School of Education, Harvard University, Cambridge, MA.

Butler-Kisber, L. (1991). Teaching and administration: Making connections. *McGill Journal of Education, 26*(2), 103–110.

Butler-Kisber, L. (1997). The practical: Classroom literacy through stories, questions and action. In V. Froese (Ed.), *Language across the curriculum* (pp. 183–213). Toronto, ON: Harcourt Brace.

Butler-Kisber, L. (2002). Artful portrayals in qualitative inquiry: The road to found poetry and beyond. *Alberta Journal of Education, 47*, 229–239.

Calkins, L. M. (1991). *Living between the lines*. Portsmouth, NH: Heinemann.

Cazden, C. B. (1988). *Classroom discourse: The language of teaching and learning*. Portsmouth, NH: Heinemann.

Cochran-Smith, M., & Lytle, S. (1993). *Inside/outside: Teacher research and knowledge*. New York: Teachers College Press.

Cooper, J. E. (1995). The role of narrative and dialogue in constructivist leadership. In L. Lambert, D. Walker, D. P. Zimmerman, J. E. Cooper, M. Dale Lambert, M. E. Gardner, & P. J. Ford Slack (Eds.), *The constructivist leader* (pp. 121–133). New York: Teachers College Press.

Corsaro, W. A. (1979). *Friendship and peer culture in the early years*. Norwood, NJ: Ablex.

Dixon-Krauss, L. (1996). *Vygotsky in the classroom: Mediated literacy instruction and assessment*. White Plains, NY: Longman.

Edelsky, C., Altwerger, B., & Flores, B. (1991). *Whole language: What's the difference?* Portsmouth, NH: Heinemann.

Erickson, F., & Wilson, J. (1982). *Sights and sounds of life in schools: A resource guide to film and videotape for research and education*. Ann Arbor: University of Michigan, Institute for Research on Teaching, College of Education.

Fogarty, R. (1999). Architects of the intellect. *Educational Leadership, 57*(3), 76–78.

Ford Slack, P. J. (1995). Reflections on community: Understanding the familiar in the heart of the stranger. In L. Lambert, D. Walker, D. P. Zimmerman, J. E. Cooper, M. Dale Lambert, M. E. Gardner, & P. J. Ford Slack (Eds.), *The constructivist leader* (pp. 159–170). New York: Teachers College Press.

Fosnot, C. (1992). Constructing constructivism. In T. M. Duffy & D. H. Jonassen (Eds.), *Constructivism and the technology of instruction: A conversation* (pp. 167–176). Hillsdale, NJ: Erlbaum.

Gardner, H. (1983). *Frames of mind: The theory of multiple intelligences*. New York: Basic Books.

Gardner, H. (2000). *Intelligence reframed: Multiple intelligences for the 21st century*. New York: Basic Books.

Goswami, D., & Stillman, P. (Eds.). (1987). *Reclaiming the classroom: Teacher research as an agency for change.* Upper Montclair, NJ: Boynton/Cook.

Graves, D. H., & Sunstein, B. S. (Eds.). (1992). *Portfolio portraits.* Portsmouth, NH: Heinemann.

Hogan, K., & Pressley, M. (1997). *Scaffolding student learning: Instructional approaches and issues.* Cambridge, MA: Brookline Books.

Hollingsworth, S. (1994). *Teacher research and urban literacy education: Lessons and conversations in a feminist key.* New York: Teachers College Press.

John-Steiner, V. P., & Meehan, T. M. (2000). Creativity and collaboration in knowledge construction. In C. D. Lee & P. Smagorinsky (Eds.), *Vygotskian perspectives on literacy research: Constructing meaning through collaborative inquiry* (pp. 31–48). Cambridge, UK: Cambridge University Press.

Lather, P. (1986). Research as praxis. *Harvard Educational Review, 56,* 257–277.

Lee, C. D., & Smagorinsky, P. (Eds.). (2000). *Vygotskian perspectives on literacy research: Constructing meaning through collaborative inquiry.* Cambridge, UK: Cambridge University Press.

Matthews, A., & Payne, D. (1993, April). *Integrating research into everyday classroom settings: Students' perspectives.* Paper presented at the Annual Springboards Language Arts Conference, Montreal, QC.

Maykut, P., & Morehouse, R. (1994). *Beginning qualitative research: A philosophical and practical guide.* London: Falmer.

Perkins, D. N. (1999). The many faces of constructivism. *Educational Leadership, 57,* 6–11.

Schön, D. A. (1983). *The reflective practitioner: How professionals think in action.* New York: Basic Books.

Schön, D. A. (1987). *Educating the reflective practitioner: Towards a new design for teaching and learning in the professions.* San Francisco: Jossey-Bass.

Seidman, I. (1998). *Interviewing as qualitative research: A guide for researchers in education and the social sciences* (2nd ed.). New York: Teachers College Press.

Tannen, D. (1984). *Conversational style: Analyzing talk among friends.* Norwood, NJ: Ablex.

Walker, D. (1995). The preparation of constructivist leaders. In L. Lambert, D. Walker, D. P. Zimmerman, J. E. Cooper, M. Dale Lambert, M. E. Gardner, & P. J. Ford Slack (Eds.), *The constructivist leader* (pp. 171–189). New York: Teachers College Press.

Weiler, K. (1988). *Women teaching for change: Gender, class and power.* South Hadley, MA: Bergin & Garvey.

Willinsky, J. (1990). *The new literacy: Redefining reading and writing in the schools.* New York: Routledge.

Wood, D., Bruner, J. S., & Ross, G. (1980). The role of tutoring in problem-solving. *Journal of Child Psychology and Psychiatry, 17,* 89–100.

Zimmerman, D. P. (1995). The linguistics of leadership. In L. Lambert, D. Walker, D. P. Zimmerman, J. E. Cooper, M. Dale Lambert, M. E. Gardner, & P. J. Ford Slack (Eds.), *The constructivist leader* (pp. 104–120). New York: Teachers College Press.

7

White Water during Inquiry Learning: Understanding the Place of Disagreements in the Process of Collaboration

MARION A. BARFURTH
University of Ottawa

BRUCE M. SHORE
McGill University

Teacher:	Did you do it [demolish it] to improve it or . . . ?
Patricia:	No, because when we tried it with the motor, the motor wasn't strong enough to turn our big gear. So we had to make all of our gears smaller.
Jeff:	It's no harder to turn this [picks up axle with a large gear on it] than it is to turn this [points to what Patricia has in her hand].
Patricia:	Yes, it is easier to. Jeff it is easier to turn [Jeff cuts her off]
Jeff:	Patricia, is it harder to turn this [turns axle with the large gear in his hand] or this [turns axle with the medium gear that Patricia has installed on invention]. What's the difference? There's no difference [turning the two axles]
Patricia:	No, there is no difference between this and this, but for this turning this [puts the large gear up against the medium gear] there are more spikes to turn than for this [points to medium gear] turning this [points to small gear at end of axle].
Jeff:	That's not true though, because that's about half and that's [pause 2 seconds]. This [points to medium gear] has twelve on it and this had twenty-four.
Patricia:	Stop. Jeff stop.
Jeff:	GRRRR . . . [making a growling sound]

In this chapter, we will take a very close look at what happens in a classroom in which inquiry learning is combined with emerging robotic-like technology designed to support scientific investigation. Modeled on scientists engaging in scientific problem solving and thinking, inquiry learning is recognized for its potential impact on the development of scientific understanding. However, the actual implementation of inquiry learning in the elementary school classroom, as we will see, can lead to the emergence of some nontraditional and unexpected learning processes. The more we understand about learning from a combined social interaction and individual cognition perspective, the better positioned we are to improve design, educate teachers, and support learners' development of scientific understanding.

Research has begun to show that the active and engaging process that accompanies inquiry learning is highly effective in developing scientific understanding (Bransford, Brown, & Cocking, 2000; White & Frederiksen, 1998). In addition to our knowledge about inquiry learning, emerging educational technologies and tools are providing new contexts in which scientific understanding can be developed.

Science educators and researchers both recognize that the implementation of inquiry learning in classrooms creates unique opportunities for learning, opportunities that may include working on current and authentic science problems rather than textbook problems, working with real and sometimes messy data, and working with others to solve complex problems. Not only are children encouraged to learn through an active process, they often work in collaboration with others. The word "collaboration" typically suggests the notion of harmony. However, when classroom tasks require shared thinking and effort, the occurrence of disagreement with respect to understanding and other stages in learning become par for the course.

Combining peer collaboration with inquiry learning into classroom-based activities opens the possibilities to witnessing and understanding new learning processes that might be quite distinct from traditional classroom behavior and learning. As this chapter demonstrates, from the surface, children's disagreements can be seen as alarming and unproductive in a classroom context and a barrier to inquiry-driven learning, but, when examined closely, they may in fact be extremely productive and a wellspring for collaboration.

Collaborative Inquiry, Cognition, and Learning
Collaborative inquiry is often implemented in the classroom with plentiful guidelines available to teachers on the various objectives, stages, and "how to" information (National Research Council, 2000). Despite a well-planned lesson, the processes that children actually undertake may be unlike those that have been described in these teacher's manuals. Learning events such as disagreement, when unexpected, can be quite unnerving and even lead to the teacher stopping the collaborative process altogether. Hence, the more we truly understand about the many different forms learning can take, the better position we are in to scaffold the development of genuine scientific understanding.

A good understanding of the learning processes in learner-directed activities such as inquiry learning is important in order to succeed at the implementation stage in the classroom. Add collaboration with peers during inquiry learning, call it collaborative inquiry, and now the puzzle just got larger, and the number of unexpected possibilities and tangents just grew. One such unexpected possibility is children disagreeing over their scientific beliefs and understandings. And, yet, from a science-education perspective, it is exactly these overt expressions of beliefs and understandings about science that can lead to authentic learning and change. The more one understands substantiated disagreements and is able to identify if there is, in fact, a constructive role for these, the more equipped one is to support collaborative inquiry. This is not to say, however, that all collaborative inquiry necessitates the presence of overt disagreement.

The active and engaging processes that accompany inquiry learning are highly effective in developing scientific understanding (Bransford et al., 2000; White & Frederiksen, 1998). In addition, emerging educational technologies are providing new contexts and tools that support the inquiry learning process both in and beyond the classroom. Examples of these contexts include the use of real science data shared over the Internet or what Feldman, Konold, and Coulter (2000) called "network science" (p. 5).

Much of the research on inquiry learning has focused on teaching and instruction for how to implement inquiry learning into the classroom (Schmidt, 1999; VanFossen & Shiveley, 1997), how to manage the classroom (Looi, 1999; Pappas, 2000), the role of technology (Edelson, Gordin, & Pea, 1999; Maor & Taylor, 1995), teacher questioning (Roth, 1996), and school administration issues around inquiry learning (Emihovich & Battaglia, 2000). Research on children's learning processes that occur during inquiry learning has begun to emerge. These studies address learning processes that include conceptualizing questions, constructing hypotheses, and reaching consensus on solutions (Lonka, Hakkarainen, & Sintonen, 2000; Bevevino, Dengel, & Adams, 1999) and social dimensions of learning (Hodson, 1999).

From a psychological perspective, the role of shared thinking on cognitive development is addressed in both Piagetian theory and the cultural-historical approaches inspired by Vygotsky and his followers. In her chapter, "Cognition as a collaborative process," Rogoff (1998) reviewed the theoretical roots and contemporary research in this important area. The analytical framework developed and used for the disagreement data reported in this chapter was designed using the distinction suggested by Tudge and Rogoff (1989) between intersubjectivity (a process that takes place across people), later called a social move, and perspective-taking (individual processes working on socially provided information), later called a cognitive move.

Collaborative Inquiry in the Classroom
Common images of classroom learning typically depict children working individually at their desks or tables or doing small group work huddling around a

project or some other shared form of activity. Collaborative inquiry typically is construed as convergent, as cooperation, everyone being supportive to each other. It is rarely reported that children disagree or argue over their understanding of and beliefs about the issue or task at hand. However, powerful learning takes place when ideas and wills collide and push at each other, not always politely at a given moment. When working on a real problem during which one is truly struggling to construct meaning or find a solution, the process can be quite intellectually stimulating and challenging all at once. When the solution path is unclear, unknown, and never before seen, however, the process can be quite challenging, messy and not always successful (Zack & Graves, 2001).

It may be that children do not get or do not take advantage of opportunities to express, defend and discuss their true scientific beliefs and understandings in the classroom. Both children and adults tend to carefully guard their scientific beliefs to avoid the embarrassment of revealing misconceptions or misunderstandings. However, developmental psychology suggests that cognitive conflict, assimilation, and accommodation (Piaget, 1977) as well as social interaction, language, and cognitive artifacts (Vygotsky, 1978) are all important pieces to building understanding and conceptual change.

Science Education and Inquiry

The importance of learning science through inquiry has been recognized by the science-education community as can be seen in *Inquiry and the National Science Education Standards* (National Research Council, 2000). By design, inquiry learning fosters critical thinking, problem solving, analysis, and many other forms of higher-order thinking skills (Byers & Fitzgerald, 2002). During inquiry learning, distinctive teaching and learning processes are fostered. For example, teaching during inquiry learning may focus on teaching students' metacognitive (self-monitoring, planning, etc.) and higher-order thinking skills (analysis, synthesis, critical thinking, and problem solving) (Manconi, Aulls, & Shore, in this volume). Although advances have been made with respect to the impact of using inquiry learning in the area of science education, further investigation on the actual processes that occur with this approach is critical to successful implementation in the classroom context. The more we know about how learners learn during inquiry, the better positioned we shall be to inform teachers about what to expect and how to support the learner.

The School Setting

You open the door and before you have time to take a breath, you know that you have entered a different kind of school. The walls are covered with children's projects and artwork, there is a humming sound that fills the large entrance hall and corridor leading up to the classrooms. We are in a private, progressive, nondenominational elementary school. It is located in Montreal, Quebec, with instruction being done in both English and French. Different subjects are taught in different languages and vary by grade level.

Following my registration at the front office, I (Barfurth) move up a floor to where the classrooms are located and see a level of activity that resembles a beehive. With an eggbeater in hand, the science teacher is leading a discussion on the different and observable components of simple machines. The spoken language of the science teacher is French and that of the computer teacher is English.

Surveying the classroom, there are 25 children between the ages of 9 and 10 years. For this particular activity, the children have been reorganized into a combined (about half-and-half) fourth and fifth grade group. Dividing and recombining homeroom groups is done throughout the week to encourage collaboration and friendships across different age levels. The children are sitting or standing around small tables and chairs in clusters of four and five. On the tables there is a container with LEGO brand construction blocks, gears, and pulleys. In addition, each table has a small electric motor, some light sensors, and a platform on which to mount their construction. The children have been asked to invent a simple machine that demonstrates the principle of mechanical advantage using the LEGO construction material. They are instructed that when they are ready, they can test their invention using the motor and program it using a modified version of Logo that has commands to control the current to a set of wires and read information from light sensors.

The children have been assigned into groups of four under the guidance of the homeroom and computer teachers. Jeff and Patricia (all names have been changed to preserve anonymity) are in grade five and are described by the teacher as both being bright, verbal, and assertive children. The two Grade 4 children, Kenny and Filene, are described by the teacher as gentle, very attentive in group work, and as having good verbal ability. The Grade 4 children were selected on the basis of the teacher's judgment that they could "stand up" for themselves when working with Jeff and Patricia.

It is now several weeks into my observing and video capturing of one group of four children inventing, designing, building, and testing a structural robotic invention that incorporates and illustrates the principle of mechanical advantage. Close up and well within the intimate boundaries of this group of children's learning space, Patricia and Jeff were working with Kenny and Filene. The following disagreement was recorded:

Patricia: And then 'cause. You know what we could do, we could put a big gear here like another big gear.
Kenny: No, it will slow it down.
Filene: We don't have any big gears.
Kenny: Plus we don't have it. Plus it will ooh.
Patricia: We could put the small one attached here [points to first axle large gear] and here [looks like the second axle medium gear].
Kenny: [Playing with a LEGO chain.] But the big gear, if we put a big gear it will go much slower cause the big gear ahh is much slower. If we add

a big gear here [points to third axle area] it won't go as fast Filene. Believe me.

Filene: Oh because this one [nods her head]. I get it.

Kenny: No because the big gears are slower. Some girls are just [he is cut off by Patricia]

Patricia: [sliding a fourth axle onto the invention with the small gear on the inside] No [to Kenny], but this one [points to small gear attached to the big gear] will go even faster.

Not Your Typical Classroom Discourse!

The exchanges are not the kind of discourse typical to a fourth or fifth grade classroom. In fact, in a seven-week observation period while working "collaboratively" on the mechanical advantage task, 24 disagreements were identified with this one group of four children. The unprecedented nature and frequency of such discourse invites many questions for teachers, school administrators, parents, and researchers. For example, what should one think about these heated exchanges occurring in the classroom? Should they be stopped at the onset or can one find indicators of learning despite the surface appearances? If so, what could these indicators tell us about a collaborative inquiry learning process for learning science that we did not already know or have access to?

While trying to unearth the scientific concept of mechanical advantage, the children had many heated episodes in which their scientific beliefs and understandings were brought out into the open and challenged, defended, modified, or confirmed. Not unlike adults struggling to build new understanding and change in perspectives, these children were going head-to-head with their beliefs and understandings of a complex notion that very often led to overt disagreement and evidence seeking.

Conceptual Framework

At the core of the conceptual framework used to analyze the disagreements is the distinction between intersubjectivity and perspective-taking (Tudge & Rogoff, 1989). Intersubjectivity has been used from a Vygotskian perspective as the process that takes place across people, whereas perspective-taking (from a Piagetian perspective) is an individual process working on socially provided information (for more detail see Rogoff, 1998). These distinctions between intersubjectivity and perspective-taking were transposed into the analytical framework developed and used to explore the children's disagreements. Specifically, the analytical framework developed used two important and distinctive perspectives on the same action, that of *social move* and of the *cognitive move* (Barfurth, 1994).

Evidence of Collaboration

The data used in this study were collected in the classroom over a two-month period. During the assigned computer and science periods, the children worked

Table 7.1 List of Social and Cognitive Moves

Social Moves	Cognitive Moves
Antecedent	Initiate a topic
Opposition	Add a new aspect
Resolution	Integrate others position
Consensus	Modify content
	Maintain same position
	Ask for explanations or clarifications
	Quit or take an observatory role

twice a week in small group collaborative work, designing, building, and programming a robotics project that incorporated the notion of mechanical advantage. The principal data-collection tool was a video camera placed on a tripod next to the group of four children. In addition to the camera, an extending microphone was placed on the table to better capture the conversation between the children.

In order to examine the transcription of 24 disagreements collected during the two-month period that the children were working on the task, a coding schema was developed to look at each utterance from two perspectives described earlier, that is, the social move perspective and the cognitive move perspective (Barfurth, 1994). The social move perspective examined the discourse as a pattern between individuals. The social perspective emulated the main structural features of a disagreement used in the sociolinguistic tradition (Eisenberg & Garvey, 1981), namely, antecedent, opposition, resolution, and outcome. The cognitive move perspective allowed the data to be examined looking at the individual processes working on socially provided information, that is, what an individual decides to do in light of what others have said. The social and cognitive moves identified in this study are listed in Table 7.1.

Table 7.2 provides an example of the coding of a disagreement in the last illustration from the social move and cognitive move perspectives. Each utterance is assigned two codes. This was done for all 24 of the disagreements and then used for the analysis.

The analysis then looked at all these variables from three different perspectives: individually, in parallel, and then sequenced.

Independently: Reveals the composition of the disagreements from either a social or cognitive move perspective.

In parallel: Reveals the cognitive moves taking place during the social moves or vice versa.

Sequentially: Reveals the interaction between the cognitive and social moves.

The children's social and cognitive moves during the 24 disagreements were examined independently. The results for the social moves (Figure 7.1) revealed that the children were in fact disagreeing. The high number of occurrences

Table 7.2　Disagreement Coding of Social and Cognitive Moves

Utterance	Social Move	Cognitive Move
0. Patricia: and then cause. You know what we could do, we could put a big gear here like another big gear	Antecedent	Initiate a topic
1. Kenny: No, it will slow it down.	Initial Opposition	Add new information
2. Filene: We don't have any big gears	Resolution	Add new information
3. Kenny: Plus we don't have it. Plus it will ooh.	Opposition-asserts alternative position	Modify position
4. Patricia: We could put the small one attached here [points to first axle, large gear] and here [looks like the second axle medium gear]	Resolution	Add new information
5. Kenny: [Playing with black LEGO chain] But the big gear, if we put a big gear it will go much slower cause the big gear ahh is much slower. If we add a big gear here [points to third axle area] it won't go as fast Filene. Believe me!	Opposition-asserts alternative position	Add new information
6. Filene: Oh! Because this one [nods her head] I get it!	Resolution	Integrate other's position
7. Kenny: No, because the big gears are slower. Some girls are just//	Opposition-asserts alternative position	Maintains same position
8. Patricia: [Is sliding a fourth axle onto the invention with the small gear on the inside] No [to K], but this one [points to small gear] attached to the big gear will go even faster.	Outcome	Add new information

reported for the Opposition and Resolution moves reflected an active process between these two categories.

The quantity of contributions to the disagreement was much lower for the fourth grade pair (27% of all utterances during the disagreements) than the fifth graders (73% of all utterances during the disagreements). Also, there was a difference between the grade levels with respect to the total number of Resolution and Opposition moves. Figure 7.1 shows that the fourth-grade children demonstrated more Resolution than Opposition, the opposite of the fifth-grade participants. This difference could simply be a result of the characters of the individual students making up the two pairs. Nonetheless, the overall pattern of contribution to the disagreements revealed that both grade levels were capable of participating in this rather sophisticated and involved process required for complex disagreement.

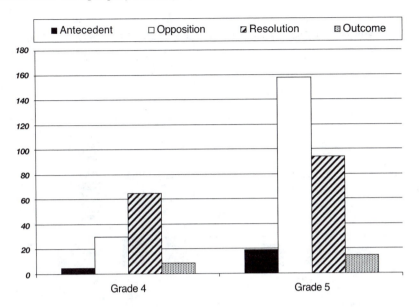

Figure 7.1 Social moves of children in disagreement.

The children used a variety of cognitive moves, although some were used more than others. Although all of the available moves were used by both pairs of children, there was a difference in the frequencies between the two grade levels. This is consistent with the dominance pattern of the fifth-grade pair described earlier. Despite this, and quite interestingly, the graph in Figure 7.2 reveals an overall similar pattern of use of the cognitive moves between the two age levels. For both levels, the two most frequently used were Adding new information (46%) and Maintaining the same position (27%). Adding new information to the disagreement reflected the children's thinking and their active involvement in understanding and finding a solution, cognitive features that every teacher seeks during learning. Some background knowledge about the disagreement process helps to further interpret the cognitive move of maintaining one's position. It does not automatically imply "stubbornness" or "saving-face" on the part of a participant. At times, when the children were putting forth new ideas or understanding that may have been correct, they would still be met with opposition on the part of the other participants. The idea had to be repeated or paraphrased. In theses cases, maintaining one's position was required to make one's point to the group. At times, sheer stubbornness did occur. In a similar vein, the opposite was also possible. New information could be added, the person was not challenged, and therefore did not have to maintain his or her position. Although it went unchallenged, it could also be incorrect.

The collaborative process can be seen further in the use of the other moves that occurred. More specifically the three moves under the heading Integrate other's position, Ask for an explanation, and Modify one's position all suggest very "collaborative" actions on the part of the children during a disagreement.

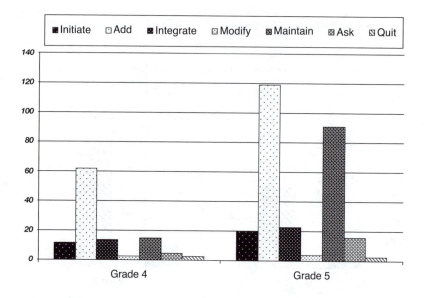

Figure 7.2 Frequency change between Grades 4 and 5.

Combined, they accounted for 17% of the cognitive moves. Their presence suggested that, although the children were disagreeing, they did use cognitive strategies that demonstrated they were learning from each other in constructive ways.

Comparing the individual children's participation, a pattern of a 70 to 30% split between the fifth and fourth grade children was sustained with respect to the overall distribution of the cognitive moves. The fourth grade children had a very low percentage for Maintain position (14%) and a high percentage for Modify one's position (43%) and Integrate other's position (38%). In contrast, the two fifth grade children did a lot of Maintaining of one's position and what they did the least (relative to themselves) was to Modify one's position. From these group differences it appears that, in an overall sense, the fourth grade children's cognitive moves were much more pliable than those of the fifth grade children.

In Parallel

The cognitive moves that took place during the different social moves were examined through direct matching of the coding for each utterance, that is, in parallel.

Not surprisingly, two cognitive moves accounted for 82% of all the cognitive moves during *opposition*. These were *Add new information* and *Maintain the same position* (see Figure 7.3). Looking at these moves in parallel with the social move of *opposition* reveals a lot about the nature of the opposition that took on the form of *Maintaining one's position*. As we have already seen, this could be a very justified strategy. At other times, the opposition meant opposing but included *Adding new information* to the issue at hand. Therefore, the social role of opposition during the disagreements was not just about negation; rather, it was

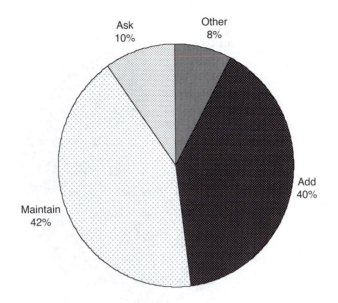

Figure 7.3 Breakdown of cognitive moves during opposition.

elaborate and at times constructive. It played a role in the overall process towards understanding and resolving the issue at hand.

Three cognitive moves accounted for 94% of all the cognitive moves during resolution moves (see Figure 7.4). These were *Add new information* (67%), *Integrate others' position* (14%) and *Maintain the same position* (13%). The remaining 6% were distributed evenly over *Initiate a new topic, Modify your own content,* and *Ask for an explanation.* The use of the cognitive moves during resolution moves as a whole tells us that the children actively sought ways to resolve their disagreements, not only through adding new aspects to the disagreement, but also through more interactive actions such as integrating, modifying, and asking.

The three cognitive moves that took place during the outcomes of the disagreements in descending order of importance were *Maintain the same position* (34%), *Integrate others' position* (22%), and *Add new information* (17%) (Figure 7.5). An interesting balance between maintain and integrate terminate a number of the disagreements. Adding new information at the end of a disagreement is perhaps a little more unexpected. A closer look at the data with respect to this result revealed that two out of the four disagreements coded with this as an outcome were interrupted by an adult intervention and therefore terminated, but not necessarily resolved. The other two involved a shift to a new focus as a result of adding a new property.

Sequentiality
The results reported in this section focus on the sequenced analysis that juxtaposes the social move with the cognitive move and reveals the different sequencing of

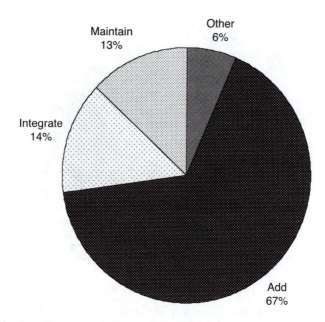

Figure 7.4   Cognitive moves during resolution moves.

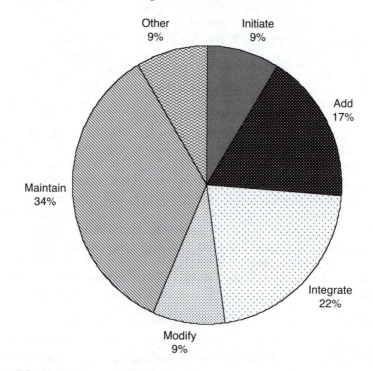

Figure 7.5   Main cognitive moves during outcome.

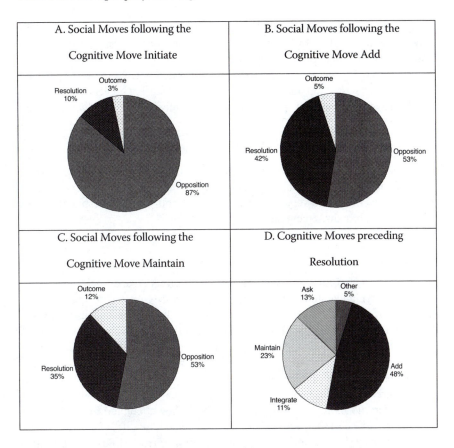

Figure 7.6 Dynamic between social and cognitive moves.

strategies that occurred during the disagreements (Barfurth, 1994). This method originated in the biological sciences and was first adapted in discourse analysis by Eisenberg and Garvey (1981). It allows one to examine events from the perspective of paired sequences, in other words, the number of times that strategy X is followed by strategy Y. In order to do this, the social and cognitive moves were examined from a two-act sequential perspective. This was obtained by forming couples with the sequence of every two events. The purpose of doing this analysis was to investigate whether certain moves incited others during disagreement.

The dynamics between the social moves that follow a cognitive move are both revealing and informative. They provide more information about the collaborative process, while, at the same time, corroborating what has been seen in previous results. Some of the highlights include the three cognitive moves, *Initiate a new topic* (see Figure 7.6-A), *Adding new information* (see Figure 7.6-B), and *Maintaining one's position* (see Figure 7.6-C), followed by opposition 87%, 53%, and 53% of the time, respectively. This suggests that the children were highly engaged in their work and that suggestions were not necessarily immediately integrated. It also confirms the disagreement process seen here from a different perspective than presented earlier.

Figure 7.6-D provides a vivid portrait of the collaborative process as revealed by this kind of sequential analysis. This particular snapshot depicts the cognitive moves that most frequently preceded the social move of *Resolution*. They are *Adding new information* (49%), *Maintain one's position* (23%), *Asking a question* (13%), and *Integrating another's position* (11%). This confirms that during the attempts to resolve the disagreements, the children used a multitude of cognitive strategies that went beyond maintaining one's position to adding, asking, and even integrating what others have proposed. The use of these different cognitive strategies illustrates very legitimate forms of collaboration despite the overt social process of a disagreement.

Discussion

The social and cognitive perspectives provide an effective analytical framework for the further understanding of underlying processes related to collaborative inquiry learning. This leads to the general and heightened anomalous result that disagreements can be viewed as a legitimate form of "collaboration." From a social perspective, it may appear that children are not collaborating, but, from a cognitive perspective, they are in fact working hard at both understanding (learning) and resolving the problem at hand.

Disagreements can be constructive and productive in the learning process. The children did more than oppose each other. They attempted to resolve their oppositions. The children were able to discuss, defend, modify, and actively seek solutions during disagreements. Because this all occurred while on-task, it also demonstrated their active involvement in understanding the scientific concepts at hand during a design task using the robotics material.

The opposition during disagreement was more than negation. Rather, it was elaborate and even constructive negotiation toward achieving the final product— an invention that demonstrated mechanical advantage. The children did not just give in to one another or blindly surrender their own ideas. They insisted on explanation and evidence as they worked on their task. Opposition played a role in the overall process toward understanding and resolving the issue at hand.

Resolution of the disagreements consisted of more than the addition of new information; at times, it also involved more interactive actions among the children. These include integrating other children's ideas, modifying one's own ideas, and asking others for clarification and explanation. All these strategies lead to sound and successful collaborations.

The results also suggest that, in addition to the metacognitive methods promoted in inquiry learning, we also should develop teaching approaches to foster learning through disagreements that perhaps include the teaching and learning of constructive argumentation.

Conclusion

This chapter begins to demystify the negative view that disagreement in the classroom is counterproductive to learning. It raises questions such as: Can the creative solution, the learning, have occurred without the disagreement or conflict? Is the learning better for the conflict? Does the teacher's job shift from avoiding conflict to lighting little fires but teaching the children to stay within certain boundaries of civility that do not impede the benefit of the disagreement? That is a much more demanding teacher task than banning or more gently avoiding conflict.

Effective collaborative inquiry in an elementary school classroom contains what is essentially a contradiction or barrier for many teachers, that is, disagreement. It is interesting that the thesis defense in the medieval university was called the disputation, and that debate is an important element of collegial intellectual life and democratic government. There are other places in our society where we value disagreement—why not the classroom? Do we have to see inquiry in education as a subversive force, not only requiring new skill, but actually requiring a different psychological and social conceptualization of the teacher? Is teaching not a safe, protective, warm, and cozy profession for nurturing people, but might it also demand the selection or education of people who revel in a little intellectual sparring match, who know how to put up the creative dukes and when and how to back off gracefully and say "I learned from you"?

Then there is another level of barrier or surprise in inquiry as central to the curriculum. The teacher needs to have another set of skills that we not think are not taught in any teacher-education curriculum. We already recognize the need to (a) be able to adapt to the selection of subject matter, (b) optimize conditions for successful individual learning, and (c) even, in some cases, help children learn to work together to define and achieve common goals. The missing piece is teaching teachers and children to not avoid disagreement but let it hang out and to deal with it, to enjoy the battle of ideas and wills while learning to do so civilly and without racism, sexism, or ageism. How does that impact on the culture of a school? On the relations among children? On the relations among teachers? On the environment the principal or head teacher endorses and creates between herself or himself and the teachers. How is dissent dealt with? Is it true that if you are not in agreement with us you are against us? These are some of the big lessons and big challenges to making collaborative inquiry work in a classroom.

References

Barfurth, M. A. (1994). *The collaborative process as seen through children's disagreements while learning science.* Unpublished doctoral dissertation in educational psychology, McGill University, Montreal, QC.

Bevevino, M. M., Dengel, J., & Adams, K. (1999). Constructivist theory in the classroom: Internalizing concepts through inquiry learning. *Clearing House, 72,* 275–278.

Bransford, J. D., Brown, A. L., & Cocking, R. R. (2000). *How people learn: Brain, mind, experience, and school.* Washington, DC: National Academy Press.

Byers, A., & Fitzgerald, M. A. (2002). Networking for leadership, inquiry, and systematic thinking: A new approach to inquiry-based learning. *Journal of Science Education and Technology, 11,* 81–91.

Edelson, D. C., Gordin, D. N., & Pea, R. D. (1999). Addressing the challenges of inquiry-based learning through technology and curriculum design. *Journal of the Learning Sciences, 8,* 391–450.

Eisenberg, A. R., & Garvey, C. (1981). Children's use of verbal strategies in resolving conflicts. *Discourse Processes, 4,* 149–170.

Emihovich, C., & Battaglia, C. (2000). Creating cultures for collaborative inquiry: New challenges for school leaders. *International Journal of Leadership in Education, 3,* 225–238.

Feldman, A., Konold, C., & Coulter, B. (2000). *Network science a decade later: The Internet and classroom learning.* Mahwah, NJ: Erlbaum.

Hodson, D. (1999). Building a case for a sociocultural and inquiry-oriented view of science education. *Journal of Science Education and Technology, 8,* 241–249.

Lonka, K., Hakkarainen, K., & Sintonen, M. (2000). Progressive inquiry learning for children: Experiences, possibilities, limitations. *European Early Childhood Education Research Journal, 8,* 7–27.

Looi, C.-K. (1999). Interactive learning environments for promoting inquiry learning. *Journal of Educational Technology Systems, 27,* 3–22.

Maor, D., & Taylor, P. C. (1995). Teacher epistemology and scientific inquiry in computerized classroom environments. *Journal of Research in Science Teaching, 32,* 839–854.

National Research Council (2000). *Inquiry and the national science education standards: A guide for teaching and learning.* Washington, DC: National Academy Press.

Pappas, M. L. (2000). Managing the inquiry learning environment. *School Library of Media Activities Monthly, 16*(7), 27–30.

Piaget, J. (1977). *The development of thought: Equilibration of cognitive structures.* New York: Viking.

Rogoff, B. (1998). Cognition as a collaborative process. In W. Damon (Series Ed.) & D. Kuhn & R.S. Siegler (Vol. Eds.), *Handbook of Child Psychology: Vol. 2. Cognition, perception and language* (5th ed., pp. 679–744). New York: Wiley.

Roth, W.-M. (1996). Teacher questioning in an open-inquiry learning environment: Interactions and student responses. *Journal of Research in Science Teaching, 33,* 709–736.

Schmidt, P. R. (1999). Inquiry and literacy learning in science. *Reading Teacher, 52,* 789–792.

Tudge, J., & Rogoff, B. (1989). Peer influences on cognitive development: Piagetian and Vygotskian perspectives. In M. H. Bornstein & J. S. Bruner (Eds.), *Interaction in human development* (pp. 17–40). Hillsdale, NJ: Erlbaum.

VanFossen, P. J., & Shively, J. M. (1997). Things that make you go "Hmmm . . .": Creating inquiry "problems" in the elementary social studies classroom. *Social Studies, 88,* 71–77.

Vygotsky, L. S. (1978). *Mind in society: The development of higher psychological processes.* Cambridge, MA: Harvard University Press.

White, B. Y., & Frederiksen, J. R. (1998). Inquiry, modeling, and metacognition: Making science accessible to all students. *Cognition and Science, 16,* 90–91.

Zack, V., & Graves, B. (2001). Making mathematical meaning through dialogue: "Once you think of it, the Z minus three seems pretty weird." *Educational Studies in Mathematics, 46,* 229–271.

8

The Embodied Conductor: Concert Pianists, Diaper Dancers, and the Fine Art of Creative Variability in Performance

PHILIP COHEN

Concordia University

> *In vain, the sage with retrospective eye,*
> *would from the apparent what*
> *conclude the why.*

Alexander Pope

Music performance is a creative act. When done well, like learning and teaching at their best in any discipline, it is a form of inquiry, a complex cognitive, intuitive and expressively directed experience supported by well-learned skills, deep knowledge, and an open mind. Too often the musical performer is seen as a direct medium for the composer, but we know that different performers interpret the same composition differently. Differences in performance by the same musician, and differences sometimes created "on the fly," in addition to intentional improvisation, are uncannily similar to inquiry and creative productivity in more familiar school subjects. At the same time, creative variability, especially in musical performance, contains some inherent paradoxes. We shall examine how these contribute to the cultivation of creative variability in real time.

To the theater director and theorist Constantine Stanislavsky, improbable logic is most convincing when it is accepted by both the communicator and the audience "as if" it is experienced as a real event (Stanislavsky, 1936). The "as if" paradox is immediately evident in the directly communicated experience of a live theater, dance, or music performance. On-stage spellbinders greet their audience with the understanding that they are collectively suspending disbelief.

Music is then a highly complex behavioral system that is at once intelligible, emotionally evocative, and untranslatable. The cognitive paradoxes that define the musical experience can be inferred from the complex web of structural, biological, and perceptual factors that enter into musical communication. In effect, the performer must organize these disparate factors into a coherent, relational whole in order to unravel the music in real time. The audience, in turn, can be assumed to experience the result as meaningful from beginning to end even though, or perhaps because, it cannot be defined. Understood from this perspective, a musical performance can be considered the most nonverbal and least explicable of the performing arts.

The Leonardo Project at Concordia University set out to study high-level musical performance from a unique perspective. With the aid of a Seagram Foundation Grant for Innovation in Academic Research, psychologist Norman Segalowitz as Project Director and I as Artistic Director undertook to study a cross-section of aspiring, career-track and established artist-performers representing most major instruments and voice from a live, on-stage, real-time, exploratory perspective. The on-stage environment included a small recital hall, two state-of-the-art concert grand pianos linked to monitors, cameras, and professional video and sound-recording facilities. These have provided us with an indispensable working environment for gathering data about the processes, conditions, and paradoxes that enter into a performer's cultivation of creative variability in a live performance. Although our exploratory focus has been on high performance, we have paid special attention to learning aspects that have the potential of impairing performance at all levels of competence.

The solo pianist. The art of a solo virtuoso pianist is a special case of performance creativity. It draws on a written text that can exist only when it is heard (Taruskin, 1995); it expresses itself nonverbally by means of abstract sounds and a physically demanding regimen; its expressive movements are wide-ranging and highly complex, yet are confined by a seated position before an immobile instrument and a stage empty of other musicians. The artist is alone, scrutinized, and vulnerable. As such, a solo piano performance "in the moment" is experienced as an individually directed event in a uniquely structured context. My working reference postulates an organizing principle modeled, in part, on the orchestral conductor: An embodied or external "conductor" delegated to cause, direct, and maintain the composed experience and, by extension, the "being in the moment" response. Here, I develop the theme of paradoxical causality largely from the perspective of the pianist as a solo performer immersed in the "being in the moment" phenomenon. Variously described as the "sweet spot," "the zone," or simply as "being on," the moment is aimed for by virtually every player in every performing discipline, whether an actor playing Juliet, a golfer competing in a tournament, or a pianist maneuvering her way through a Beethoven sonata. You know you are "in the moment" when you find yourself simultaneously playing and not playing, doing and not doing, being moved and not being moved by the music. It manifests itself as an uncanny, apparently spontaneous suspension of disbelief that blurs all normal distinctions between subjective experience and objective fact (Nachmanovitch, 1990).

Improvising, the creative component of performance, depends on "being in the moment." The performer can plan to improvise at any point or do so spontaneously, but will not practice the specifics. Improvisation cannot have a script. The musician can only practice the process, but every end-product is unique. This is particularly so in the performing arts, where disparate modes of apprehension must synchronize and unfold in real time to form an undivided and convincing experience, most convincing when it blurs the normal distinctions between subject and object. The need for clarification of this merger between intentionality and spontaneity, between deep knowledge and the urge to navigate uncharted waters is implicit in the cognitive spin-offs that have emerged in recent years. These attempts to redefine nonstandard ways of knowing in terms of distinctive modes of embodied, "off line," metacognitive, and extracognitive cognition (Atran, 1996; Shavinina & Seeratan, 2004; Tambiah, 1996; Wilson, 2002).

This chapter discusses paradoxical cognition and creative variability in their theoretical, research, learning, and developmental contexts. These include research issues in creativity and performance, a bioesthetic hypothesis, cross-sensory modal parallels and explorations, the "as if," "seeing as playing with" model of paradoxical cognition, naïve and acquired musical bodies, a performance-specific vocabulary, and a sketch-test-and-digress model for learning, research, and cross-sensory modal verification. Each of these areas poses distinct questions on the issue of performance creativity, its cultivation, and communication. The paradoxical model of cognition articulates between conventional and nonconventional ways of knowing.

The chapter explores complex musical performance from an "on-stage" bioesthetic perspective that focuses on a performer's ability to creatively vary a notated score spontaneously in repeated live performances of the same work. The perspective has been developed out of (a) a cross-disciplinary frame of reference, (b) a cross-sensory mode of cognitive organization, and (c) a critical review of received and conveniently accepted wisdoms about high ability and its cultivation. Understood as a whole, these have broad implications for learning that are of interest to students, teachers, and pedagogical theorists across disciplines.

Neuroimaging and Expertise

The past quarter century has seen a marked increase of scientific interest into the neurobiological, cognitive, and "expertise" aspects of musical performance. The growth of neuroimaging studies, in particular, is a development of major significance. A case in point is the mounting evidence from these studies that highly skilled performers achieve an impressive degree of neural plasticity. Perhaps related to brain plasticity is a series of PET-scan studies conducted by Parsons (2001) that suggested the existence of neural anatomical systems for processing music (melody, harmony, and rhythm) throughout the left and right cerebral as well as cerebellar hemispheres.

The inherent complexities—for researchers as well as performers—are dramatically evident in the multilayered sensori-motor environment within which music exists, an environment that is simultaneously in motion and in a state of flux (Lovelace & Parton, 2001). Further complications enter with Brust's (2001) observation that "pitch, timbre, duration, loudness and rhythm . . . are most likely processed through separate circuits" (p. 143). Related esthetic and cognitive difficulties also arise from the varying interpretations researchers assign to the significance of deviations from the musical score, whether by means of accent (Drake & Palmer, 1993), expressive modification (Sundberg, Friberg, & Fryden, 1991), or alterations in tempo between performances of the same work (Desain & Honing, 1994; Mackenzie & Van Eerd, 1990). Sundberg, for example, accepted invariance as a given, and provided 15 rules for explaining durational and related varieties of expressive deviation while Palmer (1997) speculated that "relational invariance (in tempo) would support the existence of a generalized motor program" and that "lack of relational invariance suggests a failure of transfer of learning; practicing a pattern at a different rate than the intended performance might be counterproductive" (p. 131). Palmer's argument for relational invariance in practice would be more convincing had she factored in the qualifying distinctions that occur between different modes of variable response. These modes cover a broad spectrum of possibilities that range from an accidental or momentary impulse to an apparently spontaneous reshaping of structural relationships into an esthetically convincing whole. She also might have included the necessary risk factor in any creative activity (Simonton, 2004).

Although neuroimaging and invariance studies offer insights into a wide range of performance-related issues, there has been relatively little in the way of substantial research into the interplay of biological, esthetic, developmental, and cognitive dimensions that enter into music performance as a formally shared creative activity and experience akin to research or inquiry in the academic world. Palmer (1997) touched on this point in her review of the methodological problems faced by researchers. These begin with the lack of objective criteria for determining representative performances, "given the large variations that can occur between competent performances of the same music" (p. 118). As a consequence, "most experimenters opt for a recognized level of performance expertise" (p. 118). In addition, they often "bypass complexity issues by using simple or reduced musical compositions as experimental stimuli" (p. 118).

Palmer's methodological concerns are implicit in Balzano's (1989) observation that performance is a "hybrid term" that has a different meaning for a performer than it has for a research scientist (p. 437). The artist sees the performance of a musical work as an expressively communicated experience that is complete in itself. When the researcher reduces, simplifies, or generalizes from a "brief snippet of behavior" (Balzano, 1989, p. 437), the performer's understanding of the experience is altered (Balzano, 1989). From a related perspective in nonverbal behavior studies, Scherer and Ekman (1982) suggested that it is best to "rely on a field study when the laboratory environment cannot effectively approximate certain real-life environments that are essential to the research" (p. 116).

Palmer (1997) concurred, but argued that a complex discipline such as music makes it necessary to gather "converging evidence" (p. 118) from a wide range of exploratory and experimental studies. When these are understood as complementary rather than unrelated, they are more likely to provide a body of meaningful contributions to the broader research picture.

The venerable nature-nurture debate (Galton, 1892) continues to examine musical potential from a variety of traditional perspectives, notably early promise, hours spent practicing, and evidence of "expertise" (Ericsson, Krampe, & Tesch-Römer, 1993; Howe, 2004; Sloboda, 1990; Sloboda, Davidson, Howe, & Moore, 1996).

Music school evaluations (Gruson, 1988), retrospective studies of famous musicians (Howe, 1999), and teachability (Subotnik, 2004) are the reference bases for most of these and similar research efforts. Less evident in these studies are correlations between motivational factors, support systems, mentor-student relationships, and context-related practice in the acquisition of high musical ability (Greenspan, Solomon, & Gardner, 2004). Current research into the nature of talent, expertise, and neural loci is undoubtedly providing a valuable body of information on music performance as a highly skilled activity. There is also a growing recognition that music (like other complex performance) is more than a total of basic elements, notably rhythm, melody, harmony, and timbre (Gabrielsson, 1986). These studies, however, have not addressed the question of how a complex network of biological, esthetic, and cognitive factors can be effectively synchronized for creatively varied spontaneity on-the-wing. Neither has research considered the generating dynamic that distinguishes creative variability as an art from expert performance as a skill.

These methodological challenges confirm Dunsby's (1989) observation that analysis alone cannot account for how a performer actualizes his or her interpretation of a given score. We could add, neither can it tell us where it will go at any particular moment during the performance (Barenboim & Said, 2002; Lebrecht, 1992; Pressing, 1988; Taruskin, 1995). This said, there is general acknowledgment of causal relationships between patterns of expression and various aspects of musical syntax and structure. These include the influence of meter on durational length and onset stress (Palmer & Kelly, 1992), clarity of execution (Sloboda, 1983), and degree of loudness (Sloboda, 1985). Palmer (1997) noted, however, that "in all these findings there is no one set of necessary and sufficient cues to denote meter" (p. 118).

Movement.   A number of studies offer general insight into movement as a fundamental dimension of the musical experience. These include a time-keeper (inner clock) model that generates rhythm and timing as opposed to a motor control model in which rhythm and timing generate movement (Palmer, 1997), and musical motion in perception and performance (Repp, 1998) with comments on its theoretical and empirical implications (Shove & Repp, 1995). From a variety of related perspectives, Gabrielsson (1986) noted "the ever changing interactions" and "overlapping of meaning" (p. 162) between musical components during performance. Clynes and Nettheim (1982) examined the neurobiology of rhythm, time, and pulse as the contributing factors in the musical experience, Clynes (1986) discussed cognition "beyond the score" (p. 171), and Repp (1995) related expressive timing to global tempo and perception. Most revealing is Truslit's *Shaping and Motion in Music,* written in 1938 and translated by Bruno Repp (1992) from the original German. Repp's comments on this late-discovered manuscript are worth repeating here: "It [Truslit's work] is probably the most coherent and convincing theory of the basis of common music experience—of musical as distinct from musicological listening" (p. 277). Repp noted that, although Truslit's work "lacks the methodological sophistication of contemporary studies . . . this lack of rigor is made up by depth of insight and breadth of view . . . we can still benefit from" (p. 265).

Creative variability.   There can be little doubt, however, that a supremely accomplished artist is distinguished by the ability to produce a signature performance that transcends interpretative norms and stands as a work of art in its own right. Take, for example, successive live performances of the same work by a master pianist. No two will be alike, yet each will bear the artist's expressively timed signature (Szpilberg, in preparation). The artist's signature will be evident in the apparently spontaneous restructuring of the work as a whole: Tempo, rhythm, articulation, nuance, dynamic patterning, emotive tone, and overall shape converge into a distinct, logically coherent, musical experience. Equally striking will be the stability of the overall time frame. Successive performances will typically vary from each other by a few seconds—independent of the length of the work (Szpilberg, in preparation). This interplay of biological, esthetic, and cognitive resources is the primary research focus in the Leonardo Project, in particular, how these modalities relate to and merge with each other into a unified whole while the music is in motion. Because a live music performance can only exist as it unfolds in real time (Cohen, 1996), the merging process implies the existence of a unifying entity (or entities) capable of directing the flow while simultaneously anticipating and guiding the structural and expressive relationships as they happen. This requires making decisions that by-pass normal reflective considerations. Decision and response must be perceived as undivided, or they risk losing the sense of immediacy without which esthetic coherence in real time is impossible.

The creative experience; speculation and theory.   What compels an actor, musician, dancer, or poet to draw us into his or her imaginary world, to enthrall us with gestures, images, tones, and word play before fading into the shadows of memory? Why do we, in those brief moments of enchantment, believe what they imagine? To begin with, the realms of intuition and esthetic sensitivity are not confined to the literary, visual, and performing arts. The human imagination has an inexhaustible wealth of verbal and nonvebal vocabularies at its disposal. These allow for a mixing and matching of the somatic vocabularies of movement, gesture, touch, and tone with intuitive, esthetic and rational modes of understanding. In their analyses of Nobel laureates' understanding of scientific intuition (physics, chemistry, and medicine), Marton, Fensham, and Chaiklin (1994) noted how virtually every laureate echoed Poincaré's dictum that in mathematics "By logic you prove. By intuition you discover" (1913/1963, p. 208). To Paul Dirac, the 1963 laureate in physics, it was "more important to have beauty in one's equations than to have them fit experiment" (p. 47). It would then seem that the creative entente that binds intuition and esthetic reference to logical proofs spans the sciences generally as well as the arts (Shavinina & Seeratan, 2004). It is by elegance that they "know."

There is a growing assortment of diverse research perspectives and loosely agreed-on assumptions about the nature of creativity and its communication. Equally inevitable has been the growth of across-the-board theories that attempt to bring order to the what, the why, and the how of the phenomenon. Csikszentmihalyi (1998), for example, offered a systems approach as an alternative to Maslow's (1963) argument that creative endeavor exists almost entirely in the process. The systems approach distinguishes between the domain (a symbolic or cultural aspect of the individual's environment) and the field (the social aspect). The former is where rules are set, skills are honed, and novelty brings a fresh perspective to tradition and general practice. According to Csikszentmihalyi, novelty achieves creative status when it is acknowledged by the field, that is, by peers, critics, and others in a position to decide what is worth passing on to posterity and what is not.

Simonton (1999b) proposed a more detailed and comprehensive emergenic-epigenetic model that assumes superior creativity to be contingent on a multiplicity of necessary given and acquired "structures." Inspired in part by Campbell's (1960) model of creativity as a Darwinian process of variation, selection, and fitness, Simonton (1999a) saw these structures as emerging in gradual stages during the course of long-term interactions between the internally developing organism and appropriate environmental stimulation. Rather than being "pre-wired at birth," they periodically cross and blend physical, physiological, cognitive, environmental, social, cultural, predispositional, "luck of historical timing," and related imperatives. The configuration as a whole is both dynamic and specific to the individual.

Weisberg (1993) has argued that "there may be no thinking except creative thinking, since our ordinary functioning involves successful adaptation to novel situations" (p. 242). Having stripped creativity of its élitist trappings, Weisberg then redefined it as "a goal directed production of a novel work" that is assessed (by the field) to be of value, and can be of influence when it is "incorporated by others" (p. 248). It achieves genius status once it has become widely influential and judged to be of inestimable value. Creativity and genius are therefore reinstated, but with an important proviso: There is nothing special about the way the great creators think that cannot be learned by just about anyone. "If in place of the genius view we adopt a conception of creative thinking as ordinary, it changes the approach to maximizing individuals' creative output," and as a consequence "we don't need a special theory of creativity, but a more complete theory about how we think" (pp. 262–264). Whatever the merits of Weisberg's assertion that creative thinking is everyday thinking, it treads on shaky ground by suggesting that (a) genius is contingent on wide acceptance and (b) that "ordinary functioning," however mundane, is no different than an original, highly complex scientific or artistic work (Grotowski, 2002; Lecoq, 2001; Repp, 1992). The "can be" and "will be" distinction between one's potential and capacity for achievement is very real. To ignore it is to ignore the complex of given and acquired generating conditions (Simonton, 1999b) that enter into the realization of one's potential and, from the perspective of this chapter, the "teachability" question (Subotnik, 2004).

A view from the stage.   Nonconventional ways of knowing are basic to the "on stage" explorations conducted by director-actor teachers in experimental theater, dance, and movement over the past half-century. Jacques Lecoq (2001, also cited by Murray, 2003), Charles Dullin (see Murray, 2003), Jerzy Grotowski (2002), and Peter Brook (in Croyden, 2003), among others, have delved into the workings of the creative experience from the perspectives and methodological criteria of an on-stage firing line in a state of flux. Inspired in part by the long-term seminal research of Constantine Stanislavsky (1936) in theater, Rudolf Laban (1976) in dance, as well as the provocative theories of Antonin Artaud (1958), and the mime teacher Jacques Copeau (in Murray, 2003), they share an overriding emphasis on challenging every "truism" embedded in mainstream authority, tradition, and common practice. Creative authenticity, as they see it, begins when actors and directors feel compelled to transcend the comfort levels that come with well-worn techniques of speech, gesture, everyday logic, and formulas for "success." Artaud's argument for a theater capable of expressing "life in its immense, universal aspect" (1958, p.116) is echoed in Dullin's proposal for a revitalized stage experience that should not confine itself to mirroring everyday reality. It should draw instead on the "power of the imagination" to express "internal poetic laws" (Murray, 2003, p. 164). Although their methods for tapping the poetically charged imagination differ from each other in particulars, there is general agreement on the central role of "the actor's body, its movement and its stillness" (Murray, 2003, p. 5) in bringing a vision of poetic authenticity to the stage experience. The subtext in these efforts is that poetic laws issue a poetic license to form constructs that shape a vision of the human experience that differs profoundly from the constructs that govern prose, reasoned argument, and numbers. Poetically licensed constructs as such live by logical paradoxes that are native to every creative art (see, for example, Picasso in Podoksik, 1996; Ravel, 1937). Grotowski summarized the logical paradigm by asserting that "there are two kinds of logic, formal and paradoxical" (Grotowski, 2002, p. 248).

The somatically based explorations emerging from experimental theater, dance, and movement are unquestionably a provocative counterpoint to contemporary scientific research into the nature of creativity and its communication.

Documented in unedited audio and video recordings, analytical notes, commentaries and interviews, these broadly diverse stage practices share one common purpose: To make dramatic sense of the paradoxes embedded in the symbiotic relationship between movement and poetically experienced human awareness. The coexploratory orientations, the atmosphere of restless invention, the emphasis on open-ended process, and the explicit dismissal of both domain and audience evaluations *per se* as valid measures of creative worth distinguish their methodological practices and raison-d'être.

The bioesthetic hypothesis. Exploratory research (1992 to the present) conducted by the author at Concordia University's Leonardo Project is studying creative variability in terms of the expressively timed synchronization of a musician's biological, esthetic (i.e., bioesthetic), and cognitive resources. The biological and esthetic aspects are expressed in a single image in order to distinguish the intent of the study from that of a biomechanical model. Biological in this context refers to (a) the expressive parallels that can be drawn between auditory, tactile, visual, and kinesthetic modes of apprehension; and (b) cross-sensory synchronization during performance. Cognition here refers to the perception of an embodied or external conductor delegated to organize the performer's bioesthetic resources. The embodied conductor causes synchronization to occur by directing the music through various nonsounding "batons" of the body (e.g., expressive gestures). The external conductor causes the action to occur through a sounding reference (the music as a baton) or a nonsounding reference apart from the music or the body. The first phase of the study (1992–2002) was conducted "on-stage" in a real time, hands-on, coexploratory setting designed to establish criteria for the analyses of logical and paradoxical constructs involved in the cultivation of creative variability in highly skilled performance (Cohen, 1996; Palmer, 1997; Scherer & Ekman, 1982).

The cultivation of a musically inventive consciousness is the ground rule for achieving the paradoxical fusion of variable repetition and nonrepeatability from one performance to the next. My point here is that the phenomenon seems to be contingent on modes of preparatory cognition that are creatively focused and internalized (Shavinina & Seeratan, 2004). When successful, the internalizing process facilitates the "being in the moment" experience of simultaneously "playing and not playing" or "doing and not doing."

The bioesthetic hypothesis shares an emphasis with experimental theater, dance, and movement on the body's expressive gestures as a nonverbal, subjectively directed means of communication. It also recognizes the role of paradox as an essential "poetically licensed" aspect of the creative process. The main distinction lies in the bioesthetic premise of an organizing principle (an embodied or external conductor) capable of being tested and verified objectively by visual, aural, and tangible (hands-on) means. The cross-modal method of verification developed in the explorations allows both the performer and the observer to evaluate the effectiveness of the self-conducted responses.

The distinctive feature of an embodied or external conductor is its function as a delegated cause rather than a focus of attention. It relies, as a consequence, on a paradoxical articulation between acting and being acted upon: The performer observes the music unfold while the delegated conductor causes it to happen. The directive to get off oneself to perform one's best suggests an affinity with "the external focus of attention" proposed by researchers from William James (1890) to Singer and Cauraugh (1993) and Wulf and Prinz (2001). The cognitive implications, however, of a causal imperative point to a very different mode of organization.

Creative variability in performance. Creative Variability in real time can be said to occur when a performer spontaneously recasts a previously composed work into a novel musical experience. The piece can be of any length or degree of complexity. There is neither anticipation nor reflection in the unfolding process, but rather an ongoing sense of inevitability by which musical intention, response, and movement are experienced as indivisible. Most significant is the immediacy with which an unpremediated turn of phrase will develop into a unified musical experience that is as surprising as it is memorable. Biologically, creative variability is contingent on a number of interrelated factors, namely (a) homeo-rheusus (Waddington, 1968)—the ability to maintain balance in an unstable environment; (b) a spontaneous readjustment of breath (biological) rhythms; (c) a high degree of cross-sensory synchronization; and (d) a sketch, test, and digress model of practice, rehearsal, and verification. The model is based loosely on the notebooks of composers and visual artists as well as the rehearsal techniques of the orchestral conductor, Wilhelm Furtwangler (Barenboim & Said, 2002; Lebrecht, 1992). Delegated embodied and external conductors serve as organizing causes capable of being cultivated and tested in practice and performance.

Creating the experience. The issue of real-time creative variability in musical performance that I am addressing in this chapter focuses on the central role of paradox in shaping the causal relationships between biological organization and expressively directed timing. Paradox, in this sense, forms the logical reference for the context-specific and interactive vocabularies developed in the Leonardo Project's long-term real-time explorations into the bioesthetic and cognitive dimensions of creativity variability. By mixing and matching standard and nonstandard modes of cognition, these vocabularies help generate cross-sensory synchronization between a musician's aural, kinesthetic, tactile, and visual modes of expression. In terms of expressively determined timing, creative variability can be understood as a function of (sensed) esthetic judgments that are experienced biologically and communicated in real time. These expressively timed relationships between successive actions organize and direct the biological responses that, in turn, are communicated directly to the listener. As a working reference, the bioesthetics of expressive timing can be said to have its roots (or essential references) in the primary sense experiences of rocking (rhythm), touch, emotive tone, gesture, movement, balance, energy, and momma-dadda baby babble.

As I have indicated, the experience is most real when it is perceived as magical—ideally a spellbound interlude for both performers and listeners that is at once a sleight-of-hand balancing act and an immersion in the collective experience.

Creative variability in real time can occur in any form of solo or ensemble from an unaccompanied song to a conducted orchestral or choral performance. It can be triggered by just about any conceivable performing situation: the ambience of the hall, a receptive or nonreceptive audience, an injury, the quality of the instrument, a memory lapse, a momentary error in judgment, frustration, or an unexplainable whim. Whatever the inspiration may be, the player turns the situation to creative advantage. The ideal result will be a collective experience that is as much of a surprise to the performer as it is to the audience. And no matter how many revelations may occur in subsequent performances of the same work, no two will be perceived as esthetically alike.

The composer creates the music. The performer creates the experience.

Musical Performance as a Creative Act: The Paradoxical Imperative

My bioesthetic hypothesis argues that the usual distinction made between a created work and an interpreted performance is semantic. Is the pianist who mesmerizes her audience less inventive than the composer who provided the written score? Although composer and pianist are locked in a symbiotic relationship, it is undeniable that it takes more than mere reading skill to breathe life into an arrangement of cues on a page (Barenboim & Said, 2002; Taruskin, 1995). Our explorations suggest that the underlying creative process rests on establishing a generating mode of spontaneous translation between esthetic intention, somatic response, and the courage to risk (Nachmanovitch, 1990; Simonton, 2004). In other words, to be creatively "on" begins with a body and brain that are on playing terms (more specifically, an acquired musical body-brain in a duo with its naïve musical body-brain).

Simonton (2004) picked up on stage wisdom and carried the logical argument over the edge to a stochastic world view, where chance and genius provoke each other into the act of creating. It is a scenario whereby "accident and error . . . the unexpected and unforeseen . . . luck, random, casual and haphazard contingencies are part of the game" and where "exceptional creators . . . exploit chance to produce genius" because they "have the capacity and the inclination to ensure that luck is on their side" (pp. 65–67). "Capacity and inclination" recall Pasteur's classic remark about chance favoring "the prepared mind" (Beveridge, 1957, p. 46). In a performing art, chance favors the prepared body through the ability to take off from a cue.

The communication of a creatively achieved image is normally received as a mood or emotive tone. This remains so even when the work is considered abstract. Although we all live with moods, artists live with both the subjective experience and the need to design a structure that will communicate that particular subjective experience—a double life with all the makings of an ideal scenario for communicating the "tragic world view," if not always in a mood of "robust health" (Rothenberg, as cited in Gutin, 1996, p. 82).

If creativity is paradoxical, then musical performance as a creative activity is the ultimate footnote to Zeno's paradox of motion and plurality. How do you make sense of complex patterns of sounds and silences—at once invisible, abstract, and emotionally evocative—traveling through time and space at varying speeds, tones, intensities, and textures? No wonder Claude Levi-Strauss (Storr, 1992) called music "the supreme mystery of the science of man . . . the only language with the contradictory attributes of being at once intelligible and untranslatable" (Cytowic, 2002, p. 319). The embedded contradictions do not automatically negate performance analyses, since, as Hilton (1987) argued, these "may be justified as a study of one of the most elaborate behavioural systems man has invented" (p. 5).

This said, untranslatable attributes do not, as a rule, qualify as the ideal scenario for a clear-cut inquiry into the workings of an experience and those who create it. And, as Arnold Ludwig (1995) noted, interviews and standard questionnaires are not always the best way to go given the prevalence of contradictory theoretical and diagnostic assumptions about how a performing artist should be expected to respond. This is particularly so with performing artists whose long and often grueling years of apprenticeship tend to get lost in process and invented in hindsight. As a consequence, asking a performer "what makes you tick" questions may seem irrelevant to some, an imposition to others, and an invitation to play word games for the rest (Pinker, 2004).

An interview some years ago with Evgeny Kissin is a case in point. When Kissin, unquestionably one of the greatest pianists of our day, was asked how he chose his encores, he answered, "They come to me." When asked how he judged an audience, he answered, "I feel something in the air." When asked how he decides when he is ready to play a piece, his answer again floated by with a nebulous "This is always very clear to me" (A. Solomon, 1996, p. 114). Kissin, who can be articulate and intellectually convincing when he is talking about music, had this to say about his reluctance to engage in discussions about himself as a musician: "Speaking in words is much less for me. In fact, I don't know how to convey through speech at all. What I have to say, the music says it. For me there is no translating this" (A. Solomon, 1996, p. 120). It is instructive here to mention that Kissin's teacher, Anna Pavlova Kantor, made it a practice never to touch the keyboard during a lesson. Instead of demonstrating for her students, she would inspire and guide them by "speaking with an expressiveness that goes beyond the specific meaning of her words" (A. Solomon, 1996, p. 119).

There may be a more fundamental issue here: How does one reconcile the translation problem between two diametrically opposed modes of communication? On the one hand, we have the prosaic language of evidence premised on objective fact. On the other hand, the "untranslatable" language of music—untranslatable, that is, when confronted with the vocabulary of "objectively" based information. When, for example, highly accomplished musicians speak of music as their first language, they mean that the experiential "truth" for them lies embedded in the poetry of expressly colored sound relationships and gestures. To speak in dispassionate terms about their musical art is to speak in a foreign tongue.

We then have two very different views—methods, if you wish—of human communication. The first is premised on objective criteria, something you can point to, explain, and ideally verify with numbers. The second is premised on inference and the emotive directness of sound qualities and gestural relationships—things you can hear, see, feel, and imagine, but cannot verify objectively. The syntax of the former is subject-verb-object and logically apprehensible. The syntax and logical fluidity of the latter is paradoxical and the experience is esthetic (or, as some have suggested, extracognitive; Shavinina & Seeratan, 2004). A creative scientist may feel comfortable discussing the place of esthetic experience in his or her discipline. To a performing artist, on the other hand, the virtue of the experience rests in its inexplicability. It can only be communicated in its own terms or in those of another art (Podoksik, 1996; Ravel, 1937; Stanislavsky, 1936).

When understood as a measure of unconventional thinking and acting, paradoxical logic is the logic of art. It is also a generating force in the interplay of biology, esthetics, and cognition that marks variability in a performing art as a creative act. Creative variability, in this sense, implies a measure of unpredictability. It follows that "acting out" an unpredictable formal event demands a risk-taking imperative—a daunting challenge for the unprepared body. I coined the term "paradoxical causality" to introduce certain cognitive alternatives to the norm in practice and rehearsal. These aim at preparing the performer, with minimum reflection, to reorganize her musical resources when inspiration beckons or the musical flow unexpectedly veers off course.

The poetic license implied in the term paradox allows for causal relationships to be perceived between normally disparate phenomena. In a performing situation, these can be delegated to cause timed expressive actions within as well as outside one's own body. For the prepared and the daring, paradoxical causality offers an excursion into any realm of the imagination, with a return ticket that includes a fail-safe peek beyond the "thin partitions" that divide madness from creativity (Dryden, 1983, p. 360). As such, it can be a valuable border-crossing pass on the artist's journey.

Live, unfiltered, and in the moment.   With the possible exceptions of mime and dance, a live musical performance is unlike that of any other physical activity. It is direct, not filtered through words on a page or virtual images on a canvas or screen. It demands qualities of skill that are poetic and rhetorical rather than mechanical. It is essentially nonverbal (even when sung); it involves very complex, esthetically directed physical organization because the performer is visible and his or her physical comportment is part of the esthetic. In addition, so-called art music and most popular genres are played to the listeners, rather than played with them in the manner typical of many traditional cultures. Finally, traditional cultures fix their classics in the remote past, whereas western art music is distinguished by a constantly evolving repertoire in which classics emerge, are replaced, rediscovered, and reinterpreted over cycles of time. For this, there is wisdom to be garnered from the playroom.

The art of pretend: "As if" and "seeing as."   Graham is engaged in conversation with his family of stuffed animals. The conversation is animated. He speaks and each animal answers with its own distinctive voice. Graham is four years old. Listener (flipping on his tape recorder): Graham, if you had to make a wish, what would you wish for more than anything else in the world? Graham (without hesitation): I wish all my animals were alive. (Leonardo Project Archives, February 28, 2003, audiotape.) Graham dissolves two contradictory thoughts into a single image. He knows it is just a wish. To make the wish more real he acts it out with his animals. In effect, he causes them to respond "as if" they were alive. Graham's "as if" is a classic example of how our naïve cognitive resources can help our acquired resources harness the improbable to creative advantage. Not a delusion, but an illusion made real.

> *To create an illusion is mankind's one great superiority.*

> **Maurice Ravel**

As a prelude to introducing our embedded conductors and their diaper-dancing muses, I will begin by expanding upon the logic of stage communication.

Constantine Stanislavsky (1936) never tired of reminding his acting students of the self-evident fact that imagination is the source of all art and that a stage play—or for that matter, any created experience—is meant to be communicated "as if" it is real. "As if" is the "lever" by which we "lift ourselves out of everyday life on to the plane of imagination" (p. 59). To Jacques Lecoq (2001), the illusion of "as if" is an article of faith that permits you to don your stage mask and "seek truth in illusion, not lies" (p. 163). The job of the creative artist, then, is to shape a vision of reality that is so convincing that the only logical response for the observer will be to suspend disbelief and enter fully into the experience. To the poet Jan Zwicky (2003), however, the "as if" leap of faith becomes a "seeing as," a form of cognition born of metaphor and experienced as a recognition that one can identify with and act upon. The performer is acting an emotional experience while the listener is experiencing the acted emotion. Both don their stage masks and each knows the rules of the game: Keep suspending disbelief and the magic will continue. Disbelieve and it is over. The role of the audience, then, is to surrender to the illusion, whereas that of the performers is to keep it going until the curtain descends, the house lights brighten, and the masks are removed. In the game of music, the mystique is all the more intriguing because it is achieved and communicated nonverbally. At a more fundamental level, the nonverbal character of the musical experience is reflected in the mirror image of esthetic values and biological organization that makes communication possible.

For the ultimate tribute to the power of "as if," consider the ancient practice of burying actors at a cross-roads with a stake through their hearts. So unearthly was their magic that people feared for the sanctity of their souls. Ghosts with demonic powers were known to weave spells with unforeseeable consequences for the innocents above ground. For the playwright David Mamet, this tribute to their art is "an awesome compliment" that every player should "aim for." Beats a standing ovation. (Mamet, 1999, pp. 6–7).

The Leonardo Project's "on stage" environment (in conjunction with our field studies) has been designed to serve as the sounding board for work on a broad range of critical, coexploratory, and developmental experiments, all conducted from the perspective of maximizing creative potential.

The setting is intended to facilitate an open-ended exchange between performance analysts, coaches, and performers on relevant issues as they arise. The long-term aim of the exchange is to establish a body of pedagogical, practical, and theoretical cross-references for subsequent experimental and exploratory studies. The umbrella scheme is important because our "in-house" population consists of a diverse group of graduate students (professional level pianists enrolled in interdisciplinary programs), aspiring performers (mainly piano, voice, and strings), performer associates (teacher-performers), artist associates (career-track professionals), and visiting artists on voice and most traditional instruments. All sessions are videotaped and remain unedited for feedback, analysis, testing, and archival reference. The bottom line asks why some people bring a distinctive, creatively focused character to their performances while others don't. And, by implication, why some who should create don't and some who shouldn't do.

The "live, as it happens" performing environment has made it possible for us to conduct long-term explorations into the predisposing conditions of creative variability from a perspective that cross-refers rational, paradoxical, and frankly contradictory views of cognitive organization (Atran, 1996; Grotowski, 2002; Simonton, 2004; Tambiah, 1996). This perspective has helped us make working sense of the prerequisite conditions to spontaneity "on the wing," in particular, how a unique "artist's signature" causes a "one time" performance "to unfold as a whole with as much of a surprise for the performer as it does for the listener" (Szpilberg, 2006, personal communication).

Homeorheusus—The Balancing Act

There are performing situations in which the precisely timed synchronization of a player's musical resources is no longer an option, typically when the ebb and flow of the musical soundscape engages the artist in an intricate balancing act that keeps her on edge from the first to the last measure (Cohen, 1996). The most promising developments to date have emerged from the concept of an embodied or external conductor delegated to synchronize the timing of a performer's biological, esthetic and cognitive resources as a whole. Delegating cause particularly emerges in a musical soundscape in which the ebb and flow requires a

balancing act that must be capable of sustaining itself despite changes in emphasis and unanticipated contingencies (Cohen, 1996). Consider, for example, the
gymnastics demanded of a pianist maneuvering through the Piano Sonata in
B Minor by Franz Liszt. The Sonata is not only a virtuoso blockbuster, but, in
the hands of a sensitive artist, a sublimely expressive masterpiece. From the
opening motives, the pianist will be engaged in juggling a wide spectrum of
emotionally toned shifts of tempo, texture, articulation, dynamics, and mood
inflections—punctuated by timed silences and abrupt changes in direction that
cover the entire keyboard. The pace will be unrelenting: Typical are lengthy pas-
sages at great speed, in multiple "voice" parts with each voice developing out of
its own center of balance and its particular direction of movement. Clearly not a
job for an unprepared conductor.

Cross-sensory integration.   The challenge to surefootedness in the balancing
act begins in the dark recesses of overlapping auditory, tactile, visual, kinesthetic,
and related constraints that greet the pianist attempting to make sense of a complex musical score. A certain degree of cross-sensory decision making—even
confusion—is inevitable before the strands can be untangled and reorganized
for performance. The first step is to achieve a workable integration of these otherwise loosely engaged modalities. Cross-sensory integration occurs when two
or more sensory modalities are perceived to be functioning in tandem (Lovelace
& Parton, 2001). The pairings may be involuntary (e.g., synesthetic) or voluntary (e.g., parasynesthetic, metaphoric). In a musical performance, the modalities
normally present at any one time are aural, visual, tactile, and kinesthetic. The
relationships of these modalities to each other and the focus of attention at any
particular moment in time depend on the nature and complexity of the work
and the performer's command of it as a whole. The performer who is "on" from
this perspective is perceiving the groupings in terms of an interwoven whole in
motion.

Cross-sensory expressive parallels.   The most striking characteristics shared
by the sensory modalities are in the expressive analogies that can be drawn
between tone, touch, gesture, and gaze. Take, for example, a decisive gesture, a
piercing cry, a stabbing touch, a sharply articulated chord, a gritting of the teeth,
a penetrating gaze, and the parallels become immediately evident. The rapport
between nonverbal signals accounts for why an orchestra of over one hundred
musicians will respond instantaneously to the expressive gestures of a conductor, no matter how varied or complex these gestures may be. The "how" includes
the synchronization of the conductor's intentions with the expressive mobility of
his or her eyes, hands, fingers, torso, legs, and "scatting" movements of the lips,
each of which can function, separately or in tandem, as a conducted cause. In
the hands of a sensitive conductor the sequencing of these gestures—silent for
the most part—will convey expressive information precisely and nonverbally in
real time.

Timing the cause.   The most important consideration here is that the conductor is the only musician who is not making audible sounds. This tells us that the expressive parallels between modalities can form causal relationships; any one mode can cause one or more of the other modes to respond. The orchestra is caused to play by the conductor's gestures and the mode-to-mode "translation" is perceived as instantaneous. A striking example of immediacy of response between musicians can be seen and heard in a videotaped performance directed by Carlos Kleiber, one of the preeminent conductors of the twentieth century (1989). Timing, in this sense, can best be described as "biological or breath rhythm" and should not be confused with metronomic time beating (Lebrecht, 1992).

Timing the poetically moved performer; bioesthetic or biomechanical?   Does it really make any difference whether a performer's skills are optimized from a bioesthetic or a biomechanical perspective? The answer depends on what we mean by optimize. Let's say we are interested in what makes a good stand-up comic tick. We might begin by checking his breathing, pulse, muscle tone, speed of response, speech patterns, tongue, larynx formation, and posture. We might narrow it down to comparing the comic's use of the "voiced" with the "voiceless linguadental fricative continuant" (Miller, 1986, p. 99). These are all biomechanically measurable and, taken as a whole, may add up to something meaningful for pedagogues as well as researchers. The stand-up comic, however, is guided by the old show biz maxim: Make 'em laugh, make 'em cry . . . and make 'em wait. The art is in the timing. Timing is the measure of how well the comic can "pull off" the act of playing with the audience's expectations, how he or she can time a shift from, say, a giggle to a sigh or a pause and bring it all together in the final run at the big laugh. It's all in the comic's turn of phrase, tone of voice, gestures, body language, and projection; how he or she judges the shape and tempo of the buildup to the punch line—the momentary cliff-hanger, the surprise twist, and shared laughter. These are timed, sensed judgments that add up to a bioesthetic experience for both the comic and the audience.

Although this example of how a stand-up comic might time an act is oversimplified, it illustrates an important distinction between a bioesthetic and biomechanical perspective on human performance. The latter confines itself, for the most part, to optimizing the readily quantifiable attributes of the performer. This knowledge is invaluable insofar as it can help the performer to improve his or her technical command by reducing strain and increasing strength, flexibility, and endurance. It does not, however, relate the mechanical factors to the context-specific esthetic that identifies the particular experience as a well-timed joke (Ramachandran & Blakeslee, 1998).

> *Gesture precedes knowledge.*
> *Gesture precedes thought.*
> *Gesture precedes language.*
>
> **Jacques Lecoq**

Gestures, as Oliver Sacks (2000) has pointed out, are the nongrammatical expressive movements that everyone makes. These movements can be anything from a dismissive shrug of the shoulders to the threat of a clenched fist or a whole body signal that communicates expectation, apprehension, or relief. Gesture is the chameleon of human communication. It can adopt any guise, enter into a liaison with any sense modality, sphincter, or joint. As the silent partner to spoken words, it also can reveal meanings that the speaker would prefer remain unsaid (Ekman & Rosenberg, 1997). Scowl, furrow your brow, adopt a steely-eyed gaze, bare your teeth, roar, and your gesture becomes a universal signal. Smile, bow to your guests, and the gesture obeys a social convention. Invent a sequence of expressive gestures, and they will tell a story in dance or mime (Trumble, 2004). Movement, touch, and expressively directed sound are the primary means of preverbal communication (expressively directed sound can be understood as audible movement). As such, the way we move both carries and is shaped by our earliest means of communication. At the gestural levels of mime, music, dance, and social interaction, complex qualities of expressive communication depend on the cultivation—consciously or otherwise—of a coherent vocabulary of movement. From this perspective, a stutter or performance block is a persistent obstruction of music in motion. As a consequence, mime, music, dance, and related phenomena that exist only while in motion cannot be effectively "translated" into everyday language, whether by means of a "name," an abstraction, a description, or a static notation.

Gestures, however, do not need a Charlie Chaplin or Fred Astaire to tell a story. Some of the most revealing insights into the human condition can be observed in a hospital waiting room or a game of chance. Take the following unspoken scene from the film, *Twenty Four Hours in the Life of a Woman* (Bouhnik, 2003).

Scene: Casino. A roulette game. The players are silent, waiting for the decisive roll of the dice. The camera pans slowly around the table, pausing briefly to focus on the hands of each player. Faces are briefly off-camera. One player is tapping impatiently on the table. Another is sliding the chips back and forth; the movements are cautious, the hand indecisive. A third is clutching the chips with a clawlike grip: Is it a good luck squeeze or is he shielding them from prying eyes? The fingers of the next player are spread out stiffly and immobile as if holding their breath while the hands of a fifth player hang loosely on the table, resigned to whatever the coming roll of dice will bring. The camera keeps scanning from one pair of hands to the next, revealing the story of the moment in gestural vignettes of hope, resignation, despair, occasional relief, and momentary triumph.

Gestures also can speak in a sign language so unique that it cannot be related to either inborn signals or conventional movements (Sacks, 2000). The theater director, Peter Brook, described one such language in the following scenario.

Scene: Theater of the Deaf. Two actors are discussing a performance of Tchaikovsky's *Swan Lake* ballet. The dialogue ranges from the story line to gossipy comments about the dancers' costumes and hairstyles. They "speak" in the "verbal vernacular" of the deaf, a "semi-spontaneous" vocabulary analogous to slang and distinct from conventional sign language. Eye movements are precisely coupled with arms, hands and fingers that "dance" with the speed "of a virtuoso pianist" and "a sensitivity that goes far beyond that of the most trained technique of a ballet dance or mime" (Croyden, 2003, pp. 85–86). Equally impressive was how precisely the actors were able to synchronize their eye movements with each other's gestures (Croyden, 2003).

Gestures, then, have the capacity to range from universal signals to the most intimate articulations of local dialects. As such, they reflect virtually every nuance of spoken language (Sacks, 2000). A sequence of expressive gestures, with no objective reference can also be spontaneously invented and communicated. As such, they simulate poetry.

Touch. The most direct and perhaps least ambiguous means of nonverbal communication is touch. A pianist's touch is often considered the measure of his or her artistic sensibility. Chopin's outstanding palette of touch colors was considered the musical signature of a master pianist (Eigeldinger, 1986). Touch, or contact gesture, is also the performing reference for individuals who are either hearing- or visually impaired. In my program notes to *Hands,* a recording by the blind jazz pianist and concert improviser, Dave Mackay, I related how he hears and plays through his hands (Cohen, 1982). I later asked Mackay to practice rapid leaps to specific tones from the extreme octaves of the keyboard in both directions. His accuracy after less than a dozen attempts was precise and repeatable over time. Mackay claimed he felt his hands carrying the sounds through space to their destinations. Mackay's cross-modal associations are consistent with Pascual-Leone's observation (Motluck, 2005) that the accomplished Braille reader recalls touch through the visual cortex.

> *By the deficits we may know the talents,*
> *by the exceptions we may discern the rules.*

Lawrence Miller

Sing through your fingers.

Frédéric Chopin,
in Eigeldinger, 1986, p. 45

The preceding examples illustrate the potential of touch to communicate beyond its given sensory mode—a phenomenon that is dramatically evident with individuals who would otherwise be considered musically disadvantaged. Ronald, a tone-deaf preteen pianist bypassed his apparent musical disability by sensing the expressive contour of the musical line when I played through his hands. He not only remembered the feel of the line, but could (a) expand expressively on it, (b) transfer what he learned to new music, and (c) vary the phrasing in subsequent performances. At age 10 he performed the first movement of a Bach concerto with a major orchestra in a young people's concert. He subsequently learned to improvise. When asked what he likes about music, Ronald answered, "The rhythm or something."

Much less evident is the ability of profoundly deaf individuals to perform music at a high technical and artistic level. The deaf virtuoso percussionist Evelyn Glennie described the experience as a "form of hearing" that resonates in specific areas of her body. "Sometimes," she said, "the sound almost hits you in the face" (Riedelsheimer, 2004).

Glennie's observations are confirmed in an ongoing field exploration with Lorna, a profoundly deaf 17-year-old music conservatory student. Now in her fifth year of study, Lorna learns through the teacher's expressive gestures and direct hands-on-hands touch. She feels the music in her hands and "hears" it vibrating in her legs. Over the years she has won prizes in conservatory and local music competitions. These accomplishments are footnotes to the inspiring saga of Helen Keller. Despite being profoundly deaf, blind, and mute, Keller was capable of learning almost entirely by touch to write, read, lecture, and publish her autobiography. Cynthia Ozick (2003) concluded that Keller's legacy—what she "saw"—is "proof of the real existence of the mind's eye" (p. 32).

Bioesthetically Determined Timing

Bioesthetically determined timing provides the most direct route of inquiry toward understanding the nature of creative variability and, in particular, how it may be cultivated and acted upon in music performance. From this perspective, bioesthetically conceived judgments may be considered a distinctive form of cognition, a way of knowing that relates the artist's musical intentions to his or her precision of execution. The cultivation of this way of knowing is best understood in the context of the special dynamic that exists between one's Naïve and Acquired Musical Bodies. We'll begin with Kessie and Sionna.

In the beginning was the foot.

**Marvin Harris,
in Ehrlich, 2002, p. 68**

The diaper dance: Babbling bipeds at play—step one in a case study. Kessie is curious. Everything in the house, everything she sees, must be tested. Things to touch. Things to hold. Things that move. Things to taste, to knock over. A cup, a vase, a wine glass—big, small, heavy things. The magical sound of a jar exploding as it hits the dining room floor. Bits and pieces that burst and bounce and disappear around and under the table. Must be important because Mommy always rushes over to pick Kessie up. Dangerous? A mess? She couldn't care less because Kessie is 14 months old. And she can walk, diapers and all, and see and do things she never knew existed. Could Kessie be thinking, "I walk therefore I am?"

It's a new beginning, so Kessie is fascinated with the look of things, how they feel, how they move, how they hit the ground with a crash and become little pieces. But Mommy is worried. She can't take her eyes off Kessie for a moment. She thinks, "if only I could distract her." And then the inspiration, "Of course, a recording! That's it! Anything with a beat will do." The music begins. Kessie stops in her tracks. Her face lights up. Her body bounces and shakes to the beat. She giggles. When the music gets excited, Kessie beams. When it speeds up Kessie speeds up. When it slows down, Kessie slows down. When it stops, she stops, or demands more.

Mommy and Daddy are impressed. So are all the relatives and friends. Kessie is musical. A natural. Could be a prodigy. And she's so cute when she giggles. They hug her and they all agree that, "Kessie dances and giggles, therefore she is a dancing musician." Well, maybe. You see, many walking 14-month-olds—diapers and all—shake, bounce, and giggle to the beat. The band plays and they move. Sometimes big people also lighten up, beat time to the music, and giggle. I say sometimes because big people can choose not to lighten up or giggle. They can even choose to frown at what they are hearing or ignore it completely. But they will rarely deny the organizing power of the musical experience. The purpose of music is to move them, and they know it.

Does Kessie have another epiphany: "I dance therefore I am?"

The immediacy of the musical response in the untutored toddler suggests that music is an evolutionary gift shared by most of us. Let's call this gift our Naïve Musical Body. But does our shared inheritance include the ability to invent and perform music?

Like Kessie, Sionna is 14 months old. And like Kessie, music makes her dance and giggle with delight. But Sionna has two things Kessie doesn't have; she has a piano and a Daddy who is a musician. Sionna loves to play the piano. Her favorite technique of tone clusters is full of surprises; palms, knuckles, and fists alternate between the right and left hand, fast, slow, subdued, heaven-storming, and punctuated by airborne flourishes with both hands. But Sionna isn't just interested in virtuoso pyrotechnics. She also enjoys spending intimate moments at the piano experimenting with a single key, tapping it with her finger, rocking it from side to side, sliding it back and forth. And, because she often plays the piano from the vantage point of her high chair, curling her feet up and against the keyboard. It feels good and helps with the beat.

But Sionna's greatest joy is making music with her Daddy. Sometimes Daddy will sit next to her and play a little tune on the piano. At other times, he will play something on his trumpet. Sionna never fails to "answer" his tune with one of her own, anything from a hands-together tone cluster to a sequence of single notes. She may even vocalize her answer. The question-and-answer game (technically a call-and-response dialogue) will continue back and forth until Sionna launches into a surprise solo, elaborating on one of her favorite sound-effect tunes. An alert listener might even detect a suggestion or two of Daddy's tune. When she's finished, Sionna acknowledges the enthusiastic applause with a big smile.

And Sionna's epiphany, is it "I play therefore I am?" Or is it more prosaic; "Daddy plays and I play, therefore I am just like Daddy?"

We don't, of course, know whether Kessie and Sionna really had epiphanies. But we can be reasonably certain that they respond "as if" the music causes them to respond. There is neither anticipation nor reflection. We can, as well, be reasonably certain that the toddlers' admirers were delighted in the experience. At the very least, "She responds in time therefore she must be musical."

Does Sionna have a head start? It would seem so. She plays the piano and her daddy plays with her. Her tone clusters, her sliding and tapping, her question-and-answer games of gestures and sounds, her rhythmic energy; and her world applauds. But is Sionna really playing the piano or is she having fun playing *with* the piano? How about her gestural experiments? Do they confirm she is a born musician or is she a mime with a scientific bent? Assuming that she opts for a career in music, will Sionna's early experiments prepare her for formal study? It looks like a head start. The question is, in what? And will she carry it through if and when she begins formal music study?

What do a diaper dancer and a diapered pianist tell us about making music?

(a) Delight: The facial responses and baby babbling of both children register delight. They gesture expressively and maintain body movements that mime and synchronize with the music. They are having fun. Music is play. It plays with you.

(b) Timing: Precision of beat is the most striking musical response of both children. Both modify their beat and expressive movements in time with simple changes in the tempo or meter. When the music shifts from triple to duple time, Kessie immediately alters her response from a sequence of vertical movements to a side-to-side shifting of the hips. Sionna maintains a steady beat with Daddy but will occasionally "take off" by increasing the speed of her improvisation, apparently carried away by the excitement of the game.

(c) Movement: Kessie stabilizes her movements with feet planted in the ground. Her knees and upper limbs synchronize and shake to the beat and the after beat. Sionna stabilizes and concentrates her power of "attack" by placing her legs against the keyboard.

(d) Concentration: The immediacy and rhythmic precision of Kessie's opening response suggests that she synchronizes her rhythmic movements to the sound on cue. There is no evidence of anticipation, reflection, or doubt. Her attention remains constant as long as the music keeps playing. In subsequent "performances" she attempted to initiate the experience by turning on the radio or record player. Sionna stays focused as long as necessary in order to "play out" a keyboard game or a call-and-response exchange with her daddy.

(e) Repetition: Kessie enjoys dancing to the same piece over and over. There is no evidence of boredom.

(f) The mimicking ear: Sionna's experience making sounds on the piano may account for her ability to vocalize the timbre and pitch of her daddy's trumpet and to pick up on his beat. Given her environment, we could go out on a limb and say that, like Yvgeny Kissin, music is her first language (A. Solomon, 1996) and that her level of fluency has its roots in her primary experience (understanding) of communication as a call and response duo between baby babble and momma-dadda intonations, caresses, rocking, and approval (Trumble, 2004). Listening to music and playing duos with daddy expands on the emotive qualities of these exchanges (Menn & Stoel-Gammon, 1995).

What makes these primal games shared experiences are the expressive gestures to organized sound. Shared, because they are acknowledged, more precisely because they are unconditionally acknowledged. It is also a tease: Not the whole story, but a prelude to making music. And that, as we shall see, is the rub: "Our genes," noted the biologist Paul Ehrlich, "do not shout commands. . . . At the very most, they whisper suggestions" (Ehrlich, 2002, p. 7).

The Acquired Musical Body

> *He [the composer-pianist Camille St. Saens] knows everything,*
> *but he lacks inexperience.*
>
> **attributed to Hector Berlioz**

Kessie and Sionna have a wealth of inexperience. Their innocence is reflected in their delight in playing games with the magical sounds of music: Mimicking the tones, bouncing to the beat, and giggling to the applause. And the genes keep whispering positive messages. By all appearances, the diaper-dancing scenario suggests a promising career in music. With this in mind, how might an élite music school determine the teachability of these two inexperienced but eager music lovers?

Much of our received wisdom on teachability deals with "knowing the talents" (Subotnik, 2004). An experienced musician "knows" the real talents because these have an apparently better than average ear, better than average memory, better than average reflexes, better than average concentration, and "something special" that a musician just "knows" (Barenboim & Said, 2002). And, often enough, the real talents lack inexperience.

The rules for identifying musical promise are discerned from the average and the exceptions are just that, exceptions. Should either Sionna or Kessie test above average, she will be seriously considered. If she tests on or below average, she will be advised to lower her expectations. She might conceivably improve over time if she can sum up enough determination to continue trying. Unfortunately, as things often go in these matters, a poor bet is unlikely to receive the quality of training she needs to beat the statistics. Such is the teachable musical body.

In the event that Sionna and Kessie are served an eviction notice they will find themselves in the company of a veritable *Who's who* of eminent creative artists among the legions of rejects, quitters, and "unteachables" (Ludwig, 1995, pp. 51–52). These include Beethoven and Ravel. Beethoven's counter-point teacher, Johan Albrechstberger, complained that Beethoven "learned absolutely nothing and will never accomplish anything decent" (M. Solomon, 1998, p. 98). Ravel failed five times to qualify for the Prix de Rome (a prize awarded by a Conservatoire-appointed jury that was intended to establish one's official status as a composer of merit). Because of his alleged neglect of his studies, Ravel's piano teacher, Charles de Beriot, labeled him "a criminal" (Korman, 1996, pp. 38–40).

It would seem from the evidence that the unteachables include both the supremely gifted who resist being taught and those who wish to learn but lack the necessary teachable qualities. Echoing the playwright David Mamet's negative assessment of theater schools as useless because all they teach you is "how to obey, and obedience in the theater will get you nowhere" (Mamet, 1999, p. 19), the distinguished choreographer Mark Morris had this to say about the education of music students: "Imagination has been wrung out of these people and it's tragic. Really, musicians have lousy rhythm" (Keller, 2004, pp. 23–24)—a conclusion Morris reached after coaching élite school students in the dance rhythms underlying works they were performing. However presumptuous his generalization may be, Morris touched on a recurring problem in the education of the gifted: the contradictions that arise when a "nothing but the best" learning concept (Kogan, 1987) is designed to favor reliability (technical correctness) at the expense of invention (original expression) on the assumption that identifying the talents and assessing their teachability is the way to go (Subotnik, 2004; also see Kingsbury, 1988).

But remember: Our genes can only whisper suggestions. With this in mind, we might ask, what Evelyn Glennie's and Lorna's genes might have whispered into their deaf ears about making music? Or, for that matter, what message the tone-deaf ears of Ronald might have received from his genes? And what does their success, against all the odds, tell us about teachability?

The answers can, in part, be deduced from the bottom-line contradictions common to highly selective disciplines. In the performing arts, the bottom line is a tug of war between the pull to create and the push to keep the audience and the critics happy. This is particularly so in the education of professional musicians wherein the emphasis tends to be on technical expertise, style, and correct performance practice. The creative aspect is, for the most part, left to its own devices, with the implicit assumption that you either have what it takes or you don't. It's a jungle out there and it takes time, effort, and money to pursue questionable goals. All things considered, losers are bad news for a top-line music school and the reputations of its artist teachers. The system, as a consequence, tends to favor the readily teachable student. Needless to say, this leaves little room for pedagogical experimentation with potential losers—however the exercise might be rationalized as a contribution to higher-order skill and creativity.

Performance Blocks—When Those who Should Create Cannot Create

It would seem that teachability at any age involves more than identifying one's potential as a performing musician (Cohen, 1986). It has as much to do with how readily otherwise competing academic, pedagogical, domain, and media doctrines of "correctness" accept received wisdom about the unteachability of those who seem to lack the magic touch. The assumption is not confined to the winner's circle or to music but permeates virtually every form of performance education.

Technically correct and performance-blocked.   What is less evident is how an overemphasis on being correct might contribute to the formation of performance blocks, notably the debilitating "paralysis through analysis" syndrome that can frustrate the best efforts of anyone who goes public (Cohen, 1992). In bioesthetic terms, a performance block is a persistent disruption of the embodied conductor's ability to expressively direct and maintain musical motion in real time. The symptoms include lapses in the performer's physical organization, memory, timing, affect, and concentration (Chan, 2005). Whatever the cause may be, the result will include feelings of insufficiency, failure, and humiliation. All things considered, an obsession with correctness may set the stage for a performance block that can adversely affect the ability of a sensitive musician to demonstrate her potential.

Exploring the unpredictable: Redirecting performance-blocked attention. An "on stage" study conducted by the author explored a novel bio-esthetic approach to the resolution of long-standing performance blocks. The study examined (a) the effectiveness of expressively improvised gestures in drawing the performer's attention away from the anticipation of blocking, (b) the role of cross-modal expressive synchronization as a factor in real-time creative variability and, (c) by extension, to examine the issue of why some musicians have the prerequisite qualities of technical skill, knowledge and motivation yet fail to realize their potential, whereas others, apparently less equipped, excel despite the odds. Five career-track pianists whose aspirations were put on hold by debilitating performance blocks participated in the study. Each had shown musical promise as a child and, as an adult continued to score above average in aural memory and related measures of performance musicianship. Participants were told that the purpose of the explorations was to have fun playing games with so-called correct positions. They were instructed to improvise "dancelike" arm, hand, finger, gesture, and postural movements. The musical score was obliquely referred to as "not necessary to improvise on." Improvisatory sequences were not to be repeated in practice sessions, open rehearsals, and formal performances. Distractions and occasional obstructions were introduced without notice during each performance in order to test the musical stability of redirected attention. Total preparation time averaged three weeks. All sessions were videotaped for later analysis.

EXPLORATION 1:   A. C., solo pianist; music performed, Joseph Haydn—Sonata in D Major, Hob. XV1:37, first movement (Documentary Recording: *The Leonardo Project: Shaping the invisible,* Discovery Channel, Canada, 1994).

INSTRUCTIONS: Improvise all movements from a standing position while wearing a blindfold and dishwashing gloves; visual cues were therefore blocked and tactility was reduced. The pianist began with her left leg resting on the keyboard while her right hand searched for and "found" the opening motif. Both sides of the body immediately snapped into place at full speed. Throughout the performance she "danced" from side to side, bending and straightening her knees, swinging her arms above and below the keyboard, palms and fingers sliding back and forth and to the side of the hands. Most significant was the cross-modal synchronization of movements with the larger phrase units and the rhythmic pulse of the music. Balance throughout was adjusted without compromising the musical line. Despite the gloves, the player claimed to "hear" the music in her fingers.

EXPLORATION 2:   A. C. and T. P., duo pianists at one piano; music performed, P. D. Q. Bach—Sonata Innamorata (Documentary report on the Leonardo Project: *Beyond 2000,* Australian TV, 1994).

INSTRUCTIONS: Improvise gestures at close quarters, however cramped or obstructed. The performance was marked by considerable interlocking of hands and spontaneous shifts of body position. Obstructions were frequent and often playful. In an inspired moment worthy of the slapstick comedian Chico Marx, the treble (upper keyboard) pianist slid to the floor, played the foot pedal with his right hand, and the keys with the back of his left hand. The bass (lower keyboard) performer simultaneously rose, walked around the seat to the upper register, completed her duo partner's phrase, then returned to her position in the bass. During a subsequent exchange the treble pianist—still in slapstick mode—bent forward to play a series of notes with his nose. Both performers maintained their balance and cross-modal synchronization despite the frequency of direct interferences with each other's movements. Most significant was the imaginative, precisely timed, and often humorous interplay between distractions and response throughout the performance.

EXPLORATION 3:   M. T. and C. G., duo pianists at two pianos separated at a distance of sixteen feet with visibility confined to the head movements of each pianist; music performed, Arthur Benjamin—*Jamaican Rhumba* (Documentary report on the Leonardo Project: *City Beat,* Canadian Broadcasting Corporation, CBMT- TV, Montreal, 1993).

INSTRUCTIONS: Improvise gestures from a standing position. At random intervals, I attempted to obstruct or distract each player's vision, balance, hand or body position. The obstructions included "hands on" shifting of their head movements, covering their eyes or hands, swinging their arms back and forth, and pushing their bodies out of position. The players responded to my intrusions with playful gestures of resistance or by adjusting their movements. In either circumstance the musical flow remained unimpeded.

EXPLORATION 4:   D. B., an affect-blocked teen-age pianist-composer and the author (as conductor and duo pianist). The two pianos were separated at a distance of 18 feet. Music performed (a) conducted and accompanied improvisations and (b) conducted and accompanied rehearsal of Ludwig van Beethoven, Sonata op. 27, no. 2 (Minuet) (Videotaped recording: Leonardo Project Archives).

INSTRUCTIONS: Improvise in a duo with the author. I created obstructions by rapidly shifting attention from either conducting or improvising to conducting while improvising. This involved abrupt changes in tempo, meter, dynamics, and character that were communicated by means of highly expressive contrasts in gesture, facial expression, and tone. Our tonal and gestural game-playing *caused* the affect-blocked pianist to communicate his musical ideas expressively and on cue without reflection. This established a model for his subsequent development over a period of six years.

   In summary, the study supported the bioesthetic premise of timing as a para-doxical synchronization of one's biological and esthetic resources. Although the sample is admittedly small, coherence and creative variability were achieved by a reprieve from acquired assumptions about correct performance. All participants made a flowing performance possible by *playing with* dancelike biological rhythms. Esthetic order was ensured by shifting back and forth across tactile and gestural sensory modes. Distractions and obstructions seemed to encour-age fluency of execution. All participants reported the "being on" experience of simultaneously playing and not playing. The spirit of play and unfettered involve-ment suggested a reactivation of the naïve musical body's immediacy of response. The results are consistent with the Leonardo Project's exploratory studies of per-formers considered to be performance-impaired. In short, the participants spon-taneously exhibited qualities of on stage compatibility that challenge received assumptions about learning and teachability (Cohen, 1986).

Musings on creatively directed learning.   Whether or not an indefinable some-thing can be taught, let alone explained, may be a matter of debate. One can, how-ever, be reasonably certain that the challenge involves nonverbal, poetic, rhetorical and playful "as if" qualities that resist objective analysis. Picasso (see Podoksik, 1996) and Ravel (1937) have argued that these qualities are shared by all artists, independent of their particular domain. It follows that a creatively inspired issue is best explained through example, that is, by demonstration, suggestion, infer-ence, or simulation. An explanatory vocabulary of expressive movement is, for this reason, a given component in the bioesthetic approach to optimizing perfor-mance excellence. All things considered, creative variability rests on actualizing shifting structural relationships as they move through time.

Overcoming Barriers to Achieving Creative Variability in Performance

Barrier 1: Timing.   The inherent variability of musical timing is unquestionably the most perplexing developmental challenge faced by a performing artist. This is a formidable task when one considers that, to most music students, good timing means playing in time to a regular beat: something you can count and check with a metronome (Barenboim & Said, 2002; Morris cited in Keller, 2004). To play expressively is usually associated with a generalized concept of emotion tied to the right sound. Expressively directed timing, in contrast, depends on (a) the perceived qualitative relationships between shape, nuance, emotive tone, rhythmic stress, and the overall structure of the music as it unfolds in real time, and (b) the specific relational patterns that expressively link harmonic, melodic, and textural durations, amplitudes, articulations, assonance, and rhythmic stress (Gabrielsson, 1988). The timing and expressive communication of any one of these patterns will be influenced by a change in the relationship between any one or more of the preceding factors. An accomplished artist is distinguished by the ability to vary these relationships while simultaneously maintaining or establishing a fundamental beat in repeated performances of a work. How this is achieved assumes a high level of biological, aesthetic and cognitive organization. It is here that the concept of an embodied or external conductor can be understood to synchronize a performer's resources "on cue" for creative variability. In this regard, I have suggested that the perception of a cause is generally more useful than the fact of a cause. A violinist, for example, may produce a more precisely focused musical line if she perceives the sound of the string causing the bow stroke rather than the more obvious fact that the reverse is true (i.e., she has delegated the cause to an external conductor). Carried a step further, if she perceives the sounding string to cause a lyrical bow stroke, the resulting musical line may not only be expressively specific, but it will allow for varied "colorings" and expressively directed timing each time it is repeated. Similarly, a pianist may perceive a legato (connected) sequence of tones in the right hand to cause an accompanying portato (slightly detached) sequence in the left hand. The timing of the causal sequence will have demonstrated a crucial step towards resolving problems of coordination. There are related situations in which simply observing the rise and fall of a sequence of keys will improve accuracy of touch and timing.

Barrier 2:   Masks that inhibit emotional authenticity. Emotional authenticity is the ground rule for many creative artists. It is a journey, according to Lecoq (see Murray, 2003), that follows a path without end where one's intuitive and esthetic "knowing" is tested in episodes of chaos, obstruction, and illusion. Grotowski (2002) described the journey as a "via negativa" where the acquired "masks" that inhibit emotional authenticity are dispensed with, in particular those that come with theater props, technological gimmicks, social status, and the need for audience approval. To the poet Stephen Spender, the journey is a "spiritual compulsion," a "necessity," rather than something you just feel like doing (Spender, 1970, pp. 62–63). Under the circumstances, the creative norm becomes a paradoxical mix-and-match of remote and contradictory associations in which metaphors, images, and sound associations have the right-of-way to blend cross-phenomenal and primordial references into conclusions that run the gamut from the profound to the banal and absurd.

Barrier 3: Overemphasis on technique. Working professionals, for whom music is rarely a first language, are generally obliged to acquire and maintain a musical vocabulary from scratch. This involves a challenge that is compounded by the complexity and sheer physical difficulty of much of the serious repertoire. In the best of musical worlds, creative freedom and its technical and physical correlates would complement each other at every step in the artist's journey. In the real world, their relationship is a lifelong balancing act between what comes first, technique or esthetic invention. Technique usually wins out and, as a consequence, methods abound to serve the unquenchable need to achieve technical perfection, even though "the musician's intentional focus . . . is grounded in the esthetic dimension of the piece being learned" (Segalowitz, Cohen, Chan, & Prieur, 2001, p. 147). In this regard, Fraser (2003) took issue with the "bulging muscle emphasis" (p. 3) of many technically focused methods, while Pascual-Leone (2001) cautioned musicians about the danger of dystonia as a consequence of repetitive practice. Many professional musicians are so obsessed with technical issues that it is not uncommon for them to define musicianship in terms of a paradoxical double standard of expertise and an indefinable "something." This brings us to the question of whether an indefinable something can be taught, let alone explained. A student of mine once interviewed a celebrated Russian pianist for a newspaper article. The interview took place immediately after the final concert of a lengthy North American tour. The pianist was clearly not in the mood for an in-depth probe into his psyche as artist and man. He fielded her questions politely enough until she asked him how he practiced. Annoyed, he winced, shrugged his shoulders, and asked, "What do you want to know?" "Well, I play the piano and I'm interested in how you go about practicing. Do you have any special method or. . . ." He interrupted her: "How do I go about practicing? All you people think about is technique, technique, that's all I hear everywhere I go. . . . Okay. You want technique? [dismissively] I practice Hanon exercises." "But," she countered, "do you sound like *me* when *I* practice Hanon?"

Barrier 4: Rehearsing for replicability. The ability to achieve creative variability in real time is formed during inventively focused practice and rehearsal. This remains true, despite the fact that many intuitive performers can achieve a remarkably well timed sense of immediacy, particularly while improvising, without prior knowledge of technical or esthetic aspects (Nachmanovitch, 1990; Pressing, 1988). In this regard, it is perhaps significant that the effect is rarely achieved by a trained classical performer who is unprepared to "take off" spontaneously. Conductors, notably Furtwangler, Celibidache, Zimmerman, and Kleiber have shown that by rethinking the purpose of rehearsal, striking improvements in spontaneity become possible. According to Furtwangler, the work can only be "reconstituted by forming it entirely anew" from the score . . . *"since the meaning of music still lies in its playing"* (Lebrecht, 1992, p. 84; italics added). In order to achieve the necessary depth in reconstituting the score, Furtwangler believed that it was mandatory to test the extreme ends of the musical spectrum in rehearsal, no matter how unrelated these might appear to be. He was said to "rehearse two hundred ways of saying 'no' so that on the evening of the concert" he could once say "yes" (Barenboim & Said, 2002, pp. 20–22). In other words, Furtwangler rehearsed "so that certain things don't happen," unlike most conductors who rehearsed so that "they could put the music together in the morning and then repeat it" exactly as rehearsed "in the evening" (Barenboim & Said, pp. 20–22).

Toward a Vocabulary of Esthetically Ordered Movement

When you speak about music remember words divide, tones unite.

Victor Zuckerkandl, 1973, p. 5

Zuckerkandl's generalization about the distinction between words and tones points to the "intelligible, yet untranslatable" (p. 25) paradox of the musical experience. It does not, however, take into account the more fundamental issue of how our everyday thinking tends to encourage what Rudolf Laban (1976) described as a static snapshot-like perception that creates an artificial separation of space and movement. We do not normally employ word orders and a syntax that expresses movement even when we describe the experience. Musical tones unite because they relate and move. As a consequence, music performance is best understood when it is learned in a vocabulary that meaningfully expresses the ways in which movement and relationship unite (A. Solomon, 1996).

The absence of a vocabulary of musical movement is at the core of certain generally accepted yet potentially inhibiting imperatives to creative variability. These acquired imperatives include the notated score, music theory, musicology, performance methods and pedagogies. Each of these disciplines is an essential reference for aspiring artists. Collectively, they comprise a musical map that serves as an aid to composing, reading, deciphering, explaining and, hopefully, making music. All the information in the map is *about* music. None of it is directly involved in the *act* of performing. Maps, however, and the territories they represent, have been known to get confused in translation. Self-evident as this may seem, it is astonishing how many musicians as well as laypeople assume that (a) the notation is the music and (b) a theoretical description is the experience (Ingarden, cited in Taruskin, 1995).

On this last point, background knowledge about the music will normally involve reading up on historical performance practices as well as contending schools of "correct" style, interpretation, and technique. Each of these areas is compounded by the fact that western music is often both global and regional. The documented "proofs," as a consequence, vary widely and are often controversial, leaving them open to a perpetual cycle of new proofs and challenges. Even on those rare occasions when one has access to the composer, there can be no guarantee of a helpful answer.

All things equal, knowledge, backed up by technique and native musicality will conceivably help translate music for the eyes and ears into music for the performing body. It is doubtful, however, whether an aspiring concert artist can fully benefit from a translation that excludes a working vocabulary of expressively directed movement. The translation from a document to sound motion is at the very least a craft and at its best a creatively varied experience.

Verbs in waiting.   An intriguing step toward developing a vocabulary of movement has been suggested by the physicist David Bohm. In *Wholeness and the Implicate Order* (1980), Bohm discussed the role of grammatical structure in human consciousness, behavior, social conditioning, and culture. Although he does not refer directly to music, the implications are significant. Bohm described a cognitive experiment in awareness that adopts a verb-based syntax. By assigning a "basic role to the verb," one immediately recognizes its function in describing "actions and movements which flow into each other and merge, without sharp separations or breaks" (1980, p. 30). Bohm's most significant observation was that, "since movements are in general always themselves changing, they have in them no permanent pattern of fixed form within which separately existent things could be identified" (p. 30).

Esthetic order, metaphors as cues.   Assigning a basic role to the verb makes sense in describing a music performance. Expressively directed movement, however also demands metaphoric images that establish relationships and paradoxes that cause tones to unite meaningfully. The success of these cue images depends on how well they can generate an esthetically ordered response. In the most general sense, esthetic order can be described as the perception of beauty. In a music performance it refers to the shaping qualities that generate and maintain spatial and temporal relationships. Theoretically, anything goes, from the emotive qualities of tone to articulation, rhythmic and durational flexibility, textural balance, elegance of line, and brilliance of attack. It is, for the most part, a matter of context and perceived internal relationships. Musicians often employ commonly used metaphors as cues to the interpretation of a musical passage. They speak of a warm or brilliant or sweet tone, a cool interpretation, a well shaped phrase, an exquisitely shaded musical line, harmonic coloring, a biting attack or *jeu perle*. A directive to play louder (*forte*) or softer (*piano*) while factually precise, is esthetically imprecise when compared to play it more brilliantly or conversely with a sweeter, more tender line (Cohen & Chan, 2003). The neuropsychologist Richard Cytowic (2002) noted parallel observations in everyday life that illustrate the fundamental role of metaphoric relationships in human discourse.

Taken literally, none of these metaphoric pairings makes sense, yet they are immediately understood by musicians and sensed by the listener. Unfortunately, the practice is rarely cultivated beyond a response to a given cue, as if getting it as described is the only possible way of expressing the music. Contrast this conventional response with Beethoven's image of an "as if" sculpture that "rises," "grows," and forms itself into a complete musical work. "I *hear and see* the image in front of me, from every angle, *as if it had been cast*" (Rothenberg, 1990, p. 28; italics added). Beethoven then hears the idea although he is deaf; he sees the sound as though it is an image; the image stands before him "as if" it is a sculpture. It's not just that Beethoven had a bigger, richer metaphor bank than ordinary mortals. What he cultivated is the ability to see, hear, touch, and imagine sounds that blend with and move improbabilities that have the power—in the heat of a cross-modal image—to explode into a probability. The transformation from inconceivable to real captures movement, time, and revelation in a tantalizing microsecond. The image conveys more than the sum of its parts.

To sum up, reading a musical text as literal information is to perceive it as a static representation that can be identified because one can see it on a page. To play what one sees requires translating the mute dots on the page into the language of sound motion. Translation begins when the distinction between a static representation and a continuum of unfolding sound relationships is made clear. Once understood as such, these relationships are perceived as if ready to spring into musical motion. It is here where metaphors, analogies, paradoxes, and verb relationships offer images and insights capable of illuminating qualities in the particular musical experience that defy literal description. In the playing scheme of things, a context-specific image becomes a cue to translate the notation from a sequence of discrete entities to verbs in waiting—an act of transformation that triggers patterns of meaningfully structured biological and esthetic responses. These cue-images illustrate why connecting and relating are what making music is all about with the added bonus that it feels more like fun than work.

Translating from a notated score to an audible performance can be greatly facilitated when we use verb-based references and the movement-friendly vocabularies of metaphor, analogy, cross-sensory imagery, and paradoxical causality. These share poetic qualities (Lecoq, 2001) that stimulate imagination and generate images of movement and subjective experiences that transcend the "tyranny" of language as description.

Summary: Timing the Acquired Musical Body

Our *what* and *how* review of the paradoxes involved in timing the Acquired Musical Body has looked at delegated causality from the perspectives of cross-sensory organization, esthetic ordering, balance, and the expressive nature of kinesthetic experience. We have made the sobering note that some people "get it" without knowing the facts. What they get is the ultimate paradox of "being on" or "in the zone," the sought after "sweet spot" that makes a performance a cherished memory. The description is familiar but the logic governing its apparent contradictions normally rests below the threshold of consciousness. The experience relies on paradoxical logic and its mystique relies in its unpredictability.

In this regard, paradoxical logic is implicit in the notion of delegating bioesthetically directed timing to a team of "as if" embodied and external conductors. As such it is an open-ended process that is geared toward cultivating modification and renewal. To cultivate is esthetically friendly: It suggests a commitment to nature and personal enhancement. To develop, in contrast, can be a deceptively neutral concept. For many late-striving performers, it evokes dark undertones: memories of imposed regimens, exams, judges, destructive criticism, and potential failure.

Grotowski (2002), Lecoq (2001), and Picasso (cf. Zervos, 1985) would add that the long-term cultivation of creative awareness resides in shedding one's counterproductive responses (Bjork & Bjork, 1992). Picasso described his own process as "a sum of destructions" (Zervos, 1985, p. 49) that he achieved partly by creating problems and working them through until a novel solution presented itself. Lecoq's "journey" followed a similar path by introducing apparent obstructions (contextual interferences) that open up alternative possibilities (Battig, 1999), whereas Grotowski explained his "via negativa" as "an eradication of blocks" rather than a "collection of skills" (Grotowski, 2002, p. 17). The experience of creating obstructions and pursuing them into unknown territory is much like attempting to coax a phantom image into life. Creative awareness grows—is cultivated—in an unending process of discovery without the benefit of a known solution or a set of rules for solving it. A creatively induced problem is, from this perspective, quite distinct from that of a conventional problem-solving regimen (Simonton, 2004).

It follows that, whether an obstacle is due to an injury, fatigue, poor training, a pitch-recognition problem, or anxiety, it can be perceived as a creative opportunity rather than a hindrance. The opportunity to cultivate these experiences bioesthetically in an "as if" exploratory atmosphere is built into the Sketch, Test, and Digress model of practice.

Composing the Performance: The Sketch, Test, and Digress Model of Creative Variability in Practice

In his treatise on drawing, Rosand (2002) argued that sketching "reveals the ideas, imagination, style, the manner of thinking of the artist," and "the role of the hand in giving form to thought" (pp. 21–23). A sketch from this perspective is the artist's personal voice and a creative work in its own right. As such, it provides the artist with a sanctuary that frees him to explore, experiment, and invent without having to account for his efforts in the domain or the field. In the long term, the habit of sketching establishes an open-ended perspective on the art itself.

A personal voice is evident in the workbooks and collected sketches of many visual artists, composers, writers, and other individuals across disciplines. These fill 8,000 pages in Beethoven's workbooks (M. Solomon, 1998), and over 7,000 pages in the workbooks of Leonardo da Vinci (Nicholl, 2005). The sketches reveal the hands of a great composer and universal genius "giving form to thought(s)" that are often breathtaking in their diversity and ingenuity (M. Solomon, 1998).

Sketchings are not necessarily preparatory exercises related to a work in progress. Picasso, Leonardo, and Beethoven (Kerman, 1971) seemed to enjoy playing with ideas for no other reason than the fun of it. For Leonardo, any available scrap of paper was inspiration enough to scribble away on the thought of the moment. One such thought expanded into a pictographic arrangement of jokes, riddles, puzzles, and cryptic asides composed in cartoonlike drawings and words written in mirror image (Marinoni, 1974/1990).

Sketching the ebb and flow of musical time. Sketching is not confined to notebooks. Wilhelm Furtwangler has shown that it is possible to achieve striking improvements in spontaneity by rethinking the purpose of rehearsal. His approach was diametrically opposed to the conventional method of preparing the orchestra to repeat the music exactly as it was rehearsed (Barenboim & Said, 2002). Furtwangler's rehearsal method illustrates an essential prerequisite to creative variability in performance: Spontaneity is more likely to occur when chance is prepared. Whether the conductor stands before an orchestra or is embodied within a soloist, the seeds of inspiration are brought to life when unlikely possibilities are explored, probabilities are played with, and risk becomes an opportunity.

Cross-modal sketching—a vocabulary. The immediate aim is to have the aspiring artist experience the distinction between willing an action and observing a response. The distinction is made clear in hands-on demonstrations that verify the experience in concrete terms. This involves adopting a cross-modal vocabulary that evokes a creative focus and maintains it through sketching in practice, rehearsal, performance, and postperformance analysis. The vocabulary is in three complementary modes of communication: (a) a performance-specific terminology, (b) nonverbal expressive gesture, touch and movement, and (c) paradoxical cognition (embodied and external conductors). Concepts and theoretical descriptions that might inhibit the translation from score to sound are initially avoided (Cohen, 1998). From a developmental viewpoint, the verb associations, images, paradoxes, and somatic analogies express self-actualizing relationships that are universally intelligible. These include cues to personal and creative responsibility (compose your performance), esthetic discrimination (audition your conductor), imagination (delegate the cause), observation (the "on" experience), and esthetic perception (a scale is a melody). Each is intended to encourage the aspiring artist to experiment with possibilities that are in and out of the box.

The most compelling argument for a sketch, test, and digress model of practice lies in its role as a medium for cultivating the entente between esthetic intention and biological rhythms. The process clarifies the role of expressively directed gestures, touch qualities, and movements in communicating the musical line. These relationships breathe life into a musical motive or phrase by perceiving it as analogous to, say, a gentle (lyrical), expansive (warm), or panting (agitated) breath.

From workaholic to playaholic. Sketching, testing, and digressing are mediums for creative exercise in which ideas are played with, in and out of context. An exhaustive attention to expressive options and their cross-modal relationships distinguishes the regimen from "practice makes perfect" models that aim for replicability with minimum risk (Palmer, 1997). The distinction does not automatically exclude repetitive practice from leading to an inspired performance. It does, however, assert that a performer who has experienced a range of bioesthetically synchronized possibilities is more likely to know and act on the difference between a safe bet and a risk worth taking. The difference lies in an embodied cognitive set that is fully equipped to "wing it" rather than wait for the inspired moment. Like a visual artist's or composer's sketch pad, the process opens up options for "playing with" the possibilities before exhibiting them.

Verification—a bioesthetic perspective. The rationale, therefore, for the sketch, test, and digress model is musical and poetic imagery. The model rests primarily on testing and verifying causal variations in movement, tactility, and perception on a given cross-sensory "practice" theme. Repetition "when or where necessary" may be part of the process, yet will rarely be treated as an exercise independent of a specific musical context. A scale, for example, may be heard as a melody that is "composed" and "conducted" with a variety of melodic inflections, articulations, and "interpretations." The testing of the melody—how it is perceived and cognitively organized from one variation to the next—may involve the incorporation of "hands-on" conducted gestures that are esthetically analogous, tangible, visible, audible, and expressively verifiable. Expressive verifiability, can, as a consequence, be confirmed from perspectives that are experienced simultaneously as both subjective and objective. The cue-based vocabulary best suited to translating the whole into a unified action may rest on generating images that include a quality of touch, an unfolding gestural shape, a rhyme scheme, or a seemingly remote mythological association. These "as if" experiences elude literal explanation yet open up the sketching and testing experience for evocative, open-ended interpretations. Most significant is the immediacy with which most performers are able to suspend disbelief and enter the "being on" mode, thereby reducing the need to deal with nonmusical practice issues and potential blocks. It follows that verification can be achieved from a bioesthetic perspective when thinking (cognition), acting (biological response), and esthetic ordering (perception) are synchronized so as to ensure maximum advantage for the whole. This assumes an overriding logic capable of harmonizing the normally disparate forces of acting and thinking about acting.

Speculations and Thoughts: Reconciling the Paradoxes between Naïve Response and Acquired Knowledge

The real challenge for the aspiring or performing musician involves coming to terms with an art that is at once pragmatic, poetic, and physically demanding. Reconciling these apparent solitudes is what makes communication between performers and listeners both vital and mutually gratifying. The subtext here is that a performer, teacher, or coach has little to gain from treading semantic hay with competing "experts" on whether the ability to make music is an innate gift, a developed skill, a hybrid of sorts, or a matter of luck and circumstance. At their best, the what, the how, and the why of the experience can be valuable references insofar as they contribute to transforming the incomprehensible into a memorable experience.

Embodied conductors, concert pianists, and diaper dancers—when learning comes full circle. A parting reflection is in order on the ententes among paradoxical logic, creative variability, and the on-stage cast of real and imagined characters responsible for translating their relationships into a musical experience (I write this with my ears attuned to my cautionary note in the previous paragraph). The effectiveness of the imagined conductor's ability to convey a performer's musical intentions is always conditioned by input from the performer's instinctual (naïve) responses and acquired understanding: a challenging balancing act given the push and pull of two-way conflicting messages. To help resolve misunderstandings that may arise, I have introduced a vocabulary that aims at overcoming some of the barriers that are likely to arise between these apparent solitudes. The vocabulary is designed to make sense of the act of playing *with* the music, and responding to it *as if* it were a playmate. With knowledge, experience, and wisdom nurtured in the playroom, the student performer is less likely to settle for anything less than a lifelong game plan: a plan dedicated to exploring the expressive riches of the creative imagination to their fullest with an in-house conductor and a diaper-dancing playmate on hand to show the way. Such is the artist's journey. "A bird sings," notes a Chinese proverb, "not because it has an answer. It sings because it has a song."

The performer creates the experience.

References

Artaud, A. (1958). *The theater and its double.* New York: Grove Press.

Atran, S. (1996). Is good thinking scientific thinking? In D. R. Olson & N. Torrance (Eds.), *Modes of thought: Explorations in culture and cognition* (pp. 261–281). New York: Cambridge University Press.

Balzano, G. J. (1989). Command performances, performance commands. *Contemporary Music Review, 4,* 437–446.

Barenboim, D., & Said, E. W. (2002). *Parallels and paradoxes: Explorations in music and society.* New York: Pantheon.

Battig, W. F. (1999). The flexibility of human memory. In L. S. Cermak & F. I. M. Craik (Eds.), *Levels of processing in human memory* (pp. 23–44). Hillsdale, NJ: Erlbaum.

Beveridge, W. I. B. (1957). *The art of scientific investigation* (3rd ed.). New York: Vintage.

Bjork, R. A., & Bjork, E. L. (1992). A new theory of disuse and an old theory of stimulus fluctuation. In A. Healy, S. Kosslyn, & R. Shiffrin (Eds.), *From learning processes to cognitive processes: Essays in honor of William K. Estes* (Vol. 2; pp. 35–67). Hillsdale, NJ: Erlbaum.

Bohm, D. (1980). *Wholeness and the implicate order*. London: Routledge & Kegan Paul.

Bouhnik, L. (Director). (2003). *Twenty-four hours in the life of a woman*. Film based on the 1913 novella by Stefan Zweig.

Brust, J. C. M. (2001). Music and the neurologist: A historical perspective. In R. J. Zatorre & I. Peretz (Eds.), *The biological foundations of music* (pp. 143–152). New York: New York Academy of Sciences (*Annals*, Vol. 930, No. 1).

Campbell, D. T. (1960). Blind variation and selective retention in creative thought as in other knowledge processes. *Psychological Review, 67*, 380–400.

Chan, A. (2005). *Unblocking performance blocks: An interdisciplinary approach towards an exploratory study on the nature of musical performance blocks in "late arriving" pianists*. Unpublished Doctoral Thesis in Music and Psychology, Concordia University, Montreal, QC.

Clynes, M. (1986). When time is music: Music beyond the score. In J. R. Evans & M. Clynes (Eds.), *Rhythm in psychological, linguistic and musical processes* (pp. 171–189). Springfield, IL: Thomas.

Clynes, M., & Nettheim, N. (1982). The living quality of music: Neurobiological basis of communicating feeling. In M. Clynes (Ed.), *Music, mind and brain: The neuropsychology of music*. New York: Plenum Press.

Cohen, P. (1982). *Hands: Dave Mackay and Vicky Hamilton* (recording program notes). Los Angeles: Discovery Records (catalog number DS 868).

Cohen, P. (1986). Interpreting the musical performer: An integrated plan of study. In *Quel enseignement musical pour demain? La formation du musicien professionnel*. Colloque International de Pédagogie Musicale (Ministère de la Culture, UNESCO et al.) Cannes, France. Paris: L'Institut de Pédagogie Musicale. (Proceedings, pp. 145–168.)

Cohen, P. (1992). *Musical virtuosity and human potential: Towards an artist/scientist perspective*. Keynote Address presented at the Conférence multidisciplinaire sur la performance musicale avancée [Multidisciplinary conference on advanced musical performance]. Leonardo Project, Concordia University, Montreal, QC.

Cohen, P. (1996). *Performance creativity: Towards the development of a bio-aesthetic theory of complex music performance*. Paper presented at the annual meeting of the Learned Societies of Canada, St. Catherines, ON.

Cohen, P. (1998). *Composing a performance: Metaphor and the art of textual translation*. Lecture and master class presented at the Hyde Park Performance Group, Chicago.

Cohen, P., & Chan, A. (2003, October). *Measures and the muse*. Poster presented at the Centre for the Study of Learning and Performance Research Fair, Concordia University, Montreal, QC.

Croyden, M. (2003). *Conversations with Peter Brook, 1970–2000*. New York: Faber & Faber.

Csikszentmihalyi, M. (1998). Creativity and genius: A systems approach. In A. Steptoe (Ed.), *Genius and the mind: Studies of creativity and temperament* (pp. 39–64). New York: Oxford University Press.

Cytowic, R. E. (2002). *Synesthesia: A union of the senses* (2nd ed.). Cambridge, MA: MIT Press.

Desain, P., & Honing, H. (1994). Does expressive timing in music performance scale proportionally with tempo? *Psychological Research, 56*, 285–292.

Dirac, P. A. M. (1963). The evolution of the physicist's picture of nature. *Scientific American, 208,* 45–53.

Drake, C., & Palmer, C. (1993). Accent structures in music performance. *Music Perception, 10,* 343–378.

Dryden, J. (1983). [From] Absalom and Achitophel: A poem. In A. W. Allison, H. Barrows, C. R. Blake, A. J. Carr, A. M. Eastman, & H. M. English, Jr. (Eds.), *The Norton anthology of poetry* (3rd ed.) (pp. 356–369). New York: Norton.

Dunsby J. (1989). Guest editorial: Performance and analysis of music. *Music Analysis, 8,* 5–20.

Ehrlich, P. R. (2002). *Human natures: Genes, culture, and the human prospect.* New York: Penguin.

Eigeldinger, J.-J. (1986). *Chopin: Pianist and teacher as seen by his pupils* (N. Shohet with K. Osostowicy & R. Howat, Trans.). Cambridge, UK: Cambridge University Press. (Original work published 1970)

Ekman, P., & Rosenberg, E. L. (1997). *What the face reveals: Basic and applied studies of spontaneous expression using the facial action coding system (FACS).* New York: Oxford University Press. (Second edition published in 2005)

Ericsson, K. A., Krampe, R. T., & Tesch-Römer, C. (1993). The role of deliberate practice in the acquisition of expert performance. *Psychological Review, 100,* 363–406.

Fraser, A. (2003). *The craft of piano playing: A new approach to piano technique.* Lanham, MD: Scarecrow Press.

Gabrielsson, A. (1986). Rhythm in music. In J. R. Evans & M. Clynes (Eds.), *Rhythm in psychological, linguistic and musical processes* (pp. 131–167). Springfield, IL: Thomas.

Galton, F. (1892). *English men of science: Their nature and nurture.* London: Macmillan.

Greenspan, D. A., Solomon, B., & Gardner, H. (2004). The development of talent in different domains. In L. V. Shavinina & M. Ferrari (Eds.), *Beyond knowledge: Extracognitive aspects of developing high ability* (pp. 119–135). Mahwah, NJ: Erlbaum.

Grotowski, J. (2002). *Towards a poor theatre.* New York: Routledge.

Gruson, L. M. (1988). Rehearsal skill and musical competence: Does practice make perfect? In J. A. Sloboda (Ed.), *Generative processes in music* (pp. 91–112). Oxford, UK: Oxford University Press.

Gutin, J. A. C. (1996). *That fine madness.* Boone, IA: Discover.

Hilton, J. (1987). *Performance.* London: Macmillan.

Howe, M. J. A. (1999). *Genius explained.* Cambridge, UK: Cambridge University Press.

Howe, M. J. A. (2004). Some insights of geniuses into the causes of exceptional achievements. In L. V. Shavinina & M. Ferrari (Eds.), *Beyond knowledge: Extracognitive aspects of developing high ability* (pp. 105–117). Mahwah, NJ: Erlbaum.

James, W. (1890). *The principles of psychology* (Vol. 2, pp. 520–526). New York: Holt.

Keller, J. (2004, July 11). Let's play the music (and dance): Mark Morris proves he can give anyone rhythm—even musicians. *New York Times,* pp. 23–24.

Kerman, J. (1971). Beethoven's early sketches. In P. H. Lang (Ed.), *The creative world of Beethoven* (pp. 21–23). New York: Norton.

Kingsbury, H. (1988). *Music, talent and performance: A conservatory cultural system.* Philadelphia: Temple University Press.

Kleiber, C. (1989). *New Year's Eve Concert in Vienna* [December 31, 1989], Vienna Philharmonic Orchestra. Deutsche Grammophon DVD and program notes, catalogue number 0730249. (Re-released in 2004.)

Kogan, J. (1987). *Nothing but the best: The struggle for perfection at The Juilliard School.* New York: Random House.

Korman, P. (1996). *Intention, creative variability and paradox in recorded performances of the piano music of Maurice Ravel.* Unpublished doctoral thesis in music, Concordia University, Montreal, QC.

Laban, R. von (1976). *The language of movement: A guidebook to choreutics* (L. Ullmann, Ed., with annotations). Boston: Plays.

Lebrecht, N. (1992). *The maestro myth: Great conductors in pursuit of power.* London: Simon & Schuster.

Lecoq, J. (2001). *The moving body: Teaching creative theatre.* (D. Bradby, Trans.). New York: Routledge.

Lovelace, C. T., & Parton, S. (2001). Integrating sensory integration. *Trends in Cognitive Sciences, 5*(2), 48–49.

Ludwig, A. M. (1995). *The price of greatness: Resolving the creativity and madness controversy.* New York: Guilford Press.

Mackenzie, C. L., & Van Eerd, D. L. (1990). Rhythmic precision in the performance of piano scales: motor psychophysics and motor programming. In M. Jeannerod (Ed.), *Attention and performance: Motor representation and control, 13,* 375–440. Hillsdale, NJ: Erlbaum.

Mamet, D. (1999). *True and false: Heresy and common sense for the actor.* New York: Vintage Books.

Marinoni, A. (1990). The writer: Leonardo's literary legacy. In L. Reti (Ed.), *The unknown Leonardo* (pp. 56–85). New York: Abradale Press. (Original work published in 1974)

Marton, F., Fensham, P., & Chaiklin, S. (1994). A Nobel's eye view of scientific intuition: Discussions with the Nobel Prize winners in physics, chemistry and medicine (1970–86). *International Journal of Science Education, 16,* 457–473.

Maslow, A. H. (1963). The creative attitude. *The Structuralist, 3,* 410.

Menn, L., & Stoel-Gammon, C. (1995). Phonological development. In P. Fletcher & B. MacWhinney (Eds.), *The handbook of child language.* Cambridge, MA: Blackwell.

Miller, R. (1986). *The structure of singing: System and art in vocal technique.* New York: Schirmer.

Motluck, A. (2005, January 29). Senses special: The art of seeing without sight. *New Scientist,* issue # 2484, 29 January 2005.

Murray, S. (2003). *Jacques Lecoq.* New York: Routledge.

Nachmanovitch, S. (1990). *Free play: Improvisation in life and art.* Los Angeles, CA: Jeremy Tarcher.

Nicholl, C. (2005). *Leonardo da Vinci: Flights of the mind.* New York: Penguin.

Ozick, C. (2003). What Hellen Keller saw. *The New Yorker, 79*(16). Retrieved from http://www.newyorker.com/printables/critics/030616crat_atlarge on September 11, 2006. [Also reproduced in C. Ozick (Ed.), *The din in the head* (pp. 11–32). Boston: Houghton-Mifflin.]

Palmer, C. (1997). Music performance. *Annual Reviews of Psychology, 48,* 115–138.

Palmer, C., & Kelly, M. H. (1992). Linguistic prosody and musical meter in song. *Journal of Memory and Language, 31,* 525–542.

Parsons, L. M. (2001). Exploring the functional neuroanatomy of music performance. In R. J. Zatorre & I. Peretz (Eds.), *The biological foundations of music* (pp. 211–231). New York: New York Academy of Science (*Annals,* Vol. 930, No. 1).

Pascual-Leone, A. (2001). The brain that plays music and is changed by it. In R. J. Zatorre & I. Peretz (Eds.), *The biological foundations of music* (pp. 315–329). New York: New York Academy of Science (*Annals,* Vol. 930, No. 1).

Pinker, S. (2004). How we may have become what we are. In J. Brockman (Ed.), *Curious minds: How a child becomes a scientist* (pp. 81–89). New York: Pantheon, Random House.

Podoksik, A. (1996). *Pablo Picasso: The creative eye (from 1881 to 1914)*. (V. Pozner Trans.) Bournemouth, UK: Parkstone/Aurora.

Poincaré, H. (1963). *Mathematics and science*. New York: Dover. (Original work published in 1913)

Pressing, J. (1988). Improvisation: Methods and models. In J. A. Sloboda (Ed.), *Generative processes in music* (pp. 129–178). New York: Oxford University Press.

Ramachandran, V. S., & Blakeslee, S. (1998). *Phantoms in the brain: Probing the mysteries of the human mind*. New York: Morrow.

Ravel, M. (1937). *Recollections of my lazy childhood*. (D. Taylor, Trans.). Paris: Paris-Soir.

Repp, B. H. (1992). Music as motion. A synopsis of Alexander Truslit's (1938) Gestaltung und Bewegung in der Musik. In *Status Report on Speech Research, #SR-111/112* (pp. 256–278). New Haven, CT: Haskins Laboratories. [This report was later published as Repp, B. H. (1993). Music as motion: A synopsis of Alexander Truslit's "Gestaltung und Bewegung in der Musik" (1938). *Psychology of Music, 21,* 48–72.]

Repp, B. H. (1995). Quantitative effects of global tempo on expressive timing in music performance: Some perceptual evidence. *Perceptual Psychophysics, 13,* 39–57.

Repp, B. H. (1998). Musical motion in perception and performance. In D. A. Rosenbaum & C. E. Collyer (Eds.), *Timing of behavior: Neural, computational and psychological perspectives* (pp. 125–144). Cambridge, MA: MIT Press.

Riedelsheimer, T. (Screenwriter & Director). (2004). *Touch the sound: A sound journey with Evelyn Glennie*. Documentary film distributed by Celluloid Dreams.

Rosand, D. (2002). *Drawing acts: Studies in graphic expression and representation*. New York: Cambridge University Press.

Rothenberg, A. (1990). *Creativity and madness: New findings and old stereotypes*. Baltimore, MD: Johns Hopkins University Press.

Sacks, O. (2000). *Seeing voices*. New York: Vintage.

Scherer, K. R., & Ekman, P. (1982). Methodological issues in studying non-verbal behaviour. In K. R. Scherer, R. Klaus, & P. Ekman (Eds.), *Handbook of methods in nonverbal behaviour research* (pp. 16–18). New York: Cambridge University Press.

Segalowitz, N., Cohen, P., Chan, A., & Prieur, T. (2001). Musical recall memory: Contributions of elaboration and depth of processing. *Psychology of Music, 29,* 139–148.

Shavinina, L. V., & Seeratan, K. L. (2004). Extracognitive phenomena in gifted, creative and talented individuals. In L. V. Shavinina & M. Ferrari (Eds.), *Beyond knowledge: Extracognitive aspects of developing high ability* (pp. 73–102). Mahwah, NJ: Erlbaum.

Shove, P., & Repp, B. H. (1995). Musical motion and performance: Theoretical and empirical perspectives. In J. Rink (Ed.), *The practice of performance* (pp. 55–83). Cambridge, UK: Cambridge University Press.

Simonton, D. K. (1999a). *Origins of genius: Darwinian perspectives on creativity*. New York: Oxford University Press.

Simonton, D. K. (1999b). Talent and its development: An emergenic and epigenetic model. *Psychological Review, 106,* 435–457.

Simonton, D. K. (2004). Exceptional creativity and chance: Creative thought as a stochastic combinatorial process. In L. V. Shavinina & M. Ferrari (Eds.), *Beyond knowledge: Extracognitive facets in developing high ability* (pp. 39–72). Mahwah, NJ: Erlbaum.

Singer, R. N., & Cauraugh, J. H. (1993). To be aware or not aware: What to think while learning and performing a motor skill. *Sport Psychologist, 7,* 19–30.

Sloboda, J. A. (1983). Communication of musical metre in piano performance. *Quarterly Journal of Experimental Psychology, A35,* 377–396.

Sloboda, J. A. (1985). Expressive skill in two pianists: Metrical communication in real and simulated performances. *Canadian Journal of Psychology, 39,* 273–293.

Sloboda, J. A. (1990). *The musical mind: The cognitive psychology of music.* New York: Oxford University Press.

Sloboda, J. A., Davidson, J. W., Howe, M. J. A., & Moore, D. G. (1996). The role of practice in the development of performing musicians. *British Journal of Psychology, 87,* 287–309.

Solomon, A. (1996, August 26 & September 2). Questions of genius: What has made Evgeny Kissin the most phenomenal prodigy of our time? *The New Yorker,* pp. 114, 120.

Solomon, M. (1998). *Beethoven* (rev. ed.). New York: Schirmer.

Spender, S. (1970). The making of a poem. In P. E. Vernon (Ed.), *Creativity* (pp. 61–76). Harmondsworth, UK: Penguin.

Stanislavsky, C. (1936). *An actor prepares.* (E. Hapgood, Trans.). New York: Routledge.

Storr, A. (1992). *Music and the mind.* New York: Free Press (Simon & Schuster).

Subotnik, R. F. (2004). Transforming elite musicians into professional artists: A view of the talent development process at the Juilliard School. In L. V. Shavinina & M. Ferrari (Eds.), *Beyond knowledge: Extracognitive facets in developing high ability* (pp. 141–145). Mahwah, NJ: Erlbaum.

Sundberg, J., Friberg, A., & Fryden, L. (1991). Threshold and preference quantities of rules for music performance. *Music Perception, 9*(1), 71–92.

Szpilberg, A. (in preparation). *Timing the muse: Creative variability in complex musical performance, its implication for the development of a general theory of complex human performance.* Unpublished doctoral dissertation in Music, Theatre, and Psychology, Concordia University, Montreal, QC.

Tambiah, S. J. (1996). Relations of analogy and identity: Towards multiple orientations to the world. In D. R. Olson & N. Torrance (Eds.), *Modes of thought: Explorations in culture and cognition* (pp. 34–35, 44, 48). New York: Cambridge University Press.

Taruskin, R. (1995). *Text and act: Essays on music and performance.* New York: Oxford University Press.

Trumble, A. (2004). *A brief history of the smile.* New York: Basic Books.

Waddington, C. H. (1968). The basic ideas of biology. In C. H. Waddington (Ed.), *Towards a theoretical biology* (vol. 1) (pp. 1–32). Chicago: Aldine.

Weisberg, R. W. (1993). *Creativity: Beyond the myth of genius.* New York: Freeman.

Wilson, M. (2002). Six views of embodied cognition. *Psychonomic Bulletin and Review, 9,* 625–636.

Wulf, G., & Prinz, W. (2001). Directing attention to movement effects enhances learning: A review. *Psychonomic Bulletin and Review, 8,* 648–660.

Zervos, C. (1985). Conversation with Picasso. In B. Ghiselin (Ed.), *The creative process* (pp. 55–60). Berkeley: University of California Press.

Zuckerkandl, V. (1973). *Man the musician: sound and symbol.* (N. Guterman, Trans.). Princeton, NJ: Princeton University Press.

Zwicky, J. (2003). *Wisdom and metaphor.* Kentville, NS: Gaspereau Press.

Other Documents Cited

Beyond 2000. Australian TV (report about the Leonardo Project).

City Beat. Canadian Broadcasting Corporation, CBMT-TV, Montreal, QC (report about the Leonardo Project).

Leonardo Project Archives (audio, video).

Shaping the Invisible. Discovery Channel (Canada) (report about the Leonardo Project).

9

Creating Change: Teachers' Reflections on Introducing Inquiry Teaching Strategies

F. GILLIAN BRAMWELL-REJSKIND
McGill University

FRANCES HALLIDAY
Western Quebec School Board, Central Quebec School Board, and McGill University

JUDITH B. MCBRIDE
Riverside School Board and McGill University

> *"You know the guard that's in the front there [on a roller coaster]?*
> *It's gone (laughter). Kids are flying all over the place.*
> *And as a teacher you're just hanging on. . . ."*

Teacher

Introducing inquiry approaches to teaching into traditional classrooms requires major changes in the way teachers plan, carry out, and evaluate instruction. As with other post-modern approaches (Doll, 1993) such as feminist pedagogy (Forrest & Rosenberg, 1997) and joint curriculum design (Gross, 1997), educational principles and practices differ from those of traditional pedagogies in crucial ways (Brooks & Brooks, 1993). They share a constructivist vision of learning, respect diversity, validate multiple sources of knowledge, and emphasize collaboration rather than competition. They require students to take significant responsibility for their own learning, thus replacing teacher authority with shared authority and decision making. They view official curricula as broad outlines from which teachers and students further develop the curriculum together in interaction with each other and their particular environments (Brooks & Brooks, 1993; Doll, 1993; Gross, 1997).

Changing one's practice is difficult and teachers generally are believed to be resistant to change (Clifton & Roberts, 1993) and to require extensive support and incentives to motivate them to change (Duke, 1993; Firestone & Pennell, 1993; Odden & Kelley, 1997). Nonetheless, many teachers continually strive to improve their practice and to acquire new teaching strategies on their own initiative. Frequently, these are the excellent, innovative teachers whom reformers wish to retain in teaching (Weld, 1998), and who potentially will lead the way to broader reform (Aaronsohn, 1996).

Innovative teachers should be considered creative (Rejskind, 2000). Studies of creativity have generally focused on the creative giants; however, as Gardner (1988) noted, it is important also to study ordinary expressions of creativity to determine if the process, personality, and environmental influences remain the same. Innovative teachers provide a good example of "everyday creativity." They fit Taylor's description (1975) of inventive creativity: ingenuity in applying readily available materials or ideas to problems. They also fit Kirton's (1976) description of creative adaptors: individuals who make incremental improvements within existing paradigms and structures. As Hogan and Morrison (1996) have pointed out, such "small innovations . . . accumulate to major revolutions" (p. 350).

Although a great deal is known about creativity and creative individuals in other fields, there have been few studies of creative teachers. The creative problem-solving process is broadly consistent across fields (Tardiff & Sternberg, 1988), but a great deal of what is known about creativity is domain-specific (Csikszentmihalyi, 1990; Gardner, 1994). Furthermore, the field of education differs in significant ways from fields such as art, literature, and science which are typically the focus of creativity research. In particular, creative individuals in those fields typically work alone or with a small group of collaborators. Teaching, however, is an intensely interpersonal act. An equally important difference is found in the use of time: Artists, scientists, and writers create their product on their own schedules and take the time needed to perfect their works. For teachers, lack of time is a perennial problem (Wagner, 1998) leaving them with little left for reflection. Because of these differences between teaching and other fields, it is not clear which aspects of knowledge about creativity can validly be applied to teachers. Thus, in this chapter we will use the framework of creativity to focus on nine teachers who, on their own initiative, introduced inquiry strategies into their teaching. We ask why they engaged in change, and their perceptions of the benefits, the drawbacks, and the barriers to making that change, and draw links to other studies of innovative teachers as well as to creators in other fields.

Method

The data in this chapter are taken from interviews with teachers who had been introduced to inquiry through the use of RE-ACT (Halliday, 1986), and had at least two years' experience using inquiry in their teaching. RE-ACT is a teacher-designed program that leads students through the process of carrying out original inquiry projects. It explicitly teaches strategies needed to formulate research questions, to make decisions about what information they need, where to find it, how to collect, evaluate and integrate it; and how to report their conclusions. Three were teachers enrolled in a graduate education program. They were introduced to RE-ACT through participating in a summer enrichment program for 9- to 15-year-old students. This course lasted 3.5 hours a day for 20 days. All three teachers had participated for at least two years and had shared responsibility for planning and delivering a classroom inquiry program in at least one of those years. At the time of the interviews, all three had less than five years' classroom teaching experience. One was working as a free-flow special-needs teacher in an elementary school and another was teaching secondary science and history. The third was employed as a school counselor.

Six secondary school teachers had been introduced to RE-ACT through McBride, a colleague at their school. They included both novice teachers with less than five years and veterans with more than 20 years' service. All continued to use inquiry in their teaching at the time of the interviews. One of these teachers had also spent one summer at the enrichment program directed by Halliday. They discussed using inquiry to teach a variety of subjects, including geography, science, moral and religious education, history, and economics.

Neither group of teachers can be considered typical or representative of teachers in general. Rather, they were selected because they were adopting inquiry, for them a new and relatively unknown approach to teaching. Nonetheless, the information they provided can be helpful in suggesting the advantages and problems that are likely to be encountered by teachers who try to adopt an inquiry methodology in today's schools. Additionally, by voluntarily adopting a new teaching approach they can accurately be described as innovative teachers who fit Taylor's (1975) definition of inventive creativity.

The interviews took place during the year that followed two years' participation in the RE-ACT program. The three teachers who collaborated in the summer program were interviewed by Halliday, the program coordinator, and a colleague from the university who had attended one of the two summer sessions. The secondary school teachers were interviewed by McBride, a teacher-researcher at the school concerned. Because of the interviewers' close involvement with RE-ACT, it is possible that the participants presented a more positive picture than they otherwise would have.

The interviews, which lasted about an hour, were informal, taking the form of a conversation among small groups of colleagues. Guiding questions included: "What are the advantages to using an inquiry-oriented curriculum?" and "What are the constraints and barriers?" However, the discussion ranged widely over teachers' experiences with and thoughts about RE-ACT and inquiry approaches to teaching generally. The interviews were taped and transcribed. A grounded theory approach (Strauss & Corbin, 1990) was used to analyze the data.

Results and Discussion

Two major themes, student learning and the need for change, emerged from the many advantages, drawbacks, and barriers to an inquiry-oriented curriculum that the informants discussed. Student learning was central: If these teachers had not believed that student learning benefited from inquiry, they would not have used it. They also spoke at length about change: the need for educational change, the difficulties in making changes, and their own motivation to make change. Related topics included changes in teacher-student and student-student relationships, issues of the formal curriculum and student evaluation, time constraints, and the impact of others' expectations.

Interwoven throughout the interviews were issues of control. Giving students increased control over their learning and behavior was perceived to be a core aspect of inquiry. Furthermore, this change in teacher-student relationships was believed to be partly responsible for the improvements in students' learning. Conversely, most of the barriers to using inquiry were associated with aspects of education over which teachers lack control. However, control *per se* was not important to teachers. Rather, they saw it as a tool to influence students' learning. Consequently, it is not given much emphasis in this chapter; readers interested in the issue will find it dealt with in more detail in Rejskind, Chennabathni, McBride, and Halliday (1998).

Change

It is not surprising that our informants talked about change, because the interviews focused on the changes they had made in the past two years as they integrated inquiry into their classrooms. A significant portion of the talk about change, which will not be discussed here, simply contrasted inquiry and traditional ways of teaching. Of interest in this chapter is teachers' talk about why they changed, advantages that resulted from change, how difficult it was to change, and how they were supported (or not) in the change process.

One characteristic of teachers who engage in innovative educational practices is their willingness to embrace change (Aaronsohn, 1996; Gross, 1997; Westberg & Archambault, 1997). All the teachers in this study were willing to make the effort needed to change. Indeed, four secondary school teachers were not only willing to change, but they also identified themselves as individuals who actively seek ways to change their teaching. One teacher recognized that "I was the type of person that needed to change" so she "went around looking at what should I change and what was out there," and another noted that "I'm always interested in finding out new things and things that might help me."

As with the teachers in Gross's (1997) study of teachers learning to design curriculum jointly with their students, and Aaronsohn's study (1996) of teachers in the process of changing to student-centered teaching, the teachers in this study did not change for the sake of change alone. Rather, there was a constant search for ways in which to better meet the needs of their students. They were aware of wide-ranging, major changes in society that have resulted in students who do not respond well to traditional ways of teaching. Furthermore, they believe that as students go through life, they will need skills that are not developed by traditional methods of education. Consequently, they believed that changes in education are needed to respond to the changes in students and society. One secondary school teacher in particular had a lot to say about changes and the implications they have for education:

> It's just that education is coming a lot from the outside. Before it was the teacher's domain, the teacher was the giver of information, but if we go back to from five years ago until now with the Internet, with the computer, the access to the computer and the Internet, we have to teach students to select the information, because it's going to be totally useless, it's going to be just garbage if they can't select, and if they can't have maps to guide them through all this selection and come up with something. And I'm starting to see it now in the interviews I see on television about Internet and computers, they can be just games and garbage, or it can be really a tool.

These changes in society are deeper and wider than the knowledge explosion, computers, and Internet access. Consistent with the teachers in Gross's (1997) study, these teachers believed that societal changes have already resulted in a change in the needs with which students come to ordinary classrooms:

> And from the clientele that we have, kids from broken homes, kids from overworked parents . . . the economy, we will have to deal with kids a lot more on an individual basis than we have been doing. This whole last century we've dealt with kids in classrooms and we've disregarded the extremities, low functioning or high, sort of always aimed for the middle and covered our bell curve. It's worked. If you parallel that to the Industrial Revolution, kids who could work on an assembly line, sit down quietly and work with their fingers on an assembly line is how we have been training our kids. Now society has changed.

One difference in particular was noted by several teachers. In recent years, all the school districts in which our informants teach have integrated special-needs children into regular classrooms, often with limited support and education for teachers. When this is added to societal changes, teachers perceived that students come to schools with a much wider variety of needs than they have been prepared to handle. Furthermore, this variety of needs is difficult to accommodate in traditional classroom, particularly in secondary schools: "A lot of our kids now need individual help, and we're going to lose a lot of them if we can't give individual help." All teachers made statements indicating that they saw inquiry as a tool that could be used successfully to adapt to this changed clientele.

The teachers also recognized that changes occurring in society would place demands on students that cannot be met through teaching the traditional curriculum in traditional ways. No longer can educators identify a core curriculum with the assurance that mastering it will prepare students for life. Rather, these teachers perceived that students need to develop into adaptable and independent learners. They recognized that the knowledge explosion demands that students learn new skills; they valued inquiry for its emphasis on skills that students can transfer to a variety of situations, in contrast to the traditional curriculum with its focus on facts to be memorized. The teachers referred to this as a change from teaching content to teaching process.

> I think it [RE-ACT] emphasizes the process as the content rather than the subject matter content being supreme and I think that primacy of process is a really important advantage to the students because this process is something that will take them through and help them to cope with many of the different challenges that they may face . . . but knowing the difference between liver warts and mosses I don't think is such a big deal in most people's lives.

This privileging of the process over memorizing specific facts is a central feature of inquiry and other constructivist approaches. It was the central concern of the student-centered teacher studied by Aaronsohn (1996) and a major concern of the constructivist teachers in Gross (1997). It probably is an aspect of inquiry that requires a major change in educators' beliefs about learning and the evaluation of learning.

The picture of the teachers that emerges from their reflections about change is consistent with the description of other creators. When one informant identifies herself as "the type of person that needed to change" she fits Barron, Montuori, and Barron's (1997) description of creative people as individuals who "want to create above all. . . . It is a primary and intrinsic motive" (p. 13). It is also consistent with Rossman's (1931) description of inventors whose primary motive for inventing was "love of inventing" (as cited in MacKinnon, 1978, p. 87) and Martindale's contention (1989) that creative people like novelty.

The recognition of the need for educational change in response to societal change reflects a sensitivity to the environment, sometimes referred to as openness to experience, that is characteristic of creative people (Getzels & Csikszentmihalyi, 1976; MacKinnon, 1978; Martindale, 1989; Rogers, 1959). Through their openness to their experience of the world around them, and to their own inner voices, creators identify problems which are of interest to their field. Problem identification is certainly the first step in the creative process (Feldhusen & Treffinger, 1980; Ghiselin, 1955; Wallas, 1926). Some have argued it is the most important step (Csikszentmihalyi, 1990; Starko, 1995). In Einstein's words "The formulation of a problem is often more essential than its solution. . . . To raise new questions, new problems, to regard old problems from a new angle, requires creative imagination and marks real advances in science" (cited in Csikszentmihalyi, 1992, p. 20). Smilansky and Hallberstadt (1986) provided evidence that creativity is partly the ability to pose high-level problems and questions. Thus, when they identify the needs for change in education, and look for ways to bring it about, these teachers closely resemble creators in other fields.

Relationships

Teaching through inquiry changes the way that students and teachers interact. The teachers recognized that they had changed from being the students' source of information to functioning more as guides. In one teacher's words "You're not the center anymore . . . you start the work and they take it and they run with it." Others referred to it as giving students "freedom," "ownership," or "control" over their work. This change in students' and teachers' roles resulted in a corresponding change in the relationships in the classroom. Teachers used a variety of metaphors to describe their new roles. One said "I like to think of myself as a tow truck company . . . and maybe they got a flat tire happening and if I was their tow truck, I'd just come around and get it going." Another teacher described inquiry as a highway and the teacher as the person with the map.

All teachers viewed this change as a valuable aspect of inquiry; for one it was so important that she added inquiry to her arsenal of teaching strategies because "inquiry curriculum fills in the spot where you give freedom to the student." Yet being in control of student behavior and learning is a defining characteristic of teachers' roles (Clifton & Roberts, 1993; Doll, 1993), and as Jervis and McDonald (1996) noted, the dominant culture of teaching holds teachers responsible for students' learning; consequently teachers who make students responsible are seen as shirking their responsibility. In addition, standardized tests and state- or provincewide final exams hold both teachers and students accountable for students' mastery of the prescribed curriculum. Equally important, the teachers themselves accepted this responsibility. Even in the summer program, where there was no pre-set curriculum or student evaluation, the teachers felt responsible for the students' learning and reported experiencing anxiety about giving up control "because I wanted them to learn everything I thought they had to learn."

Students were not, however, given unlimited freedom. Rather, teachers made the decision to restrict or extend students' freedom on the basis of its potential influence on learning, and the extent of students' freedom varied from teacher to teacher. One secondary teacher, for example, was concerned with the need for control over students' behavior when he weighed the merits of students working in their classrooms or going to the library.

> The only thing with the library is that they're walking all over the place, and you have to walk all over the place too. . . . I prefer the classroom, less chaotic, but I think the kids got more information and more learning done when we went to the library.

The most common limit placed on students was to restrict their choice of specific topics for projects to subjects identified by the teacher and relevant to their course. This allowed students to have some control over what they studied while ensuring that the requirements of the prescribed curriculum were met. At other times, in order to ensure that students acquired specific skills, teachers specified the resources that students were to use or placed restrictions on the ways they were to present their projects. Several teachers indicated a need to carefully monitor students' progress to make certain that work was progressing satisfactorily. When students were not on the right track "you point them in the right direction as much as you can without interfering, without actually saying 'do this.'"

The teachers described how they gave varying amounts of freedom to students, based on their judgment of students' ability to make good use of it. "Students whom I can trust were dispatched to their various activities . . . and I basically rode shotgun over the rest."

By setting pedagogical limits at the same time as giving students a greater say in their learning, these teachers were able to establish a negotiated curriculum without turning control over to the most vocal or disruptive minority. This is similar to the approach taken by other student-centered (Aaronsohn, 1996) and constructivist teachers (Gross, 1997). It allowed them to reap the motivational and learning benefits of students having increased input without incurring the educational disadvantages noted by Ennis (1995) when control over activities was simply given to the most vocal students.

As the teachers were able to develop a new balance between their control and students' freedom, other aspects of classroom relationships changed. One of the summer school teachers, whose great respect of students permeated all parts of her interview, perceived the new way of relating to students to be the most positive aspect of inquiry.

> They were always free to not take my suggestion so it was always, we had such a team, I like team spirit and I like for the students to feel that I'm no different from them . . . In fact many times I thought my suggestions were great and they would totally bypass them. And often the kids came up with better suggestions than me.

All the teachers who learned about inquiry through the summer program referred positively to this change in student-teacher relationships, and many at the secondary school also viewed the changes positively. However, in the latter setting, teachers also noted that the changes were not always positive. As previously discussed, some students who had been successful in traditional classrooms were reluctant to change which sometimes resulted in conflict between teachers and students, and made teaching more difficult. For example, one teacher described a problem getting a student to select a topic: "It wasn't without a great deal of pain, sort of analogous to a tooth extraction without a needle. . . ."

In addition to the change in teacher-student relationships, teachers noticed students interacting in new ways. "And you'd have questions going back and forth. Kids going—ask this kid, I don't know, but this kid over here might know." Furthermore, as the nature of the interaction changed, a wider range of students gained recognition: "What the students themselves found was it wasn't the person who said everything who came up with the answers. We had discussion in class one day where one of the quieter kids in the class said no that's not true."

The teachers valued the new relationships between students, believing that the social skills they were learning would serve them well in the future. As with any change, however, students had to learn new skills in order to work together successfully and this held the potential for failure. "We had really only one group that sort of self-destructed at the end because the guys really didn't get along nearly so well around the project as they did wandering the halls at lunch." However, this struggle itself was considered to be a useful experience for students. "Yeah, but that's a real life skill, being able to communicate and work in groups. Even though kids get frustrated by it, it's really important that kids develop those skills, so inquiry kind of encourages this kind of situation."

The students' responses to the introduction of new teaching approaches were consistent with those reported by Aaronsohn (1996) and Gross (1997). In the studies of teachers who introduced joint curriculum design (Gross) and student-centered teaching (Aaronsohn) into their classrooms, both found students generally gave positive responses to the new relationships that developed. Yet those students, too, needed help to make teamwork successful, and some needed reassurance and support from their teachers to make the transition successfully. We, too, have had similar experiences with university students who are engaging in inquiry for the first time.

In their willingness to change their relationships with students and in so doing to go counter to the belief that teachers have sole responsibility for student's learning and behavior, our informants again demonstrated a similarity to other creative individuals who act independently and take risks; they are demonstrating their "courage to go naked" (Barron, Montuori, & Barron, 1997, p. 203).

Learning

Creativity research frequently focuses on creative products, whether an invention, a novel, a building, or a work of art. For the teachers in this study, their creative "product" was, clearly, their students' learning. Student learning is the core task of teaching (Rosenholtz & Simpson, 1990) and the most compelling source of motivation for many teachers (Butt, Raymond, McCue, & Yamagishi, 1992; Gross, 1997; Lortie, 1975; Sederberg & Clark, 1990). Furthermore, a focus on instructional goals is typical of all expert teachers (Borko & Livingston, 1989), and improved student learning was the motivation that drove the teachers described by Gross (1997) and Aaronsohn (1996) to begin and to continue in their efforts to use postmodern methods. Halliday developed RE-ACT to improve student learning, and McBride introduced it to her students and school for the same reason. Consequently, it is not surprising to find that the reason our informants introduced inquiry into their classrooms was their belief that it improved students' learning. They identified many changes in learning including greater enthusiasm, more independence, more students succeeding, and learning new types of skills. In the words of one teacher,

> I think that it's a lot more rewarding to see the students so much more engaged, so much more interested, learning so much better. The kinds of things that you've been slaving away trying to teach them in the past in the more traditional methods and I think when you see that the things that they've been having so much trouble with finally click in because they've been able to process them themselves and sit there and really have a good think about it is a lot more rewarding than they finally memorize the lines.

The teachers appreciated students' increased enjoyment of the learning process. Words such as "fun," "interest," and "enthusiasm" were scattered throughout the interviews. "We had a lot of fun that summer." One teacher even identified fun as one of the reasons that she got into inquiry: "And it sounded like fun. It sounded like the kind of thing that I would enjoy doing myself, so that means it will be more enjoyable for the kids if I enjoy it. That's how I got into it." However, the fun was important because it led to greater learning. "One of the advantages that immediately comes to mind is the fun the kids [have] *learning*" (italics added). Equally important, and closely related, students' enjoyment resulted in a greater willingness to work: "I loved the fact that both of the students stay way past 12 o'clock to work and without complaining. *Without complaining!* I was floored."

Some teachers were explicit about the relationship between students' increased interest and their increased control over their learning tasks. "I think one of the major advantages is the increased interest, usually. Not always, but usually. Students are much more interested in this kind of thing because it's their own." And, "the fact that they've selected their topic or their subject makes them very keen on getting to where they want to go." A teacher from the summer school was even more emphatic about the need for students to have control: "I think for them to be enthusiastic they have to feel . . . that they are contributing that you are not taking over, that it's their baby that they can do as they see fit with minimal intervention from you." Clifton and Roberts (1993) note that the growing variability in students makes the teachers' role of motivating them to learn increasingly difficult. Thus, inquiry approaches to teaching and learning provide a useful tool in dealing with this reality of modern classrooms.

Another change that resulted from the introduction of inquiry was that it allowed students both to work and to learn on their own, which several teachers valued. Initially, some students had difficulty adapting because "some kids need some kind of structure. . . . I found a lot of the kids can't make up their own mind." However as students acquired the appropriate skills they learned to work independently. Teachers were pleased by this because it meant that students could be relied on to work without constant supervision.

I couldn't get there on time and I was so worried because I thought they would be sitting there doing nothing but no, no, they were outside doing exactly what we had planned for the next day and I was thrilled.

The teachers also considered independent learning to be a life skill that students could carry with them to new situations both in school and beyond. "The thing is when you do [use inquiry], it's memorable, and the next time when you have another problem they have these strategies they can say, look, this is how we solve the problem. So they start to become independent."

Yet another perceived change was that the nature of learning changed in inquiry classes. In the words of one teacher, inquiry represents "a whole different outlook on what education is, what learning is." One secondary teacher was explicit about the nature of the different outlook: "I think this [RE-ACT] emphasizes the process as the content rather than the subject-matter content being supreme." This was highly valued by the teachers. As with students' increased independence, teachers perceived the mastery of the process of learning to be more useful than learning facts, because the skills involved can be applied to new situations both in and out of school that help prepare students to adapt to change: "I am fine tuning and giving them skills that they'll be able to use throughout their lives, not just in school or in university, but whenever they have to tackle anything new on the job." Indeed, some teachers were able to observe the transfer of skills to new situations. "I didn't do inquiry with [a particular] class but I could see the skills you [McBride] were teaching when I was doing my regular teaching . . . I didn't have to guide them. They knew exactly what we're doing."

The teachers who worked at the summer program believed that students would remember content better when they learned through inquiry because "it's not only a matter of understanding, it's a matter of finally internalizing it and taking ownership of the information." This internalization was possible because students' control over their learning allowed them to build on the knowledge that they brought into the situation. "In inquiry your past knowledge kind of interacts with your present knowledge, it's always interacting with your present knowledge, you know, what you come with is what you use and . . . you incorporate it." Only two of the teachers who came to RE-ACT through the secondary school referred to the importance of prior knowledge, and they saw it primarily as a motivational tool. "I had kids come into my class with knowledge that they were able to use because of the situation there, the learning situation, which is very powerful." This difference between the two groups probably arose from the emphasis that the summer school instructor (Halliday) placed on the role of prior knowledge in learning.

An important perceived benefit of using inquiry was that it allowed all students to experience success. "I see inquiry as everybody succeeding, no one failing." This is consistent with the experiences of Halliday and McBride, both of whom began using inquiry with low-achieving students. It is also consistent with related literature. The teacher with whom Aaronsohn (1996) worked initially changed to student-centered teaching in an attempt to reach low achieving students, and then transferred the approach into an integrated setting to teach all students. Gross's teachers (1997) also found that low-achieving students improved when joint curriculum design was introduced, and Baum, Renzulli, and Hébert (1995) showed that inquiry projects helped reverse underachievement in gifted students. There are several possible reasons for this change.

One of the reasons for the increased success rate lies in the nature of RE-ACT itself, which systematically teaches students the component skills of defining questions, collecting, evaluating, synthesizing, and reporting information. Many students who succeed with traditional methods learn some of these skills intuitively; teaching them explicitly makes them available to all. As well, the ongoing evaluation that is part of RE-ACT also allowed for correction of students' misunderstandings as they arose. The resulting change was not initially anticipated by all teachers, however. One reported observing a group of students " . . . that surprised me. They weren't very talented students, but they followed all the steps and they did very well."

Another factor that contributes to success for all students arises from students' increased control over their learning. One consequence, noted earlier, is that students were more enthusiastic about their learning and as a result often worked harder, presumably increasing their chances of success. Also, by choosing their own topics, students were able to build on knowledge that they had acquired outside of school. Not only did this enrich their learning but also, as one teacher noted, it motivates students: "I had kids come into my class with knowledge that they were able to use because of the situation there, the learning situation, which is very powerful for them. It's very self-affirming, very nice." Such increases in motivation can have more impact on the learning and performance of low-achieving students than on the students who are already earning high marks, thus leading to success for more students.

In addition to its influence on motivation, giving students more freedom in their work allows students who learn differently from the majority to build on their past learning and to work from their strengths.

> It puts everybody on an equal basis. It lets kids work from where they
> are so there is no stigma of everybody has to be doing the same things
> with the same expectations because right away when you teach like that,
> a third of the class is not going to meet those expectations.

Similarly, teachers perceived that students' increased say in their learning and evaluation allowed them to use their strengths to demonstrate learning that might otherwise go unrecognized.

> It allows them to express themselves in a way that's appropriate for them.
> The kid that hates writing isn't going to give you a written report. He's
> going to give you something that's much more exciting and much more
> to his/her ability.

Furthermore, when students are reporting on their own work in their own way, they sometimes take on new confidence. One of the summer-school teachers described how nervous she was on behalf of two very shy students whose turn it was to report their work to the class. "I said, oh my God how are they going to present? And I had no problem, they were blaring away at the end, it's this special relationship that the student has with their own work." This special relationship allowed these two students to demonstrate learning that likely would have been overlooked in traditional classrooms.

Yet another factor contributing to inquiry bringing success to all students resulted indirectly from students' ability to work more independently. "I could push my brighter students out of the room and they could go off and do their own thing. I just put them in the library." As a consequence, teachers are freed up to spend more time working with students who particularly need help. "Before inquiry you had to deal with the whole class as well as with the behavior problems. With inquiry, you only have to deal with the behavior problems because the other kids are working you can really focus in."

The cumulative result of these changes is that low-achieving students suddenly appear to be much stronger academically than was previously apparent. "But it was certainly something that I did not expect, that sort of night-and-day difference. Usually when kids are performing that poorly, they don't, there is not this huge difference." For these teachers, facing great pupil diversity in their classrooms, this was an important advantage of using inquiry. The effectiveness of inquiry-based instruction with low achieving students is also an important finding when viewed in conjunction with the resistance presented by some high achievers. Inquiry strategies are widely accepted in gifted education; these results demonstrate that it can be successful with all students.

As with creative individuals in other fields, these teachers were very focused on improving their "product"—their students' learning. They tried inquiry, and continued to use it because they believed that students learned better, that they enjoyed learning more, that they learned important life skills through the use of inquiry, and that more students succeeded with inquiry than with traditional approaches to teaching. This intense focus on a self-selected task is characteristic of creative individuals generally (Amabile, 1996; Csikszentmihalyi, 1988; Perkins, 1981; Starko, 1989); Barron, Montuori, and Barron refer to it as the "dedication to mastery" (1997, p. 171).

Barriers

The teachers in this project viewed both inquiry and change positively, yet encountered barriers to both. Although some were barriers to introducing inquiry specifically, others were simply related to the process of change itself.

Much as they valued change, our informants confirmed that it was not an easy process. Every teacher considered change per se to be difficult not only for themselves but also for their students. "I think it's very difficult to open yourself to change, because it's always hard to try something new." Later in the interview, the same teacher identified the comfortable feelings associated with traditional approaches as one source of the difficulty. "I find I tend to slip back into that traditional role which is very familiar to me. It's comfortable. I'm quite comfortable getting up and performing for a bunch of students." In contrast, change tended to produce feelings of anxiety. Another teacher found it was "kind of scary for me in the beginning." In another interview two teachers compared using inquiry strategies in their teaching with being on a roller-coaster ride.

> You know the guard that's in the front there? It's gone (laughter). Kids are flying all over the place. And as a teacher you're just hanging on. . . . (Teacher)
>
> Oh, you're not down there with the power switch? (Interviewer)
>
> Oh, I wish. No way I'm at the back of the train going oh, no, oh, no. . . . (Teacher)
>
> You're either at the back of that roller-coaster train or at the very front, but you're never safe in the center of it. You know, you're either being whipped around at the end or watching that hill come up to you as you're going down in the first car. (Teacher)

Not only is change uncomfortable, it also requires extra effort to develop new practices with which to replace well established routines. "It's really hard to use inquiry as a teaching method because it means that you have to do a lot of thinking, a lot of preparing." Furthermore, these new skills take time to develop, which exposes teachers to the risk of making mistakes as they learn.

> I had to figure out how to do it. You know, I had to know how much information to give the kids. And sometimes I didn't give them enough and sometimes I just gave them way too much, so that it was too easy for them.

Consistent with other reports of innovative teachers, the informants in this study considered change to be an ongoing process. One secondary teacher, for example, discussed changes she was planning for the following year, noting that "it gets more inquiry and more self-directed as time goes on" because "I think as a teaching method you still have to grow into it. I don't think you can learn to use constructivism or inquiry or anything like this right off the bat."

Unlike most professionals who work with clients one at a time, teachers who are experimenting with new ways of doing things make their mistakes in front of entire classes, and must answer to parents and principals as well. Thus, change is indeed a risky business and our informants recognized that inquiry approaches were not suitable for all teachers. "You also need the ability to accept ambiguity. And to have things thrown at you. But it's not for everybody."

Other researchers (Aaronsohn, 1996; Butt, Raymond, McCue, & Yamagishi, 1992; Duke, 1993; Gross, 1997; Westberg & Archambault, 1997) also reported that teachers believe that changing their teaching methods requires a willingness to take risks. Barksdale-Ladd and Thomas (1996), Gross, and Aaronsohn, too, observed that change was gradual, that mistakes were made in the process, and that at times teachers felt inadequate and insecure as they struggled to change. As well, there are again clear parallels to creative individuals in other fields. Barron, Montuori, & Barron (1997) concluded that "This journey into the unfamiliar can be scary" (p. 57) and there is agreement that risk-taking is characteristic of creative individuals in other fields (Gardner, 1994; MacKinnon, 1978; Martindale, 1989; Starko, 1995; Sternberg, 1988).

Student resistance. Another barrier to change that our informants faced was student resistance. Most students are highly motivated by the changes that inquiry brings to the classroom (Aaronsohn, 1996; Rejskind & Halliday, 1997; Gross, 1997). However, all the teachers noted that some of their students found the change difficult. Students, too, were more comfortable doing things in familiar ways, and some actively resisted inquiry:

> In my grade nine . . . class, where I had the very bright students and they had been trained in the old system of doing research, I had quite a battle with that class. They did not want to change their ways, they did not want to answer questions, they did not want to develop a question, they did not want to omit things that were not under the umbrella of the question. It was a fighting battle all the way to make them do a research project through the inquiry method.

Unlike traditional projects, in which students simply gather information and report it back to the teachers, RE-ACT requires students to formulate research questions, and to make decisions about what information they need, where to find it, how to collect, evaluate and integrate it; and how to report their conclusions. Because the emphasis is on the process, the common student strategy of simply copying information is no longer sufficient. Some teachers thought that students' lack of the skills needed to carry out inquiry was responsible for their resistance. One secondary teacher noted,

> And the students, again the students, they're not ready. They really are not ready to do this kind of research because they've been so spoon-fed all through their school career. They don't, they are not taught to think, they're taught to listen and sort of absorb information, so this is difficult for them.

The reason most frequently cited for students' resistance to the new way of doing projects was that it affected their marks "if their success has been in marks. If they know what the teacher wants—all the stuff written out, it's nice, it's pretty and if that's the only way they've ever had success they're going to have a hard time." This was particularly a problem in some secondary school subjects where students—and by extension, teachers—are evaluated on provincewide examinations that were designed to evaluate learning that has been acquired through traditional methods of instruction. Although the provincial curriculum is changing, its implementation is slow and not yet reflected in the high school leaving examinations.

Student resistance particularly was an issue for the secondary school teachers in this study. It meant that in addition to having to develop new skills themselves, and to help students develop skills, they also had to find ways to overcome students' resistance: "The students aren't ready for it so you really do run into a lot of resistance and so you have to develop methods of getting around that resistance." This is consistent with the report by Gross (1997) that some students needed teacher support in making the transition to joint curriculum design. Aaronsohn's (1996) study of a student-centered teacher also identified successful students as the most resistant to change. However, the teachers described both by Aaronsohn and Gross also experienced resistance from low achieving students who had figured out how to get by without doing much work when more traditional teaching methods were used. Because the group work entailed by the new approaches made students' lack of effort much more visible, it led to the peers of low performing students pressuring them to pull their weight. At the university level, too, students frequently resist the opportunity to engage in inquiry, and we have observed students to drop a course when it required them to participate in such learning. Consequently, teachers who contemplate a change to inquiry and other constructivist approaches need to be prepared to counter student resistance.

Lack of education. Absence of appropriate support is another barrier for teachers. They considered their ongoing search for better ways of teaching to be a part of their professional development. However, they reported receiving little help from the educational establishment. One experienced teacher complained:

> I've known mechanics, when they have to be retrained . . . they go away for two weeks and they keep their regular salary and so on and they are trained. I know people who work in, for instance, in banks, and when they bring in a new program, if it takes let's say four or five days to train the person, they're trained. It becomes part of their job. But if you look at teaching, if you want to upgrade yourself you do it during the summer, you do it during the evening.

Even when there was an official decision to introduce a new teaching method, these teachers felt that they were not thoroughly trained. Rather, "It was having a ped day [i.e., a one-day session] here, a ped day there, and then saying here're the books. Do it." Once change had been initiated teachers perceived little ongoing support as they implemented it. Several teachers would have welcomed more feedback: "I really would benefit to have somebody every once in a while come into my classroom and look at a lesson and say at this point, you know . . . just evaluating it on a more regular basis."

Colleagues. Not only did teachers find little support in the educational establishment, but their perceptions of others' expectations were actually potential barriers to using inquiry. Some teachers feared that their colleagues would find it threatening because "these kids are having fun, they like it and then might even start, if they're a little smarty pants and old enough, to question other teachers. Why don't you do it like this?" Yet another possibility that concerned participants was that teachers could receive poor evaluations based on traditional standards because "You'd walk in and if you didn't know, you'd think it was chaos. Utter and total chaos. This teacher has no control. The kids are talking, it's somewhat noisy. . . ." Having control over students' behavior—keeping order—is the first, most basic requirement of successful teaching; to be seen as a teacher who cannot keep control is to be considered incompetent. Teachers are also expected to be in control of their students' learning, so that giving control to students, a central aspect of inquiry, also can be seen as inappropriate teacher conduct (Jervis & McDonald, 1996). Considering that several of our informants did not have permanent positions, the possibilities of making mistakes and of being misjudged as not being in control of one's class are not trivial concerns. Similar to the observations in this study, Butt, Raymond, McCue, and Yamagishi (1992) concluded that intercollegial relationships were the predominant theme in the professional development of the two teachers whose life histories they traced, and they feature heavily in Aaronsohn's report (1996) of one teacher's change to student-centered teaching. Furthermore, these relationships, too, were a barrier rather than a support for change. Aaronsohn's teacher, for example, experienced the fear of being misjudged and considered to lack control over students when she instituted student-centered teaching. Similarly, Herzog (1995) reported that some teachers were threatened by her success with nontraditional approaches, and Aaronsohn (1996), Gross (1997), and Boxall (1995) all described situations in which other educators were barriers to teachers' development. Therefore, teachers who decide to use inquiry strategies in their teaching need to be prepared to face resistance from colleagues and students who prefer to continue with more traditional approaches to education.

That our informants persevered with their changes in spite of the possibility of being misunderstood by their colleagues is consistent with interpreting their innovativeness as an act of creativity. Barron, Montuori, and Barron (1997) referred to the willingness of creative persons to take such risks as "the courage to go naked" (1997, p. 203) and it is a well-documented characteristic of creative individuals in other fields (Gardner, 1994; MacKinnon, 1978; Martindale, 1989; Starko, 1995; Sternberg, 1988).

Curriculum and evaluation. Curricula and evaluation are not inherently problematic for teachers who wish to use inquiry in their classrooms. As Gross (1997) observed, the curriculum is a useful guide for teachers who want to use jointly constructed curricula. In fact, our informants used the curriculum to direct students' choice of topics for their inquiry projects. Equally, the ongoing evaluation that is inherent in RE-ACT was partly responsible for the broad-based success, as can be seen from one teacher's description of what evaluation meant to her:

> You have to check the process, you're the teacher you have to keep notes on the children, how they're doing. But I see inquiry as everybody succeeding, no one failing. . . . You keep tabs on every kid and how they're doing, when they are stuck you point them in the right direction as much as you can without interfering, without actually saying do this. . . . I'll be saying most of what you're doing is very good, try this if you're stuck or do this if you need some of my help or my attention, but it's not a 'this is right, this is wrong' process. Everybody's going to get it right.

Nevertheless, several teachers experienced problems around issues of curriculum and evaluation. Another teacher noted, for example, that the kind of ongoing evaluation that was necessary when using inquiry strategies could be "very difficult for teachers because teachers are generally trained to assess based on the response given. They are not necessarily trained to evaluate processes." He also considered that the conflict between an inquiry focus to instruction and the need to prepare students for external examinations designed for a traditional approach to curriculum and evaluation could constrain teachers' in their use of inquiry. "As long as the subject matter . . . is going to be primary over anything else for evaluation of courses, then inquiry is going to have a lot of trouble moving it to especially the senior high school classes." Similarly, another secondary teacher found that the rigid demarcation of learning into courses, and the resulting need for course-specific grades, caused practical problems in evaluating students' inquiry products. When students worked on one project for two or more courses, which is a frequent occurrence when inquiry strategies are used, grading was affected. "Evaluation is a problem for teachers sharing kids. Who grades what? When? How much weight does each phase warrant?"

The concerns raised by the teachers are consistent with the observation made by Brooks and Brooks (1993) that fragmentation of curriculum and pressures of time to cover curricula that are heavily laden with facts to be memorized are problematic for constructivist teaching. Under these conditions, Brooks and Brooks concluded, testing drives teaching as teachers prepare their students to do well on their tests.

It was only in the context of these traditional aspects of evaluation that teachers saw curriculum and evaluation as potential problems. In traditional, modernist classrooms the curriculum is believed to represent the core knowledge necessary for students to know about a field. Grades, then, have the purpose of determining how much of this body of knowledge has been acquired by students. Traditional approaches to education assume a norm that all students should strive for and against which all should be measured (Doll, 1993). Postmodern constructivist pedagogies, on the other hand, consider that the purpose of curricula is to set broad outlines; the enacted curriculum is developed jointly by teachers and students in interaction with each other and their particular environments (Brooks &

Brooks, 1993; Doll, 1993; Gross, 1997). Evaluation is conceived as being ongoing, clarifying for both teachers and students the progress that students are making. It identifies students' strengths and also areas in which they may need to improve. At the end of a project, it does not ask "how much of this do you know?" but, rather, "what do you know?" (Doll, 1993).

Students' expectations for traditional evaluation also caused problems for some of our informants. As previously discussed, students who had earned high marks under traditional teaching methods resisted the new regime.

> The kids who were quite capable and who were getting eighties, eight out of ten, eighty per cent, they weren't really pleased. . . . These kids were very satisfied getting their eight. They were very satisfied being successful how they were working. It's very threatening, and it's very confusing to have to change, especially, you know, when it was working, in those cases where the kids didn't feel that there was anything wrong with the way they were learning.

Two teachers observed that students needed ongoing evaluation to give them a sense of security in their progress, and both felt they had to react to that need.

> Kids need validation and if you can't give them "this is what I wanted, this is the answer," it's very threatening for them, it's very hard. You have to build in evaluation for them. You have to have different ways of them being able to see their progress, to evaluate themselves, because they need that. They really need to feel that they are going somewhere.

However, although these two teachers shared a perception of students' needs for evaluation, the solutions they undertook were quite different. One responded by instituting frequent evaluation which gave the students' feedback and at the same time kept their behavior more under his control:

> I found it important to evaluate them on each stage, and they know that they are going to be evaluated on each stage, whether it's the opening discussion of a project or a story that they might be working on, and they, you tell them ahead of time I want this done this period and at the end of the period they have to hand it in. Otherwise you'll find they'll say oh, we're still discussing it, we'll hand it in later. We're still in the discussion part of it. So, I found it's very important to do that.

The other teacher, in contrast, tried to find a way to decrease her students' dependence on her:

> I've been working on having the kids design their own evaluation rubrics so they're actually looking at what they have to do to achieve a certain grade, and I'm giving them the Ministry [of Education] guidelines for the first unit that they have to do in biology, and the kids are going to develop their own evaluation guide from that.

This experiment in turn raised another issue, that of time. "It's going to be time-consuming though. I've got to figure out how to make it manageable."

Time.   The organization of time, as well as a lack of time, is a problem for most teachers (Wagner, 1998). Not surprisingly, then, problems of time presented several barriers to the use of inquiry. School schedules made it difficult to find the blocks of time needed. "In our schools in Grades 4 and 5, the science teacher is not the home room teacher; he is there for two 45-minute periods per week. So that's a time constraint but it's also a timetable constraint." Schedules were particularly problematic when students were bused. Other authors have noted that scheduling, particularly in secondary schools, hampers attempts to move away from traditional teaching methods and have suggested that block scheduling may help to solve these problems (Reis & Renzulli, 1986; Weld, 1998; Lybbert, 1998). Even when schedules were not an issue, the time needed for students to master the assigned curricula often conflicted with the time necessary to carry out inquiry projects. "The content courses can be so vast that you know, you've got to get through so much material . . . that it becomes difficult, because it [inquiry] does take more time." This was perceived to be more of a barrier by the secondary-school teachers whose students were faced with provincial exams based on the assigned curricula. Similar problems have been reported by teachers in other studies (Aaronsohn, 1996). Generally, when inquiry is used, teachers and students study fewer topics, substituting depth of understanding for breadth of knowledge (Weld, 1998).

Three teachers also pointed out that inquiry demanded more of their own time. This was partly because the approach was new to them, but also because they sometimes needed to be available to students outside of class time. Halliday, too, found that inquiry approaches demand a great deal of teachers' time. That these teachers were prepared to take the time is consistent with Weld's observations concerning one inquiry teacher, and his contention that exemplary teachers generally commit a great deal of time to the improvement of their craft (1998). It is also supported by Aaronsohn (1996) and Gross (1997), and by Westberg and Archambault (1997), who reported that teachers who were willing to embrace change were also prepared to spend considerable time and effort to make the changes.

There is wide agreement that the creative process takes a great deal of time (Britton & Glynn, 1989; Tardiff & Sternberg, 1988); Gruber and Davis (1988) noted that "the single most reliable finding in our studies is that creative work takes a long time" (p. 265). Teachers, however, have full schedules with very little time for reflection (Wagner, 1998). Indeed, expert teaching has been characterized as an improvisational act (Borko & Livingston, 1989; Moore, 1993) particularly when teachers use constructivist approaches such as inquiry. Thus, it is not surprising to find that these teachers identified lack of time available to them as a barrier to innovation. This observation concerning the role of time represents an important difference between creative teachers and creative individuals in other fields. It is worth further study to explore the impact of time on teachers' creative behavior.

Resources. A mismatch between students and the resources available sometimes presented a barrier to the use of inquiry. The textbooks available in secondary schools were geared to students achieving at grade level and did not readily accommodate the wide range of abilities in typical classrooms. Additionally, a "second language problem" was also noted by some teachers. Language could be a barrier when students with different mother tongues worked together on their projects and also when "they come to want to do research and all their resources are now in a second language, so it lowers the level at which they can do their research."

School level. Because the barriers to the use of inquiry strategies for teaching are much greater in secondary than elementary schools, several teachers suggested that they be mainly used in elementary schools where teachers have more control over grading, schedules, and curricula. However, that could exacerbate one source of many secondary school problems: An important developmental task for early adolescents is to become more independent. Yet as adolescents move from elementary school to secondary school they frequently have less rather than more control over their learning (Eccles & Midgley, 1990). Giving students more freedom in elementary school without making corresponding changes at the secondary level could increase adolescents' alienation from school. Reform is needed that provides space for constructivist approaches to be part of the curriculum at all levels of education. Fortunately at least some of the new curricula in Quebec, as elsewhere, are starting to make this transition and school leaving exams are gradually being given less importance in determining students' grades.

Support for Change

Although colleagues were sometimes viewed as potential barriers to change, teachers did find support for developing inquiry strategies from a small group of colleagues at school and at the university. Consistent with Westberg and Archambault's (1997) observations, the school-based teachers referred to their colleagues as their main source of ideas and support. In one case it was a deliberate search:

> I searched, I really looked for people who could help me, and I didn't recognize it at the time, but what I was doing was looking for mentors. And I've found one in every single school I've worked at. . . . I didn't have to experience all those mistakes, all the dead ends that some other people ran up against before they found their way around.

In the other cases, finding support was more happenstance. One informant recounted that "I had never done [a particular course] before so I went into it in a situation where I recognized that you [another teacher] would be a good resource." They believed that this had been possible because they were working together in a small school in which all teachers shared the same staff room and interacted with each other. They made a point of meeting once a week to discuss their experiences introducing inquiry into their classrooms. These informants described other schools in which teachers were segregated by subject, which they felt made such cross-fertilization less likely.

In addition to finding support from colleagues, the teachers who were introduced to inquiry through the summer program identified the university as source of support for change. All three referred to a university course in research methods that they felt had made it possible for them to use inquiry strategies effectively. This course was not about inquiry *per se;* rather, the teachers were required to plan a small research project, from start to finish, on their own or in small teams. The participants recognized that "this research method (course) was inquiry and it was hard." However, having been through this inquiry experience themselves gave them both a better understanding of the inquiry processes that their students' were engaged in, and also the confidence in themselves to risk using inquiry with their own students. One informant explained that if she had not taken the research course, then the summer class:

> would have been a very miserable experience because I would have been doing everything and they would have just been tagging along and we'd be getting maybe one source of information, maybe two, and I would be thinking, Wow, am I doing well. But if I hadn't gone through the process I wouldn't know. You have to do it yourself to know.

In his teaching prior to taking research methods, one teacher had tried to get away from traditional types of school projects. However, on reflection he realized that his earlier attempt "was lacking a certain something. And I think that was . . . the analysis part" that he learned how to do in the research course. Actually having done a research project himself had "given me certainly a different view of the whole inquiry process."

It was also in a university course that McBride met Halliday, was exposed to RE-ACT, recognized its potential power for her students, and introduced it into her school. A second teacher from the high school also spent one summer with the summer-school program run by Halliday. Thus, indirectly the university also supported the change in the secondary school. Ongoing contacts between the school and university continue to be a positive force for both partners.

The observations about change and professional development made by these teachers are consistent with other literature on innovative teachers. Other researchers have noted that collaboration with colleagues is an important source of support in teachers' professional development (Brooks & Brooks, 1993; Gross, 1997; Westberg & Archambault, 1997). Dantonio (1995) documented the ineffectiveness of relatively short workshops and demonstrated that peer coaching is more effective in bringing about teacher change. Similarly, Westberg and Archambault (1997) found that effective teachers engaged in a variety of forms of collaboration to support their attempts to change. For the teacher with whom Aaronsohn (1996) worked, the colleague was a university instructor; only very gradually was she able to find other teachers who developed into a mutually supportive group. Fullan (1996) concluded that traditional schools do not support teacher networking and recommended that specific strategies need to be developed to use this resource for change.

The need for support from others has been noted in studies of creative individuals in other fields. Gardner (1994) reported that both professional and personal supports were crucial to the development of the creative giants that he studied, and Murdock, Isaksen, and Trincanati (1993) found mentors had a powerful influence on the creative researchers they studied. Once again, we can see clear parallels between these innovative teachers and creative individuals in other fields.

Conclusions and Implications

The informants in this study were motivated to use inquiry in their teaching in order to improve their students' learning. In the process, they found increased student enjoyment in learning, and more rewarding teacher-student relationships. The primacy that they place on students' learning, with improved classroom relationships being a valued bonus, is consistent with other reports of teachers who change their practice (Aaronsohn, 1996; Butt, Raymond, McCue, & Yamagishi, 1992; Gross, 1997; Weld, 1998). Equally consistent with other reports (Butt, Raymond, McCue, & Yamagishi, 1992; Clifton & Roberts, 1993; Gross; 1997; Herzog, 1995; Weld, 1998) the barriers that they perceived to using inquiry were related to systemic resistance to change in the educational system. Particularly in secondary schools, the inflexible use of time and traditional forms of evaluation pose real problems for the use of inquiry in classrooms.

In addition to their similarity to other innovative teachers, our informants resemble creative achievers in other fields in several significant ways: their openness to experience, their willingness to take risks, their independence of judgment, their ability to cope well with novelty, their use of metaphoric thinking. Above all, they are motivated by a deep drive to do their task better. Amabile (1996) described artists and writers who are committed to the task of writing or art; these teachers are committed to the task of getting their students to learn as effectively as possible.

Most research and thinking about teacher motivation has centered on educational reform. In particular, the concern has focused on how best to attract and retain high quality teachers, and how to motivate all teachers to improve their teaching. One approach has focused on using teacher compensation to bring about change, raising questions such as, what should teachers be compensated for, how to determine who should be rewarded, and the nature of the incentives to be employed. The most commonly proposed rewards are extrinsic, primarily financial, and administered at the board or district level (Frase, 1992; Odden & Kelley, 1997). Alternative approaches to educational reform, currently receiving increased attention, include school restructuring and the empowerment of teachers (Payzant, 1992). In these models, reform is focused at the school level and teachers are given the authority to decide how best to meet students' needs, usually with input from the school community. However, the impetus rarely comes from the teachers; rather, it is generally mandated at the board or district level.

Research on creativity clearly demonstrates that innovators in other fields are intrinsically motivated, and that extrinsic rewards of the kind envisioned by the teacher compensation movement are frequently detrimental to their creativity (Amabile, 1996). However, school restructuring, teacher compensation, and teacher empowerment approaches typically are instigated by educational administrators and often require the participation of a majority of the teachers in a given school. The excellent, innovative teachers whom reformers wish to retain in teaching (Weld, 1998), and who potentially lead the way to broader reform (Aaronsohn, 1996), strive to improve their practice on their own initiative. They are not likely to be primarily motivated by extrinsic rewards and pressures. Furthermore, because these innovative teachers do not represent the views of the majority in a school community, it is not likely that their ideas would be adopted for schoolwide change, and peer pressure would probably make it difficult for them to implement the kind of change that we have tracked in this study. Therefore, it is not surprising to find that recent research indicates that the traditional approaches to change have not been very successful (Frase & Poston, 1992).

If one is truly committed to a constructivist view of learning, then it has to be applied equally to teachers' change and growth. This would imply multiple paths to the growth, multiple goals, and multiple ways for teachers to demonstrate their growth. It cannot be assumed that all teachers will want to adopt inquiry, or any other specific approach. As one of our informants noted, you cannot impose inquiry because "you would have to change a lot of people's ways of thinking and seeing what school is." Furthermore, "dictating or imposing something on the teacher will backfire. You have to open up, show it, and keep your classroom door open and showcase it . . . and invite other teachers into your classroom and show them what you are doing." These suggestions are consistent with the type of environment that has been shown to support creativity in other fields. Creativity flourishes when individuals are given support to follow their own visions. Administrators can support innovative teachers through such actions as rearranging students' and teachers' schedules to make more flexible use of time, finding funds to provide teaching materials and teacher release-time, and valuing teachers' efforts in discussions with parents, students, and other teachers. Such support has been evident both in the summer school and in the secondary school from which these teachers were drawn.

The model of teacher empowerment described by Barksdale-Ladd and Thomas (1996) is more appropriate for innovative teachers than are the school or district-level actions often advocated in the educational reform literature. In their study of eight teachers they demonstrated that empowerment did not come from workshops or in-service activity but from the teachers' own realizations that there was a need for change, followed by a personal search for relevant professional education and experience. As they applied their new understanding to their classroom instruction, the teachers grew in confidence and continued to change. Consistent with this approach Westberg and Archambault (1997) concluded that teachers who successfully implemented new practices needed both autonomy to follow their own goals and administrative support to make changes needed to implement their new approach. To this end, Weld (1998) made a plea for educational administrators to lead through facilitation, and Duke (1993) suggested that a multitrack system be put in place to encourage teacher growth and to support teachers who undertake the risks inherent in change. A model of change based on this approach would allow considerable variety in teachers' learning and development and result in rich and varied schools. Just as students need a variety of paths to learning, so, too, do teachers.

References

Aaronsohn, E. (1996). *Going against the grain: Supporting the student-centered teacher.* Thousand Oaks, CA: Corwin Press.

Amabile, T. M. (1996). *Creativity in context: Update to "The social psychology of creativity."* Boulder, CO: Westview Press.

Barksdale-Ladd, M. A., & Thomas, K. F. (1996). The development of empowerment in reading instruction in eight elementary school teachers. *Teachers and Teacher Education, 12,* 161–178.

Barron, F., Montuori, A., & Barron, A. (Eds.). (1997). *Creators on creating: Awakening and cultivating the imaginative mind.* New York: Putnam.

Baum, S. M., Renzulli, J. S., & Hébert, T. P. (1995). Reversing underachievement: Creative productivity as a systematic intervention. *Gifted Child Quarterly, 39,* 224–235.

Borko, H., & Livingston, C. (1989). Cognition and improvisation: Differences in mathematics instruction by expert and novice teachers. *American Educational Research Journal, 26,* 473–498.

Boxall, W. (1995). Making the public private. In D. Thomas (Ed.), *Teachers' stories* (pp. 152–162). Buckingham, UK: Open University Press.

Britton, B. K., & Glynn, S. M. (1989). Mental management and creativity. In J. A. Glover, R. R. Ronning, & C. R. Reynolds (Eds.), *Handbook of creativity* (pp. 429–440). New York: Plenum.

Brooks, J. G., & Brooks, M. G. (1993). In *search of understanding: The case for constructivist classrooms.* Alexandria, VA: Association for Supervision and Curriculum Development.

Butt, R., Raymond, D., McCue, G., & Yamagishi, L. (1992). Collaborative autobiography and the teacher's voice. In I. F. Goodson (Ed.), *Studying teachers' lives* (pp. 51–98). New York: Teachers College Press.

Clifton, R. A., & Roberts, L. W. (1993). *Authority in classrooms.* Scarborough, ON: Prentice Hall Canada.

Csikszentmihalyi, M. (1988). Society, culture, and person: A systems view of creativity. In R. J. Sternberg (Ed.), *The nature of creativity: Contemporary psychological approaches* (pp. 325–339). New York: Cambridge University Press.

Csikszentmihalyi, M. (1990). The domain of creativity. In M. A. Runco & R. S. Albert (Eds.), *Theories of creativity* (pp. 190–212). Newbury Park, CA: Sage.

Csikszentmihalyi, M. (1992). Motivation and creativity. In R. J. Runco (Ed.), *Genius and eminence* (2nd ed., pp. 19–33). New York: Pergamon Press.

Dantonio, M. (1995). *Collegial coaching: Inquiry into the teaching self.* Bloomington, IN: Phi Delta Kappa.

Doll, W. E., Jr. (1993). *A post-modern perspective on curriculum.* New York: Teachers College Press.

Duke, K. L. (1993). Removing barriers to professional growth. *Phi Delta Kappan, 74,* 702–704, 710–712.

Eccles, J. C., & Midgley, C. (1990). Changes in academic motivation and self-perception during early adolescence. In R. Montemayor, G. R. Adams, & T. P. Gullotta (Eds.), *From childhood to adolescence: A transitional period?* London: Sage.

Ennis, C. D. (1995). Teachers' response to noncompliant students: The realities and consequences of a negotiated curriculum. *Teaching and Teacher Education, 11,* 445–460.

Feldhusen, J. F., & Treffinger, D. J. (1980). *Creative thinking and problem solving.* Dubuque, IA: Kendall/Hunt.

Firestone, W. A., & Pennell, J. R. (1993). Teacher commitment, working conditions, and differential incentive policies. *Review of Educational Research, 63,* 489–525.

Forrest, L., & Rosenberg, F. (1997). A review of feminist pedagogy literature: The neglected child of feminist psychology. *Applied and Preventive Psychology, 6,* 179–192.

Frase, L. E. (1992). The effects of financial and nonfinancial rewards: Program description and research results. In L. E. Frase (Ed.), *Teacher compensation and motivation* (pp. 217–238). Lancaster, PA: Technomic.

Frase, L. E., & Poston, W. K. (1992). Effective teacher incentive programs: Diversity and effectiveness without state funding. In L. E. Frase (Ed.), *Teacher compensation and motivation* (pp. 141–147). Lancaster, PA: Technomic.

Fullan, M. G. (1996). Turning systemic thinking on its head. *Phi Delta Kappan, 77,* 420–423.

Gardner, H. (1988). Creative lives and creative works: A synthetic scientific approach. In R. J. Sternberg (Ed.), *The nature of creativity: Contemporary psychological approaches* (pp. 298–321). New York: Cambridge University Press.

Gardner, H. (1994). *Creating minds: An anatomy of creativity as seen through the lives of Freud, Einstein, Picasso, Stravinsky, Eliot, Graham, and Gandhi.* New York: Basic Books.

Getzels, J. W., & Csikszentmihalyi, M. (1976). *The creative vision: A longitudinal study of problem-finding in art.* New York: Wiley.

Ghiselin, B. (1955). *The creative process.* New York: Mentor.

Gross, P. A. (1997). *Joint curriculum design: Facilitating learner ownership and active participation in secondary classrooms.* Mahwah, NJ: Erlbaum.

Gruber, H. E., & Davis, S. N. (1988). Inching our way up Mount Olympus: The evolving systems approach to creative thinking. In R. J. Sternberg (Ed.), *The nature of creativity: Contemporary psychological perspectives* (pp. 243–270). New York: Cambridge University Press.

Halliday, F. (1986). *RE-ACT teaching strategies of research and inquiry: Making the inquiry process work for kids.* Unpublished report, Faculty of Education, McGill University.

Herzog, M. J. R. (1995). Breaking tradition: The experiences of an alternative teacher in a rural school. In D. Thomas (Ed.), *Teachers' stories* (pp. 152–162). Buckingham, UK: Open University Press.

Hogan, R., & Morrison, J. (1996). Managing creativity. In A. Montuori (Ed.). *Unusual associates: A festschrift for Frank Barron* (pp. 344–351). Cresskill, NJ: Hampton Press.

Jervis, K., & McDonald, J. (1996). Standards: The philosophical monster in the classroom. *Phi Delta Kappan, 77,* 563–569.

Kirton, M. J. (1976). Adaptors and innovators: A description and measure. *Journal of Applied Psychology, 61,* 622–629.

Lortie, D. C. (1975). *Schoolteacher: A sociological study.* Chicago: University of Chicago Press.

Lybbert, B. (1998). *Transforming learning with block scheduling: A guide for principals.* Thousand Oaks, CA: Corwin Press.

MacKinnon, D. W. (1978). *In search of human effectiveness: Identifying and developing creativity.* Buffalo, NY: Creative Education Foundation.

Martindale, C. (1989). Personality, situation, and creativity. In J. A. Glover, R. R. Ronning, & C. R. Reynolds (Eds.), *Handbook of creativity* (pp. 211–232). New York: Plenum.

Moore, M. T. (1993). Implications of problem finding on teaching and learning. In S. G. Isaksen, M. C. Murdock, R. L. Firestien, & D. J. Treffinger (Eds.), *Nurturing and developing creativity: The emergence of a discipline* (pp. 51–69). Norwood, NJ: Ablex.

Murdock, M. C., Isaksen, S. G., & Trincanati, N. S. (1993). A community of scholars: Antecedents of the 1990 International Working Creativity Conference participants. In S. G. Isaksen, M. C. Murdock, R. L. Firestien, & D. J. Treffinger (Eds.), *Understanding and recognizing creativity: The emergence of a discipline* (pp. 83–104). Norwood, NJ: Ablex.

Odden, A., & Kelley, C. (1997). *Paying teachers for what they know and do: New and smarter compensation strategies to improve schools.* Thousand Oaks, CA: Corwin Press.

Payzant, T. W. (1992). Empowering teachers and enhancing student achievement through school restructuring. In L. E. Frase (Ed.), *Teacher compensation and motivation* (pp. 453–481). Lancaster, PA: Technomic.

Perkins, D. N. (1981). *The mind's best work.* Cambridge, MA: Harvard University Press.

Reis, S. M., & Renzulli, J. S. (1986). The secondary triad model. In J. S. Renzulli (Ed.), *Systems and models for developing programs for the gifted and talented* (pp. 267–305). Mansfield Center, CT: Creative Learning Press.

Rejskind, G. (2000). TAG teachers: Only the creative need apply. *Roeper Review, 22,* 153–157.

Rejskind, G., & Halliday, F. (1997, May). *Motivation in inquiry teaching and learning.* Paper presented at the annual meeting of the Quebec Association of School Administrators & the Quebec Association of School Board Administrators, Quebec City, QC.

Rejskind, G., Chennabathni, R., McBride, J. B., & Halliday, F. (1998). Issues of control in an inquiry teaching method. In J. Ross Epp (Ed.), *Centering on . . . the margins: The evaded curriculum.* Proceedings of the Second bi-annual Canadian Association for the Study of Women and Education International Institute (pp. 33–40), Ottawa, ON.

Rogers, C. R. (1959). Towards a theory of creativity. In H. H. Anderson (Ed.), *Creativity and its cultivation* (pp. 69–82). New York: Harper.

Rosenholtz, S. J., & Simpson, C. (1990). Workplace conditions and the rise and fall of teachers' commitment. *Sociology of Education, 63,* 241–257.

Sederberg, C. H., & Clark, S. M. (1990). Motivation and organizational incentives for high vitality teachers: A qualitative perspective. *Journal of Research and Development in Education, 24,* 6–13.

Smilansky, J., & Hallberstadt, N. (1986). Inventors versus problem solvers: An empirical investigation. *Journal of Creative Behavior, 20,* 183–201.

Starko, A. J. (1989). Problem finding in creative writing: An exploratory study. *Journal for the Education of the Gifted, 12,* 172–186.

Starko, A. J. (1995). *Creativity in the classroom: Schools of curious delight.* White Plains, NY: Longman.

Sternberg, R. J. (1988). A three-facet model of creativity. In R. J. Sternberg (Ed.), *The nature of creativity: Contemporary psychological perspectives* (pp. 125–147). New York: Cambridge University Press.

Strauss, A. L., & Corbin, J. (1990). *Basics of qualitative research: Grounded theory procedures and techniques.* Newbury Park, CA: Sage.

Tardiff, T. Z., & Sternberg, R. J. (1988). What do we know about creativity? In R. J. Sternberg (Ed.), *The nature of creativity: Contemporary psychological perspectives* (pp. 429–440). New York: Cambridge University Press.

Taylor, I. A. (1975). An emerging view of creative actions. In I. A. Taylor & J. W. Getzels (Eds.), *Perspectives in creativity.* Chicago: Aldine.

Wagner, T. (1998). Change as collaborative inquiry: A constructivist methodology for reinventing schools. *Phi Delta Kappan, 79,* 512–517.

Wallas, G. (1926). *The art of thought.* New York: Harcourt Brace.

Weld, J. (1998). Attracting and retaining high-quality professionals in science education. *Phi Delta Kappan, 79,* 536–539.

Westberg, K. L., & Archambault, F. X., Jr. (1997). A multi-site case study of successful classroom practices for high ability students. *Gifted Child Quarterly, 41,* 42–51.

10

Teacher Models of Teaching Inquiry

ANN ROBINSON

University of Arkansas at Little Rock

JULIA HALL

Benton School District, Arkansas

> "Tell me more about what you are doing with your Culture Fair. Are some teachers more effective than others at getting their students to engage in inquiry?"
>
> "I don't really know. Some kids seem to do better with certain teachers, but it's not clear."
>
> "So, what is the important issue for you, then?"
>
> "Well, I'd like to get more teachers involved or maybe more committed to teaching inquiry as a part of Culture Fair, but beyond it, too."

This brief interchange (or one very nearly like it) was the beginning of an action-research project involving the use of inquiry in a junior high social studies and English culture fair in an inner city International Studies/Gifted and Talented specialty school. Out of the questions we shared over the course of several discussions, an inquiry on inquiry took shape. The first author is a university teacher educator and researcher with an interest in teacher thinking and teacher professional development. The second author is a junior high school teacher with a background in social studies. Both share interests in curriculum development and have formal professional preparation in gifted education.

This chapter traces our investigation of one aspect of inquiry—the models that teachers carry with them when they engage in a sustained inquiry project with their students. Our assumption was that if we could hear what teachers had to say about inquiry, we might be able to describe patterns of teachers' thinking about this complex instructional approach. If we could describe the teachers' models of teaching inquiry, we might plug a gap in the existing literature. A review of inquiry teaching by Flick (1995) concluded that the current literature focuses primarily on the role of the student in inquiry rather than on the role of the teacher. The research done on teachers within the framework of inquiry has focused largely on the science classroom (Crawford, 2000; Falk & Drayton, 2000; Flick, 1996; Flick & Dickenson, 1997; MacKenzie, 2001; Tobin, Kahle, & Fraser, 1990). There is a need to investigate teachers whose inquiry teaching occurs in other subject-matter domains or whose approach may be more general and less content-specific. To understand what roles teachers play, what classroom conditions they set, and what specific teaching behaviors they use to encourage inquiry, we believed the place to begin was with what teachers themselves believed about inquiry and inquiry teaching.

First Efforts in our Inquiry on Teachers' Beliefs

Our first pass at getting at teachers' beliefs (which was one of convenience) produced useful, but relatively thin data. It was undertaken as a basis for developing a structured interview protocol for Culture Fair teachers the following year. The first author was teaching a current issues seminar course in gifted education; the focus of the seminar that semester was on classroom practices and curriculum and included the use of interactive journals. It was no trouble at all to "try out" inquiry prompts with this group of in-service professionals as part of the interactive journal. To get an initial impression of what teachers thought inquiry was, the first journal prompt focused on teachers' definitions of inquiry: *As teachers we are often encouraged to provide opportunities for inquiry for our students. What is inquiry? Offer your definition. How do you encourage inquiry in your students?*

Of the 13 in-service professionals attending the seminar, 10 responded that inquiry meant questions. They offered a range of definitions related to questioning. For example,

> "When the concept of inquiry comes to mind, I automatically think of 'asking questions.'"
> "Inquiry is finding an answer to a question or concern that a person has."
> "Open ended and initially undirected questioning." And,
> "Inquiry? I don't have a well thought out definition. I try to offer students questions instead of answers."

Responses from the remainder of the seminar participants did not specifically mention questions, but conceptualized inquiry as a "sequential process," "any method by which a subject's knowledge content is increased," or "a type of 'debate.'"

A month later in the seminar, the 13 educators were given a second journal prompt focusing on inquiry. By that time in the semester, they had been asked to select an area of inquiry of their own for seminar discussions, had been given an assignment to complete computer searches on their topic using two different databases, and been given the opportunity to search for library and Internet sources relevant to their inquiry topic. In essence, they had been engaged in inquiry themselves rather than guiding the inquiry of their students. The second prompt focused on reflection:

> After having begun your own inquiry into an issue or topic of interest to you in this class, revisit your thoughts on inquiry. What does it mean to you now? Re-read your journal entry of 1/20. How are your thoughts this week and your thoughts two weeks ago similar? How are they different?

Overall, the educators did not acknowledge that their definitions of inquiry changed. However, their later journal entries were longer and more elaborated. Nine of the educators specifically commented on the frustrations and constraints of doing their inquiry projects. They noted the lack of time, the lack of resources, and the lack of their own focus as barriers to inquiry. In several journal responses, teachers mentioned that doing an inquiry project themselves for the seminar course gave them insight into how inquiry and independent projects must feel to their students.

> "Inquiry still means seeking answers. However, I now understand how frustrating it can be if my students meet some of the obstacles I have met (lack of time and resources)."
> "The most frustration has come because of the distance to good research materials. I understand better as a student that access is most important!"
> "Seeking out and searching for information can be a very time consuming task and the information can come in many forms. For example: printed material, videotapes, audiotapes, computer, people, etc. Making contacts for materials, equipment, or to set up and meet to talk to people also takes time so inquiry is not a quick, run-out and get this done in 10 minutes type of thing."

Context of the Investigation into Teaching Inquiry

The seminar participants' journal responses were a useful starting place for understanding teacher beliefs about inquiry, but we needed the opportunity to investigate inquiry teaching *in situ*. We also needed the opportunity to get expanded and extended information from teachers through interviews in which probes and follow-up questions would help us to tease out teachers' thinking about inquiry teaching and their approaches to it. That opportunity presented itself through the second author's implementation of an inquiry-based Culture Fair in her urban school. We organized our study of teacher beliefs about inquiry teaching to coincide with the Culture Fair cycle that began following a vacation break in March.

The Culture Fair was an annual event for seventh-grade students at this school. Held each spring, it was designed to be the culmination of a significant part of the year's work in two required core subjects: English and social studies. Based on an idea published by Patricia and Peter Watson in *Cultural Fair:*

A Resource Guide (Watson, & Watson, 1991), students were required to plan a project that focused on a cultural theme or issue, narrow down this project to a specific topic, research this topic, draw appropriate conclusions from the data collected, and present the findings by preparing reports, graphs, drawings and diagrams as necessary. Students received instruction in both English and social studies classes and worked on the project for much of the fourth quarter of the school year. On completion, students earned credit for their work in both English and social studies.

In addition to class credit, students entered their projects into a schoolwide competition that took place in the school gymnasium and looked very much like a science fair (i.e., a collection of projects or investigations on cardboard backboards set up on rows of folding tables). Projects were grouped into nine categories: genealogy, migrations, heritage, economics, arts and crafts, settlements and groups, customs, special events, and general culture. Each category of projects was judged by a team of two or three community experts, usually adults working in a job related to the general field of study. The students were asked to present their projects to the judges and answer questions. The judges were given a scoring rubric and asked to evaluate the level of mastery each student had attained in five key categories of accomplishment: (a) knowledge of subject, (b) level of completion, (c) creative effort, (d) method, and (e) presentation. The rubric included a description of what a project ranging from the highest performance level, *exceptional,* to the lowest performance level, *fair,* would look like. Judges were then instructed to determine place awards by considering the number and categories of *exceptional* and *very good* marks. The day after the judging, an awards assembly was held for all Culture Fair participants. All students were recognized at this assembly and personally handed a Certificate of Participation. First, second, third, and honorable mention ribbons were awarded in each category (if earned). In addition, 10 Spirit ribbons were awarded to recognize those students who really caught the spirit of multicultural and international inquiry. Perhaps they did not produce the best projects but they were willing to take on a challenge, work hard, and really try to learn something new about some aspect of culture in which they were interested. The recipients of Spirit ribbons were determined by teacher and judge nomination.

Overall, the Culture Fair had been designed to meet the following objectives:

1. To expose all of the school's seventh-grade students to the study of different cultures and to encourage an awareness of and an interest in multicultural and international issues.
2. To expand several of the key components (research skills, writing, world geography, and cultures) in the seventh-grade English and social studies curricula by giving students the opportunity to involve themselves in an in-depth investigation of a cultural issue.
3. To reinforce principles of the scientific method by applying this method to investigations in other areas of study.

4. To assist seventh-graders in their transition to the competitive world of junior and senior high school by providing an opportunity for them to develop their own interests, talents, and confidence in their abilities, without the discouragement of stiff competition from older students.

At the time of this study, the Culture Fair had been in place at the school for four years. It was a schoolwide event that encouraged participation in a common learning experience by both identified gifted students and students who were not so identified. For many of the nonidentified students, the seventh-grade Culture Fair was the first time they had been asked to complete an extended project and report the results to an adult they did not know personally. Thus, the activity involved students of varying abilities, their teachers, and community adults in a common enterprise, but one with opportunities for individual choices in terms of topic or researchable question, use of resources, and engagement with the project.

Teacher Participants

In this environment, seven junior high school teachers were interviewed as they carried out this long-term inquiry project with their students. Of the seven teachers interviewed, three were English and four were Social Studies teachers. Two of the teachers were male, and five female. Four of the teachers were African American, three were Caucasian. Two of the teachers were in their first year of teaching, two had taught more than one year but fewer than five years, and three had more than 20 years of teaching experience. Four had taught Culture Fair to their students in previous years, three were teaching Culture Fair for the first time.

Focus of the Teaching Inquiry Interviews

The semistructured interviews were designed to elicit teacher thinking about the definitions, approaches, procedures, and students' accomplishments during the course of the inquiry project. Building on what we had learned from the journal prompts used in the seminar course, we developed a more elaborated set of interview questions for the Culture Fair teachers (see Table 10.1).

Teachers agreed to two interviews during the "Culture Fair season." The interviews were conducted by the first or second author before the teachers began teaching Culture Fair that year, and after the culminating event some two months later. The first interview focused on the teachers' definitions of inquiry, the ways they saw themselves and their students using inquiry, and how they determined the success of inquiry for their students. The second interview focused on the teachers' feelings about having been involved in a school-wide inquiry project, what advice they would give to other teachers, and what benefits they believed their students to have gained from participation.

Table 10.1   Abbreviated Interview Protocols (the full text of questions and follow-up probes is available on request from the first author at aerobinson@ualr.edu).

Interview #1

Prepared questions for the semistructured interview conducted shortly after the introduction of Culture Fair to students.

1. When I say the word inquiry, what do you think of?
2. If you had to define inquiry, how would you define it?
3. When do you see yourself using inquiry?
4. When do you see your students using inquiry?
5. What do you do to get started teaching inquiry?
6. What do you do when a student "gets stuck"?
7. How do you tell when inquiry is really working in your classroom?
8. What would you describe as a successful result of inquiry?
9. How would you describe a successful Culture Fair project?
10. Overall, if you were to characterize your approach to inquiry, what would you say?

Interview #2

Prepared questions for semistructured interview near the end of students' final presentations of their inquiry projects.

1. At this point in the Culture Fair season, how do you feel about Culture Fair?
2. How did you go about teaching Culture Fair this year?
3. What was the most difficult part of teaching inquiry?
4. What do you think your students have gained?
5. What advice would you give to a teacher undertaking Culture Fair for the first time?
6. Given a choice among the various teaching strategies you use, is inquiry one you would choose on your own? Why or why not?
7. Any final thoughts on inquiry?

Patterns of Teachers' Beliefs

The interviews, conducted during teachers' preparation periods, were tape-recorded and transcribed. The transcriptions were read independently by the two authors who subsequently met to discuss the patterns each noted in the teachers' responses. Coding was initially done within each question. Then, coded data were read across questions to establish more general patterns. In the preliminary analysis, three patterns of teacher thinking about inquiry teaching emerged: question-driven, resource-driven, and discovery-driven.

Question-Driven

The question-driven pattern was characterized by a focus on the value of inquiry as a way for students to generate good questions. Recall that, in the initial journal prompts from the group of teachers in the seminar course, the majority included questions as part of their definition of inquiry. In this more extensive interview process, we learned that the importance of questions extended beyond the teachers' definition of inquiry to include what skills or dispositions they wanted their students to develop—a questioning attitude and the skill of asking good questions. Teacher E(1), who was responsible for the English component of the Culture Fair, commented about her students in the following way:

> They know that Ms. _____ doesn't want babies. I always say I don't want babies; I don't want thin, skinny sentences or questions. I want FAT. I want big, fat questions that cause me to just sit and think. And I don't want an answer that you could . . . a question that can be answered with yes, no, the colors blue, black. No. We want you to think. We want others that [*sic*] read your project to think as well. I think we want open-ended questions.

Another English teacher, E(2), focused on the importance of questions when asked about the deliberate or happenstance nature of inquiry. During the course of the first interview, the interviewer asked if inquiry was taught specifically—did the teacher set out to teach it? Or did it just happen? The teacher's response indicated that question development played a significant role in his approach to inquiry both within the context of the formal curriculum and in the day-to-day events of the classroom. He came to the realization about his focus on questions after recalling an earlier teaching experience. Students in his class were noisy and were punished with a mandatory essay. He reflected on this experience and the students' subsequent objections to such treatment by challenging them the next day to ask him questions about why he took such action. From this teacher's point of view, the disciplinary event was an inquiry opportunity in the same way that Culture Fair was an opportunity to ask good questions. When asked to give an overall characterization of his approach to inquiry, Teacher E(2) stated "in a sense . . . the questions that I ask, the questions that they ask me, we get right down to the nitty-gritty."

The importance these teachers placed on questions also was reflected in their reports on the ways in which they taught the inquiry process. Questioning was seen as a way to understand the world. Open-ended questioning was seen as the way to guide students through the inquiry process. Inquiry assignments were presented as a series of questions to explore. When students encountered problems, teachers reported that problems were solved by asking more questions. When asked how she dealt with students who got stuck while in the midst of an inquiry project, E(1) said that she responded by asking questions about the questions they were asking, because "maybe they were written in a way where possibly if you rewrite them or rethink them, you would be able to come up with a different way of asking that question and your answers would be found there." Finally, success on an inquiry project was measured by how they used their questions—if students asked and answered questions that allowed them to delve deeper that was deemed a good project.

In summary, the question-driven pattern of teacher thinking was characterized by its focus on the question as the key to successful inquiry. Questioning was explained as a way to understand the world. In some cases, the question was viewed as a way to narrow down a topic. In other cases, the question was valued for itself: It was seen as a way to encourage students to be critical thinkers. To borrow a phrase from advertising, "inquiring minds want to know."

Resource-Driven

The resource-driven pattern of teacher thinking was characterized by teachers' concerns about information accessibility, the use of multiple sources, and teaching students a system of keeping information organized. When asked to define inquiry, these teachers tended to focus on information as the key word. Teacher SS(4), a social studies teacher, stated, "To me when I think of inquiry, I think of inquire, which means to ask or to find information, to find facts and then to take that information and try to make some kind of understanding of it." Teacher SS(3) commented, "I think the most difficult part of inquiry is getting the information and getting it organized."

In this model of teacher beliefs about inquiry, teachers viewed their role as one of facilitating inquiry by guiding students toward rich resources when possible, and by recognizing that resource availability often constrained the course of inquiry for their students. Teacher SS(3) noted the reality of doing interest-based inquiry in the schools: "A lot of times the original question ends up changing as they realize that this is what they found, and this is what they are writing about, and it's not relating to the question that they originally wanted to do." These comments do not necessarily refer to the experience of revising the focus as a project progresses because new insights take the inquirer in new directions, rather, because the information available is only tangentially related to the topic of interest. Therefore, the student's final inquiry product is guided by what is accessible rather than what is important to the original question. Recall that the teachers undertaking inquiry in the context of the graduate seminar reported similar resource constraints and frustrations.

The resource-driven approach to inquiry is a very pragmatic one. If students were to carry out inquiry successfully, the teachers realized that materials could be a key variable in student progress and motivation. Teachers chose to handle the issue of scarce resources in different ways. Some teachers guided students early into topics and questions that they felt were sufficiently supported by materials in the school and in local and university libraries. Their approach was to head off frustration by suggesting alternative topics or questions. Other resource-driven teachers chose to let students uncover the resource difficulties themselves as part of the inquiry process. In some cases, these teachers knew that little information was likely to be available; in others, the teachers themselves were uncertain about the richness or the accessibility of needed resource materials. These teachers stepped in with support and assistance when the student hit a resource barrier, but they were less likely to redirect the project focus until the student encountered problems.

Once students had access to the information they needed, these teachers also put great emphasis on teaching students what to do with the information in a very concrete manner. Teacher SS(1) described teaching Culture Fair as "a building process that . . . works its way up." Teacher E(3) stated that one of her main goals teaching inquiry was to make sure the students stayed on "the right track." Many of these teachers used very specific steps, requirements, and deadlines to guide their students through the inquiry process. Providing a concrete model of a final inquiry product for students was also often a part of the resource-driven approach. A source of frustration for one of these teachers seemed to be the individual nature of the inquiry process. Teacher SS(4) commented, "It would be nice if we had a real method of teaching it (inquiry) rather than doing it individually." Success for these teachers seemed to be measured by how well students met the specific requirements and learned some new information about their topic. As E(3) said, "I consider it to be successful if they have gone through the process, step-by-step . . . and done the best that they could do."

Discovery-Driven

A third pattern of teacher thinking about inquiry was characterized by personal growth for the teacher and by exposure to something new and exciting for the students. The teacher whose predominant approach was discovery-driven offered herself as a role model of inquiry. When asked how she taught inquiry, Teacher SS(2) commented she did this by practicing it herself. She further elaborated by stating that "one thing that I've done in my 23 years of teaching is I never do the same thing twice. So I have inquiry for myself. . . . We're always discovering new material. There's always something to discover."

Unlike the resource-driven teacher, the discovery-driven teacher did not bring in a previously completed student product from another class to show the students. Showing students a finished product tended to produce "copycats" or what Teacher SS(2) described as "fill-in-the-blank products." The discovery-driven teachers also did not focus on requiring specific steps. The goal was to submit an interesting and creative end-product, one that would allow a student to, in the words of Teacher SS(2), "transfer that [interest] to anyone that comes by, particularly the judges, then you've done yourself, you know, a wonderful favor."

Attitude toward inquiry seemed to be of vital importance in the discovery-driven approach. These teachers focused on keeping their students interested in their topics and, thereby, in the inquiry process. Their advice to teachers struggling with any part of teaching inquiry was to keep it fun and meaningful to their students. A large part of success for the discovery-driven teacher was measured by the amount of enthusiasm and pride students took in their end-products. Success was also determined by how much students talked about their projects and seemed to have gained personal meaning from them. As Teacher E(2) stated that it was a "real [sic] good sign if . . . once they have found this information out . . . that it becomes the topic of their conversation when they are speaking to their teacher." Teacher SS(2) answered the question as to how she would describe a successful result for an inquiry project as "satisfying for the individual student. Questions that they have had to think about and sift through mentally to come up with an end-product that they felt comfortable and proud of with new knowledge that will spur them on for more inquiry." Thus, one important characteristic of the discovery-driven approach to inquiry is its recursive nature—the project might be done, but a successful journey of inquiry was never finished. As teacher SS(2) elaborated, "And so when you get through, I feel like you feel you have finished that particular path . . . I mean not finished it . . . but reached a plateau where you're satisfied with it. And I think that's important. That's a good feeling."

Final Thoughts and Future Directions

Through an action research project, we investigated teachers' reports of their approach to inquiry teaching. We reasoned that if we listened to teachers' thinking about inquiry, we might have a better understanding of what works for teachers in this complex instructional practice. Although we began our conversations wondering if some teachers were better at reaching students through inquiry teaching than others, we did not carry out the current action research project in a way that allows us to answer that question. It seemed premature. Rather, our inquiry took us in the direction of characterizing teacher approaches as they emerged from the teaching-inquiry interviews.

First, we found three relatively distinct patterns: question-driven, resource-driven, and discovery-driven. These models seemed to us to capture the constellation of definitions, processes, procedures, strategies and desired outcomes, but the teachers themselves on whom these models are hypothesized are not "pure types." Teachers seemed to have preferred approaches, but we saw at least one teacher of the seven who demonstrated both question- and discovery-driven approaches in some ways. Four teachers, the largest group, were predominantly resource-driven in approach. The least predominant approach was discovery-driven. Future research will help us to refine these designations. We may find that any of the three general patterns will subdivide or that the least frequent approach is better subsumed under another.

Second, although the general patterns were distinctive, there were specific areas in which they showed similarities. Three were noticeable: process-orientation, motivation, and the strategy for maneuvering a student through an inquiry barrier. Examples of student barriers were inability to identify or articulate a distinct interest, inability to focus on a question, difficulty organizing information for a long-range project, operating with a book-report rather than investigation mentality—in summarizing information rather than using it as evidence, and being impatient with ambiguity. Students wanted to get the answers and "get done" with the product. In contrast, across all approaches, teachers tended to focus on the process of inquiry rather than the tangible product or the expected outcome. The processes considered most important differed across the approaches, but the tendency to focus on process did not. This diminished focus on the actual product took us by surprise. The context of the Culture Fair clearly emphasized a fully elaborated product, including a short report and a visual display. Over the years of Culture Fair implementation, a specially designed rubric was added to aid judges in making decisions for Assembly recognition. Thus, the product focus, the rubric, and the visibility of the fair forum itself would seem to make the end point of the Culture Fair very salient to the participating teachers. Although references to the product were not absent (recall that one discovery-driven teacher initially commented that the product let her know how inquiry was working in her classroom), these references did not swamp any of the approaches. It may be that provision of the rubric allowed teachers to turn their attention to inquiry teaching elsewhere in the Culture Fair context. The display and the rubric may have functioned as givens.

Future research on inquiry teaching in contexts that do not provide guidance for desired end performances may give a different picture of teacher preoccupations. In addition to a focus on process, the three approaches all addressed student motivation in some way. For some teachers, enthusiasm and satisfaction were noted; for others, effort was key. The final overarching similarity across approaches concerned students who "got stuck." Most teachers, whatever the predominant approach, believed that individual assistance was needed to boost the student over the barrier. Phrases such as "one-to-one," "tutoring," and "meet outside class" peppered the comments of the teachers. Even a first-year teacher who had yet to participate in a full Culture Fair cycle and who began her comments to the "stuck" question by suggesting that she would have to start at the beginning to reteach inquiry to her class, ultimately thought aloud and led herself to the conclusion that she would use individually tailored focusing questions to extract her students from the mire.

Third, we do have questions about which we would feel comforted by having definitive answers. In the spirit of inquiry, however, we have more questions and fewer answers at the end of this action research project than when we began. We suspect that the teachers' definitions of inquiry do, in fact, affect their facility with it. Many teachers in the initial seminar had relatively impoverished and unidimensional definitions focused on question asking. Although we agree that questions are central to inquiry, these were not elaborated models of questioning which might support an inquiry environment. In terms of the Culture Fair teachers, we suspect that the definitions and approaches articulated by these teachers affect how inquiry is actually taught in the classroom and how students see inquiry because of their teachers' actions. We did not observe teachers in the classroom, so at present we cannot state that teachers' beliefs and actions are aligned. We do not know if a teacher's previous experience with inquiry was an important variable. It would seem likely that such complex instruction would be more comfortably handled with experience, but our interviews of the Culture Fair teachers were not structured in a way to tap this information. It seems logical that teachers who build up mental models of inquiry in the classroom through repeated experience with it would ultimately be guided by richer and more elaborated definitions of inquiry. It would be interesting to investigate the relationship between prior experience, richness of definition, and the teachers' ability to negotiate around a barrier or inquiry trap. We suspect that impoverished definitions make teacher traps more likely.

Numerous questions might be asked from the students' perspective. For example, are students more likely to engage in inquiry spontaneously if they are matched in preferred approach with a teacher whose predominant approach is similar? We don't know. We did not question students about their reactions to their teachers' guidance during the Culture Fair season. We suspect that students and teachers who have very different inquiry styles may find that a barrier, but we do not yet know. We can only imagine how a highly organized, resource-driven teacher might respond to a discovery-driven student. The mismatch between the perceptions of the two might present barriers to both the student and the teacher. Finally, we suspect that teaching-inquiry approaches also affect how teachers use evaluation and grading in the context of inquiry. For example, how are evaluation and grading used by teachers when a rubric is not supplied and when it is? And what effects do we see on students' responses to inquiry under both of these conditions?

Although we have many unanswered questions and we have put forward our models of teaching inquiry as hypotheses not yet fully tested, we do believe that inquiry is a basic skill of learning. Furthermore, we believe that as teachers we should develop a love of inquiry rather than a distaste for research assignments in our students.

References

Crawford, B. A. (2000). Embracing the essence of inquiry: New roles for science teachers. *Journal of Research in Science Teaching, 37,* 916–937.

Falk, J., & Drayton, B. (2000, April). *The inquiry-based classroom in context: Bridging the gap between teacher's practice and policy mandates.* Paper presented at the annual meeting of the American Educational Research Association, New Orleans, LA.

Flick, L. B. (1995, April). *Complex instruction in complex classrooms: A synthesis of research in inquiry teaching methods and explicit teaching strategies.* Paper presented at the annual meeting of the National Association for Research in Science Teaching, San Francisco, CA. (ERIC Document Reproduction Service ED 383 563)

Flick, L. B. (1996). Understanding a generative learning model of instruction: A case study of elementary teacher planning. *Journal of Science Teacher Education, 7,* 95–122.

Flick, L. B., & Dickinson, V. L. (1997, March). *Teacher intentions, teaching practice, and student perceptions in inquiry-oriented teaching.* Paper presented at the annual meeting of the National Association for Research in Science Teaching, Oak Brook, IL. (ERIC Document Reproduction Service No. ED 407 254)

MacKenzie, A. H. (2001). The role of teacher stance when infusing inquiry questioning into middle school science classrooms. *School Science and Mathematics, 101,* 143–153.

Tobin, K., Kahle, J. B., & Fraser, B. J. (1990). *Windows into science classrooms: problems associated with higher-level cognitive learning.* New York: Falmer Press.

Watson, P., & Watson, P. (1991). *Culture fair: A resource guide.* St. Louis, MO: Milliken.

11

Teachers' Use and Understanding of Strategy in Inquiry Instruction*

LYNN MANCONI, MARK W. AULLS, AND BRUCE M. SHORE
McGill University

The purpose of this qualitative multicase study was to find out how experienced teachers who do and do not use inquiry-teaching methods in their classrooms vary in their knowledge of inquiry. The hypothesis was that the inquiry teachers would have a more detailed and complex understanding of inquiry than those teachers who did not use inquiry in their classrooms, and that the structure of their knowledge would include more concepts found in the expert literature on inquiry than for the noninquiry teachers.

Empirical investigations of inquiry-based instruction have demonstrated that, when inquiry is properly implemented, students (a) become active learners, (b) are efficient problem solvers and critical thinkers, (c) know how to apply their knowledge in new situations, and (d) are able to learn new content on their own (Brown & Campione, 1994; Crawford, 2000). However, when teachers do not fully understand what an inquiry approach entails, difficulties arise because students try to grasp with concepts that are beyond their level, they are not given sufficient time to think, and they fail to see the connections between their learning and their daily lives (Brown, 1994).

---

* This chapter was derived from Lynn Manconi's PhD dissertation about teachers' understanding of inquiry (Manconi, 2003) that also partially tested the Aulls-Shore four-property framework of inquiry in education (Shore, Aulls, & Rejskind, 1999). The research was cosupervised by Bruce M. Shore and Mark W. Aulls, and conceived and designed collaboratively by all three chapter authors.

The Multifaceted Nature of Inquiry

There is legitimate justification for confusion over the meaning of inquiry from a teacher's perspective. One reason is that the meaning of inquiry is multifaceted. For example, when inquiry is presented as a group activity, it can still be a truly personal experience. The success derived from inquiry learning is not necessarily dependent upon solving the problem at hand, but on students' awareness of a growing ability to apply their ideas, skills, and judgments to solving a problem (Henson, 1986). Another multilevel dimension of inquiry instruction involves learning about the topic or subject matter being investigated while simultaneously learning about the process of inquiry (Tamir, 1983).

There exists a notion that inquiry is synonymous with other terms, such as problem solving, discovery learning, creativity, research, and the scientific method (Manson & Williams, 1970). These terms are often used interchangeably in the inquiry literature. However, some terms refer to teaching methods, such as discovery learning, whereas others signal intellectual processes such as, problem-solving, research, and the scientific method. This distinction between inquiry as an intellectual activity of the learner, inferred from what the learner does, and inquiry as instructional conditions created by the teacher, and the learner and teacher together, also can cause confusion over the nature of inquiry instruction (DeBoer, 1991; Tamir, 1983).

Establishing an integrative definition of inquiry that could be applied, if possible, to all school subjects might assist teachers at a variety of grade levels to have a common point of departure in interpreting, evaluating, and utilizing this approach in the classroom (Cox, 1968). Yet, reputable scholars in different disciplines and subject areas have not established a mutually acceptable meaning for inquiry as instruction or learning (DeBoer, 1991; Henson, 1986; Joyce & Weil, 1980; Rogers, 1990; Short & Burke, 1996). One assumed reason for this lack of consensus up to this time is that each discipline or subject-matter domain usually has its own inquiry methods and language that students learn as a function of the central phenomenon of scholarly study (Rogers, 1990).

From a different perspective, all inquiry embodies processes such as creative or critical thinking. Nonetheless, what counts as valid creativity or critical thinking will be determined by the criteria of the forms of knowledge embraced in the specific discipline. "There is no way in which historical and scientific inquiries can be merged into some general inquiry skill—the things one has to do to carry them on are markedly different because they call for the marshalling of different bodies of information and insight into radically different conceptual schemes" (Rogers, 1990, p. 75). Wineburg (1991) also supported the notion of a general inquiry theory as being problematic when comparing historical inquiry to problem solving in more highly structured domains: "Historical understanding can be thought of as a beginning where problem solving in other domains ends. In history, outcomes are often known. Rather than arriving at a solution by maneuvering through a 'problem space' of a pre-existing template, patterns and moves, historians dwell in an 'explanation space' in which they already possess the solution but must reconstruct the goal and state of the world from it" (p. 10).

Reconceptualization or reorientation of inquiry has been a prime consideration in many fields of study: natural sciences, social sciences, humanities, and mathematics education (Shubert, 1989). The National Committee on Science Education Standards and Assessment (National Research Council, 1996) described an inquiry curriculum as involving students asking questions, formulating hypotheses, searching for and generating information, suggesting and testing experiments, collecting and analyzing information, and discussing and evaluating their findings against prior knowledge and schemas. In short, the trend toward inquiry instruction has developed consistently in North America and has been a recurring part of educational reforms since 1930 (Rogers, 1990). However, for some reason, inquiry teaching is not being widely incorporated into elementary and secondary classrooms in North America to the extent that many university educators hoped it would be (DeBoer, 1991).

Although variations in methods for carrying out research assume importance in many fields of study, at or beyond university, the importance of inquiry as an element in a program of general education has been questioned. Kliebard (1968) proposed that inquiry may fail in the classroom, not so much as a result of failing to match the kind of inquiry process to a subject—although that is important—but, rather, as a problem of clarifying common conceptualizations of inquiry instructional practices among teachers who intend to teach content through inquiry in comparison to those who have no such intention. This concern appears still to be relevant today.

Another issue is that the inquiry literature needs extensive conceptual organization that reflects current views of the nature of instruction. Within a grant application by Shore, Aulls, and Rejskind (1999), Aulls and Shore proposed a four-property framework of inquiry learning and instruction for describing the nature of inquiry instruction. This framework was used in the dissertation research from which this chapter is derived (Manconi, 2003) to organize the review of the literature on inquiry. Aulls and Shore's proposed definitions of the four properties of inquiry are that inquiry can be conceptualized as follows:

1. Inquiry as Process: The inquiry process is driven by the student's own curiosity, wonder, interest, or passion to understand an observation or solve a problem. The process begins by the students noticing something that intrigues, surprises, or stimulates a question. What is observed often does not make sense in relationship to the students' previous experience or current knowledge. The process can be defined as teaching students to become inquirers. Students learn generalizable process skills that are specific but that carry broad transferability across many subject-matters. Crucial to cultivating students' inquiry skills is teaching them thinking skills. The process of teaching inquiry ensures that the learners will internalize inquiry learning in their lives. Process also includes the manner in which content

and strategies are jointly constructed by a teacher and students in a classroom or by participants in inquiry in some other setting than schools. The learning process is primarily directed and controlled by the learners.

2. Inquiry as Content: As the process unfolds more observations and questions emerge, providing an occasion for deeper interaction and relationship with the phenomena, or subject matter at hand. This opportunity for reflection provides greater potential for further development of understanding the concepts. It places emphasis on the process through which subject-matter is learned and taught, with content serving as a vehicle to develop the process. The information transfer is measured by content, skills, attitudes, aspirations, and knowledge. Inquiry provides an opportunity to teach content at a deeper level and to apply knowledge. Inquiry can be integrated into all subject areas. For example, a specific lesson may incorporate all the steps of inquiry or focus on only one of them.

3. Inquiry as Strategy: Action is then taken through continued observations, raising questions, making predictions, testing hypotheses, creating theories and conceptual models. The students must find their own individual way through this process. The students rarely follow a linear progression but, rather, go back and forth from their predictions to their hypotheses, as they express their thinking. This entails the techniques, the methods or the procedures used to develop the process skills. For example, problem-solving strategies are being taught in order for students to arrive at their own solutions. Teachers who use inquiry need to incorporate planning or organizational skills into the curriculum and make them an integral part of their teaching; for example, students are taught to think ahead before they start to evaluate, and to revise their plans as necessary.

4. Inquiry as Context: Along the way, the students are collecting and recording data, making representations of results and explanations, drawing upon other resources such as books, multimedia, the internet, parents, and other people in the community. Making meaning from the experience requires reflection, conversations, and comparison of findings with others, interpretation of data and observations, and applying new knowledge to other contexts as one attempts to construct a new understanding of the world. The setting for inquiry teaching involves creating the environment that will stimulate and sustain productive inquiry and provide resources both within and outside of the school setting. Inquiry can be incorporated into the classroom discourse between a teacher and a student, into small group activities, and whole group activities. For example, the way a teacher responds to a student's response can serve to provide elaboration on the topic. Students also can acquire inquiry skills through the hidden curriculum through subtle and indirect ways such as the design of the environment, wall displays, and management strategies (Shore et al., 1999, p. 12).

We organized the isolated findings of research into a conceptual framework that supported the four constructs of inquiry proposed by the Aulls-Shore framework. By presenting the inquiry literature with the use of this framework, it enabled us to discern the validity of the framework's credibility at the theoretical, empirical, and opinion levels in the literature. The literature review indicated that process, content, strategy, and context each have theories, empirical research, and opinions that are associated with each dimension. In fact, in looking at inquiry from these different dimensions revealed a complex domain made up of multiple theories, empirical studies, and expert opinions.

Descriptions of the Eight Teachers

This study used three interviews with each of the eight teachers to collect data about each teacher's knowledge of inquiry and classroom practices. Our criteria were to include two teachers experienced in inquiry from each of the elementary, secondary, and university levels. These teachers needed to have a minimum of three years experience teaching through inquiry. Teachers were also selected so that the inquiry approach was associated with learning different subjects: English as a second language, French as a second language, family-life education, physics, science, and special education. Two teachers were selected to be control cases. They did not perceive themselves to be inquiry-based. Selecting two teachers who held a traditional view of instructional practice provided a means to determine if there was a qualitative difference in their practices compared to the shared knowledge of the inquiry-oriented teachers. The eight participants also needed to be articulate, insightful, accessible, and cooperative about being interviewed three times for 90 minutes in the course of one year. Table 11.1 describes each teacher's subject taught, level of education, and years of teaching experience.

When asked to define inquiry, the inquiry teachers' prior inquiry experience acquired in an informal way and formal inquiry instruction at the university level enabled them to formulate a conceptualization of inquiry that corresponded well with the literature on inquiry. Three observations were noted regarding the inquiry teachers' knowledge of inquiry. All had some formal instruction about inquiry in their graduate studies, either from conducting research for their theses or projects, or participating in laboratory projects. Second, they all had participated in an informal inquiry activity during their leisure time, either by researching their own projects or cultivating their knowledge through reading. Third, the inquiry teachers were all experts in their domains, either by having a doctorate in the subject or having taught 25 years in the field. Teacher 2 had less experience than the other teachers, but was considered the science specialist in the school and did obtain her degree in science at the undergraduate level. It seems, therefore, in order to feel confident to teach through inquiry, that it is helpful to have expertise in the field of study. Teacher 2 explained it in these words: "To become a science specialist requires that you have a broad understanding of science. It takes someone who has done science before and has a love for science. You also

Table 11.1 Description of the Eight Teachers

Teacher	Subject Taught	Level of Education	Years of Teaching Experience
1	French Immersion Grade 2	M.A., completing Ph.D. in Education	25
2	Elementary Science Specialist	switched from a B.Sc. to a B.Ed.	3
3	Physics High School	B.Sc. in Biology, diploma in Education	25
4	Special Education High School	B.A. in Psychology, M.A. in Educational Psychology, Certificate in Special Education, Completing Ph.D. in Educational Psychology	25
5 (Noninquiry Teacher)	Teaching English as a Second Language Adult Education	B.A. in Fine Arts, M.A. in Fine Arts, Certificate in teaching English as a Second Language	10
6 (Noninquiry Teacher)	Vocational Training Adult Education	B.A. in Early Childhood Education then switched to Guidance Counselling, M.A. in Career Development	5
7	Family Life Education University Level	B.A. in Child and Abnormal Psychology, Certificate in Family Life Education, M.Ed. in Educational Psychology, Completing Ph.D. in Educational Psychology	20
8	Physics University Level	Honor's degree in Physics, M.A. in Physics, Ph.D. in Physics	25

need to understand the hands-on aspect of science." Teacher 3 also supported this inference by stating, "A teacher needs to know the content of the subject matter and needs to have expertise in the field to teach inquiry. You have to know your content, otherwise students pick up on a lack of knowledge like that."

The noninquiry teachers admitted they were not familiar with this approach. They did not learn about inquiry in their formal studies, and neither did they engage in an inquiry activity at home. They also had difficulty defining inquiry and could not provide many examples or expand on the term.

The Characteristics of Inquiry

A second research question looked at the similarities and differences in the characteristics of inquiry when comparing the teachers' descriptions of the meaning of inquiry to the descriptions of inquiry found in the literature. From the inquiry teachers' statements emerged 19 common characteristics that could be categorized under the four Aulls and Shore properties of inquiry (Shore et al., 1999). This ability to meaningfully fit the teacher-based statements into the literature-based categories formed the basis of the validation of the four constructs. Table 11.2 combines a summary of the main characteristics that all six experienced inquiry teachers expressed in common compared to a number of inquiry characteristics that were relevant from Manconi's (2003) coding and categorization of the inquiry literature.

Table 11.2 reveals the high consistency between the coding system based on the literature meanings and the categories based on the inquiry teachers' own remarks. The Aulls-Shore framework originally placed teacher and student roles, as well as student talk under the strategy heading rather than context, but these arose as distinguishing elements in both inquiry teachers' responses and in the research literature. This supports the conclusion that the inquiry teachers' understanding of inquiry was well matched to the meaning of inquiry revealed in the literature. It also provides a first round of support for the Aulls-Shore four-property framework of inquiry in education (see *Inquiry in Education,* Volume I).

Table 11.2 does not include a column for the noninquiry teachers' comments because the characteristics listed are specifically related to inquiry teaching. The noninquiry teachers either did not express any of these characteristics in their interview statements, or their comments differed from those of the inquiry teachers. Some noninquiry teachers' comments about the constructs of process, content, and context presented in Table 11.2 for the inquiry teachers are nonetheless interesting. In contrast to the inquiry teachers, Teachers 5 and 6 believed the teacher's role was to teach content. Both wanted their students at their desks, working on their workbooks in silence. They implemented activities that corresponded to the course's objectives, but did not mention any transfer of knowledge other than how the students attain the specific objectives. Teachers 5 and 6 evaluated the students' work and behavior but did not refer to students' process skills. For example, Teacher 6 asked her students to explain how they arrived at their answers but did not teach strategies to integrate or facilitate the process. Teacher 5's content consisted of having the students master grammar and vocabulary. The noninquiry teachers considered themselves a resource to their students by being able to provide them with information and answers. The goal of the noninquiry teachers was to provide their students with basic information, follow instructions, and complete assignments according to their specifications. Another distinguishing feature was that the noninquiry teachers felt it was necessary to plan everything and did not consider involving the students in the planning and organization of the activities. In both cases, Teachers 5 and 6 provided no evidence of joint curriculum construction throughout their interviews.

Similarly to the inquiry teachers, Teachers 5 and 6 complained they lacked time. Teacher 5 responded that she could not afford to take the time to ask the students to explain their responses or verify their understanding. The noninquiry

Table 11.2   Characteristics that All Six Inquiry Teachers Expressed in Common
Compared to Inquiry Characteristics Derived from the Literature

Inquiry characteristics derived from the literature	Inquiry characteristics expressed by all six inquiry teachers
PROCESS	**PROCESS**
• PROCESS—SELF EFFICACY: Through inquiry, students gain understanding of acquiring, validating, and using their own knowledge.	1. Students explain, develop, and are aware of their thought processes.
• PROCESS—STUDENTS FIND OWN ANSWER: Teacher redirects students' questions, students are encouraged to arrive at their own answer.	2. Teacher waits for a response, lets students figure it out.
• PROCESS—INTRINSIC MOTIVATION: Emphasizes internal rewards from the successful pursuit of one's own ideas. The motivational processes the student experiences as an inquirer, and as an independent and autonomous learner.	3. Independent work is for designing programs, labs, or projects.
• PROCESS—STUDENTS LEARN GENERAL PROCESSING SKILLS: Students learn generalizable process skills that carry broad transferability across subject matter, includes steps of thinking (process skills) into real life.	4. Teacher teaches strategies to integrate and facilitate the process.
CONTENT	**CONTENT**
• CONTENT—SUBJECT MATTER: The inquiry process is given emphasis as the subject matter is learned and taught.	5. Emphasis is not on the subject matter; the content emerges as the focus is placed more on the processes of inquiry.
• CONTENT—SKILL-BUILDING EXERCISES LINKED TO LEARNING: Skill-building exercises linked to ongoing learning.	6. Objectives incorporated through projects, labs, and assignments.
• CONTENT—TEACHER EVALUATES STUDENTS' GROWTH: Teacher evaluates students' growth instead of facts acquired, looks at the individual. Teacher evaluates process skills rather than content knowledge.	7. Teacher evaluates how students learn based on strengths and weaknesses.

Table 11.2 *(continued)*   Characteristics that All Six Inquiry Teachers Expressed in Common Compared to Inquiry Characteristics Derived from the Literature

Inquiry characteristics derived from the literature	Inquiry characteristics expressed by all six inquiry teachers
STRATEGY	**STRATEGY**
• STRATEGY—CREATIVITY FOR STUDENTS: Teacher recognizes and promotes students' creativity, believes in students' capabilities, and encourages them to learn on their own.	8. Students are encouraged to learn on their own.
• STRATEGY—PROBLEM SOLVING: Strategies to maximize students' thinking through problem solving.	9. Students engage in problem solving.
• STRATEGY—TEACHER'S QUESTIONS: Strategies are based on teacher's questions leading students to explore, explain, support, and evaluate their ideas. Students observe, make predictions, investigate, record, or chart their data.	10. Students think, observe, reflect, investigate, write results, and draw conclusions. 11. Students talk to each other about strategies and results.
• STRATEGY—TEACHER'S GUIDANCE: Guidance ranges from little teacher guidance to a very structured teacher-directed approach.	12. Teacher provides guidance.
CONTEXT	**CONTEXT**
• CONTEXT—TEACHER DISCOURSE: ASKING QUESTIONS AT A HIGHER ORDER THINKING LEVEL: The teacher asks questions which are at a higher order thinking level (Bloom's Taxonomy).	13. Teacher asks higher-order thinking questions.
• CONTEXT—TEACHER DISCOURSE: BASED ON STUDENTS' IDEAS: Teacher's questions are based upon students' ideas; teacher incorporates the students' ideas in teaching.	14. Students are encouraged to come up with their own ideas.
• CONTEXT—AMOUNT OF TIME REQUIRED: The amount of time needed to satisfy the students' quest. This also includes teacher's use of own time for preparation of material and extra-curricular time offered to students.	15. Inquiry takes time.

Table 11.2 *(continued)*   Characteristics that All Six Inquiry Teachers Expressed
in Common Compared to Inquiry Characteristics Derived
from the Literature

Inquiry characteristics derived from the literature	Inquiry characteristics expressed by all six inquiry teachers
• PROCESS—STUDENTS' TALK ENCOURAGED: Classroom norms are that students talk more than the teacher, a student-centered approach.	16. Teacher is student-centered.
• CONTEXT—TEACHER DISCOURSE: TEACHING BASED ON QUESTIONS: Teacher to class discourse: The purpose is to question the students and not tell the students what to do.	17. Teacher and students communicate through discussion and discourse.
• CONTEXT—STUDENTS' DISCOURSE: Student-to-student discourse: Students are free to exchange and discuss ideas amongst themselves.	
• CONTEXT—USE OF RESOURCES: Use of resources such as parents, mentors, colleagues, computers, lab equipment, use of classrooms, even the teacher.	18. Teacher uses everything and everyone who is available.
• STRATEGY—TEACHER'S ROLE AND RESPONSIBILITIES: Teacher has the last word, structures, takes charge of the situation, and the students are aware of the rules and routines.	19. Teacher manages and has some structure.

teachers' reasons for wanting more time differed from those in the inquiry teachers' statements. Teacher 5 wanted to be able to cover more topics and Teacher 6 wanted to spend more individual time with her students. Last, Teachers 5 and 6 made no statements about their students being motivated about their class work; instead, they both agreed it was the teacher who needed to be motivated.

Use and Understanding of Strategy in Inquiry
Instruction by Inquiry and Noninquiry Teachers

Strategy was one of the four inquiry constructs in which the differences between the noninquiry and inquiry teachers were most apparent. Examples of strategy characteristics from Table 11.2, supported by the teachers' statements and citations from the inquiry literature, illustrate these differences.

Students are encouraged to learn on their own.   All the inquiry teachers believed it was necessary to provide structure, direction, and guidance at the beginning of their courses, then gradually withdraw these and enable the students to learn on their own. The inquiry teachers provided their students with the opportunity to discover solutions on their own by allowing them the freedom to explore. This was supported by Germann (1989) in his description of inquiry teaching in which the teacher provides little guidance and specific expectations are minimal so that students are free to explore and learn independently. Teacher 4 commented that, by the end of the year, her students no longer even needed a teacher. Teacher 7 explained, "I am the creator of climate and conditions, it's a little hard to describe because it's setting things up, but it's not controlling them." Teacher 8 provided direct instruction to teach problem skills but during the discussion periods he remained silent to allow his students an opportunity to talk to each other. These statements were also supported by Herron (1971), who argued that the highest level of inquiry is achieved when students have the greatest amount of independence. Sizer (1984) also agreed that students learn to become responsible for their own learning in inquiry instruction.

Teachers 3 and 4 had their students submit proposals for their projects. Before this, they taught their students how to plan and organize themselves so they could complete their projects on time. Doherty and Evans (1981) agreed that students need to establish a schedule for long-term projects, because it is important to organize their work within a time frame.

The noninquiry teachers neither encouraged the students to question themselves nor allowed them an opportunity to explore. Teachers 5 and 6 were more teacher-centered. Teacher 6 admitted that only once did she allow her students to explore using the Internet. She did not do it again because she felt that the activity was not sufficiently structured. Teachers 5 and 6 did not teach their students how to organize their work or plan in advance. Also, by placing restrictions upon the students' freedom to explore and by not encouraging their students to question themselves, they created a barrier to implementing inquiry. According to Newmann (1991), there is a need to be reflective in inquiry, to take the time to think problems through for oneself, rather than to act impulsively or to automatically accept the view of others.

Students engage in problem solving.   Problem solving also arose as an important concept for the inquiry construct of strategy. Teacher 1 stressed how she found it important to show her students that there were different ways to solve a problem: "When there is a conflict, I tell the children to listen to all the versions, take two minutes to reflect, talk about it, and try and find a solution. If a child arrives with a solution, I emphasize to the group that this is not the only way. There is more than one solution." Teacher 3 also asked questions that rarely had one solution, in fact he kept encouraging his students to find alternative answers: "Folks, here are five resistors, I would like to have a resistance of 80 ohms. Tell me how many different ways can you add up these particular things in series and parallel and give me that value?" He also had them search for alternative ways in a more general way: "Here is an electric circuit diagram, question it; there are probably three ways to do it. Hunt for them, go!" Teacher 8 also tried to teach his students about thinking in alternative ways: "There is this attitude amongst students that there is a right and wrong way. I try to legitimize the idea of alternative." Teacher 3 hoped his students would gain insight into how to approach a problem: "What I simply hope for is that my students have gained insight into just simply how to approach a problem. I'm talking about how to plan something when they're panicky. When they have a dilemma, they will know how to deal with it." According to Woods (1989), in order to develop problem-solving skills, a teacher needs to assume the role of facilitator and coach, rather than lecturer and provider of information. Regardless of the discipline they taught, the inquiry teachers had their students engage in problem-solving, ranging from solving mathematical problems to resolving conflict situations. The inquiry teachers spent a lot of time teaching problem-solving strategies because they believed their students needed to learn how to use these strategies in order to be able to solve problems. Teacher 4 explained her view: "In math, there are certain operations that the kids need, but there are also certain problem solving strategies as well. By basic operations, I mean adding and subtracting, multiplying, and dividing; there's nothing more to math than these four operations. And the kids have a hard time getting past that, so I don't deal with that. I deal with the strategies in problem solving; that's where my concern is: Can they unpack a problem?" Scott's (1977) description of a guided discovery approach is consistent with Teacher 4's approach to teaching problem solving. In the guided discovery approach, the teacher is feeding positive information about the techniques for efficient problem solving back to the students and then helping the students to internalize these techniques.

Newell and Simon (1975) defined problem solving from an information-processing view: "Problem-solving is a search for the best of a set of paths that may surmount the obstacle and lead to the goal state" (p. 150). Teacher 8's description of how he taught problem solving is similar to this view: "The one thing I have to do in some of these courses is teach them how to solve a problem. I spend a fair amount of time on ways to solve problems. The class gets into small groups and works for about ten minutes on the problem that has been posed on a transparency. It's not a numerical problem; it's a qualitative problem. Then, they debate the question, both for themselves and the rest of the students. I do not interfere. I do not want them to have any hint of my own views. Then, the issue is related through a historical question. Eventually, using a laser disk demonstration it clarifies the experiment. So, this was a question that was answered by some little experiment. At the end, they were all given the critique to take home. They had to clearly state the two positions and give arguments for both positions."

Schoenfeld (1989) explained how teachers also can stimulate reflection by checking in with students as they are problem solving, ask what they are doing, why they are doing it, and how will it help. These approaches not only make students more aware of their methods but also increase their consciousness of their own thought processes, an important ingredient in the development of internal monitoring. In order to assess their students' problem-solving strategies, Teachers 1, 2, 3, and 7 had their students explain how they solved their problems. Teacher 3 explained this concept well: "By explaining how they figured out the problem, I could see that the students were engaging in critical thinking. This provided me with an opportunity for the assessment of that thinking and the strategies that the students were using. The students' knowledge was expressed by problem-solving." Glover, Ronning, and Bruning (1990) agreed with Teacher 3; they described problem solving as an active process that depends on knowledge.

There was no evidence of Teachers 5 and 6 teaching problem-solving strategies. Teacher 6 made just one related comment: "If my students did engage in problem-solving activities, they would need to use various strategies." She did not discuss what these various strategies entailed and never referred to problem solving again in her interviews. The observation that the noninquiry teachers did not teach problem-solving strategies or have their students engage in any problem-solving activity suggests, perhaps, that they were not problem solvers themselves. Polya (1981) supported this assumption, having proposed that in order to effectively teach problem solving, teachers need to be problem solvers themselves. Problem solving is an integral part of inquiry and without it, inquiry is not possible.

Students think, observe, reflect, investigate, justify, verify, and write results and conclusions.   Inquiry requires teachers to create learning experiences in which students must identify problems for investigation, predict outcomes relative to these problems, test these hypotheses against evidence, draw conclusions about the validity of these hypotheses and, finally, either devise new hypotheses for testing or apply these conclusions to new data (Byer, 1987). The inquiry teachers described inquiry as beginning with a question. This was followed by having the students think, reflect, predict, investigate, collect and compare data, write their results, justify and verify results, and draw conclusions. The inquiry teachers placed importance on students' predictions. Teacher 2 described how she evaluated the students' predictions: "Most of the time I tell my students, 'I am not interested in whether your prediction is correct. I'm interested in why you think that. I'm interested in your explanation, your observations, and all that you did.' So, all the time I am asking them what they think and to express what they think. A prediction is as good as the reasons you had for it and it's not really about if it worked out."

Equally important were the students' explanations about whether the experiment or project was a success or not. Teacher 3 described his approach: "I have my students learn or try to understand that, if their experiment didn't work, you do not throw your hands up into the air and say, 'Oh this lab is done, I'm a goner.' I stress to them to look if their experiment is legitimate and if it has no holes in it in terms of method. Then they can tell me the sort of things they suspect that went wrong; that's equally important."

Published research appears to be supportive of this perspective. The process of testing a hypothesis is the key to inquiry. It is here that learning takes place, for it is in doing this that data are located, used, pulled apart, refitted, and manipulated over and over again. In the process of testing the hypothesis against evidence, patterns or relationships are perceived and which either support, modify, or negate the hypothesis (Beyer, 1971). For the inquiry teachers, the hypothesis served as a guide to the inquiry that followed, by which students attempted to verify the elements of the problem, to see whether those elements did indeed relate to the proposed solution, and to determine whether the solution held up or others needed to be generated.

The inquiry teachers also placed a considerable amount of emphasis upon the writing process. Even in the younger grades, Teachers 1 and 2 had their students writing all the time. Teacher 1 said: "They are writing all the time, this is a big part of the project. At each phase of the project, the children have to write what are their strengths, their challenges, how are they going to meet those challenges, and what will be the method they will use to help them." Teacher 2 described her approach in getting her students to write: "The students have to make predictions, then make observations. In a lot of cases, I try to make it so that they design how they are going to do the experiment. They carry out the activity and then compare it to their predictions. Then, they describe what they observed. We struggle with that difference, between observations and results. I have to teach them about how to have ideas and opinions based upon what they have observed. And then afterwards, I want them to write down their results and justify them in their conclusion. Almost every time they do anything, they have to also give me written work."

Torrance (1965) believed it was the teacher's role to develop in students' skills for formulating hypotheses, procedures for testing them, and methods for reporting the results. None of these components was found in the noninquiry statements. Their lessons did not begin with a question nor were their students asked to think, reflect, predict, investigate, and write their results. These characteristics are essential components for inquiry instruction and, without these basic procedures, the instruction these students receive will be based solely on memorization of factual content.

Students talk to each other about strategies and results.   Through inquiry, students learn how to work with others in exploring different ways of looking at problems, and how to make conclusions on the basis of the data (Joyce & Weil, 1980). The inquiry teachers considered discussion amongst the students to be an important element of the inquiry process. Teacher 1 stressed, "It is through discussion and discourse that we favor critical thinking by confronting our ideas with other people's ideas." Teacher 2 felt that discussion throughout inquiry was essential: "The students are hearing each other's ideas most of the time." Teacher 7 added, "Learning happens through discussion and discourse." Teacher 8 set up the discussion for his students, then refrained from talking while his students presented their arguments: "I literally do nothing more than provide a vehicle for discussion." This approach was supported by Welch, Klopfer, Aikenhead, Glen, and Robinson (1981), based on their observations of an inquiry classroom. They found student formulations of responses were listened to, clarified, and deliberated with a high frequency of student-student interactions. In direct contrast, Teacher 5 did not want her students talking to each other during class time. "I am very severe about having complete silence in the class because I teach individualized instruction, so it's important that there is silence in the class." Teacher 6 led the class discussions and did not have her students discuss the issues amongst themselves. She felt that she needed to control the class discussion so that the students would follow the discussion at hand and not deviate from the subject. The absence of class discussion or class discussions completely controlled by the teacher can also be considered as barriers to implementing inquiry.

The inquiry teachers recognized that students providing feedback to each other was often more constructive than receiving it from the teacher. Orlich et al. (1985) supported this assumption that peer approval or feedback is considered by many students to be more important than teacher approval. Short and Burke (1996) added that providing opportunities for students to construct and explore their understandings with others through conversation and dialogue is another important factor that needs to be integrated within inquiry instruction.

Teacher provides guidance.   Far from diminishing the role of the teacher, an inquiry approach imposes new demands on teachers as they plan and orchestrate classroom activities providing stimuli and structure to support the students' own inquiries (Richards, 1991). Teacher 1's description of herself as an orchestra leader related well to the literature: "With this approach, you become an orchestra leader. I find this is the role I use the most. I do the supervision to see if the teams have worked well. But, at the same time, you have to let go, it's the sharing of power. I tell my students, 'I can help you, but you yourself can help search.'" This leads to what the inquiry teachers said about being supportive, that is, creating conditions for students to discover on their own. Teacher 7 believed that you could not empower someone simply by giving them power: "You have to create conditions in which they discover and use the power themselves. I think this is an important aspect of teaching, because if you think of power not just in terms of knowledge but constructiveness, it is all about gaining power as a learner. To be able to recognize the fact that you can construct your own knowledge. By having the students recognize that and being aware of it, you are creating conditions to enable that." Teacher 8 agreed: "I'm pointing out directions, but I feel that you can't climb a mountain for someone, for somebody who never climbed it. You can guide by indicating what to do and provide tools, but that's as far as it goes. I told my students, 'That as far as understanding these concepts, you can look at things many times and then suddenly, it will come to you.'"

Cole (1989) claimed that a teacher needs to be competent, supportive, and assume a proper but nontraditional role. A supportive teacher arranges appropriate experiences for the students to encounter, but does not force the students to a particular observation, interpretation, or conclusion, and encourages the students to create their own organization of their experiences. Inquiry teachers also described being supportive as being open and willing to listen to the students. For example, Teacher 3 described it as taking on another role: "I guess to a certain extent another part of my role is to be open enough to be able to have the kids come to me and honestly tell me how they feel."

Facilitating was defined by the inquiry teachers as providing students with suggestions and ideas, and pointing out directions when students appeared to be stuck. When Teacher 4 observed a student experiencing difficulties, she did some scaffolding with that student, and described this as facilitating. Teacher 1 told her students, "I am there to facilitate. I plan everything with my students, which makes me more of a facilitator." Teacher 7 described herself more as a facilitator than a guide: "I see my role as a facilitator because I am creating experiences that are going to allow people to bring their ideas out."

The inquiry teachers interpreted guidance to mean asking students questions to get them thinking, to lead students to what they have learned, and what they need to learn. Teacher 7 found that the process gets supported by the guidance: "I question my students to further elaborate on what they mean. So, in a sense, it's drawing out so that they can internalize their thoughts, and also that others can hear them. It's also about helping them move on to the next level. I ask them, 'What does this all mean? How might you apply it?'" Teacher 8 described himself as a guide in this process: "I am guiding the questioning in class and creating the atmosphere where they will hear different points of view, and conceptual conflict will occur. I think of myself as a guide in this process."

Teachers 2, 3, and 4 felt that, at the beginning, the students required help leading up to ideas, because at first the students did not know anything about what they were doing. Then, as students understood more, the teachers provided less structure, but continued to provide input. Teacher 3 expanded on this: "At the beginning, I have to really lead them because they don't know anything about what they are doing. I find that they need an awful lot of leading up to ideas." Teacher 2 also proceeded similarly: "I guide them a lot in the beginning. I guide them by asking questions. I like to show my students how their thinking fits in." In the framework of inquiry, students are gradually introduced to methods of asking questions efficiently in order to obtain the facts and to eliminate irrelevant information about the objects, events, and conditions in the experiment (Scott, 1977). Teacher 2 also considered herself as a facilitator and a guide: "I think I am a facilitator and a guide. I facilitate what's going on in class. I hope to get them what they need and help to get them to cooperate. I help to stimulate them if they don't have ideas." Wilson (1974) defined guidance in accordance with the inquiry teachers' perspective: Guidance consists of a series of cues and feedback that supports investigations, identifies profitable or unprofitable areas of inquiry, suggests valid experimental procedures, outlines ways to quantify results, relate factual data and sources for information, and encourages learners in order to develop persistence.

The literature cautions about not providing answers too readily, and this was the prominent difference between the inquiry and noninquiry teachers. Balzer (1970) described how an inquiry teacher needs to be flexible to deal with alternative patterns of exploration. As questions and problems arise, the teacher must use care in releasing information. Voicing a fact known by the teacher may permit the class to proceed to further questions; in other cases, release of information may resolve the matter and make continued inquiry impossible. Teacher 2 was very adamant about not telling the students the answers: "Rarely do I tell them the answers. I think that telling them the answer would shut them off instead of turning them on. Instead, I guide them by asking questions and show students how their thinking fits in. Sometimes I may give them some background information as it becomes relevant to guide them through, but I do not tell them what is happening nor tell them what to predict, nor tell students what I think." Teacher 8 also mentioned that he did not give a hint of his views but would wait a long time for students to provide answers.

The noninquiry teachers interpreted guidance differently from the inquiry teachers. Instead of questioning their students, Teachers 5 and 6 considered guidance to mean helping their students by showing them how to do things or indicate to them the correct response. Teacher 6 did not wait long for a response and usually wanted only one answer: "I ask them a question, before saying the answer. Sometimes my students' responses are variable, so I tell them what I want as a response. If we are talking about behaviors at work, I just want one answer." She felt that by telling her students the answers she was helping them. Teacher 5 realized during our interview that she often gave her students the answer and mentioned to me that she would be making efforts in the future to wait and have her students answer. She made an interesting comment regarding exam questions: She felt that the questions on the provincial English exam were not clear to the students, that the exam questions were not obvious since the questions did not have part of the answers in them. This is in direct contradiction to Teachers 2 and 8 who preferred questions that were not obvious, meaning that the students had to figure out on their own the answers (and sometimes first restructure the question toward that goal—see Austin & Shore, 1995).

Teacher 5 often made many references to the verb "show": "My role as a guide is to show them the way. I just show them the way to the right answer. It is really important to show them how to read instructions because I want to be a guide for them. What I try to do the most is, when I explain to them, I point out to them what is good." Teacher 6 used a similar approach: "I am there to help them. So, I guide them and I accompany them. My students are at a presecondary level, so I have to help them with their calculations. They are students who require help for understanding certain things. I have to give them clues."

Contrary to portraying herself as an orchestra leader like Teacher 1, Teacher 5 saw herself as a captain: "I see myself as a captain and it's my job to see that everything is okay." Teacher 6 considered herself not necessarily as an authoritative teacher: "I am there to help them, to structure them, and to supervise. I am there to guide them in their development." Overall, the noninquiry teachers' approach was to direct their students by telling them what to do and did not offer opportunities for students to discover on their own.

With respect to giving feedback, Teachers 5 and 6 used feedback as a way of correcting their students by pointing out to them their mistakes. As Teacher 5 put it, "Students are able to receive my criticism about their behavior or their work. And when they have the right answer, I say 'This is good' and then I explain to them why it is good." Teacher 6 gave her students feedback about their hygiene: "I comment on their appearance. I tell them for work they need to look and smell nice." The inquiry teachers appeared to utilize feedback differently; they gave their opinions about their students' work, but did not criticize it. Teacher 2 told her students if they were off-base, but did not tell them they were wrong. Teacher 3 provided his students with suggestions and clues on how to improve their projects. Also, Teacher 1 expected her students to provide her with feedback on their work and progress. She felt that her students knew what needed to be corrected: "I take the time to read and comment on what the children have written. The children know what needs to be corrected. I believe in using lots of feedback, and coming back and asking them, 'How have you learned?'"

For these sample characteristics of strategy, it was stressed by the inquiry teachers that teachers need to facilitate, entice collaboration among their students, provide clues and not the answers, and most of all provide scaffolding. These characteristics were all absent in the noninquiry teachers, which created a further barrier to inquiry learning to take place. This was supported by Uhlhorn (1971) in that learners need to be self-directing and free from the reliance of teachers' direction and guidance, both characteristic of conventional teaching. Husén and Postlethwaite (1996) claimed that by having a teacher encourage students to raise questions to which answers are to be sought by inquiry and not given by the teacher, students gain the opportunity to show initiative, use their own ideas, and challenge rather than accept until they find supporting evidence.

Summary of Inquiry Teachers' Profile for the Use of Strategy

Following is a brief résumé of how the inquiry teachers differed from the noninquiry teachers with respect to the construct of strategy based on an analysis of each inquiry teacher's emphasis on the construct of strategy derived from their interview responses. In other words, it is an account of how the teachers described their use of strategy in their own words. The noninquiry teachers are not included because they made very few comments concerning the construct of strategy, which resulted in an insufficient lack of data to be able to form a profile.

For the construct of strategy, Teacher 1 linked the teaching and use of strategies to the process. "I model a lot the kind of attitude that I want from them. By showing them the steps, I do not have to provide them with any solutions. I find it important to show them there are different ways to solve a problem. I question my students all the time. It obliges the students to sit down and think about solving the problem by themselves." Teacher 1 provided guidance to her students by teaching them how to plan and organize themselves, how to problem solve, how to talk and discuss, and how to learn to work in teams and learn from each other. Teacher 1 also shared the power with her students. She planned everything with them and delegated to the students the responsibility for their own learning.

Teacher 2 had two outstanding concepts for strategy: (a) promoting risk-taking, respect, and self-esteem; and (b) being a model and guide for her students. "The risk-taking plays into my strategy, because I think that risk-taking can also affect inquiry in the first place. The risk-taking also has to do with the students' self-concept, because if the students are insecure they might not want to do an honest self-evaluation. The process of self-evaluation is then linked to the teacher guiding the students' thinking processes: "I try and stimulate their thinking because I think a good important part of the students' learning to inquire for themselves is to understand how they think."

Teacher 3 placed the most emphasis on the construct of strategy. He claimed that he used inquiry as a teaching tool to help motivate his students and spark their creativity: "In a way, I look at inquiry learning as a device to motivate my students. I think what I do is that I give them a kind of staging area where they could be creative." Teaching his students strategies such as how to plan and organize, study, and problem-solve were given priority in his teaching approach. Teacher 3 provided guidance to his students when they were participating in an inquiry activity: "I guide them and have input into their projects. I watch them, and question how they are setting up their strategies and research."

Teacher 4 defined strategy as the teacher teaching the students different strategies and processes or the students themselves using the strategies in their research. Teacher 4 explained: "I model strategies for the students. I go through the whole process of teaching them to write research questions. I initiate the process in that I am modeling processes for them. I deal with the strategies in problem solving. The students have to know how to use each of the strategies discreetly. They also have to know how to pull all the strategies together and use them as a research method." Teamwork was also emphasized, in that, Teacher 4 believed that her students could learn from each other.

Teacher 7 considered strategy not as a method but more as a foundation for planning and organization, which, in turn, supports the process and content of learning. She found that this could be achieved through role-modeling, facilitating, and creating experiences for the students: "To develop openness and authenticity, I do a lot of role-modeling. I create experiences that are going to allow people to bring out their ideas, I see this as facilitating." Teacher 7 also modeled strategies for her students with the goal to promote problem solving and having them gain new knowledge and attitudes.

Teacher 8 spoke about the importance of teaching strategies: "For problem-solving you have to talk about strategies and how to do it. You need direct guidance. I try and give them strategies, which are descriptions. I am guiding questioning in class. The ideal thing is to throw out questions and try and get people to start questioning themselves."

He adapted his courses according to his students' suggestions and provided them with a choice when they did their free writing. He used a student-centered approach and acted as a resource to his students. Teacher 8 stated: "The students start discussing the reading material. I am really there as the resident expert." His students were given the responsibility to further their own learning by using the class time to discuss issues and concepts that needed clarification. His students solved problems in teams and Teacher 8 stressed the importance of collaborative learning.

Practical Implications

These common characteristics from Table 11.2 reveal a pattern of inquiry teaching that is supported by the literature and by six inquiry teachers' conceptualizations of inquiry. The noninquiry teachers, also well regarded as caring professionals, did not share these characteristics in their statements. Therefore, we feel confident that these characteristics are properties of inquiry teaching, and not just good teaching in general. We have validated their importance to inquiry, based on what the literature predicted and by comparing qualitatively what the noninquiry and inquiry teachers said.

It was the difference in the use of the four constructs that distinguished the inquiry teachers from the noninquiry teachers. For illustrative purposes in this chapter, we have addressed only the construct of strategy. If one were planning to provide teachers with an in-service education on inquiry, how would the construct of strategy in inquiry be explained? How would strategy need to be defined in order to distinguish it from a more traditional approach to teaching?

Strategy incorporates facilitating, wherein teachers provide students with suggestions and ideas, and point out directions when students appear to be stuck. Strategy also encompasses guidance. Teachers ask students questions to get them thinking, to lead students to what they have learned and what they need to learn. Teaching problem-solving strategies plays an important role in inquiry because students will need to learn how to use these strategies in order to be able to solve problems. Teachers can stimulate reflection by checking in with students as they are problem solving. The teachers can ask what their students are doing, why are they doing it, and how will it help. These questioning strategies not only make students more aware of their methods but also increase their consciousness of their own thought processes, an important ingredient in the development of internal monitoring (Schoenfeld, 1989).

Students' predictions are a highly emphasized aspect of strategy. Teachers create learning experiences in which students must identify problems for investigation. The hypothesis serves as a guide to the inquiry that follows, students attempt to verify the elements of the problem, see whether those elements did indeed relate to the proposed solution, and determine whether the solution held up or others needed to be generated. A considerable amount of attention is also placed upon the writing process within the strategy construct. Students communicate the solutions of their problem in writing. Inquiry and learning are facilitated because writing requires that new connections be made, ideas be selected, and new relationships between facts and ideas be discovered (Germann, 1989).

Conclusion

This study found that those teachers who did not use inquiry in their classrooms did not possess a clear understanding of inquiry and implemented a traditional teacher-directed approach to instruction. Teachers who possessed a clear conceptualization of an inquiry approach to teaching were able to transfer their knowledge and expertise to their students, who could then better understand what is involved and intended in the inquiry process. Teachers' understanding of inquiry, and more specifically, the ability to identify and implement the characteristics of the construct of strategy, are essential in order to successfully teach inquiry in the classroom. The absence of this background knowledge and expertise will become a barrier for teachers who attempt to implement inquiry-based teaching and learning in their classrooms.

References

Austin, L. B., & Shore, B. M. (1995). Using concept mapping for assessment in physics. *Physics Education, 30*(1), 41–45.

Balzer, L. V. (1970). Teacher behaviors and student inquiry in biology. *American Biology Teacher, 32*, 26–28.

Beyer, B. K. (1971). *Inquiry in the social studies classroom: A strategy for teaching.* Columbus, OH: Merrill.

Brown, A. L. (1994). The advancement of learning. *Educational Researcher, 23*, 4–12.

Brown, A. L., & Campione, J. C. (1994). Guided discovery in a community of learners. In K. McGilly (Ed.), *Integrating cognitive theory and classroom practice: Classroom lessons* (pp. 229–270). Cambridge, MA: MIT Press.

Byer, B. (1987). *Inquiry in the social studies classroom: A strategy for teaching.* Columbus, OH: Merrill.

Cole, H. P. (1989). Process curricula and creativity development. *The Journal of Creative Behavior, 3*, 243–259.

Cox, C. B. (1968). An inquiry into inquiries. In R. F. Allen, J. V. Fleckenstein, & P. M. Lyon (Eds.), *Inquiry in the social studies: Theory and examples for classroom teachers* (pp. 42–45). Washington, DC: National Council for the Social Sciences.

Crawford, B. A. (2000). Embracing the essence of inquiry: New roles for science teachers. *Journal of Research in Science Teaching, 37*, 916–937.

DeBoer, G. E. (1991). *A history of ideas in science education: Implications for practice.* London: Routledge.

Doherty, E. J. S., & Evans, L. (1981). Help! Need direction in independent study? *GCT, 4*, 43–46.

Germann, P. J. (1989). Directed-inquiry approach to learning science process skills: Treatment effects and aptitude-treatment interactions. *Journal of Research in Science Teaching, 26*, 237–250.

Glover, J. A., Ronning, R. R., & Bruning, R. H. (1990). *Problem-solving: Cognitive psychology for teachers*. New York: Macmillan.

Henson, K. T. (1986). Inquiry learning: A new look. *Contemporary Education, 57,* 181–183.

Herron, M. D. (1971). The nature of scientific inquiry. *School Review, 79,* 171–212.

Husén, T., & Postlethwaite, T. N. (Eds.). (1996). *The international encyclopedia of education* (2nd ed.). Oxford, UK: Pergamon Press.

Joyce, B., & Weil, M. (1980). *Models of teaching* (2nd ed.). Englewood Cliffs, NJ: Prentice-Hall.

Kliebard, H. M. (1968). The search of modes of inquiry. In R. F. Allen, J. V. Fleckenstein, & P. M. Lyon (Eds.), *Inquiry in the social studies; theory and examples for classroom teachers* (pp. 50–54). Washington, DC: National Council for the Social Sciences.

Manconi, L. (2003). *Teachers' understanding of inquiry*. Unpublished doctoral dissertation in educational psychology, McGill University, Montreal, QC, Canada.

Manson, G. A., & Williams, E. D. (1970). Inquiry: Does it teach how or what to think? *Social Education, 34,* 78–81.

National Research Council (1996). *National science education standards: Observe, interact, change, learn* (7th ed.). Washington, DC: National Academy Press.

Newell, A., & Simon, H. A. (1975). The functional equivalence of problem solving skills. *Cognitive Psychology, 7,* 268–288.

Newmann, F. M. (1991). Promoting higher order thinking skills in social studies: Overview of a study of 16 high school departments. *Theory and Research in Social Education, 19,* 324–340.

Orlich, D. C., Harder, R. J., Callahan, R. C., Karvas, C. H., Kauchak, D. P., Pendergrass, R. A., et al. (1985). *Teaching strategies: A guide to better instruction* (2nd ed.). New York: Heath.

Polya, G. (1981). *Mathematical discovery: On understanding, learning, and teaching problem solving*. New York: Wiley.

Richards, J. (1991). Mathematics discussions. In E. von Glasersfeld (Ed.), *Radical constructivism in mathematics education* (pp. 13–51). Dordrecht, Netherlands: Kluwer.

Rogers, P. (1990). Discovery learning, critical thinking and the nature of knowledge. *British Journal of Educational Studies, 38,* 3–14.

Schoenfeld, A. H. (1989). Teaching mathematical thinking and problem solving. In L. B. Resnick & L. E. Klopfer (Eds.), *Toward the thinking curriculum: Current cognitive research* (pp. 83–103). Washington, DC: Association for Supervision and Curriculum Development.

Shore, B. M., Aulls, M. W., & Rejskind, F. G. (1999). *Inquiry teaching and learning: Strategic demands and context*. Unpublished manuscript, McGill University, Montreal, Quebec. (Team standard research grant application to the Social Sciences and Humanities Research Council of Canada, funded from 2000 to 2003.)

Shubert, W. H. (1989). Reconceptualizing and the matter of paradigms. *Journal of Teacher Education, 40,* 27–32.

Scott, N. C. (1977). Inquiry strategy, cognitive style, and mathematics achievement. *Journal for Research in Mathematics Education, 8,* 132–143.

Short, K. G., & Burke, C. (1996). Examining our beliefs and practices through inquiry. *Language Arts, 73,* 97–104.

Sizer, T. R. (1984). *Horace's compromise: The dilemma of the American high school*. Boston: Houghton Mifflin.

Tamir, P. (1983). Inquiry and the science teacher. *Science Education, 67,* 657–672.

Torrance, E. P. (1965). *Gifted children in the classroom*. New York: Macmillan.

Uhlhorn, K. W. (1971). The challenge of inquiry teaching in science. *Contemporary Education, 42,* 238–240.

Welch, W. W., Klopfer, L. E., Aikenhead, G. S., Glen, S. D., & Robinson, J. T. (1981). The role of inquiry in science education: Analysis and recommendations. *Science Education, 65,* 33–50.

Wilson, J. T. (1974). Processes of scientific inquiry: A model for teaching and learning science. *Science Education, 58,* 127–133.

Wineburg, S. S. (1991). Historical problem solving: A study of the cognitive processes used in the evaluation of documentary and pictorial evidence. *Journal of Educational Psychology, 83,* 73–87.

Woods, D. R. (1989). Problem solving in practice. In D. Gabel (Ed.), *What research says to the science teacher* (pp. 97–121). Washington, DC: National Science Teachers Association.

12

The Hidden Curriculum and Multicultural Education: A Potential Barrier to the Implementation of an Inquiry-Driven Curriculum

Francesca Luconi
McGill University

The origins of inquiry-driven curriculum in the United States can be traced back to Dewey's curriculum ideology of progressivism that emphasized a problem-centered curriculum, reflective thinking, and discovery learning (Dewey, 1938; Eisner, 1992; Engle, 1986) and the Academic Reform movement of the 1960s and 1970s that included the New Social Studies movement. This movement aimed at the revision of the conventional curriculum areas so as to teach the structure of disciplines (Schwab, 1968) and the inquiry strategies used by scientists (Haas, 1979). A variety of factors influenced the limited implementation of inquiry instruction at the time, including (a) inadequate design for teaching inquiry skills to teachers and students, (b) deficient teacher education, (c) limited availability of inquiry materials, (d) concern about students' preparation and ability to use inquiry strategies, and (e) perception of being a type of instruction difficult to manage (Jantz, Weaver, Cirrincione, & Farrell, 1985; Hill, 1985; L. R. Nelson & Drake, 1994; VanSickle, 1985).

Fenton (1991) and Massialas (1992), leaders of the Academic Reform movement particularly drew attention to the hidden curriculum as one of the factors that contributed to the failure of such reform. Massialas (1992) claimed that the hidden curriculum is a powerful force that "as opposed to the formal curriculum, is responsible for as much as 90 percent of all learning taking place in the school" (p. 123). Hoping to avoid the same mistakes in the future, this chapter discusses the arguments presented by the leaders of the New Social Studies movement. In light of the demographic changes of classroom composition, it is today even more urgent to investigate the effects of the hidden curriculum in teaching and learning in multicultural classrooms (Luconi, 1996).

In the 1990s, our global society became increasingly multilingual and multicultural. This trend will continue in the third millennium with the expected increase of minorities in North American, Australian, and European schools, paralleled by a decrease of the Caucasian population (Edmonston & Passel, 1992). Bailey (1990) argued that, historically, African Americans and Hispanics have done poorest in terms of educational achievement, therefore employers and educators need to make a concerted effort to help these groups to participate in the globally competitive American economy of the third millennium. However, despite the interest of numerous task forces in making science education more accessible to all students by increasing the number of minorities in scientific professions, Rosenthal (1996) claimed that science-education reform of the nineties failed to reach this goal in higher education. The gap between what is fostered by the systemic reform in science and mathematics education and what teachers implement in their classrooms was documented by Knapp's (1997) comprehensive review of current systemic reforms in mathematics and science in the United States, supported by the National Science Foundation (NSF), state governments, and school districts (S. G. Grant, Peterson, & Shojgreen-Downer, 1996).

The specific purpose of this chapter is to advance the claim that the hidden curriculum might become a barrier to the successful implementation of an inquiry-driven curriculum in a multicultural classroom that includes students of different ethnicity, gender, socioeconomic status, and ability. The rationale for this claim is based on the historical background of inquiry-driven curriculum and the complex teaching dilemmas of a multicultural classroom. This analysis is grounded in a critical-pedagogy theoretical framework and adopts a sociolinguistic micro-ethnography perspective. Critical theorists (e.g., Cornbleth, 1990) emphasized the need to consider the social context of instruction and the redefinition of hidden curriculum (Giroux, 1981). In the past, researchers and practitioners were oblivious to this fundamental aspect of instruction because the majority of investigations were framed by the mainstream positivistic paradigm that considered knowledge to be neutral, objective, and universal. Feminist and African American scholars challenged the dominant paradigm and introduced the idea that knowledge is "transformative" because it reflects multiple voices, power relations, and the cultures of the social scientists (Banks, 1995; Sleeter, 1995).

In order to justify the importance of investigating the hidden curriculum in inquiry instruction, the literature was reviewed in a variety of fields, (a) curriculum, (b) inquiry-instruction, and (c) multicultural education. This chapter includes studies that explicitly use the terms "hidden" or "implicit curriculum" as well as those where the hidden curriculum is inferred (e.g., Ginsburg & Clift, 1990) as a prelude to the suggestion that multicultural education might prevent or limit the negative effects of hidden curriculum during the implementation of the inquiry-driven teaching and learning in a heterogeneous classroom.

Definitions

Multicultural Education

Multicultural education is a philosophical concept and an educational process. As an educational philosophy and ideology, multicultural education originated in the U.S. civil rights movement of the 1960s and 1970s (C. A. Grant & Tate, 1995). Multicultural education is controversial and has provoked both conservative and radical critiques (Sleeter, 1995). Banks (1995) nevertheless maintained that there is a developing consensus among multicultural specialists about the goals of multicultural education, namely, "to reform the school and other educational institutions so that students from diverse racial, ethnic, and social-class groups will experience educational equality . . . and to give male and female students an equal chance to experience educational success and mobility" (p. 3). In order to achieve these goals, multicultural education requires the integration of five dimensions: curriculum content, knowledge construction, prejudice reduction, equity pedagogy, and empowering school culture and social structure. Multicultural education is associated with institutional changes in order to achieve educational equality. However, two of the barriers that limited the attainment of this goal have been to narrowly reduce multicultural education to a curriculum reform through content integration and the gap between theory and practice because of a variety of factors such as inappropriate teacher-education programs (Darling-Hammond, 1995).

Inquiry-Driven Curriculum

Inquiry is a multifaceted concept (Aulls & Shore, 2008) that can be described as a way of thinking, an attitude toward learning and teaching in solving problems under investigation (Merwin, 1976). The multifaceted nature of the concept of inquiry is reflected in the variety of terms used in the literature, which make it difficult to investigate and define. In the social studies, inquiry has been defined as in-depth study (Rossi, 1995), the structure of a discipline (Schwab, 1968), an inquiry approach (L. R. Nelson & Drake, 1994), issue-centered instruction (Shaver, 1992), reflective inquiry (Massialas, 1992), and discovery learning (Bruner, 1960). In science, inquiry has been identified as problem solving (Welch, Klopfer, Aikenhead, & Robinson, 1981), an approach to teach science (Cummins, Pinar, & R. Good, 1989; Tamir, 1983), inquiry teaching, discovery learning, guided learning, and a heuristic method (DeBoer, 1991).

Inquiry in education has its conceptual roots in Dewey's theory of inquiry, which he called instrumental or experimental logic and considered as the "lifeblood of every science" (Dewey, 1938, p. 4). Scientific inquiry typically follows a series of steps that start with a doubt due to confrontation with an ambiguous situation that, in turn, provokes questioning. This problematic situation is resolved through guided inquiry. The first formal step is transforming the initial doubt and confusion into a statement of a problem. This phase is crucial because it will guide the selection of data, hypotheses, and conceptual structures (Dewey, 1938).

There are many versions of inquiry-driven curriculum (Joyce & Weil, 1996) as well as of inquiry-oriented teacher-education programs (Casey & Howson, 1993; Tom, 1985). In this chapter, a global operational definition of inquiry-driven curriculum is adopted so as to contextualize the interaction between the manifest and the hidden curricula. In this definition, inquiry drives subject-matter curriculum design and instruction by emphasizing the teaching of learning strategies, higher-order thinking (Newmann, 1991), critical thinking, and discussion skills (Rossi, 1995). The inquiry-driven curriculum is a problem-centered (Casey & Tucker, 1994) curriculum aimed at fostering reflective thinking and effective learning (Bruner, 1960; Wilen & McKenrick, 1989). Students identify an area of interest or a problem, frame research questions, construct knowledge on the basis of prior knowledge through the collection and manipulation of data, and present the learning outcomes to a suitable audience. The role of the teacher is that of a guide and resource person (Hammer, 1997). The librarian also can play the role of resource person in the phase of searching and evaluating resources for a research project (Wilen & McKenrick, 1989). The students' roles are to develop the research question individually or jointly and to identify resources needed for the research project (T. H. Nelson & Moscovici, 1998). From a social constructivist perspective, the inquiry-driven curriculum could be interpreted as "contextualized social process" influenced by broader socioeconomic and political forces (Cornbleth, 1990) and an "evolving construction" resulting from teacher-student interactions (Zumwalt, 1989). The negotiation of certain phases of the inquiry process includes access to the library and out-of-school facilities, time required to finalize the research project, and the evaluation of the project (Hammer, 1997; Wilen & McKenrick, 1989).

The Hidden Curriculum
One of the central goals of the school is the socialization of students through the manifest, formal, or explicit curriculum and the hidden curriculum (Morrissett, Hawke, & Superka, 1980). The former includes "what the school and its personnel set out deliberately to teach students and what the learning is as seen and felt by students" (Erickson & Shultz, 1992). In 1968, Jackson first coined the term "hidden curriculum," which he defined as all implicit norms and rules that students and teachers should master in order to succeed at school. The hidden curriculum is reflected in different aspects of the school and classroom cultural patterns (Zaharlick & Green, 1991), such as verbal and nonverbal messages (Green & Wallat, 1981), teachers' expectations, effects of cultural differences, differential student treatment, language attitudes, student status, instructional ability groupings, and the school's organizational dimension (Hernandez, 1989). The inquiry-driven curriculum integrates the two parts, the manifest and the hidden curricula. The manifest curriculum suggests what counts as academic knowledge, but since its importance is transformed by what happens in the classroom, the hidden curriculum becomes a powerful force for teachers and students to unravel and deal with (Giroux, 1981; Goodlad, 1984). The hidden curriculum filters and mediates

messages that parallel (Weisz, 1988) or contradict the manifest or explicit curriculum (Cornbleth, 1990). It is important to investigate the hidden curriculum in order to understand what is transmitted and learned in schools, to improve teaching methods, and to reveal the connections between education and the larger social order (Cummins, Pinar, & R. Good, 1989; Martin, 1976). The hidden, implicit (Cornbleth, 1990), or informal curriculum (McCaslin & T. L. Good, 1996) covers different dimensions. However, in this chapter, only those messages transmitted during teacher-student interactions are analyzed.

Hidden Curriculum Messages in Teacher-Student Classroom Interaction

Contradictory hidden curriculum messages could be a barrier to inquiry-based instruction. Casey and Tucker (1994) argued that the hidden curriculum in inquiry instruction is conveyed by the norms and rules implicit in the design of the classroom environment, the wall displays, and classroom management (Uhlhorn, 1971; Morrissett, Hawke, & Superka, 1980). Hidden-curriculum messages are also transmitted as a result of some teachers' struggles in implementing a variety of new roles during inquiry instruction, roles that differ from teacher-centered instruction and "activitymania." Inquiry instruction requires a new way of teaching involving discovery teaching (Hammer, 1997) that embodies distinctive teachers' roles and assumptions, for example, appropriate knowledge of the discipline, awareness and judgment to diagnose the students' progress and difficulties, and flexibility to plan and implement the curriculum due to the ongoing negotiation of the tension between inquiry and traditional content and the curriculum's enrichment with students' ideas. The teacher's facilitator role implies indirectly guiding inquiry by finding the delicate balance between intervening, controlling students' thinking and drilling them with facts (Brown, 1992; Schleppegrell, 1997; Uhlhorn, 1971). T. H. Nelson and Moscovici (1998) reported that during "activitymania" as opposed to inquiry instruction, teachers feel in control, unchallenged intellectually, relaxed, and that they are having fun. In contrast, during inquiry instruction, teachers lose or give up a degree of control, and they feel intellectually challenged because there are no ready-made answers to many of the problems being investigated.

In the 1960s, leaders of the New Social Studies movement (cf. Engle, 1986; Massialas, 1992) reported that the lack of teacher education to deal with conflict issues limited the success and implementation of the New Social Studies materials. Most teachers were trained in the traditional expository method that allowed them to be in complete control and to avoid controversial issues. In a classroom climate in which controversy is not to be avoided, Massialas (1963) emphasized the importance of discourse that creates the conditions to enhance appropriate questioning so that students can critically analyze social issues relevant to them. Hidden curriculum messages are conveyed by the type of discourse and the tacit rules of student participation in classroom discussion (Cazden, 1986; Edwards & Mercer, 1987). Questioning is a significant skill in inquiry instruction. Patterns of questioning reflect the hidden curriculum's messages that could communicate an open, friendly, unthreatening, and risk-taking classroom climate, or a closed type of environment where students hesitate to ask questions for fear of being ridiculed by peers or the teacher (Aulls & Luconi, 1997; Sternberg, 1994). A safe classroom climate that stimulates children's intellectual curiosity, participation, and critical thinking skills is illustrated by various teacher-researchers who emphasize the importance of the teacher's modeling the questioning process, the teacher's nonjudgmental attitude (Ciardello, 1986; Iwasyk, 1997), and the student's freedom to formulate divergent and evaluative level questions (Wilen, 1979; Wilen & McKenrick, 1989). Rossi (1995) argued that, in the context of a social studies inquiry-based curriculum, to create an "open, safe, and challenging environment" is particularly difficult due to the controversial type of knowledge, greater responsibility on the part of the student to participate, and greater flexibility expected from the teacher "in adjusting to students' choices about the use of information" (p. 109).

Teacher-Student Interactions in Science Education and the Image of Science Transmitted to Students

Cummins et al. (1989) elaborated on the effects of hidden curriculum within the teaching of science. They referred to the "bucket" image of science that chemistry, physics, and humanities students get through the hidden curriculum. Gordon (1984) had borrowed the concept of bucket image from Popper's (1972) theory of science, based on the assumption that our mind is a bucket into which materials and information enter through our senses based on our experiences. Students do not reject this image but accept it uncritically. The bucket image of science is an important factor in shaping the students' consciousness in a way that facilitates technological consciousness, that is, as "a world view in which science functions as a central metaphor" (p. 368). The bucket image contradicts the goals of the Academic Reform movement wherein students are supposed to learn critical-thinking skills and scientific thinking during inquiry-oriented instruction. Within a product-centered instructional model, science was considered as a static or slowly growing body of knowledge created by others and transmitted from teacher to students. Textbooks were considered as the main source of information, the majority of which did not relate academic content to societal or personal contexts. The bucket image of science does not support the dual nature of science as both product and process. Inquiry as a science process to be experienced was either absent or barely alluded to in most science texts (Cummins et al., 1989).

The image of science that students receive at school through the hidden curriculum does not offer a realistic image of science as experienced by scientists because it avoids the treatment of conflict by excluding discussion, indeed argument and disagreement, within the scientific community and during teacher-student interaction (Apple, 1971; Barfurth & Shore in this volume; Gordon, 1984). It portrays the scientist as a "coldly rational inductive empiricist" (DeBoer, 1991,

p. 199) and, in scientific papers, it usually sanitizes the fuzziness of scientific procedures and methods. (McGinn & Roth, 1999). McGinn and Roth (1999) offered interesting suggestions to implement "authentic science" activities that reflect a more realistic image of science grounded in "the situated, contingent and contextual nature of science, while also acknowledging the diverse range of communities and locations where science is created and used" (p. 17).

The image of science devoid of conflict is not unique to science teaching. It is also found in social studies (Apple, 1971; Massialas, 1992), and it is rooted in the epistemology that is transmitted by teacher-education programs (Ginsburg & Clift, 1990). Knowledge as given is contrary to a notion of knowledge as problematic, defined as "constructed, provisional, and tentative, subject to political, cultural and social influences" (Berlak & Berlak, 1981, p. 147). In order to change classrooms curricular practices, Tamir (1983) and T. H. Nelson and Moscovici (1998) agreed that the teacher's conception of the nature of inquiry, acquired at least in part during teacher education (and also from colleagues once employed) is a key element to take into account.

The positivist image of science is also reflected in textbooks. Pizzini, Shepardson, and Abell (1991) demonstrated that commercially published junior high school activities do not contribute to the inclusion of open-inquiry science instruction due to their emphasis on confirmation and structured level inquiry. Within Tafoya, Sunal, & Knecht's (1980) classification of inquiry activities, used by Pizzini et al. (1991), confirmation activities require that students "verify concepts or principles through a known given procedure that the student follows" (p. 113). Structured inquiry activities "present students with a problem in which they do not know the results, but they are given a procedure to follow in order to complete the activity." In contrast to confirmation and structured activities, "open-inquiry activities allow the student to formulate hypotheses or problems and the procedure for collecting data for interpretation and conclusion drawing. Open inquiry requires students to use science concepts or principles" (p. 113). Pizzini et al. (1991) asserted that it is the science teacher's responsibility to include problem-solving activities to foster open-inquiry instruction. The use of prepackaged, hands-on science activities in activitymania limits the construction of conceptual understanding and scientific literacy (T. H. Nelson & Moscovici, 1998).

Science education seen as biased against women and minority students. Stereotypes in science education constitute another dimension of the hidden curriculum that might directly or indirectly limit the participation of girls and some minority students in inquiry-driven science courses as well as in following careers in science, mathematics, and technology (Blake, 1993; Crew, 1998). Rosenthal (1996) argued that, besides lack of attention to the cultural background of students, the decrease in science-major numbers could be attributed to a variety of other factors such as inadequate or weak science background, textbook-driven laboratory activities, inadequate laboratory facilities, teacher-centered pedagogy, lack of role models for minority students, or the size of the class. The relative lack of role models for women and minority students is reflected in the demographic profile of college science professors who are predominately male, white, and over the age of 40 (Rosenthal, 1996). This stereotyped image of the scientist also emerged from a national survey in the United States of 1,500 readers of the journal *Science and Children* (Barman, 1997). In higher education, Asian American students are overrepresented in science and technology, and researchers have warned educators that behind the myth of the "model minority" there is a great variety of Asian Americans ranging from those who are highly successful to those who have recently immigrated and have problems of communicating in English (Bennet, 1995; Rosenthal, 1996). C. A. Grant and Tate's literature review (1995) described the model minority stereotype as "quiet, hard-working, nonverbal and high achieving" (p. 25). This stereotype constitutes part of the hidden curriculum and could be a burden for the student, an influence on teacher-student interaction, career aspirations, and the curriculum.

The Social Context of Multicultural Classrooms

Scholars associated with the critical pedagogy approach (e.g., Apple, 1971; Cornbleth, 1990; Giroux, 1981) have advocated systematic research into the social controlling function of the hidden curriculum because it might reproduce unequal treatment in the classroom and limit students' opportunities to learn. Empirical evidence has indicated negative effects of the hidden curriculum on minority students' academic achievement due to its greater influence than the manifest curriculum (Avery & Walker, 1993; Jacob & Jordan, 1987). In order to deal with the complexity of heterogeneous classrooms, teachers require a higher cultural awareness to recognize how ethnicity, socioeconomic status, gender, and other sociocultural factors influence and interact with the classroom culture (Hernandez, 1989). Furthermore, teachers need to be equipped with "a refined diagnostic ability, a broad repertoire of teaching strategies, . . . the ability to match strategies to varied learning styles and prior levels of knowledge . . . using inquiry and cooperative learning strategies as well as skills in classroom management. . . . Because relatively few teachers are prepared to manage heterogeneous classrooms effectively, tracking persists" (Darling-Hammond, 1995, p. 474). Darling-Hammond (1995) has argued that tracking combined with other factors limits the access to opportunities to learn for students of ethnic and racial "minority" groups in the United States.

A philosophy of teaching (cf. Pajares, 1992) is tacitly embedded and transmitted through the hidden curriculum. An example of mismatch between the teacher's philosophy of teaching and the teacher's practice is illustrated by Spindler and Spindler's (1990) ethnographic case study in which contradictory hidden-curriculum messages of unfairness contradicted the manifest curriculum of equity and fairness. Despite perceiving himself as a fair-minded person, the observed teacher verbally and nonverbally interacted more with children with a mainstream cultural background similar to his own and ignored children of a lower socioeconomic status and different ethnicity. The discrepancy between the manifest and the hidden curricula might produce potential negative effects on the self-esteem and general affective well-being of Mexican-American high-achieving teenagers, who felt marginalized in their school because their immigrant heritage was not respected (Davidson, 1992). An inquiry-driven multicultural curriculum should include cultural celebrations of a variety of ethnic groups, not only those of African Americans (Luft, 1997). In sum, the disempowering effects of the hidden curriculum transmitted by prejudices and misconceptions filtered the social interactions at school and contradicted the manifest curriculum that praised understanding and communication in a multicultural student population.

As previously noted, discourse, and specifically questioning, is an important ingredient in the successful implementation of inquiry-driven curriculum (McGinn & Roth, 1999). In a multicultural classroom, the tacit rules of discourse transmitted through hidden curriculum might not be correctly interpreted by minority students. Empirical classroom-based studies have demonstrated the influence of discourse in the opportunities that students have to display what they know (Mehan, Lintz, Okamoto, & Wills, 1995). Because the nonverbal language has been acquired unconsciously (Hall, 1989), misunderstandings might occur during interactions among students and teachers of different ethnic and cultural backgrounds. For example, some gestures (consider pointing or eating with the left hand), values and beliefs that are acceptable in some cultures are considered as vulgar and obscene in others (Rosenthal, 1996). These fundamental hidden curriculum forces may erode the social conditions necessary for students to participate equally in classroom inquiry.

Discussion and Implications

This chapter engaged claims by two leaders of the New Social Studies movement about the influence of the challenges presented by the hidden curriculum to the successful implementation of inquiry-driven curriculum, and highlighted the importance of investigating the influence of the hidden curriculum in multicultural classrooms. The literature review yielded a scarcity of empirical studies on the hidden curriculum during inquiry-based instruction in multicultural classrooms. Despite the recommendations of inquiry-instruction specialists, the impact of the hidden curriculum is still a neglected area of research. In order to capture the complexity of the hidden curriculum's influence during inquiry-based instruction, future empirical studies with combined methodology should integrate three instructional domains: curriculum, inquiry-instruction, and multicultural education.

Successful implementation of inquiry-driven curriculum cannot be taken for granted due to the mismatch between the manifest and hidden curricula. Hidden curriculum messages that contradict the formal inquiry-driven curriculum might be found in the classroom culture at different levels: (a) the nature of socioaffective and cognitive teacher-student interactions, (b) classroom climate,

(c) classroom management and locus of control, (d) teachers' and students' conception of inquiry based on their formal education and past experiences, (e) the teacher's style and philosophy of teaching, (f) discourse patterns, (g) the image of subject matter transmitted in teacher-education programs, (h) variety in teachers' roles, and (i) the teacher's differential treatment that might limit the opportunities to learn by specific types of students (e.g., women, minority, low-ability, and low-socioeconomic-status students).

Educational Implications

Inquiry-based instruction and multicultural education share some similarities. Both approaches are student-centered, value process and content, and emphasize higher-order learning skills. Their common historical roots stem from the Progressive Education movement and a constructivist conception of knowledge. The multicultural transformative approach offers the educational community several tools with which to identify aspects of the hidden curriculum that might be detrimental to the implementation of inquiry-driven curriculum, and suggests means to overcome the barriers.

In science education, a fairly recent branch called multicultural science education considers science education as a type of cultural transmission. Science teachers are encouraged to acknowledge the cultural capital of students of different backgrounds and of male and female scientists from other cultures (e.g., Chinese, Indian, or Islamic) (Krugly-Smolska, 1996; Luft, 1997), and to teach critical thinking skills in order to question the objectivity of the traditional scientific methods (Crew, 1998; Harding, 1991). Some tools have been developed to enhance transcultural understanding among young children based on similarities instead of differences among cultures. Hickey's (1997) Culture Kits offer a variety of hands-on activities that foster individualized instruction and increase children's pleasure and motivation to learn. Dialogic inquiry is a process-oriented research and pedagogical tool by which teacher-researchers investigate their students' motivation, cultural background, and related cultural issues (Schleppegrell, 1997).

Another contribution that multicultural science education offers to fight prejudice and racism is "to demystify the concept of race and show the limitations of race as a biological concept" (Krugly-Smolska, 1996, p. 78). Several authors (e.g., Apple, 1971; McGinn & Roth, 1999) have suggested focusing on the history of science in order to show the human nature of scientists and scientific debates. In order to support and encourage young women to pursue scientific careers, the MentorNet World Wide Web site (Arent, 1999) puts them in contact with mentors who are experienced women working in science-related fields.

Regarding teacher-student interactions, Rosenthal (1996) offered several recommendations for helping "limited English proficient (LEP) students" in traditional science courses. Instructors should limit the use of jokes, slang, or idioms, and explain references to popular culture. They are encouraged to mix native and non-native English speakers in student groups, to ask the opinion of an English as second language specialist for choosing a text, and allow the use of bilingual dictionaries during tests. Experienced educational anthropologists suggest that, due to the teacher's role as cultural transmitter, multicultural education "sensitivity training" should be incorporated in preservice and in-service teacher training programs (Spindler & Spindler, 1990). Furthermore, action-research studies and classroom-observation studies provide teachers opportunities to reflect and clarify their philosophy of teaching and learning so as to avoid contradictory hidden curriculum messages that might prevent students' access to opportunities to learn. Luft (1997) illustrated some of these principles with a case study of "Jill." Being in contact with a different culture, Jill, a preservice teacher and proponent of multicultural education, contrasted her beliefs about multicultural science-inquiry instruction versus traditional instruction. This kind of reflection empowered Jill to negotiate the borders of different cultures found in her teaching education and hidden curriculum messages embedded at different levels of the school and classroom cultures. Increasing preservice and in-service teachers' knowledge and awareness of the students' cultures and ethnic background facilitated the development of a more relevant inquiry-driven curriculum, especially by enhancing the quality of dialogue in the classroom.

The hidden curriculum might be a barrier to the implementation of inquiry-driven curriculum in a multicultural classroom. To avoid this, it is essential that teachers, university professors, and curriculum theorists work collaboratively. The hidden curriculum is a key element to be taken into account with regard to curriculum theory, research, and educational practice in order to reach a deeper understanding and application of equity and excellence in education.

References

Apple, M. W. (1971). The hidden curriculum and the nature of conflict. *Interchange, 2*(4), 27–40.

Arent, L. (1999). Leading women to tech fields. *Wired news update*. Retrieved August 19, 2005, from http://www.wired.com/news/culture/0,1284,19948,00.html

Aulls, M. W., & Luconi, F. (1997, May). *Pre-service teachers' conceptualization of inquiry*. Paper presented at the mid-year conference of the National Association for Gifted Children, Montreal, QC.

Aulls, M. W., & Shore, B. M. (2008). *Inquiry in education: The conceptual foundations of research as a curriculum imperative*. New York: Erlbaum.

Avery, P. G., & Walker, C. (1993). Prospective teachers' perceptions of ethnic and gender differences in academic achievement. *Journal of Teacher Education, 44*, 27–37.

Bailey, T. (1990). *Changes in the nature and structure of work: Duplications for skill requirements and skill formation*. Berkeley, CA: National Center for Research in Vocational Education.

Banks, J. A. (1995). Multicultural education: Historical development, dimensions and practice. In J. A. Banks & C. A. McGee Banks (Eds.), *Handbook of research on multicultural education* (pp. 3–24). New York: Macmillan.

Barman, C. R. (1997). Student's views of scientists and science. *Science and Children, 35*(1), 18–23.

Bennet, C. I. (1995). Research on racial issues in American higher education. In J. A. Banks & C. A. McGee Banks (Eds.), *Handbook of research on multicultural education* (pp. 663–682). New York: Macmillan.

Berlak, A., & Berlak, H. (1981). *Dilemmas of schooling: Teaching and social change.* New York: Methuen.

Blake, S. (1993). Are you turning female and minority students away from science? *Science and Children, 30*(7), 32–35.

Brown, A. L. (1992). Designing experiments: Theoretical and methodological challenges in creating complex interventions in classroom settings. *The Journal of the Learning Sciences, 2,* 141–178.

Bruner, J. S. (1960). *The process of education* (2nd ed.). Cambridge, MA: Harvard University Press.

Casey, M. B., & Howson, P. (1993). Educating preservice students based on a problem-centered approach to teaching. *Journal of Teacher Education, 44,* 361–369.

Casey, M. B., & Tucker, E. C. (1994). Problem-centered classrooms: Creating lifelong learners. *Phi Delta Kappan, 76,* 139–143.

Cazden, C. B. (1986). Classroom discourse. In M. C. Wittrock (Ed.), *Handbook of research on teaching* (3rd ed.; pp. 432–463). New York: Macmillan.

Ciardello, A. V. (1986). Teacher questioning and student interaction: An observation of three social studies classes. *The Social Studies, 77*(3), 119–122.

Cornbleth, C. (1990). Beyond the hidden curriculum. In C. Cornbleth (Ed.), *Beyond the hidden curriculum: Curriculum in context* (pp. 42–61). Basingstoke, UK: Falmer.

Crew, H. S. (1998). Transforming the hidden curriculum: Gender and the library media center. *Knowledge Quest, 26*(4), 30–33.

Cummins, C. L., Pinar, W., & Good, R. (1989, March). *The hidden curriculum within the teaching of science and its relationship to current science education goals.* Paper presented at the annual meeting of the American Educational Research Association, San Francisco.

Darling-Hammond, L. (1995). Inequality and access to knowledge. In J. A. Banks & C. A. McGee Banks (Eds.), *Handbook of research on multicultural education* (pp. 465–483). New York: Macmillan.

Davidson, A. L. (1992, April). *Border curricula and the construction of identity: Implications for multicultural theorists.* Paper presented at the annual meeting of the American Educational Research Association, San Francisco.

DeBoer, G. E. (1991). *A history of ideas in science education.* New York: Teachers College Press.

Dewey, J. (1938). *Logic: The theory of inquiry.* New York: Holt, Rinehart, & Winston.

Edmonston, B., & Passel, J. S. (1992). *The future immigrant population of the United States.* Washington, DC: The Urban Institute.

Edwards, D., & Mercer, N. (1987). *Common knowledge: The development of understanding in the classroom.* New York: Routledge.

Eisner, E. W. (1992). Curriculum ideologies. In P. W. Jackson (Ed.), *Handbook of research on curriculum* (pp. 302–325). New York: Macmillan.

Engle, S. H. (1986). Late night thoughts about the New Social Studies. *Social Education, 50*(10), 20–22.

Erickson, F., & Shultz, J. (1992). Students' experiences of the curriculum. In P. W. Jackson (Ed.), *Handbook of research on curriculum* (pp. 465–485). New York: Macmillan.

Fenton, E. (1991). Reflections on the "new social studies." *The Social Studies, 82,* 84–90.

Ginsburg, M. B., & Clift, R. T. (1990). The hidden curriculum of preservice teacher education. In W. R. Houston, M. Haberman, & J. Sikula (Eds.), *Handbook of research on teacher education* (pp. 450–456). New York: Macmillan.

Giroux, H. A. (1981). Schooling and the myth of objectivity: Stalking the politics of the hidden curriculum. *McGill Journal of Education, 16,* 282–304.

Goodlad, J. I. (1984). *A place called school: Prospects for the future.* New York: McGraw-Hill.

Gordon, D. (1984). The image of science, technological consciousness, and the hidden curriculum. *Curriculum Inquiry, 14,* 367–400.

Grant, C. A., & Tate, W. F. (1995). Multicultural education through the lens of the multicultural education research literature. In J. Banks & C. A. McGee Banks (Eds.), *Handbook of research on multicultural education* (pp. 145–166). New York: Macmillan.

Grant, S. G., Peterson, P. L., & Shojgreen-Downer, A. (1996). Learning to teach mathematics in the context of systemic reform. *American Educational Research Journal, 33,* 509–541.

Green, J. L., & Wallat, C. (1981). Mapping instructional conversations: A sociolinguistic ethnography. In J. L. Green & C. Wallat (Eds.), *Ethnography and language in educational settings.* Norwood, NJ: Ablex.

Haas, J. D. (1979). Social studies: Where have we been? Where are we going? *Social Studies, 70*(4), 147–154.

Hall, E. T. (1989). *Beyond culture* (2nd ed.). New York: Anchor Books.

Hammer, D. (1997). Discovery learning and discovery teaching. *Cognition and Instruction, 15,* 485–529.

Harding, S. G. (1991). *Whose knowledge? Whose science? Thinking from women's lives.* Ithaca, NY: Cornell University Press.

Hernandez, H. (1989). *Multicultural education: A teacher's guide to content and process.* Columbus, OH: Merrill.

Hickey, M. G. (1997). Science activities to develop transcultural understandings. *Hoosier Science Teacher, 23*(2), 53–55.

Hill, D. M. (1985). Inquiry experiences for elementary education. *Journal of College Science Teaching, 14,* 349–351.

Iwasyk, M. (1997). Kids questioning kids: "Experts" sharing. *Science and Children, 35*(1), 42–46, 80.

Jackson, P. W. (1968). *Life in classrooms.* New York: Holt, Rinehart, & Winston.

Jacob, E., & Jordan, C. (1987). Moving to dialogue. *Anthropology and Education Quarterly, 18,* 259–261.

Jantz, R. K., Weaver, V. P., Cirrincione, J. M., & Farrell, R. T. (1985). Inquiry and curriculum change: Perceptions of school and college/university faculty. *Theory and Research in Social Education, 137*(2), 61–72.

Joyce, B., & Weil, M. (1996). *Models of teaching* (6th ed.). Englewood Cliffs, NJ: Prentice Hall.

Knapp, M. S. (1997). Between systemic reforms and the mathematics and science classroom: The dynamics of innovation, implementation and professional learning. *Review of Educational Research, 67,* 227–266.

Krugly-Smolska, E. (1996). Science education in an evolving multicultural education. In K. A. McLeod (Ed.), *Multicultural education: The state of the art national study. Report no. 4* (pp. 75–79). Winnipeg, MB: Canadian Association of Second Language Teachers.

Luconi, F. (1996, June). *The hidden curriculum effects on teaching and learning in multi-cultural classrooms.* Paper presented at the annual meeting of the Canadian Society for the Study of Education, St. Catherines, ON.

Luft, J. A. (1997, October). *Border crossings: The student teaching experience of a multi-cultural science education enthusiast.* Paper presented at the Arizona K-16 Teaching Reforms Conference, Phoenix, AZ. (ERIC Document no. ED417144)

Martin, J. R. (1976). What should we do with a hidden curriculum when we find one? *Curriculum Inquiry, 6,* 135–151.

Massialas, B. G. (Ed.). (1963). The Indiana experiments in inquiry: Social studies. *Bulletin of the School of Education, Indiana University, 39,* Whole no. 3.

Massialas, B. G. (1992). The "new social studies"—Retrospect and prospect. *The Social Studies, 83,* 120–124.

McCaslin, M., & Good, T. L. (1996). The informal curriculum. In D. C. Berliner & R. C. Calfee (Eds.), *Handbook of educational psychology* (pp. 622–670). New York: Macmillan.

McGinn, M. K., & Roth, W.-M. (1999). Preparing students for competent scientific practice: Implications of recent research in science and technology studies. *Educational Researcher, 28*(3), 4–24.

Mehan, H., Lintz, A., Okamoto, D., & Wills, J. S. (1995). Ethnographic studies of multicultural education in classrooms and schools. In J. Banks & C. A. McGee Banks (Eds.), *Handbook of research on multicultural education* (pp. 129–144). New York: Macmillan.

Merwin, W. C. (1976). The inquiry method. In S. E. Goodman (Ed.), *Handbook of contemporary education* (pp. 388–392). New York: Bowker.

Morrissett, I., Hawke, S., & Superka, D. P. (1980). Six problems for social studies in the 1980s. *Social Education, 44,* 561–569.

Nelson, L. R., & Drake, F. D. (1994). Secondary teachers' reactions to the new social studies. *Theory and Research in Social Education, 22*(1), 44–73.

Nelson, T. H., & Moscovici, H. (1998). Shifting from activitymania to inquiry. *Science and Children, 35*(4), 14–17, 40.

Newmann, F. M. (1991). Higher order thinking in the teaching of the social studies: Connections between theory and practice. In J. F. Vess, D. N. Perkins, & J. W. Segal (Eds.), *Informal reasoning and education.* Hillsdale, NJ: Erlbaum.

Pajares, M. F. (1992). Teachers' beliefs and educational research: Cleaning up a messy construct. *Review of Educational Research, 62,* 307–332.

Pizzini, E. L., Shepardson, D. P., & Abell, S. K. (1991). The inquiry level of junior high activities: Implications to science teaching. *Journal of Research in Science Teaching, 28,* 111–121.

Popper, K. R. (1972). *Objective knowledge: An evolutionary approach.* Oxford, UK: Clarendon Press.

Rosenthal, J. W. (1996). *Teaching science to language minority students.* Bristol, PA: Multilingual Matters.

Rossi, J. A. (1995). In-depth study in an issues-oriented social studies classroom. *Theory and Research in Social Education, 23,* 88–120.

Schleppegrell, M. (1997). Teacher research through dialogic inquiry. *The Canadian Modern Language Review, 54*(1), 68–83.

Schwab, J. J. (1968). The concept of the structure of a discipline. In R. F. Allen, J. V. Fleckenstein, & P. M. Lyon (Eds.), *Inquiry in the social studies: Theory and examples for classroom teachers. Social studies readings no. 2* (pp. 29–41). Washington, DC: National Council for the Social Studies.

Shaver, J. P. (1992). Rationales for issues-centered social studies education. *Social Studies, 83,* 95–99.

Sleeter, C. E. (1995). An analysis of the critiques of multicultural education. In J. Banks & C. A. McGee Banks (Eds.), *Handbook of research on multicultural education* (pp. 81–94). New York: Macmillan.

Spindler, G., & Spindler, L. (1990). A case study of a fifth grade teacher and his classroom: An example of the substance of ethnographic research. *Proceedings of the Qualitative Research Conference* (pp. 5–16). Athens: School of Education, University of Georgia.

Sternberg, R. J. (1994). Answering questions and questioning answers. *Phi Delta Kappan, 76,* 136–138.

Tafoya, E., Sunal, D., & Knecht, P. (1980). Assessing inquiry potential: A tool for curriculum decision makers. *School Science and Mathematics, 80,* 43–48.

Tamir, P. (1983). Inquiry and the science teacher. *Science Education, 67,* 657–672.

Tom, A. R. (1985). Inquiring into inquiry-oriented teacher education. *Journal of Teacher Education, 36,* 35–44.

Uhlhorn, K. W. (1971). The challenge of inquiry teaching in science. *Contemporary Education, 42,* 238–240.

VanSickle, R. L. (1985). Research implications of a theoretical analysis of John Dewey's "How we think." *Theory and Research in Social Education, 13*(3), 1–20.

Weisz, E. (1988). *The hidden curriculum: The elusive side of classroom life in first grade.* (ERIC Document no. ED307991)

Welch, W. W., Klopfer, L. E., Aikenhead, G. S., & Robinson, J. T. (1981). The role of inquiry in science education: Analysis and recommendations. *Science Education, 65*(1), 35–50.

Wilen, W. W. (1979). Are your students ready for inquiry? *The Social Studies, 70,* 170–175.

Wilen, W. W., & McKenrick, P. (1989). Individualized inquiry: Encouraging able students to investigate. *The Social Studies, 80,* 51–54.

Zaharlick, A., & Green, J. L. (1991). Ethnographic research. In J. Flood, J. Jensen, D. Lapp, & J. Squire (Eds.), *Handbook of research in teaching the English language arts* (pp. 1–74). New York: Macmillan.

Zumwalt, K. K. (1989). Beginning professional teachers: The need for a curricular vision of teaching. In M. C. Reynolds (Ed.), *Knowledge base for the beginning teacher* (pp. 173–184). Oxford, UK: Pergamon Press.

13

The Role of the Teacher in Opening Worlds of Inquiry-Driven Learning with Technology

ROBERT J. BRACEWELL, CATHRINE LE MAISTRE,
SUSANNE P. LAJOIE, AND ALAIN BREULEUX
McGill University

For the past several years, we have been studying the changes in teachers' knowledge and beliefs about teaching and learning, and the changes in their teaching practice that accompany the use of the new information and communication technologies as an integral part of their instruction in the classroom. The changes that we have documented describe a radically different classroom situation from the traditional one for both teachers and students, one in which participants' roles (i.e., who is instructing) vary from time to time and from person to person, in which participants' responsibilities and expectations are much more elaborated and varied, and in which knowledge and expertise is shared across teachers and students. In particular, for the purposes of this current volume, the teachers' activities in fostering student learning emerge as very different in pattern, although not in kind, from those seen in the traditional classroom.

The Setting

We have been working with teachers and students in six different classrooms covering Grades 5, 6, and 7. The teachers are all experienced, with an average of 15 years in the profession, and with some prior experience with the use of computers in the classroom. They also volunteered for the project, agreeing to participate after consultation with board administrators and ourselves. The schools are situated in middle- to lower-class, urban, or suburban neighborhoods. The selection of schools and teachers was made in cooperation with our participating boards of education, the Protestant School Board of Greater Montreal (now the English Montreal School Board), and the Khanawake Education Center. The choice of schools in less-than-advantaged communities was a deliberate one, in that we all were interested in examining the impact and use of information technologies in such learning circumstances. As one of the principals characterized his students in a grant application to obtain funding for teacher professional development, "Many of these students can be considered to be at risk in their upcoming studies in secondary school."

Each classroom was equipped with eight to 10 networked, multimedia computers and customary peripherals such as printers, CD-ROM drives, scanners, and cameras. As well, each classroom had at least one computer with access to the Internet. The number of students in each class varied from 25 to 30; thus, there were usually three students per computer in the class.

Sources of Data

We have been collecting evidence on the changes in belief, knowledge, and practice from three sources: (a) audiotaped structured interviews of participating teachers to insure coverage of relevant topics (e.g., the importance of knowing software features, differences in learning associated with computer use, etc.), (b) journal logs recorded by research assistants who were observing classroom interaction and also helping with technical problems, and (c) videotape both of classroom activities using the computers and of interviews of teachers and students on specific topics such as grading practices. We draw on these sources of data in presenting our characterization of the changes that have occurred and the new pattern of teacher activities that has emerged.

Changes in Belief, Knowledge, and Practice

Preliminary Considerations
The best-known effort to document changes in teachers' beliefs, knowledge, and practices when using technology for instruction was part of the Apple Classrooms of Tomorrow (ACOT) Project, which took place from 1985 to 1997. The classrooms in this project were equipped with a significant number of computers and peripherals, typically six to 10 networked computers and two printers. A comprehensive description of teacher changes, together with references to earlier reports, can be found in Fisher, Dwyer, and Yocam (1996) and in Sandholtz, Ringstaff, and Dwyer (1997). This work (Sandholtz et al., 1997) identified five stages in teachers' use of technology for instruction that are described here.

1. Entry: Traditional instructional activities without integrated use of technology, concern for discipline and resource management in student use of technology.
2. Adoption: Use of technology for drill and practice activities.
3. Adaptation: Capitalization on technology effects (e.g., use of editing capabilities of word processor to support student revision skills).

4. Appropriation: Increase in project-based and collaborative activities using technology, increase in self-paced learning.
5. Invention: Integration of direct instruction and student-centered learning activities, emergence of new forms of assessment.

The first three stages represent essentially traditional forms of instruction in using information technology. However, the last two levels include elements that speak directly to inquiry-driven learning based at least in part on students' interests or on the co-construction of curriculum by both students and teachers.

The design of our research was both informed by and built on these findings, in which it was found that teachers frequently experienced difficulty getting past an initial concern with student discipline and using computing resources for more than drill and practice (the Entry and Adoption stages). First, it was clear from outcomes reported in the literature and from our own prior observations of classrooms that the mere presence of computers in the classroom constituted significant competition for teachers who wished to instruct and manage students using didactic techniques (in the apt phrase used by our French-speaking colleagues, "la pédagogie frontale"—face-to-face or frontal pedagogy). To deal with this competition, and coinciding with the introduction of the technology into the classroom, the teachers instituted a cooperative learning approach (Brown & Campione, 1994) that gave the students the skills to work both independently of the teacher and also together in small groups. Second, with the agreement of the boards and teachers, we recruited teachers in pairs from the same schools and at the same or adjacent grade levels so that there would be an accessible source of peer support in the immediate environment. Third, we wanted to document in greater detail than was available in the literature the characteristics of the teachers' changes, in order to provide an account of these changes that was more accessible and informative to both educators and researchers. Therefore, we used a structured interview format with the teachers, together with triangulating sources of evidence provided by the observations of research assistants and by the videotape record of classroom activities.

Initial Reactions

As expected, teachers showed an initial concern with discipline, with resource management, and with direct control of students' computer activities. The following comments are from interviews that were conducted with the teachers three weeks after the classroom startup:

> I find that they get engrossed in what they're doing and they forget and then the noise level just goes up and up and up and up and then if I *do* want their attention I have to turn the lights off and on. . . .

> One thing that I'm a little discouraged with in the writing is that a lot of them are still stuck on the fonts, and the colors and the size of letters and

they're trying to make it pretty and experimenting, and you've got these huge letters on the screen, but they're not really into writing.

(In response to question, "What are they doing particularly well?") Claris-Works and Geometric Golfer. Geometer's Sketchpad. I make up an activity and they have to do it. So they do it, but they're not dying to use it.

However, the teachers also immediately recognized a change in student activity:

It's amazing! I find all of a sudden, some of the students who are normally meek have taken over because that's their area of expertise and some of the others defer to them, and you have to watch that everybody gets a turn.

One thing I've noticed is that they've really developed a pride of authorship, ownership. All of a sudden they can see a product that's fairly decent. You have some kids who always want to hide their work, they never want to read it to the class, now they're sharing it, "come and look at what I wrote."

With three months of experience with the technology in the classroom, the teachers' concerns about discipline and resource management were being resolved:

. . . noise level decreasing because they're learning how to organize their work more carefully. For each project there's a different captain, and they now see that, "aha, if I'm captain next time I want them to listen, so maybe I'd better listen."

. . . in the beginning they're caught up in the mechanics and they all want to get these special effects . . . but once they experience it they go beyond it, and it's OK because they're learning how to use the tools, and then they actually go and do something with it . . . but as long as they're experimenting with the software, I think that's OK.

In large part, we think that this quick resolution of the entry and adoption problems (in comparison to that reported in the ACOT studies, for example) can be attributed to three factors. The first was implementing pedagogical practices, principally cooperative learning techniques, that complemented and served to control the student use of computers. It was not a case of simply dropping the technology into the classrooms and seeing what happened, but of dropping the technology into a pedagogical framework that allowed the technology to be used as an appropriate tool for learning (Laferrière, Bracewell, & Breuleux, 2001). Fortunately, the teachers in our study were experienced enough as practitioners to have a well-defined pedagogical framework and to be able to adapt their framework to use the technology effectively.

The second factor was a decision by the teachers to assign groups of three or four students to a home-base computer. The students of a group carried out most of their work on the home-base computer, stored their personal files on the hard disk, and were responsible for maintaining the applications, file structure, and desktop of the machine. (This is not to say that students worked solely on their home-base; certain computers were specialized for functions such as scanning, and all students used these machines at various times.) Our observation is that this decision considerably facilitated students' uptake and ownership of the use of the computers for learning. Certainly, vandalism in the form of deleting files or interfering with the functionality of systems was at a minimum in these classrooms.

The third factor, related to the second, was the recognition by the teachers that with the introduction of the technology the students were taking on more active and differentiated roles in the academic activity of the classroom. This recognition marked the starting point of a major shift in roles and responsibilities among teachers and students concerning learning.

Major Shifts in Roles and Responsibilities

The concern with control over student computer activities took longer to resolve because it is a manifestation of a larger issue, namely, making sure that the instructional activities of the classroom cover the curriculum that is prescribed for the grade level. In traditional pedagogy, the teacher deals with this issue by taking on control of the presentation and scheduling of curriculum content, as seen in the use of didactic teaching and of seatwork exercises. Of course, the fact that the curriculum is presented by the teacher does not mean that the students take it up. Even in a teacher-centered classroom, there are always differences between the curriculum as intended by the instructional designers, the curriculum as enacted by the teacher, and the curriculum as experienced by the students (for a review, see Doyle, 1992). In classrooms such as the ones we were studying, where students have access to significantly enhanced means of production, these differences become highly salient.

In the case of these classrooms, with their computing technology that permits a far greater degree of autonomy on the part of the students, much of the curriculum is both enacted and experienced by the students. The difference in the curriculum as intended versus the curriculum as enacted and experienced was noted by the research assistants observing the classrooms, both of whom were qualified teachers:

> Alison [the teacher] points out the students like to explore on the computer. It is good for me to remember this as I am so task-oriented I wonder why students are not hurrying to finish. Perhaps they are enjoying learning the software and don't feel the need to rush.

> I think that structure is necessary, but one must also ensure that students are given the opportunity to be creative or incorporate a little bit of themselves in the task.

This tension between the intended and the enacted and experienced curriculum remains an ongoing aspect of instruction in these classrooms, and has been dealt with by the teachers in a number of ways. Within the first three months, the teachers began to reflect on the integration of technology and curriculum:

> I'm going to have to go through all of my different subject areas and see how the computers fit into it.

> . . . so I'll have to see how I can modify my computer program so that the math fits into it.

The difference between action and effect presented in these two comments (i.e., does one modify the curriculum or the computer?) indicates the novelty and uncertainty of dealing with technology in the classroom. In practice, we observed that the teachers usually adapted the computer and its software to the curriculum. The example of the reading record presented immediately below is an instance of this. Of course, differences in accessibility and representation that come with the use of the technology yield their own, often unforeseen, effects.

One of the initial problems with respect to integration of technology and curriculum was that the curriculum content was in the textbooks and worksheets, and not on the computers. To deal with this, the teachers began to capitalize on the growing student expertise and sense of ownership with respect to using the technology, setting up activities using database software to input content to the computers:

> . . . a bit more into projects . . . we have the database [FileMaker Pro] and they're going to build up a file on animals.

> The most spectacular success was Filemaker Pro because we had our reading record on it. . . . It made a big difference to their reading. They read more. . . . I have them go into Filemaker, and they put in the author's name, and all the information, and then they finish reading the book and do a little summary of the literature. . . . And now the kids are looking back at the reading record . . . many of them have looked at other people's records, and looked up a good book.

These types of academic activities, which involved a more active and independent role for students, marked the beginning of a major transition in teachers' perspectives on teaching and learning over the first year, one that we labeled with the phrase, "release of agency." With respect to teaching, release of agency is the psychological decision that accompanies (indeed, allows) a teacher to make the well-documented change in roles from a didactic instructor to a coach who facilitates student academic inquiry (Means & Olson, 1994; see also references in Laferrière, Bracewell, & Breuleux, 2001, Section 2.3). An important consequence of this decision is that the teacher relinquishes the role of sole expert in all matters in the classroom:

> I find that they're learning from each other a little more than I used to think. I used to think it all came from the teacher. I'd stand up there at the front and entertain them. That's fading out a bit.

As long as we have a little head start and basically know what we're doing then we can learn as we go along. I find that preferable to waiting because otherwise you don't start anything. If you're afraid and say, "I really have to know this software inside out just in case somebody asks me a question," you never try anything. The children know we've tried it, this is interesting, and this is what we can do with it. They share because we usually have a little post mortem. We try to stop a few minutes early and they tell the class what they've discovered.

Some of my students this year are experts on it [use of Hypercard] and I'm quite happy to say, "You know more about it than I do. Why don't you go over and help so-and-so or teach me how to do it?"

It appears that one of the more significant requirements for this change in role to be effective is that the teacher is comfortable with the change. Some of the classroom activities that reassure and support teachers with respect to this change in role are explored here in considering evaluation procedures that have evolved in these classrooms.

With respect to learning, another consequence of the release of agency is that it broadens the environment for student learning and provides the context for a profile of student knowledge and skills that, although valued, are not often prominent in traditional classrooms. These include initiative, ownership, cooperation, organization, and deep learning:

Having taught LogoWriter myself to teachers in training at McGill, I could observe that Frances's students' reluctance to explore was much lower than adults. They were readily exploring the commands. (Research assistant notes)

Most of them are really responsible. . . . They have pride of ownership and they realize that the computer is not a toy . . . and that it can do a great deal.

With the computer, moreover, what is important to say is that the interaction [among the students] is smoother, not often filled with little disputes.

. . . one thing that really jumps out is the organization skills. They really learned how to organize themselves and how to plan ahead.

I notice they do things in greater depth. So instead of doing three events in language arts in a certain time, I might only do two. But when I actually look at the output and the enthusiasm, I think they have actually done as much. Previously I'd think, well, I have to cover all this, focusing on the skills that have to be learned.

The classroom environment thus becomes a much more heterogeneous one with respect to student activities than the traditional classroom, one that offers the opportunity for a greater variety in instructional techniques. Fortunately, this opportunity can be realized, because one of the other consequences of release of agency is that it frees the teacher's time to implement this variety.

New Practices and Standards in the Classroom

The freeing up of time allows teachers to be more responsive to student academic needs, consulting with individuals and groups, helping them to set priorities, guiding student learning, and assessing student performance and learning in new ways. Four typical instances of interaction from a Grade 6 class follow. The first two illustrate the changed role of the teacher in guiding and supporting student learning, and in evaluating this learning. The third and fourth interactions illustrate the changed role of the students in adopting the kinds of evaluation that have been modeled by the teacher, and in insuring that they understand the material that they have been working on. Together, these four instances demonstrate a distribution across the classroom of responsibility for learning and evaluation that serves to maintain the integrity of the inquiry process that results in learning.

Guiding Student Learning

In the first illustration, students were working in groups at the computers on projects in science and social science. The teacher moved from group to group, assessing progress and offering suggestions on what resources to access. One of the students was working on a project on the physical geography of Europe and the teacher suggested that he prepare a map showing the major mountain ranges. The true flavor of the interaction can be seen in the transcription of the teacher and student conversation:

Student: Where can I get a picture of that?
Teacher: Well, start with your atlas, and we d-, we do have an atlas on- on disk but um, it may not show what you want it to show.
Student: C-can we add the mountains, like put the mountains like (on it?).
Teacher: There's a good idea. I bet there's a way to do that.
Student: Does anybody know here in class?
Teacher: Well why don't you start working on the problem, and if I find anyone who can help you with it I'll send them to you. OK?

There are a number of noteworthy aspects of this interaction. First, the student was thinking of a computer-based presentation from the beginning, and in response to the teacher's doubt about whether the needed information exists in soft copy, asked if the mountains can be put in over an existing map. Second, the teacher immediately acknowledged this request as an innovative and worthwhile goal. Third, the student invoked potential help with this goal from other students who may know how to do it, reflecting an awareness of the distributed knowledge in the class. Fourth, the teacher acknowledged the distributed knowledge and undertook to try to bring it to the student. Over the course of the next half-hour, the teacher checked with the student at about 10-minute intervals to ascertain the progress that he was making.

Evaluating Student Learning

In the second illustration, a group of students was working on a natural science project on snakes. Again the teacher was moving from group to group assessing progress on the projects. He examined the content of the screen for this group's work, and then initiated a conversation with the group, asking:

Teacher:	What are vipers?
Student 1:	Uh, vipers are a kind of snake. Uh, some of the vipers have horns on their side.
Student 2:	Two horns like this.
Student 1:	Well, not horns, but horns like this.
Teacher:	OK.
Student 1:	Some, some of them are called tr-true vipers.
Teacher:	And are they poisonous, or are some?
Student 2:	They're poisonous.
Student 1:	They're poisonous.
Teacher:	(reading from the screen) True vipers live in Africa, Asia, Europe, and East Indies.

Again, there are a number of noteworthy aspects about this interaction. First, the teacher examined the information that the students had entered into their project files in order to determine the progress students were making. Second, he asked the direct question of the students, "What are vipers?" Thus he used this activity as an opportunity to evaluate the students' understanding of the information they had been entering, and to insure that the project information was not simply a product of copying and pasting from other sources. The teacher then returned to examining the information on the screen. Third, the interaction shows an increased integration of instructional and evaluative activities in these classes, in which the types of evaluation routines are not simply summative but are formative in guiding student learning.

Student Uptake of Evaluation Procedures

One of the most interesting outcomes of this kind of evaluation activity by the teacher was that it came to serve as a model for student interaction around project matters. In this third illustration, a group of students were conducting a peer evaluation of another group's science project on plant reproduction. One of the authors of the project also was present to provide information. The evaluation was carried out by means of a rubric that had been jointly designed by the teacher and the students, and consisted of criteria such as layout and functionality, content, and spelling and grammar. The evaluation team was working with the criterion of spelling and grammar at the time of the following interaction:

Evaluator 1:   OK, now spelling and grammar. Let's look into your information.
Evaluator 2:   We have to look at the information. Let's go to pollination.
Evaluator 1:   All right. (Reads silently.) What is an ather (*sic*)?
Author: An anther? It's the female part of the flower.
Evaluator 2:   Is it ather or anther?
Author: Anther, anther.
Evaluator 2:   But it says ather.
Evaluator 1:   Spelling mistake. OK, well we won't take that much off so don't
                 worry.

What is noteworthy about this interaction is that, in the midst of evaluating spelling and grammar, the evaluator asks a knowledge question of the author. That is, the students have adopted the same practice as the teacher in asking questions that assess the understanding and knowledge of the author concerning the information that has been entered into the project.

Student Responsibility for Comprehension

In the fourth illustration, another group of students also was working at the computers, in this instance on a social-science project. The teacher was moving from group to group when one of them requested help with the meaning of a word in a reference text, which the students were using. The interaction was the following:

Student 1:   Mr. T., do you have another word for abolish?
Teacher: OK, give me the sentence (looking at the monitor screen)
Student 1:   OK. (reading) "By 1966 the religious courts had abolished . . ." But
               we want to put it in . . .
Teacher: Abolished what?
Student 1:   " . . . abolished their duties, assumed (?) by civil courts"
Student 2:   Because what if anybody doesn't understand the word. We want
               them to understand it.
Teacher: OK. It means that it, its, they uh closed down . . .
Student 1:   The religious courts closed down.
Teacher: Right, or stopped working.
Student 1:   OK. The religious courts closed down (reaching for the keyboard).

The noteworthy aspect about this interaction is that the students were aware that they, and perhaps others, would have problems with the word abolish in this context and sought the teacher's help. It may have been that they did not understand the word, and it may have been that the syntax of the source material was problematic . . ."abolish" is a transitive verb which takes a direct object, but in this context the object noun phrase was partially reflexive on the subject of the verb, that is, "their duties" referred to the duties of the religious courts themselves. This reflexivity was not well signaled by the syntax ("their own duties" would have been better). The teacher's suggested translation may have been a little broad, but it did capture the essence of the situation. The interaction indicates the distribution across the class of standards of responsibility and accountability with respect to the knowledge that students are mastering and working with.

Discussion and Conclusion

The instructional activity that was seen in these classrooms marks a different type of pedagogy from traditional didactic instruction and seat-work activities. It is achieved through support from a number of factors. One of these was the technology itself, which provided students with representational tools that, in turn, allowed them to create explicit and public works that could be accessed by others, both students and teachers. Just as important was placing the use of the technology within a set of pedagogical practices that enabled its effective use. Especially important is the use of cooperative learning techniques and the distribution of responsibility and expertise across the members of the class. The adoption by the students of standards of comprehension and accountability for their learning that were seen in the last two illustrations should reassure both critics who fear excessive and mindless copying of material using information technologies (e.g., Armstrong & Casement, 1998) and advocates who would like to see a greater role for student-led investigation in classrooms (e.g., White, Shimoda, & Frederiksen, 2000). Finally, a consequence of these factors being in place is that the teachers had time to engage in individualized instruction for both single students and groups, and in particular were able to institute ongoing support for and evaluation of student progress.

Furthermore, it is clear from an examination of the pedagogy, that the teachers were not only addressing the cognitive demands of the students, they were also attending to their motivational and affective needs (Cordova & Lepper, 1996; Lepper, Woolverton, Mumme, & Gurtner, 1993). This was achieved in large part through the distribution of responsibility across the classroom, which provided students with a sense of ownership of academic activities, as seen in the adoption of the teachers' evaluation practices (see third illustration earlier in this chapter). It also was achieved through the interactions instituted by the teachers, as can be seen especially in the first illustration, where the teacher both guided the student toward the information resources that could prove useful and also praised the student's initiative in undertaking the mapping task.

Although the analysis of these interactions is preliminary, it is still possible to extract key instructional characteristics of situations that can lead to significant change in what is learned in these evolving, project-based investigations. First, the information provided by the teachers often occurs "on demand" because it is initiated by the students. This is in keeping with, and is a consequence of, students assuming a more independent role in the classroom for their learning. Second, in these situations, evaluation skills become a key component of tutoring. The teachers frequently began an interaction with a series of questions to the student or group of students that served to bring the teacher into the context of the student activity. This is a consequence of the evolving nature of the student projects, which requires the teachers to update themselves as to the characteristics of the projects and the students' plans for further development.

The impediment to inquiry-based learning in an environment that is rich in information technology include those that are present in traditional pedagogy, as well as the apparent distractions of the technology itself, both hard and soft. However, the introduction of information technology, if suitably mediated by the teacher, can also provide opportunities not easily matched by other instructional settings. We noticed an interesting difference between how teachers and students viewed the information technology that was present in the classroom. For the teachers, this technology was seen to be primarily an information presentation device (to put it simplistically, the closest electronic technology would be the television). It was this perspective that led the teachers initially to be very concerned with what CD-ROMs were to be purchased for the classroom. For the students, however, this technology was primarily a production device, to be used literally to make representations and presentations. This production stance underlay (to the disappointment of the teachers) the students' initial fascination with font size and colors of letters. It also provides the reason that the most used pieces of software were the word-processing program, and the object-oriented drawing program. The students' achievements in representing and displaying their knowledge were a direct result of having the means to do so using these two types of software.

The need for the teacher to be comfortable with the technology is also an important hurdle, but our experience in this study shows that the teacher does not have to master every component of the technology or function of the software. Rather, the solution to the problem of using software competently that was adopted by our teachers was to be part of the technological expertise that was distributed across students and teachers. This solution allowed the teachers to focus more frequently on their irreplaceable roles, for example, in guiding students' question asking and in the integration of evaluation, especially formative evaluation, with the ongoing experience.

In further research on this type of interaction, it would be worthwhile to gather information on how teachers respond to individual differences as seen in prior knowledge and interests of the students, on the depth and extent of scaffolding that is achieved in this way (e.g., in the first illustration, what were the characteristics of the follow-up interaction with the student concerning the making of the map?), and on the effects of this type of interaction for what students learn and the practices that they adopt for furthering their learning. In this manner, we can more carefully observe the relationship between the interaction process and learning in classroom activities that are initially ill-structured. Perhaps the most intriguing aspect of this research is that it starts to define a model of teaching in learning communities where participants deal with evolving task definitions and use information technologies to support task activities. Even though the learning tasks are ill-structured, the instructional interactions appear well structured in terms of the types of interventions and evaluations the teachers make when they intervene to support learning.

References

Armstrong, A., & Casement, C. (1998), *The child and the machine: Why computers put children's education at risk.* Toronto, ON: Key Porter Books.

Brown, A. L., & Campione, J. C. (1994). Guided discovery in a community of learners. In K. McGilly (Ed.), *Classroom lessons: Integrating cognitive theory and classroom practice* (pp. 229–270). Cambridge, MA: MIT Press.

Cordova, D. I., & Lepper, M. R. (1996). Intrinsic motivation and the process of learning: Beneficial effects of contextualization, personalization, and choice. *Journal of Educational Psychology, 88,* 715–730.

Doyle, W. (1992). Curriculum and pedagogy. In P. W. Jackson (Ed.), *Handbook of research on curriculum: A project of the American Educational Research Association* (pp. 486–516). New York: Macmillan.

Fisher, C., Dwyer, D. C., & Yocam, K. (Eds.). (1996). *Education and technology: Reflections on computing in classrooms.* San Francisco: Jossey-Bass.

Laferrière, T., Bracewell, R. J., & Breuleux, A. (2001). The emerging contribution of online resources and tools to K-12 classroom learning and teaching: An update. Retrieved August 19, 2005, from http://www.schoolnet.ca/snab/e/reports/snab_reports.asp

Lepper, M. R., Woolverton, M., Mumme, D. L., & Gurtner, J.-L. (1993). Motivational techniques of expert human tutors: Lessons for the design of computer-based tutors. In S. P. Lajoie & S. J. Derry (Eds.), *Computers as cognitive tools* (pp. 75–106). Hillsdale, NJ: Erlbaum.

Means, B., & Olson, K. (1994). Tomorrow's schools: Technology and reform in partnership. In B. Means (Ed.), *Technology and education reform: The reality behind the promise* (pp. 191–222). San Francisco: Jossey-Bass.

Sandholtz, J. H., Ringstaff, C., & Dwyer, D. C. (1997). *Teaching with technology: Creating student-centered classrooms.* New York: Teachers College Press.

White, B. Y., Shimoda, T. A., & Frederiksen, J. R. (2000). Facilitating students' inquiry learning and metacognitive development through modifiable software advisers. In S. P. Lajoie (Ed.), *Computers as cognitive tools, volume two: No more walls* (pp. 97–132). Mahwah, NJ: Erlbaum.

14

Promoting Authentic Inquiry in the Sciences: Challenges Faced in Redefining University Students' Scientific Epistemology

DEBORAH L. BUTLER, CAROL POLLOCK,
KATHY M. NOMME, & JOANNE NAKONECHNY
University of British Columbia

Calls for incorporating inquiry into science curricula have been issued for well over 30 years (DeBoer, 1991) and many benefits have been associated over time with students' participation in active, inquiry-based activities (Minner, Levy, & Century, 2004). Unfortunately, however, research consistently shows that, although there are pockets of innovation (e.g., Hofstein, Nahum, & Shore, 2001; Tamir, Stavy, & Ratner, 1998), science curricula at all educational levels may not sufficiently incorporate features of authentic scientific inquiry (e.g., Basey, Mendelow, & Ramos, 2000; Chinn & Malhotra, 2002). The result is that students may develop inadequate or incorrect conceptions about science, and about their roles as learners in science, with the potential to undermine their meaningful engagement in scientific activity and development of scientific literacy (Carey & Smith, 1993; Haury, 1993). Indeed, Chinn and Malhotra (2002) cautioned that simple, nonauthentic inquiry tasks prevalent in much instruction "may not only fail to help students learn to reason scientifically; they may also foster a nonscientific epistemology in which scientific reasoning is viewed as simple, certain, algorithmic, and focused at a surface level of observation" (p. 190).

In this chapter, we describe one attempt to overcome this problem in the Faculty of Science at the University of British Columbia (UBC). In 1994, biology instructors at UBC seized an opportunity to dramatically restructure the 1st-year laboratory experience. Moving away from experiments that focused narrowly on illustrating concepts or implementing procedures, the new laboratory experience was designed to engage students in authentic inquiry. We describe herein benefits and challenges that we have observed since the new laboratory course was implemented, drawing insights both from our experiences and on results from a systematic investigation recently undertaken to evaluate the course (Pollock et al., 2005).

We start by examining why authentic, inquiry-oriented instruction is so central to science education and by linking calls for inquiry-oriented instruction to emerging learning theories. These discussions establish a framework for our consideration of benefits and challenges associated with inquiry-oriented instruction. In subsequent sections, we briefly review challenges and benefits observed in prior research before introducing our own project and findings. We conclude by discussing implications for providing inquiry-oriented laboratory experiences for first-year undergraduate students in science.

The Centrality of Authentic Inquiry to Science Education

The images that many people have of science and how it works are often distorted. The myths and stereotypes that young people have about science are not dispelled when science teaching focuses narrowly on the laws, concepts, and theories of science. Hence, the study of science as a way of knowing needs to be made explicit in the curriculum. (American Association for the Advancement of Science, AAAS, 1993, p. 2)

In the United States, national bodies concerned with scientific research are consistently calling for a revision of science curricula so as to engage students in "scientific investigations that progressively approximate good science" (AAAS, 1993, p. 6; see also National Research Council, NRC, 1996, 2000). These national bodies argue that the goal of science education is to create a scientifically literate citizenry that understands how science works, can participate in scientifically driven discourse, and can follow the developments in science over time (AAAS, 1993; NRC, 1996). As a means of fostering scientific literacy, calls have been issued to involve students in authentic inquiry experiences across educational levels (AAAS, 1993; Chinn & Malhotra, 2002; NRC, 1996, 2000). For example, the Center for Science, Mathematics, and Engineering Education (1999) of the NRC recently issued a report calling for an ambitious revision of science education at the postsecondary level. As part of their call to action, the Center recommends a focus on inquiry not only for science majors but for all undergraduate students. They suggest that postsecondary educators should be concerned with whether "we actively engage students in science, mathematics, engineering, and technology in ways similar to how we work as scientists, mathematicians, or engineers" (p. 2).

What is authentic, scientific inquiry? The scientific method is not as rule-bound, recipe-like, or procedural as some descriptions might suggest (AAAS, 1993; Friedrichsen, 2001; NRC, 1996). Instead, real scientists engage in a dynamic, recursive cycle of activities (see Figure 14.1). These activities are highly interrelated and include (a) defining a problem and framing questions; (b) designing an approach for studying the problem, considering not only features of effective design (e.g., variables and controls) but also time and resources available; (c) conducting experiments, including selecting and setting up of equipment; (d) representing, analyzing, and interpreting data; (e) testing, extending, or generating theoretical accounts, which often includes creating rich explanations of expected and unexpected findings and/or analogical reasoning (Chinn & Malhotra, 2002; Dunbar, 2000); and (f) subjecting methods and findings to criticism by a community of researchers (Chinn & Malhotra, 2002). In authentic inquiry, investigators often revise one or more of problem statements, questions, and methods in follow-up investigations, thereby reentering the inquiry cycle back at the beginning (White & Frederiksen, 1998).

Educational researchers suggest that, to promote authentic inquiry in educational settings, inquiry-oriented instruction should involve students "in the investigative nature of science" (Haury, 1993, p. 2). Key to establishing authentic inquiry for students is providing them with opportunities to take control over the recursive cycle of inquiry activities (Friedrichsen, 2001; Haury, 1993; Minner et al., 2004). Unfortunately, unlike "the real thing," in experiments within high school science curricula usually "the question to be investigated is decided by the teacher, not the investigators; what apparatus to use, what data to collect, and how to organize the data are also decided by the teacher (or the lab manual); time is not made available for repetitions; or, when things are not working out, for revising the experiment; the results are not presented to other investigators for criticism; and, to top it off, the correct answer is known ahead of time" (American Association for the Advancement of Science, 1993, p. 6).

Educational change around inquiry learning has been slow to take place across educational levels. In their analysis of the quality of inquiry tasks in textbooks for middle school or upper elementary students, Chinn and Malhotra (2002) found little evidence of 14 features of authentic inquiry. They concluded that "inquiry activities in most textbooks capture few if any of the cognitive processes of authentic science" (p. 204). Similarly, Basey et al. (2000) assessed the laboratory curricula at six randomly selected community colleges in Colorado on a seven-point scale reflecting students' active involvement in what they defined as the basic components of inquiry (i.e., problems, variables, methods, performance, data analysis, interpretations, extensions). They found that the average number of components included in weekly laboratory curricula was quite low (from 1.6 to 2.8 components). Clearly, more work is needed to integrate key features of authentic inquiry into curricula across educational levels.

As depicted in Figure 14.1, authentic inquiry also generally occurs within a research community where new knowledge is socially constructed (Chinn & Malhotra, 2002). Not only do researchers subject reports of research to criticism by peers, a key feature of the inquiry cycle, but they also often work within collaborative teams to which individuals ideally contribute diverse perspectives

A Community of Researchers

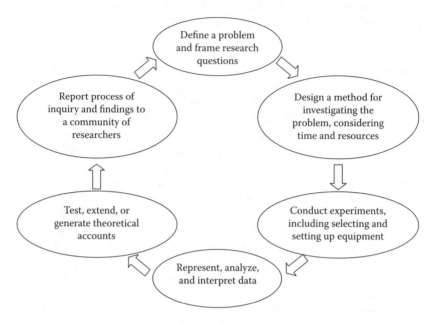

Figure 14.1   Dynamic, recursive cycles of authentic scientific inquiry.

(Chinn & Mahlhotra, 2002; Dunbar, 2000; White & Frederiksen, 1998). Thus, to promote scientific literacy, it is critical that science educators engage students in authentic and collaborative scientific processes for generating and solving problems (White & Frederiksen, 1998).

Active, Constructive, and Inquiry-Driven Learning

As described earlier, calls for inquiry-oriented science criteria have been grounded in an analysis of the nature of authentic scientific processes. But calls for inquiry-oriented instruction are also fueled by emerging theoretical perspectives on learning (Bransford, Brown, & Cocking, 2000; Harris & Graham, 1994; Paris, Byrnes, & Paris, 2001; Vygotsky, 1978). These models emphasize students' active roles in constructing knowledge through experience and the benefits of social mediation in students' development of new understandings (Bransford et al., 2000; Butler, 1998b; Harris & Pressley, 1991; Stone, 1998; Vygotsky, 1978)

Constructivist theory, for example, describes how prior knowledge is used to build frameworks for making meaning out of new information (Harris & Graham, 1994). The relevance of constructivist theory to teaching in science was demonstrated by Bransford and colleagues (2000). They described a science class in which students' prior conceptions interfered with a more scientific understanding of the earth as spherical rather than flat. Students incorporated new spherical information about earth into a revised mental model which included a pancake earth on top of a spherical one. Bransford and colleagues concluded that, "The children's construction of their new understandings has been guided by a model of the earth that helped them explain how they could stand or walk upon its surface, and a spherical earth did not fit their mental model" (p. 10). Including learners in inquiry learning affords them opportunities to test and extend current mental models in light of new information.

At the same time, it is not only students' conceptions about scientific concepts that affect what they take away from instruction. Students' conceptions about science as a field of study and about learning in science also shape the way in which they approach inquiry-oriented tasks. For example, Cartier (1997) found that students' differing conceptions about learning in a problem-based learning environment (i.e., as accumulation of details to be used later vs. development of more meaningful understanding) affected their selection of learning strategies and the quality of constructed knowledge. Educators must attend to students' initial and emerging beliefs about science and science learning if they are to support effective learning.

Thus, aside from mirroring authentic scientific processes, another compelling rationale for involving students in inquiry-based learning is that doing so provides a means for students to actively and reflectively construct rich understandings in science (Carey & Smith, 1993; Eilam & Aharon, 2003). Rather than fostering rote memory of disconnected concepts or procedural skills, engaging students in inquiry learning has been associated with students' actively searching for and constructing conceptual and procedural knowledge (Haury, 1993; Rivarola, Bergese, Garcia, & Fernandez, 1997; Zion et al., 2004) and developing richer understanding about the nature of science and scientific processes more generally (Haury, 1993; Zion et al., 2004).

Emerging learning theories also replace images of passive learners waiting to be filled with knowledge with images of students actively managing their own learning (Bertrand, 1995). Learners who self-regulate (i.e., manage) their own learning are more engaged, more independent, and more motivated because they are participants in a learning cycle (Zimmerman & Schunk, 2001). Indeed, models of self-regulated learning have been used to characterize multiple factors that impact how students engage in academic work (e.g., Butler & Cartier, 2005a; Butler & Winne, 1995; Corno, 1993, 1994; Zimmerman, 1994). Over time, these models have evolved to describe how students' approaches to learning are shaped, for better or for worse, by a combination of cognitive, metacognitive (i.e., learners' knowledge about and management of learning), affective, and motivational processes.

For example, Wolters (1998) described successful, self-regulated learners as those who set adaptive learning goals (Pintrich, 2000; Schunk, 1994), who draw on large numbers of cognitive and metacognitive strategies in order to achieve their objectives, and who modify strategies in response to challenges or changes in learning requirements (Butler & Winne, 1995; Zimmerman, 1989). Conversely, for less successful students, problems in self-regulation may arise, for example, because of low motivation, the intrusion of negative emotions, misconceptions about learning requirements, lack of awareness of good learning strategies, or lack of attention to monitoring outcomes and adjusting learning activities accordingly (Butler, 1998a, 1998c; Butler & Cartier, 2004b; Butler & Winne, 1995).

Finally, while emphasizing students' active roles in constructing and managing their own learning, emerging perspectives on learning also foreground the role of social influences (e.g., mediated instruction) in students' construction of new understandings (e.g., Vygotsky, 1978). With inquiry-oriented approaches in science, researchers have found that providing scaffolded support for students' engagement in inquiry facilitates learning about scientific concepts and processes (e.g., Eilam & Aharon, 2003; Tamir et al., 1998; Zion et al., 2004).

Benefits and Challenges Associated With Inquiry-Oriented Instruction

In the past 30 years, much research has been done linking variations of inquiry-oriented instruction to a variety of outcomes. For example, in an ambitious review of research since 1984, the Center for Science Education in the United States is examining outcomes associated with inquiry-based learning at the K to 12 levels. In a preliminary report on this research, Minner et al. (2004) described that, across 477 studies on inquiry-oriented instruction in science, the most commonly reported gains for students were in science content knowledge, inquiry content knowledge, attitudes toward science instruction, and attitudes toward science. In his review, Haury (1993) linked inquiry-based learning for middle-school students with development not only of important procedural skills such as laboratory skills, graphing, and interpreting data but also of conceptual knowledge, critical thinking, positive attitudes toward science, understanding of scientific processes, and scientific literacy.

Consistent with these reviews, recent research on inquiry-oriented curricula has documented gains for students in self-efficacy (i.e., perceptions of control over outcomes) and self-confidence (Friedrichsen, 2001), attitudes toward science (Friedrichsen, 2001), biology content learned (Wilden, Crowther, Gubanich, & Cannon, 2002), critical, independent, or analytical thinking (Hofstein et al., 2001; Rivarola et al., 1997), managing learning (Eilam & Aharon, 2003; Tamir et al., 1998; Zion et al., 2004), and understanding scientific processes (Zion et al., 2004). For example, Zion et al. (2004) described a curriculum in Israel (Biomind) designed to help students "learn about the nature of science via scientific inquiry" (p. 59). Students reported that the course contributed to their acquisition of inquiry skills such as planning and drawing conclusions. As one student explained, "I experienced scientific thinking and all the processes that a researcher goes through during his research—such as repeating the experiment, changing the experiment, examining additional theoretical material" (p. 66). Students also noted they had learned how to write up a scientific research report.

At the same time, recent research has highlighted challenges associated with implementing inquiry-oriented instruction. For example, Friedrichsen (2001) described an inquiry-based biology course for prospective elementary teachers (nonscience majors). She found that, although students eventually built increased self-confidence, felt more empowered as potential teachers, and enjoyed the focus on their own learning, many initially had reservations about the shift in instructional methods. Similarly, although Chin and Chia (2004) found benefits associated with allowing groups of ninth-grade students in Singapore to self-generate and investigate ill-structured problems, they found that a handful of students did not appreciate the move away from more teacher-centered lessons. These students "were not used to thinking hard and deeply about such issues and were unwilling to try" (p. 74). Other problems arose when group dynamics were less than optimal or group discussions strayed off-topic and when student-defined research topics were framed too narrowly.

Eilam and Aharon (2003) found that self-regulated engagement of ninth-grade students was facilitated by providing abundant time (an entire year) for students to complete an inquiry-oriented project, assigning a complex task, and shifting responsibility to students for defining, managing, and directing the project. They noted, however, that lower achieving and higher achieving students participated in the project differently. For example, higher achievers assigned themselves homework to deepen understandings or acquire new information, whereas lower achievers chose homework mostly to just finish assignments or repeat exercises. Lower achieving students also evidenced lower self-efficacy, lower motivation, and less effective emotion and motivation management (Corno, 1993, 1994).

In sum, previous research suggests that successful implementation of inquiry-oriented curricula is likely to lead to positive outcomes but may at the same time be quite challenging. Challenges can include student resistance to increased expectations for active thinking and problem solving, and problematic group interactions (Chin & Chia, 2004). The quality of students' approaches to learning may be tied to different patterns in self-confidence, emotion control, and motivation (Butler & Cartier, 2005a; Eilam & Aharon, 2003). And the persistence of prior conceptions about academic work may lead to the selection of ineffective approaches to learning (Butler & Cartier, 2004b; Cartier, 1997, 2002; Cartier, Plante, & Tardif, 2001).

Implementing an Inquiry-Oriented Curriculum at the Postsecondary Level

Teachers and researchers across educational levels have been responding to calls for inquiry-oriented curricula in science education. At the postsecondary level, science organizations as well as individual disciplines have developed resources and engaged in research studies on inquiry teaching. For example, the U.S. National Science Teachers Association (2001) has published a journal collection on investigative approaches to college science teaching. Inquiry-oriented curricula have also appeared across a range of disciplines, including geology (Leech, Howell, & Egger, 2004), chemistry (Lewis & Lewis, 2005; Rudd, Greenbowe, Hand, & Legg, 2001), and biophysical chemistry (Hutchinson, Bretz, Mettee, &

Smiley, 2005). Physiology labs have been developed in which students focus on real phenomena and are guided toward investigations that stretch their research skills (Kolkhorst, Mason, DiPasquale, Patterson, & Buono, 2001). At Michigan State University, students in an introductory course in molecular biology develop questions and then devise experiments to test their hypotheses (Luckie, Maleszewski, Loznak, & Krha, 2004). Researchers at the University of Nevada, Reno found that, when contrasted to traditional delivery methods, inquiry-oriented teaching made a significant difference in the amount of biological content learned (Wilden et al., 2002).

Following on these trends, the University of British Columbia (UBC) has revised its curriculum for 1st-year biology to include an inquiry-oriented laboratory experience, Biology 140. Previously, biology laboratories at UBC were set up to introduce students to the kingdoms of organisms. Activities were planned so that students could observe as many examples of different organisms as possible in the time available. Instructors provided questions and comments that directed students to relate structure and function or consider adaptations for survival. Students made detailed drawings with complete notes (often graded), and, on examinations, were required to identify organisms and provide accurate information about them. When an experimental approach was used, the exercises typically provided step-by-step, detailed procedures; data were analyzed by drawing graphs and inferring conclusions, usually by referring to course texts for explanations; and outcomes were known in advance. Over time, our observations were that these practices seemed to promote passive, reproduction-focused learning by students.

In contrast, the goal in Biology 140 is to support students' learning about the process of science by clarifying what science is and by providing opportunities for students to participate in the scientific method as practiced by scientists. Laboratory experiences engage students not only in designing, conducting, and analyzing experimental data but also in other aspects of authentic inquiry such as working in groups, communicating results to others, and peer review—all in a biological context. The six specific objectives in Biology 140 are for students: (a) to study the effect of one abiotic factor on a specific organism and to discuss this effect within the context of the environment in which the organism lives; (b) to design and conduct an experiment with appropriate hypotheses, controls, and replicates; (c) to analyze and interpret data; (d) to write a scientific report in the style of a journal article; (e) to present results orally to peers, and (f) to work effectively with a group on a project.

Biology 140 aims to facilitate students' taking ownership of their projects, being active participants in their learning, and focusing on the process of science rather than specific biological content. The eight-week guided program allows students to proceed stepwise through the process of the scientific method with regular feedback from instructors and peers and provides them with many opportunities to revise and repeat their experiments. The weekly concepts introduced in the course (see Table 14.1) are consistent with parameters for authentic inquiry (Chinn & Malhotra, 2002). The use of a sequential introduction of new ideas and

Table 14.1 Weekly Schedule of Biology 140

Week	Topics	Assignments	Key Features of Authentic Inquiry
Week 1	Introduction to ecosystems (biological context), division into groups and assignment of organisms, observation of living organisms.	Paragraph describing organism, library tutorial (online), research report, experimental design (online).	Group work, library research, making careful observations and combining them with a writing assignment.
Week 2	Experimental design, equipment review, development of biological questions, peer review of descriptive paragraphs.	Prepare oral proposal.	Develop questions, define a specific problem, design an experimental procedure, peer review.
Week 3	Experiment proposal. Group oral presentations followed by question and answer period.	Final proposal handed in. Students begin work on their "understanding the response" paragraphs.	Oral presentation with peer review, consider time and resources required to complete experiment.
Week 4	Trial 1 of experiment. Post-experiment modifications made and handed in as experiment summaries.	Data analysis (online).	Perform, analyze, revise, experiment.
Week 5	Trial 2 of experiment. Students hand in final experiment summaries.	Data interpretation, data analysis (own experiment), journal article review, peer review of "understanding the response" paragraphs.	Data analysis, library research, peer review.
Week 6	Data analysis (one-on-one group and instructor).	Prepare for lab exam, work on final reports (group oral and individual written report in the style of a journal article).	Critical analysis of data from own experiment, integrated with and interpreted in light of other scientists' research.
Week 7	Lab exam. Open book. New scenarios to design experiments around and analyze data.		Extend specific knowledge of own experiment to new situations.
Week 8	Group orals followed by question and answer period.	Written reports handed in.	Written assignment in format of journal article, oral presentation with peer review.

introductory exercises and assignments for all students maintains the open-ended aspect of authentic inquiry, and, at the same time, scaffolds support for students' learning (Eilam & Aharon, 2003; Fransson, 1977; Tamir et al., 1998).

The 2,000 students who enroll in first-year biology classes at UBC each year are ethnically diverse and include recent immigrants and international students. The majority of students in first-year science are from urban centers. Most students have recently graduated from British Columbia (BC) high schools. Although the scope and depth of biology course content varies from high school to high school, all students graduating from BC high schools must write provincial examinations. To be successfully admitted to first-year science at UBC, students must obtain high scores on these examinations and achieve an average of at least 89%. Thus, although incoming students at UBC are from diverse backgrounds, what they have in common is their success in high school and a belief that they are capable of continued success in university.

Contrary to the expectations of these high-achieving high school graduates, we have observed over the past decade that first-year science students typically suffer a drop in achievement at university. Students appear unprepared for the independent study that is expected of them at the postsecondary level. They tend to focus on learning specific content rather than underlying theories and processes. Although the students are well trained in memorizing, they appear unprepared to evaluate, synthesize, or apply information. Encouragingly, an initial review of outcomes associated with Biology 140 suggested that participants suffered lower failure rates (7%) as compared to those students in large lecture-based courses (10 to 15%). It also seemed that components of Biology 140 assisted students in transitioning from surface to deeper learning. These observations led us to initiate a collaborative research project to investigate these patterns further.

The Biology 140 Collaborative Project

Two goals motivated our collaborative research project. These were: (a) to investigate attitudes toward and perceptions about learning in science that students brought to first-year biology that might shape their approaches to inquiry-based learning; and (b) to examine how participation in Biology 140 influenced students' attitudes about, perceptions of, and approaches to learning in biology. In this chapter, we do not provide a full empirical report of our project (for more information, see Butler, Cartier, Pollock, Nomme, & Gagnon, 2005; Pollock et al., 2005). Instead, we provide an overview of selected findings as they relate to the benefits and challenges associated with engaging first-year biology students in inquiry-oriented instruction.

To investigate our two central research questions, a multidisciplinary team was assembled. Collaborators were drawn from the Faculties of Science and Education and included individuals with experience in varying types of research methodologies. The team constructed a research design comprising multiple, complementary strategies (see Butler et al., 2005; Pollock et al., 2005). As the project unfolded across two terms in the 2003–2004 academic year, three types of methodological tools were used in combination: (a) a self-report questionnaire, (b) course evaluations, and (c) focus group interviews.

The self-report questionnaire (Butler & Cartier, 2005b) was used to assess students' perceptions about factors related to their self-regulated engagement in an inquiry-oriented project (e.g., motivation, emotion, cognition, and metacognition; see Butler & Cartier, 2004a; Cartier & Butler, 2004). The questionnaire was administered to intact classes of students enrolled in a lecture-based course, Biology 121, at the beginning and end of each term. We created two types of samples from this set of participants, with our two main research purposes in mind. First, in each term, we analyzed pretest data from Biology 121 students with the goal of investigating perceptions about learning that first-year biology students bring to instructional contexts. Second, to evaluate benefits and challenges associated with taking Biology 140, we extracted data from a subset of students to create two comparison groups: (a) students taking Biology 140 concurrently with Biology 121 and (b) students who were neither enrolled in nor had ever taken Biology 140. In the first term, 267 students completed the pretest questionnaire. Pretest and posttest data were available for 68 of these students (18 in Biology 140 and 48 not in Biology 140). In the second term, 474 students completed the pretest questionnaire. Pretest and posttest data were available for 110 of these Biology 121 students (87 also in Biology 140 and 23 not also in Biology 140).

The second source of data we drew on were course evaluations collected each term at the end of Biology 140. At the end of the first term, 484 Biology 140 students were asked the following questions as part of their course evaluation: "Do you think that participation in Biology 140 has affected the way you think about learning in biology? If so, how has it affected your thinking?" Their responses were systematically coded to define the major themes in students' responses. For the evaluations in term 2, a 13-item questionnaire was generated that reflected the key themes derived from the thematic analysis from term 1. Students ($n = 1015$) rated the extent to which each statement was true of them on a five-point scale. Although we could not compare results for individuals from the questionnaire and evaluation data because evaluations were completed anonymously, these two sources of information provided converging evidence related to challenges and benefits for students.

The final source of data was focus-group interviews. The methodology employed for this part of the project drew on a qualitative research tradition. Ragin (1994), Neuman (1997), and Hesse-Biber and Levy (2004) concurred that quantitative techniques concentrate data to develop broader understanding of the phenomena under study, while qualitative techniques augment data to provide a clearer focus on key aspects of the phenomena. In our project, qualitative research provided us with the capacity to elaborate research questions and broaden our critical understanding of findings from the questionnaire data.

Focus groups are a recognized, highly useful qualitative method employed in a variety of academic areas including communications research, education, health research, and feminist research (Litoselliti, 2003). In the case of our project, two focus groups were constructed in order to listen to Biology 140 students talking about their learning experiences in inquiry-oriented biology laboratories. These students participated in both pretest and posttest focus-group interviews. Semistructured questions were used to launch the discussion in each focus group, probing students' perceptions about learning in science, learning in a biology laboratory, and benefits associated with Biology 140. When combined with questionnaire data, interview data from the focus groups provided a rich understanding of the complexity of students' self-regulated learning and conceptions about science associated with participating in Biology 140.

Benefits and Challenges Associated With Lab-Based Biology 140

A combination of past experiences with and data from our research project on Biology 140 have allowed us to identify a number of benefits associated with participating in an inquiry-oriented laboratory, consistent with prior research (e.g., Eilam & Aharon, 2003; Friedrichsen, 2001; Haury, 1993; Minner et al., 2004; Rivarola et al., 1997; Tamir et al., 1998; Zion et al., 2004). At the same time, we have also observed multiple challenges in developing and implementing the Biology 140 laboratory course. These challenges are of three broad types: (a) logistical challenges in providing an inquiry-oriented course on a large scale, (b) instructional challenges in supporting laboratory instructors to provide facilitative rather than directive instruction, and (c) student-related challenges that establish barriers to their productive engagement in inquiry-oriented learning. In the rest of this chapter, we discuss these benefits and challenges along with potential solutions.

Logistical Challenges and Potential Solutions
As noted earlier, up to 2,000 students enroll in first-year UBC biology courses each year. Providing inquiry-oriented experiences on such a large scale creates several logistical challenges. Consider, first, that even when working in collaborative groups of four, 2,000 students will plan 500 unique research projects, each of which will require resources that must be prepared in advance. If students were to be provided complete choice and control over projects, then it would be difficult to predict and prepare in advance the exact organisms, materials, and equipment that might be needed. Furthermore, purchasing materials for individual groups rather than bulk ordering of materials would significantly add to the cost of the program.

This first logistical challenge for Biology 140 dictates that parameters be defined to constrain students' selection of projects. To that end, six laboratories are set up in each available time period, each of which is assigned one of three different ecosystems: terrestrial, marine, or freshwater. Six organisms from each ecosystem are then chosen for their ease of culture and availability (for a total of 18 possible organisms, six in each of three ecosystems). The 24 students assigned to each laboratory classroom are clustered into six groups of four, and each of these groups is assigned one of the six organisms available within their laboratory. The result of this organizational strategy is that the demand for organisms, organism-specific equipment, and materials is distributed evenly across classrooms, time blocks, and terms. At the same time, students retain the ability to design unique inquiry projects related to a particular organism.

As another strategy for managing equipment and resources, infrastructure supports are provided to help students in identifying and procuring needed equipment. For instance, while designing experiments, students are provided with material request forms that list organism-specific materials and equipment that they can consider using. Student requests are consolidated and submitted to technicians for preparation of organisms and other materials. Use of these request forms has two complementary benefits. First, the forms provide scaffolded support to students in the planning of experiments. Second, they enable course technicians to predict and prepare required materials and redistribute equipment as needed, thereby facilitating our ability to provide open-ended inquiry opportunities for a large number of students.

Similarly, in order to keep costs at a minimum, standard lab equipment and many materials are reused. More costly equipment may be borrowed from other teaching and research labs at UBC. Unusual equipment is either made by the students or by work-study students from low-cost materials. In some cases, students provide selected materials for themselves. In this manner, students are still faced with the challenge of defining and obtaining needed equipment, as is the case in authentic inquiry. But infrastructure supports facilitate the coordination of simultaneous equipment demands from multiple groups.

A second logistical challenge related to the scale of Biology 140 is the overwhelming pressure on space. During the winter term as many as 44 three-hour lab sections may be offered per week. Materials and equipment that students use for more than one session require space for storage. Organisms that are treated for extended periods need to be cared for or incubated in special conditions. To reduce demands on space, students are encouraged to develop short-term experiments of behavioral responses that can be completed in one three-hour lab period. Nonetheless, although students' actual experiments may be conducted in three-hour blocks, their development of an inquiry project extends over multiple sessions, thereby promoting the planning, problem solving, and revising processes central to authentic inquiry. Furthermore, conditions in Biology 140 mirror constraints often faced by scientists who also must design experiments with available resources, time, space, and materials in mind.

A final logistical challenge in Biology 140 is that students are required to find reference materials from which they can develop their ideas and make comparisons. Librarians may quickly become inundated with requests for information about particular organisms by first-year students unfamiliar with library search processes. Our strategy for distributing different organisms helps in spreading out the demand for particular library resources. In addition, library staff members have designed online tutorials that familiarize students with the library and useful search engines. Biology 140 students are required to complete these tutorials as one of their course assignments. To help students access information, a reserve area in the library holds popular references with copies of materials dedicated for Biology 140 students. To help the students, librarians have developed their own reference lists of keywords and search tools for particular organisms. They provide students with tools for conducting library searches but are careful not to find information for them.

Instructional Challenges and Potential Solutions

Providing instruction within an inquiry-oriented laboratory course requires a balance between providing information, tools, and guidance to students and promoting students' self-directed (self-regulated) learning (Tamir et al., 1998; Eilam & Aharon, 2003). Developing the instructional skills required to achieve this balance can take time and sustained effort (Butler, Novak Lauscher, Jarvis-Selinger, & Beckingham, 2004). In an undergraduate course the size of Biology 140, classes are often supported by graduate student teaching assistants who have no formal teacher education or special training for facilitating self-directed inquiry. As a result, teaching assistants are often tempted to demonstrate their own knowledge and "help" students by offering explicit suggestions rather than guiding students with probing questions that would lead them to solve problems more independently. In a course with multiple sections, it is also important to establish equivalence across sections so that all students are equally supported to develop problem-solving skills rather than being directed to follow instructions.

To address these instructional challenges, extensive effort is made to train teaching assistants to be facilitators of students' self-regulated learning. All teaching assistants meet once a week with supervising faculty to review important concepts to be presented and techniques that can be useful for initiating problem solving by students. During classes, supervisory teaching faculty members are available to answer difficult questions, provide technical support, deal with unusual student issues, and ensure that safety standards are met.

Student-Related Challenges and Potential Solutions

When Biology 140 was initiated, it seemed that the course provided the first opportunity for many students to design and execute a long-term research project. Initially, students seemed to be either excited by the challenge or unnerved because there were no "right answers" to be easily found in a reference article or text. Also, consistent with Cartier's (1997, 2002) observations about challenges facing medical students in problem-based learning, we noted that Biology 140 students needed to learn new skills and adapt or abandon old approaches to learning (e.g., memorizing) that had helped them succeed previously.

Based on these observations, as Biology 140 was developed, we built in a number of supports to scaffold students' success in an inquiry-oriented curriculum. For example, to guide students through the development of projects, the process of scientific investigation is broken down into a series of steps that unfolds over an eight-week period (see Table 14.1). Students are also provided with opportunities to observe their organisms and try out potential experimental techniques before designing their own experiments. Teaching assistants facilitate students' development of research questions and protocols by asking probing questions. Frequent feedback from teaching assistants may also dispel some of the uncertainty many students experience about the inquiry process. For instance, a first writing assignment requires students to tease out relevant information about their experimental organism and present it in a specific format. Feedback is detailed and helps guide students in defining what information is valuable and how to report it.

In spite of the supports provided in Biology 140, over time we have noted some persistent challenges for students in both cognitive and social aspects of learning. For example, students sometimes become frustrated when teaching assistants attempt to facilitate problem solving instead of providing direct and ready answers (see Chin & Chia, 2004; Friedrichsen, 2001). Students also perceive that assuming the responsibility for finding appropriate information, developing and executing an experiment, and reporting results requires a lot of work. Students find it challenging to define how their research fits with the greater body of scientific literature or is relevant to the natural world. Social skills are tested in the dynamics of research groups. Presenting to an audience of peers and a teaching assistant can be intimidating, even when students have opportunities to practice by presenting an informal proposal to peers.

The student-related challenges described earlier were distilled from our observations of Biology 140 students over a number of years, but data collected more systematically during our collaborative research project allowed us to validate, extend, and better understand the patterns we were observing. For example, understandings derived from analyses of focus group data were consistent with our observation that first-year students were not always prepared for the demands of an inquiry-oriented biology course. Although students' levels of preparation seemed variable, high school experiences did not seem to prepare some students to engage in science learning at the level expected at university. As one student explained: "'Cause I've never done labs like that before. It was just that you observe in high school, and now you research why. And you do the calculations based on your lab results, and (draw) conclusions from that. So we never did that."

Focus group interviews also suggested that students may have constructed problematic conceptions about science before entering university. These views may cast science as a field of absolutes, filled with facts rather than concepts and theories. In addition, students might be unaware that science is a process that uses a particular methodology—the scientific method—to engage in research about the physical and natural world. To illustrate this problem, one student's initial thinking about biology was captured in her later description of how her thinking had changed after participating in inquiry-oriented laboratories such as Biology 140:

And by doing Biology 140 and other lab like Chemistry lab, I sort of changed my way of thinking of science, 'cause before I was always thinking biology is just they tell you all these facts, like what is going to happen, and so you just memorize it. You say OK, when particular case happens then this is a particular situation, then you are going to apply particular specific methods, or what it's going to be like. But right now, I'm more, I don't really care about the details, I care more about the process and why, I'm trying to like, there is no right answers for anything, it's just like I'm not focusing on the result I got, but more likely I'm focused on how, why would certain, why would the things end up like the way they end up with.

Unfortunately, focus group interviews also revealed that, unlike the student here, but consistent with data from evaluations and questionnaires described later, students may maintain links with prior misconceptions about science over time. For these students, the process of change may be slower because they have difficulty reflecting on what they are learning and the broader implications.

Analyses of pretest questionnaire data from term 1 ($n = 267$) also suggested that many students' perceptions of inquiry-oriented projects at the start of the term had the potential to undermine success in an inquiry-oriented laboratory. Almost half of the students reported being worried (45%) or stressed (46%) when facing an inquiry-project. This finding is problematic, not only because students who experience such negative emotions are more likely to give up but also because, in times of stress, students may adopt or revert to superficial or surface learning approaches or methods that led to success in the past, even if those strategies are no longer appropriate (Fransson, 1977).

Furthermore, many students lacked confidence in their ability to be successful (42%). Most students were confident they could follow instructions (91%), perhaps reflecting experience and comfort with procedural directions. However, fewer students were confident they could define an important problem or issue for study (69%), plan a way to study the situation (59%), or judge whether they had done a good job (51%). Fourteen percent of students prejudged inquiry projects to be too difficult for them to complete. These findings are problematic given previous research suggesting that task-specific perceptions of control over outcomes are related to task persistence and more productive use of strategies (Bandura, 1993; Schunk, 1994).

When interpreting what was required of them by an inquiry-oriented project, most students focused on positive learning goals (e.g., 88% said it was often or almost always important to understand key information about the situation). However, a substantial minority of students failed to recognize the relevance of requirements more specific to the inquiry process. For example, the percentage of students who thought that it was almost never or just sometimes important to define a problem for study, generate strategies for investigating the problem, and generate new knowledge through inquiry were 16%, 25%, and 31%, respectively. Furthermore, 33% of students felt that, in inquiry-oriented projects, it is important to memorize information.

In terms of the quality of students' engagement in inquiry-oriented learning, only 50% to 60% of students reported engaging in planning of time, methods, or resources, which is problematic considering the importance of planning to designing and enacting investigations. Consonant with their focus on positive learning goals, the majority of students reported using positive strategies for learning material presented by others (e.g., 85% reported focusing on main ideas, concepts or themes). However, even among these academically successful high school graduates, fewer reported using more active strategies associated with deeper learning (e.g., paraphrasing information; making diagrams, charts, or webs to represent connections among ideas). Forty-two percent of students reported using strategies for memorizing.

Perhaps most troubling was that among the least frequently endorsed strategies by students were ones focused on generating new knowledge through inquiry as an extension beyond just learning or memorizing information provided by others. For example, only 50% of students reported using strategies for coming up with ideas about possible inquiry procedures, whereas fewer than half reported designing inquiry projects to generate new knowledge (38%), generating alternative ways of designing an investigation (38%), or anticipating possible outcomes and adjusting procedures accordingly (46%). Thus, before engaging in inquiry-oriented learning, many first semester students appeared to experience challenging emotions, be low in self-confidence, and have limited understandings about inquiry-project requirements and of productive cognitive and metacognitive strategies specific to inquiry learning.

To further study the patterns in students' pretest perceptions about inquiry-oriented learning, we examined second semester pretest scores from all of the students ($n = 249$) who completed the questionnaire within the lecture-based course (Biology 121). We conducted factor and cluster analyses to identify groups of students who responded similarly to the questionnaire. We found four patterns in student responses that cut across and integrated emotions, motivation, cognitive strategies, and metacognition (cf. Butler & Cartier, 2005a). One small group ($n = 10$) of very excited students appeared to be very actively and productively engaged in inquiry-oriented learning. A second group of students ($n = 68$) reported higher levels of stress but were also positively engaged in learning, although not as productively as group 1 students (e.g., they reported using fewer inquiry-oriented strategies than did group 1 students). A third, unfortunately sizeable, group of students ($n = 85$) was the most highly stressed and least productively engaged. Finally, students in the fourth, also sizeable, group ($n = 86$) were most neutral emotionally and least interested in the task that they judged to be less important. These students seemed motivated to merely fulfill task requirements, reporting strategy use at low to moderate levels. These results, like those of Eilam and Aharon (2003), seemed to point to different patterns in engagement among different groups of students.

In addition to risk factors observable in these pretest data, challenges for some students seemed to remain even at the end of Biology 140. For example, when asked on course evaluations at the end of the first term, "Do you think that participation in Biology 140 has affected the way you think about learning in biology?," 15% of students said "no." Similar to findings by Zion et al. (2004), an additional 5% of comments focused on how much harder work in biology was than expected. A further 3% of comments reflected poorer attitudes toward biology, whereas another 1% of comments identified negative effects on learning of course activities. Thus, as has been suggested in prior research, perhaps some students do not respond well to courses that require more active, effortful, and self-directed learning (Chin & Chia, 2004).

Findings from our focus group interviews allowed us to link what students bring to an inquiry-oriented curriculum to patterns in how they participate in learning. More specifically, focus group data allowed us to identify three learning streams. One stream characterized participation by students who enter inquiry-oriented curricula with a better understanding of science. These students seem able to progress with fewer back-eddies in their learning process. In another stream, students are actively engaged in the active learning, inquiry-oriented format. These students appear able to integrate new experiences with prior conceptions and develop new cognitive and metacognitive strategies as they develop as self-regulated learners. But, a third stream was characterized by students' remaining unengaged in learning and tied to previous conceptions of science. In this pattern students' learning seems to progress more slowly and students are less able to appreciate "new" scientific processes. As with any defined streams, the boundaries are permeable and students almost always shift from one level to another depending on the cognitive and social demands of the task. It is the dominant pattern of their actions that defines into which learning category they fall at a given point in time.

Benefits Associated with Biology 140
Although pretest analyses of questionnaire data suggested that many students were at risk for less productive engagement in learning, and although evaluation and focus group data suggested that some students remained challenged by the end of the term, our data analyses also suggested that many Biology 140 students responded positively to the course, potentially overcoming initial challenges. One source of evidence for this conclusion was a comparison of pre- and posttest questionnaire data from term two. These data revealed several positive changes for Biology 140 students, whereas responses of non-Biology 140 students either stayed the same or became more negative. For example, more Biology 140 students were confident in their ability to complete an inquiry project at posttest (81%) than had been at pretest (58%), whereas perceptions of students not taking Biology 140 did not change. Furthermore, a greater number of Biology 140 students recognized the potential contributions of the previous literature to their understanding of their project at posttest (77%) than had at pretest (59%), whereas at posttest fewer of the comparison students appreciated the benefits of reviewing past work (a slight drop from 65% to 59%). Interestingly, more Biology 140 students reported handling

negative emotions by imagining feeling good after finishing at posttest (84%) than had at pretest (69%). In contrast, students not taking Biology 140 were less likely at posttest to use that same strategy (59%, down from 83% at pretest). Given the substantial number of students who reported experiencing stress or worry at pretest (as described earlier), it is encouraging that more Biology 140 students gained awareness of at least one strategy for managing such intrusive emotions.

Most striking in our term two questionnaire data was the large number of areas in which Biology 140 students showed no or little change, whereas students not enrolled in Biology 140 experienced marked negative changes. For example, at posttest fewer non-Biology 140 students perceived that they could succeed on an inquiry-based project with instructor help (36% compared to 61% at pretest) and these students seemed less likely to ask for help when needed (36%, down from 61%). Fewer non-Biology 140 students perceived planning to be important at posttest. Similarly, at posttest non-Biology 140 students were less likely to report using monitoring strategies, strategies for remedying difficulties, or use of internal criteria for evaluating their own performance. Fewer non-Biology 140 students reported feeling relaxed before and during the project, and fewer felt relieved or proud when finished. These results imply that the learning profiles of first-year biology students not participating in an inquiry-oriented laboratory declined sharply by the end of the year, whereas participation in Biology 140 seemed to protect first-year biology students from similar declines.

Positive outcomes for students also were suggested by the Biology 140 evaluation data in which close to three-quarters of responses were positive. Five major themes were identified among positive responses. The largest category of comments described changes in understandings about science and scientific processes (26% of comments). This broad category included increased understanding about the scientific method (15%), major shifts in thinking about how science works (6%), and increased understanding about writing in science, presentations, or library skills (5%). Examples of comments coded into this category included: "I always thought studying biology was all about memorizing specific terms but by participating in Biology 140, I could know that studying biology is related closely to my daily life;" "Now I more clearly understand what is involved in being a research scientist as I have had firsthand experience;" and, "It has made me analyze scientific data in a more clear and structured way, and also understand the underlying structure behind experiments."

A second major category reflected gains in biology-specific knowledge (16%), including increases in relational understandings (e.g., about how biology connects to the real world). A third major category included adoption of more active, analytical, critical, or reflective approaches to learning (9%). For example, one student explained that "It [Biology 140] has caused me to think more critically about the material." Similarly, another student wrote, "It [Biology 140] has made me a more critical thinker about the world around me." A fourth major, positive category included statements reflecting students' development of more positive attitudes toward biology or science (7%). Finally, a fifth category included comments describing concrete benefits accrued from participating in Biology 140 activities (5%). Taken together, themes that emerged from first-term evaluation data were consonant with findings from other research, which also has reported gains for students in knowledge about scientific processes (Haury, 1993), active, critical thinking (e.g., Hofstein et al., 2001; Rivarola et al., 1997), and attitudes toward science (Friedrichsen, 2001; Haury, 1993).

In term two Biology 140 evaluations (which used a quantitative scale based on themes found in qualitative analyses of term one course evaluations in the lab-based course), students most commonly reported gains in knowledge about biology, understanding how a scientific paper should be written, and learning about how to conduct scientific experiments (over 70% of students in each case). Thus, most students perceived gains in more content and procedurally focused aspects of what they learned. But half of the students (i.e., over 500 students) indicated that the course had changed their view of biology as a field of study, a significant change for a single-semester course. As one student put it (in an answer to term one's open-ended question, which also was asked in term two), "I thought that biology is more of memorizing than thinking, but now I think that biology is more of THINKING." Similarly, around half of the students recognized that they were actively engaged in learning and felt that they thought more analytically and critically after participating. Many students also reported understanding the contribution of group work to scientific inquiry.

Data from focus group interviews also suggested that students participating in inquiry learning may realize that science is a process of knowing that is realized through the scientific method, a powerful problem-solving heuristic. Students also may realize that participating in scientific and academic communities requires a variety of skills, academic, communicative, and social. Finally, focus-group interviews revealed that engaging in an inquiry-oriented curriculum has the potential to support, not only students' development of procedural skills and recognition of their role in scientific communities, but also a broader understanding of science. Like the student mentioned earlier who described how her conceptions about science had changed, another participant explained:

> Yeah, I think, like coming to UBC, I start to really know what science is. Like in the past, in high school, we did science like Physics, Chemistry, just only the textbook, but after coming to UBC, because we actually do a lab and we do how to analyze the research, that kind of scientific thing, and I start to really like science is, what science really is, it's tough, but interesting, yeah. And actually it achieved purpose of staying in science like, because we start to realize you know like what it really is like.

Conclusion

This chapter has provided an in-depth analysis of challenges and benefits associated with engaging first-year university students in an inquiry-based laboratory experience in biology. As has been found by others (e.g., Cartier, 1997, 2002;

Chin & Chia, 2004; Friedrichsen, 2001), our findings certainly suggest that many challenges arise when developing and implementing an inquiry-oriented curriculum. We have identified logistical and instructional challenges that emerge when attempting to create open-ended, authentic inquiry experiences for students, especially on a large scale. We also have examined how students' attitudes toward and conceptions about science, resistance to active learning, inadequate prior knowledge about inquiry processes, low perceptions of self-efficacy, negative emotions, and unproductive patterns of engagement with academic work may create obstacles to success.

But we also have identified a number of solution strategies that can be employed to counter such challenges. And, based both on our informal observations and research findings, many of our solution strategies appear to be helping. For example, solutions to logistical challenges have allowed us to engage large numbers of students in authentic, open-ended inquiry. Systematic training of teaching assistants and coordination with library staff have ensured students receive facilitative support that fosters self-regulated learning. Systematic scaffolded support coupled with timely and extensive feedback also seems to be helping in overcoming many student-related challenges. Indeed, consistent with prior research, our findings suggest that substantial benefits can be accrued by engaging students in inquiry-oriented curricula in the development of content and procedural knowledge (Haury, 1993; Wilden et al., 2002; Zion et al., 2004), positive attitudes toward science (Friedrichsen, 2001), constructive and active thinking (Rivarola et al., 1997), self-regulated learning (Eilam & Aharon, 2003; Tamir et al., 1998), and, perhaps most significantly, productive conceptions about science and how science works (Haury, 1993). Although we will certainly refine our efforts to support student learning in the months to come based on our recently collected data, overall our findings seem to highlight the potential of carefully planned and organized inquiry-oriented instruction.

References

American Association for the Advancement of Science (AAAS). (1993). *Benchmarks for science literacy.* New York: Oxford University Press. Retrieved August 12, 2005, from http://www.project2061.0rg/publications/bsl/online

Bandura, A. (1993). Perceived self-efficacy in cognitive development and functioning. *Educational Psychologist, 28,* 117–148.

Basey, J. M., Mendelow, T. N., & Ramos, C. N. (2000). Current trends of community college lab curricula in biology: An analysis of inquiry, technology, and content. *Journal of Biological Education, 34*(2), 80–86.

Bertrand, Y. (1995). *Contemporary theories and practice in education.* Madison, WI: Magna.

Bransford, J. D., Brown, A. L., & Cocking, R. R. (2000). *How people learn: Brain, mind, experience, and school.* Washington, DC: National Academy Press.

Butler, D. L. (1998a). A Strategic Content Learning approach to promoting self-regulated learning. In D. Schunk & B. J. Zimmerman (Eds.), *Developing self-regulated learning: From teaching to self-reflective practice* (pp. 160–183). New York: Guilford.

Butler, D. L. (1998b). In search of the architect of learning: A commentary on scaffolding as a metaphor for instructional interactions. *Journal of Learning Disabilities, 31,* 374–385.

Butler, D. L. (1998c). The Strategic Content Learning approach to promoting self-regulated learning: A summary of three studies. *Journal of Educational Psychology, 90,* 682–697.

Butler, D. L., & Cartier, S. C. (2004a, May). *Learning in varying activities: An explanatory framework and a new evaluation tool founded on a model of self-regulated learning.* Paper presented at the annual meeting of the Canadian Society for the Study of Education, Winnipeg, MB.

Butler, D. L., & Cartier, S. (2004b). Promoting students' active and productive interpretation of academic work: A key to successful teaching and learning. *Teachers College Record, 106,* 1729–1758.

Butler, D. L., & Cartier, S. C. (2005a, April). *Multiple complementary methods for understanding self-regulated learning as situated in context.* Paper presented at the annual meeting of the American Educational Research Association, Montreal, QC.

Butler, D. L., & Cartier, S. C. (2005b). *The inquiry learning questionnaire: A validation study.* Unpublished manuscript. University of British Columbia, Vancouver.

Butler, D. L., Cartier, S. C., Pollock, C., Nomme, K., & Gagnon, F. (2005). *First year biology students' understandings about learning in science: A self-regulated learning perspective.* Unpublished manuscript. University of British Columbia, Vancouver.

Butler, D. L., Novak Lauscher, H. J., Jarvis-Selinger, S., & Beckingham, B. (2004). Collaboration and self-regulation in teachers' professional development. *Teaching and Teacher Education, 20,* 435–455.

Butler, D. L., & Winne, P. H. (1995). Feedback and self-regulated learning: A theoretical synthesis. *Review of Educational Research, 65,* 245–281.

Carey, S. C., & Smith, C. (1993). On understanding the nature of scientific knowledge. *Educational Psychologist, 28,* 235–251.

Cartier, S. C. (1997). *Lire pour apprendre: Description des stratégies utilisées par des étudiants en médecine dans un curriculum d'apprentissage par problèmes.* Unpublished doctoral dissertation, Université de Montréal, QC.

Cartier, S. C. (2002). Étude de l'apprentissage par la lecture d'étudiants en contexte d'apprentissage par la lecture. *Revue Canadienne de l'Enseignement Supérieur, 32*(1), 1–29.

Cartier, S. C., & Butler, D. L. (2004, May). *Elaboration and validation of the questionnaires and plan for analysis.* Paper presented at the annual meeting of the Canadian Society for Study of Education, Winnipeg, MB.

Cartier, S. C., Plante, A., & Tardif, J. (2001, April). *Learning by reading: Description of learning strategies of students involved in a problem-based learning program.* Paper presented in the annual meeting of the American Educational Research Association, Seattle, WA.

Center for Science, Mathematics, & Engineering Education, Committee on Undergraduate Science Education, National Research Council (1999). *Transforming undergraduate education in science, mathematics, engineering, and technology.* Retrieved August 12, 2005, from http://books.nap.edu/html/transund

Chin, C., & Chia, L. (2004). Implementing project work in biology through problem-based learning. *Journal of Biological Education, 38*(2), 68–75.

Chinn, C. A., & Malhotra, B. A. (2002). Epistemologically authentic inquiry in schools: A theoretical framework for evaluating inquiry tasks. *Science Education, 86,* 175–218.

Corno, L. (1993). The best laid plans: Modern conceptions of volition and educational research. *Educational Researcher, 22,* 14–22.

Corno, L. (1994). Student volition and education: Outcomes, influences, and practices. In D. H. Schunk & B. J. Zimmerman (Eds.), *Self-regulation of learning and performance: Issues and educational applications* (pp. 229–251). Hillsdale, NJ: Erlbaum.

DeBoer, G. E. (1991). *A history of ideas in science education.* New York: Teachers College Press.

Dunbar, K. (2000). How scientists think in the real world: Implications for science education. *Journal of Applied Developmental Psychology, 21*(1), 49–58.

Eilam, B., & Aharon, I. (2003). Students' planning in the process of self-regulated learning. *Contemporary Educational Psychology, 28,* 304–334.

Fransson, A. (1977). On qualitative differences in learning-effects of motivation and anxiety on process and outcome. *British Journal of Educational Psychology, 47,* 244–257.

Friedrichsen, P. M. (2001). Moving from hands-on to inquiry-based: A biology course for prospective elementary teachers. *The American Biology Teacher, 63,* 562–568.

Harris, K. R., & Graham, S. (1994). Constructivism: Principles, paradigms, and integration. *The Journal of Special Education, 28,* 233–247.

Harris, K. R., & Pressley, M. (1991). The nature of cognitive strategy instruction: Interactive strategy construction. *Exceptional Children, 57,* 392–404.

Haury, L. (1993). *Teaching science through inquiry.* Columbus: OH: ERIC Clearinghouse for Science, Mathematics, and Environmental Education. (ERIC Document Reproduction Service No. ED359048)

Hesse-Biber, S. N., & Leavy, P. (2004). Distinguishing qualitative research. In S. N. Hesse-Biber & P. Leavy (Eds.), *Approaches to qualitative research: A reader on theory and practice* (pp. 1–15). New York: Oxford University Press.

Hofstein, A., Nahum, T. L., & Shore, R. (2001). Assessment of the learning environment of inquiry-type laboratories in high-school chemistry. *Learning Environments Research, 4,* 193–207.

Hutchinson, K. M., Bretz, S. L., Mettee, H. D., & Smiley, J. A. (2005). A guided inquiry experiment for the measurement of activation energies in the biophysical chemistry laboratory: Decarboxylation of pyrrole-2-carboxylate. *Biochemistry and Molecular Biology Education, 33,* 123–127.

Kolkhorst, F. W., Mason, C. L., DiPasquale, D. M., Patterson, P., & Buono, M. J. (2001). An inquiry-based learning model for an exercise physiology laboratory course. *Advances in Physiological Education, 25,* 45–50.

Leech, M. L., Howell, D. G., & Egger, A. E. (2004). A guided inquiry approach to learning the geology of the U.S. *Journal of Geoscience Education, 52,* 368–373.

Lewis, S., & Lewis, J. (2005). Departing from lectures: An evaluation of a peer-led guided inquiry alternative. *Journal of Chemical Education, 82,* 135–139.

Litoselliti, L. (2003). *Using focus groups in research.* London: Continuum.

Luckie, D. B., Maleszewski, J. J., Loznak, S. D., & Krha, M. (2004). Infusion of collaborative inquiry throughout a biology curriculum increases student learning: A four-year study of "Teams and Streams." *Advances in Physiological Education, 28,* 199–209.

Minner, D. D., Levy, A. J., & Century, J. R. (2004, April). *Describing inquiry science instruction in existing research: A challenge for synthesis.* Paper presented at the annual meeting of the National Association for Research on Science Teaching, Vancouver, BC.

National Research Council (NRC). (1996). *National science education standards.* Washington, DC: National Academy Press.

National Research Council (NRC). (2000). *Inquiry and the national science education standards: A guide for teaching and learning.* Washington, DC: National Academy Press.

National Science Teachers Association (2001). *Practicing science: The investigative approach in college science teaching.* Arlington, VA: NSTA Press.

Neuman, W. L. (1997). *Social research methods: Qualitative and quantitative approaches* (3rd ed.). Boston: Allyn & Bacon.

Paris, S. G., Byrnes, J. P., & Paris, A. H. (2001). Constructing theories, identities, and actions of self-regulated learners. In B. J. Zimmerman & D. H. Schunk (Eds.), *Self-regulated learning and academic achievement: Theoretical perspectives* (2nd ed.) (pp. 253–287). Mahwah, NJ: Erlbaum.

Pintrich, P. R. (2000). The role of goal orientation in self-regulated learning. In M. Boekaerts, P. R. Pintrich, & M. Zeidner (Eds.), *Handbook of self-regulation* (pp. 451–502). San Diego, CA: Academic Press.

Pollock, C., Nomme, K., Butler, D. L., Nakonechny, J., Cartier, S. C., & Gagnon, F. (2005). *Engaging first year biology students in a guided-inquiry laboratory: An evaluation study.* Unpublished manuscript. University of British Columbia, Vancouver.

Ragin, C. (1994). *Constructing social research.* Thousand Oaks, CA: Pine Forge Press.

Rivarola, V. A., Bergesse, J. R., Garcia, M. B., & Fernandez, A. C. (1997). A problem-based learning approach to a biological chemistry laboratory class for students of veterinary science. *Biochemical Education, 25*(1), 22–23.

Rudd, J., II, Greenbowe, T., Hand, B., & Legg, M. (2001). Using the science writing heuristic to move toward an inquiry-based laboratory curriculum: An example from physical equilibrium. *Journal of Chemical Education, 78,* 1680–1686.

Schunk, D. H. (1994). Self-regulation of self-efficacy and attributions in academic settings. In D. H. Schunk & B. J. Zimmerman (Eds.), *Self-regulation of learning and performance: Issues and educational applications* (pp. 75–99). Hillsdale, NJ: Erlbaum.

Stone, C. A. (1998). The metaphor of scaffolding: Its utility for the field of LD. *Journal of Learning Disabilities, 31,* 344–364.

Tamir, P., Stavy, R., & Ratner, N. (1998). Teaching science by inquiry: Assessment and learning. *Journal of Biological Education, 33,* 27–32.

Vygotsky, L. S. (1978). *Mind in society.* Cambridge, MA: Harvard University Press.

White, B. Y., & Frederiksen, J. R. (1998). Inquiry, modeling, and metacognition: Making science accessible to all students. *Cognition and Instruction, 16,* 3–118.

Wilden, J., Crowther, D., Gulbanich, A., & Cannon, J. (2002). A quantitative comparison of instruction format of undergraduate introductory level content biology courses: Traditional lecture approach vs. inquiry-based for education majors. *Proceedings of the Annual International Conference of the Association for the Education of Teachers in Science.* (ERIC Document Reproduction Service No. ED465607)

Wolters, C. (1998). Self-regulated learning and college students' regulation of motivation. *Journal of Educational Psychology, 90,* 224–235.

Zimmerman, B. J. (1989). A social-cognitive view of self-regulated learning. *Journal of Educational Psychology, 81,* 329–339.

Zimmerman, B. J. (1994). Dimensions of academic self-regulation: A conceptual framework for education. In D. H. Schunk & B. J. Zimmerman (Eds.), *Self-regulation of learning and performance: Issues and educational applications* (pp. 3–21). Hillsdale, NJ: Erlbaum.

Zimmerman, B. J., & Schunk, D. H. (Eds.). (2001). *Self-regulated learning and academic achievement: Theoretical perspectives* (2nd ed.). Hillsdale, NJ: Erlbaum.

Zion, M., Shapira, D., Slezak, M., Link, E., Bashan, N., Brumer, M., et al. (2004). Biomind: A new biology curriculum that enables authentic inquiry learning. *Journal of Biological Education, 38*(2), 59–67.

Author Index

Subject Index

A

Academic Reform movement, 271, 276
Ambiguity in inquiry, 36, 37, 39, 220
Apple Classrooms of Tomorrow (ACOT)
    Project, 288, 290
Audience, see also Science fairs
    examples, 69–71
    product development, 82
    role of, 86
Aulls-Shore four-property model of inquiry in
    education, 247, 251
    context as students learning from each
      other, 260–261, 265
    context as teachers providing guidance,
      261–264
    four properties of inquiry, 249–250
    process as independent learning strategy,
      257
    process as problem-solving strategy,
      257–259, 265
    validation of the four properties, 253
Authentic learning, 151, 265
Authentic science, 277; see also Authentic
    scientific inquiry
Authentic scientific inquiry, 301–304; see also
    Authentic science
    authentic inquiry, 308, 321
    definition, 302–303, 308
    key features, 309
    nonauthentic scientific inquiry, 301
Authority, see Shared authority; Teacher
    authority

B

Barriers, see also Mistakes; Obstacles
    disagreements, 150, 163
    inquiry instruction, 1–2, 5, 6–8, 40, 210
    inquiry-based instruction, 275
    inquiry-oriented curriculum, 219–227
    resistance to change, 229
    students involved in inquiry, 242–246
    teachers involved in inquiry, 237

Beethoven, Ludwig van, 188, 191, 196, 198
Bioesthetic hypothesis, 173–174
Bioesthetically determined timing, 181, 184
Biomedical timing, 181
Brainstorming, 11, 28, 51, 76, 78, 80

C

Campbell's model of creativity, 171
Canadian Cognitive Abilities Test, 10
Career development
    creative productive activities, 91
Center for Science Education in the United
    States, 306
Characteristics of inquiry
    inquiry teachers, 252, 254–256, 257–264,
      266
    noninquiry teachers, 252, 253, 256,
      257–264, 266
Cheating among professionals and scientists
    British Journal of Obstetrics and
      Gynaecology, 99
    Dr. Robert Fiddes, 99–100
    Dr. Shervert Frazier, 99
    faked data, 97–101
    Henry H. Goddard, 98
    inflated test scores, 100
    Interleuken-4A, 99
    John Darsee, Harvard Medical School, 99
    plagiarism, 97–99
    resulting from high stakes testing, 100
    Sir Cyril Burt, 98
Cheating in academics
    adolescent cheating, 94–96
    college-level cheating, 96–97
Cheating in science fairs
    causes of cheating, possible, 111–113
    fabricating data, 105
    percent who admitted to cheating, 109–110
    related to products, 103
    suspicion of cheating confirmed, 110–111
Classroom academic conversations, 31
Classroom instruction
    definition of, 13

I